# AYDEN, THE SPORTS TOWN

# AYDEN, THE SPORTS TOWN

Stories of Playing and Living in Tobacco Country

Volume 1

William Harrington and Mitchell Oakley

TOE SACK BOOKS

TOE SACK BOOKS
919-616-6870 (or) 252-412-8572

Front Cover: *Basketball, Baseball, and Football: Photo by Mitchell Oakley, Lights Graphic: creativecommons.org*

Back Cover: *Tobacco Field: Photo by Mitchell Oakley*

Cover Design: *Stuart Albright*

To learn more about this book, the authors can be contacted at:

William Harrington at billharringtoncc@yahoo.com
www.williamharringtonbooks.com

Mitchell Oakley at moakley62@embarqmail.com
www.mitchelloakley.com

**Ayden High School** *(The Wheel)*

**South Ayden High School.** *(From South Ayden High School History and Memories, Courtesy of Charles Becton)*

To all those players who cleared the way for the running backs, passed the ball to the leading scorers, and made the tough plays to save the day for the pitchers

# Table of Contents

**Ayden High School Song**

Come let us sing to dear Ole' AHS
The school of all the schools we love the best
And to maroon and white we will be true,
And to our Country's flag – the red, the white, the blue.
Our banners, they will ever float on high
And may she grow as years go passing by, passing by,
So let us all together ever stand as a band, AHS.

**Ayden Tornadoes seat cushion.** *(Photo by Mitchell Oakley)*

# Introduction

Soon after Maija and I were married, I said to her, "It's time for me to go home again."

"When is our home going to be home to you?" I was asked.

"Never!"

Realizing that answer didn't go over very well, I tried to patch things up. "I really have two homes, ours and Ayden. Sorry Dear, but Ayden will always be home to me."

Whenever I "hit the road" to go back home, something indescribable has always happened. Indescribable means just that – virtually impossible to convey in words; on the other hand, I know how this something feels, just like the tears that are welling up in my eyes at this moment. Akin to a transformation, it is filled with rich memories – recollections of my parents, of my grandparents, of my aunts and uncles – of the people I will no longer be able to visit. I have never once traveled to Ayden without thinking about my childhood: playing in the field behind the Methodist Church, in front of David "Clem" McLawhorn's ('62) house; sneaking into Dr. Grady Dixon's fenced-in side yard to watch the goldfish in his tiny pond; scrambling over the fence after Mrs. Phillips had caught my friends and me *procuring* apples from her back yard. Of course, that's not what she called it. After Mrs. Phillips made a phone call to Daddy, I told him that we were simply doing our civic duty by relieving an old woman of what must have been a strenuous task; that is, bending over to pick up all those little apples. Obviously, I'm stretching the truth. Telling Bill Harrington ('28) such an obvious falsehood would not have been a good idea. Unlike other faux pas of my youth, I did not receive a scolding from him on that occasion. I was never sure, but I suspected it was because he'd done something equally exciting – maybe in the same apple orchard when the trees were younger and they were owned by a previous "Mrs. Phillips."

Playing was part of growing up in Ayden. Eating fresh apples, wondering how goldfish "breathed" underwater in a neighbor's pond, and frolicking in a field imagining we were in the wild west are just a few of the good times I remember. To this short list, I could add so many more exciting experiences. Like everything in life, however, playtime came to an end, and it was time to go to work.

Momma ('35) and Daddy worked hard, and they expected me to do the same. First I was a Lawnmower Man and then an Iceman. When visiting home after Daddy retired, I would usually go by the dormant ice plant on 1$^{st}$ Street; sometimes I'd drive by, most of the time I walked by. I remain compelled to do this. Of course, the old tin building where we made the ice, the big silver fuel oil tank, and the little coal office are no longer there. I have vivid memories of the seven years of working at the plant to make spending money while I was in high school and later to pay my way through East Carolina College.

My family and Ayden Ice and Coal Company were synonymous. Whenever I was interviewing someone for this book and they were trying to figure out who I was, all I had to do was ask, "Remember Bill Harrington, the guy who ran the ice plant?" During the summer when the plant was running 24-7, Momma became a "short-order cook." Daddy and his boys rotated on and off the job throughout the day, and she knew we'd be hungry when we got off work. So many images of those days in the 1950s and 1960s will forever be a part of my life's early scrapbook. Simply thinking about the ice plant conjures up a multitude of pictures. My youngest brother Bob ('66) is on the platform cutting a piece of ice just the right size to load into the crusher. He uses the scoop to put the ice into a bag, hands it to a customer, and accepts 15 cents. My brother Joe ('64) and I are loading the straight-six Chevrolet truck with ice to run the country route. Daddy and I are walking around the plant deciding who is going to work 3$^{rd}$ shift. Working 3$^{rd}$ will saddle me with a tough decision: Am I going to visit my girlfriend in Grifton or am I going to go home and sleep so I'll be rested for the start of my shift at midnight? If my girlfriend wins out, Joe will have to drive the old Chevy truck tomorrow, and I'll have to sit on the passenger side and catch up on my sleep while he drives.

Jimmy Persinger ('61) and I used to walk to high school together. We walked along 6th Street hoping that a certain student of the female variety was in front of us. She had a way of gliding along in her tight skirt that drew some stares from the two of us. Just like our coaches used to tell us, timing made all the difference. If the young lady was too far ahead of us, we'd speed up our gate; then again, if she was nowhere in sight, we'd stroll along finding other things to talk about. During the early part of our senior year, especially if the girl was not where she ought to be, the talk turned to football. That year, we won the Coastal Conference championship and finished the regular season undefeated, while giving up a total of eighteen points in nine games.

*Used to be*. All of those things used to be. It's my youth that used to be. I miss it. I miss the safety and security of Ayden; I miss the warm feelings that awaited me every time I walked into Grandmamma and Granddaddy's house. I miss my family's house on Snow Hill Street where Joe, Bob and I grew up and where Momma and Daddy lived most of their adult lives. One night after Momma had passed away and Daddy had moved in with Joe and Vivian in Pinehurst, I visited the green cinder block house one last time. I sat on the couch and stared at the floor-to-ceiling gray-stoned fireplace on the other side of the family room. I'm not sure how to characterize what I did next. I talked out-loud to my family, to my relatives, to everybody who had ever been in that house. And, I spoke to the house itself. Whatever I was doing seemed to be the right thing. The house didn't say anything back to me, but I am sure it was listening. I took one final tour through my home, making sure to say good-bye to some of the most important pieces of furniture. I entered the short hallway, circled past the bedrooms, across the living room floor, and back into the family room. I slowed down as I walked between the two most meaningful articles of furniture: Momma's chair near the double front windows and Daddy's old tattered green chair beside the coffee table. Once outside on the back porch, I turned the key slowly in the lock for the last time.

The indefinable "something" that I've experienced while driving home always leads to a smile as I pass the Ayden town limit sign and drive onto 3$^{rd}$ Street. There used to be a slight dip near the intersection of 3$^{rd}$ and Juanita Streets; as strange as it may seem, arriving home wasn't quite right until I experienced that dip. Then, on one trip, that bump in the road was gone. A right onto Snow Hill Street, and I'd soon be turning into my parents' driveway. For years the grammar school where my classmates and I attended grades one through four and where Daddy attended high school, faced Snow Hill Street and stood at the intersection of Washington Street and 3$^{rd}$ Street. Now, the one-block square recreation area includes tennis courts, a playground, and Veterans Memorial Park. My family and I referred to it as the playground or the grammar school. When I visited Momma and Daddy, my children used to play on the sliding boards, the merry-go-round, and the swings. I still have a pleasant memory of watching my son Paul and my Granddaddy as they left our house, walking hand-in-hand toward the playground. Once, my first wife and our daughter, Julieanne, met a classmate of mine near the old merry-go-round. I knew who he was by her description of him. No matter what challenges I may have been facing in my busy life, visiting Ayden always returned me to the world of my family – to a time and place of unconditional love. If my blood could be magically analyzed, I am sure that the profile would include maroon and white corpuscles, each with a Tornado tattoo.

*Ayden, the Sports Town* was Mitchell Oakley's idea. I joined the publisher emeritus of *The News-Leader* in 2009 and we kicked off our journey. At first, Mitchell and I met with several people, gathered some preliminary documents, and formulated our game plan. Through this process, we became acquainted – a necessary step for two people who were going to be making dozens and dozens of decisions together. One of the first things Mitchell told me about himself was that he enjoyed "staying in the background." Judging by his newspaper editorials, I wasn't so sure about that statement. I came to realize that what he really meant was that he loved to work hard and didn't actually care who got the credit. A true friendship has grown out of our time together.

Several books have been written about high school sports in eastern North Carolina. For example, Lee Pace authored a book called

*Blackbirds: The Glory Days of Rocky Mount Athletics.* In this book and in the others, a short segment of a school's existence was carved out and highlighted. Mitchell and I wanted to do more. We decided to try and "tell it all" – starting at the beginning and riding the horse all the way to the finish line. That means going back to the first sports activities at Ayden High School 100 or so years ago and chronicling the events through the graduating class of 1971, the last group of seniors to walk the halls of Tornado country. Our aim is also to return to the 1930s in an attempt to recount the early years of South Ayden School basketball and, then, to spring forward to 1965 when the Eagles fielded their first football team.

*Ayden, the Sports Town* is a story book, a history book, a resource book ... a sports book – with lots and lots of pictures.

I have chosen to journey through the old days like a time machine. This time machine is not like the ones that have been depicted in science fiction movies; it is a 1955 fire engine red Thunderbird convertible, the neatest, sexiest car ever made. I always wanted one of those. The closest I ever came was a red Geo Tracker during my mid-life crisis before Maija and I were married in 1992. Soon after the wedding, she announced that my red convertible days were over. We needed something more practical. So, I traded my nifty little car for a dull, unsexy white Chevy S-10 pickup truck. I must admit it was better for hauling sand, rocks, lawnmowers, and all the other things needed to landscape our ten acres north of Hillsborough.

At present, I can have any car I want – in this book, of course. I invite you to climb in the front seat next to me. Like the car, the transmission is magical; it's custom built. Reverse will take us from zero to any time in the past in an instant. And then, forward will bring us back just as quickly.

As you will see, I've changed gears constantly – from a balloon ride over Ayden and back to earth again; from ballgames to a Hoover Cart Parade in the early 1930s and back to ballgames; from football in 1939 to World War II and back to the gridiron in 1946. You and I will take the red time machine to South Ayden School where we'll meet a student for a campus tour. I will welcome you to join me on a sightseeing trip through the 1950s as we bring some memories back to life. I hope you will help me put a tarp over our car before Hurricane Hazel blows it away. Once we've cleared away some of the debris from around the house, we can go in to see if electricity is still getting to the Harrington's television set, the newest piece of furniture in the living room.

Now that you have a picture of the red time machine with all its amenities, you are able to envision zipping back and forth through the decades from before Ayden was Ayden to the time in 1962 when I'll turn the keys over to Mitchell so that you can travel with him the rest of the way – from the 1962-63 school year until the last graduating class at Ayden High School in 1971.

At the beginning of my discussions with Mitchell, I lived in Efland, an unincorporated rural community west of Hillsborough. Soon after I started doing research for this book, I moved to Durham. I have made the trip through Wake Forest, Zebulon, and Wilson a zillion times to explore old newspapers and to interview past athletes – men and women who no longer looked like athletes but who had fond memories of their time at Ayden High School.

I have chosen to write in first person because I want you, the reader, to ride with me as I travel the roads on my way to Ayden. I want you to sit next to me during my interviews with players, coaches, teachers, and town's people as they attempt to answer my questions about a period of their lives so long ago. Bum ('56) and Shirley Dennis have been so gracious in allowing me to interview people in the dining room of their restaurant. They always encouraged me to use the room "in any way I wanted." Mitchell and I had many of our meetings in that room. Of course, we just happened to meet around lunch time. It's a great life – eating at Bum's and talking about old times.

From the very first time I read one of the old newspapers, I began to wonder, "Where was the Princess Theater?" Months went by before I read an article that placed the theater on $3^{rd}$ Street where Bum's restaurant is today. On the next trip, I asked Bum exactly where it had been. Parts of the theater never went anywhere. The wall between Bum's two rooms contains the wall of the old building. The outside wall next to the parking lot still contains the windows of the defunct theater. Mitchell and I were eating our barbecue and collards in what used to be the lobby of the Princess Theater.

I hoped to identify Ayden High School's first season in each of the three major sports – the first football game ever played by an Ayden eleven, the first girls and boys basketball matchups, and the first baseball team representing the Tornadoes. The first football season was described in *The Ayden Dispatch* in some detail, but accounts of the first basketball and baseball seasons were unavailable from any source. Other mysteries will pop up also. Occasionally, I felt like the detective in a whodunit novel – running down lead after lead. I was sometimes successful, and other times I decided to provide you with the clues and encourage you to make a decision for yourself.

I wanted to recreate the South Ayden Eagles' athletic program. The longest running sports were girls and boys basketball. I thought about driving my time machine back to the time when the two teams first played in their gymtorium at the South Ayden School building, or maybe the first competition was somewhere else. Like AHS's first basketball seasons, I drew a blank. There is virtually nothing about SAH girls' basketball – only a sound bite here and there. It's my best guess that Tornado basketball started in the teens or early twenties and that Eagles basketball began in the 1930s. The girls' team at South Ayden was discontinued in the mid-1960s. In addition to girls' and boys' basketball, SAH fielded a team in one more sport: football. The Eagles played on the gridiron from 1965 until 1970. As I moved through the archival materials pertaining to the South Ayden School, it became painfully clear how little I knew about my fellow Aydenites. There were two Aydens – the one where I grew up and the one I knew so little about. My ignorance was magnified as I played my Sherlock Holmes game of tracking down the facts. Placing myself in my neighborhood on Snow Hill Street and at Ayden High School was easy. Driving south of 6<sup>th</sup> Street and onto the campus at South Ayden High School shoved me into an unknown world.

The editions of Ayden's newspaper from its inception in 1912 through 1925 are forever lost. Other newspapers in the area did not follow Ayden sports during that era. I have wished a thousand times that I could talk with Daddy or Heber Cannon ('28) or Louis Prescott ('28) or Marie Spear ('28) or Hal Edwards ('29) or Estelle McClees ('29) or Dalton Sumrell ('29) or Laura Mae Griffin ('30) or Huldah Smith ('30), or Jack Collins ('31), or Preston Dunn (31), or Robert Harris ('31) or someone of their generation.

I was privileged to attend Ayden High School and to learn from our teachers and coaches on my journey to graduate in 1961. I have often thought of how lucky I was to attend a small school. In a large school I would have been lost. I would not have been able to play sports. I wouldn't have been good enough. I am not sure what would have happened to me had I not been able to play football, basketball and baseball.

Nolan "Nolie" Norman ('61) experienced Ayden – if not in a unique – in an unusual way; his family moved to Norfolk, Virginia in 1949 and returned in 1957. That school year, Nolan worked on his uncle's farm near Ayden and did not attend school. The following school year, he started playing sports at AHS and eventually became a starter in football and baseball. Unlike most Ayden athletes, Nolan experienced a huge school in Norfolk where he said he would never have been able to participate. "What is so dear to me ... I came down here to Ayden and I could be a starter on a baseball team and a football team." Nolan was also on the basketball team, but he told me he played $3^{rd}$ string "only because there was no $4^{th}$ string." I, therefore, tend to disbelieve his story about the 32 points he claims to have scored in a game.

All of my life I've been told that academics come first. Unfortunately, that notion had not fully taken hold when I attended AHS. There were educational pursuits that would obviously be instrumental when I attended college. One of the most important was offered by Mrs. Louise Little ('28) in her English class. I recall writing note cards and organizing them for my term paper, an expanded version of which I am currently employing. The leaf and bug collections I did for Mrs. Evelyn Finch's biology class were the highlights of my high school studies. I am still unconvinced about the usefulness of the following: learning the French national anthem so that I could sing it to my teacher, Mrs. Carolyn Howard, while Jimmy Persinger laughed at me in the hallway. I made it through all of those assignments; however, my dreams of scoring a touchdown, of hitting my first shot, or of stealing second base were more often on my mind. Should it have been that way? No. But, that's the way it was.

During the last football game of my senior year, I can still *see* some of the plays against James Kenan High School on November 18, 1960. Packed away in my memory somewhere is the picture of Mac Tripp ('61) running into the end zone untouched on a play Coach Tripp called an inside reverse. The only tackle I made all year occurred after James Kenan scored its second touchdown to make the score 13-12 in Ayden's favor. In those days, most teams ran for the extra point rather than kicking it. And, there was no two point conversion rule. Carroll McLawhorn ('62) hit the running back low, and I hit him high. In reality, I just helped out Carroll a little. He deserves most of the credit. Who knows if my memory is working the way it should. Writing is fun, but it also hurts sometimes. Bad memories resurface just like the good ones do. Many of you know we lost that game, 19-13. I remember someone saying afterwards that it was "one of the best high school football games ever played." It wasn't so great to me. I will never forget the locker room afterwards. In the middle of the twentieth century, men and boys weren't supposed to cry; nevertheless, there were many tears in the locker room that night.

The James Kenan game was just one of what many people in Ayden referred to as "near misses." Over time our teams had gone so far and were so good; yet, we'd been unable to win it all. There were on-the-field examples: a 25-footer at the buzzer by the opponent that went in, a layup that was missed, a critical fumble, an error. What if ... what if. There were off-the-field reasons; more than once in the middle of the 20th century, something happened off the field to deny or hamper the players in their quest to compete in the state playoffs. Pushing the broken down activity bus on the way to a playoff game in Edenton didn't help much either.

One summer night between my academic years at East Carolina College, I was called out of the stands and asked to umpire a little league baseball game. There was no umpire for the game, and I thought, "These kids aren't gonna be able to play tonight unless I do this." I'd never umpired before. As I walked to home plate, Sam McLawhorn, who had been one of my little league coaches a few years earlier, gave me a 10-second training course. "William, I don't care whether you get the calls right or not, just call them fast."

On the mound was a skinny little left-hander. I remember distinctly calling balls and strikes that night. I had never seen a "counter," the little plastic thing that umpires used to keep balls and strikes and outs, so I kept those vital statistics on my fingers. Since I didn't have enough fingers for all those numbers at once, each time there was an out, I made a line in the dirt next to my right foot. I think I did pretty well for my first umpiring gig back when I didn't need to wear glasses. I did, however, have trouble seeing from one perspective. When the pitcher turned sideways during his windup, I had trouble picking up the pitch. Maybe that was the same problem Ayden's opponents had during the no-hitters he pitched in high school.

Stuart Tripp, who coached AHS football, basketball, and baseball, used to get a question over and over again: "Which teams were your best?" As far as I know, he always answered it the same way; Coach talked about the Teedy Bullock ('52) era and the Paul Miller ('68) era. Of course, Paul was the pitcher on the mound for my umpiring debut, and Teedy and I probably set a record for the longest phone interview. (I felt like I already knew Teedy because of my Daddy's stories about him and his teammates.) I have heard both of them emphasize, "I was just one of the players on a team of great players."

When I suited up for the home football games during my senior year, running around behind the bleachers pretending to be football players was a group of kids who would end the "near misses" drought. Once their opportunity arrived, these play actors would accomplish something that not only would be a first in Tornado country but also a first in North Carolina, a record that would stand for decades.

*The time has come to crank up the Thunderbird. Hop in, we're gonna drive over to the spot where I walked down the aisle to the tune of 'Pomp and Circumstance.'*

Imagine yourself in the Ayden High School auditorium. For those of you who haven't been there, picture yourself sitting in one of the nine hundred seats with the projection room behind you and the stage in front of you. The draperies covering the huge windows on each side and the curtains currently hiding the stage are maroon with white fringe, the colors of the school.

You will be witness to a two-act play. Act 1 (Volume 1) will begin shortly. Act 2 (Volume 2) will follow after the intermission. Soon, the curtains will open for Act 1. You will be taken back more than a century to a tiny settlement without an official name. And then – street by street, house by house, business by business, church by church, and family by family – Ayden will come alive. In 1914 a two-story red brick graded school will be launched on Snow Hill Street, and the building in which you are sitting will open on September 23, 1929, seven days late. Your seat was delivered and installed at a cost of $3.45 in the summer of 1929, but some of the other "finishing touches" took a week longer than expected.

When the curtains open, the spotlight will be on sports. However, the authors of the play you are about to experience recognized an essential reality early in their work: football, basketball, and baseball do not occur in a vacuum. In addition to the interplay between the citizens, teachers, and administrators of the town and school, the athletic environment was enhanced or hindered by the events of the day. The Great Depression and World War II touched the lives of every Aydenite. The sports venues of the Ayden High School Tornadoes and the South Ayden Eagles, and their opponents were captured by the social and economic changes of the 50s and 60s. When consolidation and integration finally arrived in 1971, the two Ayden schools vanished into the past. The play in the Ayden High auditorium will begin for you shortly. Presenting the theatrical production at South Ayden High, where the curtains would have been maroon and gray, will not be possible. Those buildings have been demolished.

Rather than providing the audience with an endless string of statistics and play by play accounts of game after game, Mitchell and I have tried to weave Ayden's sports story around and through the fabric of the community – to paint a portrait of the times. Usually, the painting on the canvas is serious-minded, sometimes it's comical, and, every now and then, the image may bring a tear to your eye. Most of all, we've tried to make it authentic.

**Ayden's Sunrise**

## Chapter 1
### A Balloon Ride

The next trip in my brand new red Thunderbird takes us to the middle school cafeteria in Ayden. We've arrived just in time to join in the singing: *Happy birthday to you, happy birthday to you, happy birthday dear* AYDEN, *happy birthday to you.* It is Sunday February 3, 1991 and Ayden is 100 years old. The four foot tall cake was baked by the Commercial Foods Class at Ayden-Grifton High School, the high school that was formed in 1971 upon the consolidation of three schools: Ayden High, Grifton High, and South Ayden High.

Naturally, our transportation to the celebration is make-believe but the roads we traveled are real. I've never actually been able to understand why the route to my hometown has been so important to me. Over the years, I've taken several routes from the Raleigh-Durham-Chapel Hill area. There came a time when the modern multi-lane highways, new strip malls, and housing developments began feeling awkward – like wearing my first baseman's glove on my right hand. That's when I started driving the "back roads" through the countryside. Sure, it would be faster to zoom along on the asphalt and cement heading east. It just ain't the same, though.

Starting about the time of Ayden's birthday party, my favorite way home has taken me past Southeastern Baptist Seminary in Wake Forest, on to Zebulon, through Wilson and past Farmville. A right-hand turn at Ballard's Crossroads has been a signal to me that I have about ten miles to go. Many of you reading these lines can recite the rest of the trip and, if you were like me, you memorized that "back way" before you learned to drive: left at the bull-eye house, right at the following intersection next to a house with a detached kitchen, around a 90-degree angle curve to the left and then another right hand turn. For me, going through the next intersection at Roundtree meant thinking back to my football days when Donald Carmen ('61) terrorized the other team's offense. His family's store was located at that crossroads. The next turn and I was almost home.

For a while, it seemed that the landmarks Daddy had pointed out to me were disappearing, one by one; sometimes only an open spot remained while another familiar marker had been replaced with a new house and freshly landscaped yard. On one trip I was surprised to see that a swath of forest had been traded for a housing development. I considered the new addition a loss, but I'm sure the new home owners did not see it that way. The cerebral map of my favorite part of the trip – from Ballard's Crossroads to Ayden was changing … forever.

*Now, it's time to try out my magical car again. Let's go back 100 years and see what all of the celebrating was about. Alf Harrington is waiting for us near the post office. He's got another vehicle that will provide us with a bird's eye view of a little community in Pitt County. It is 1891.*

The sun is rising and we – just you and me – are hovering over Ayden in a hot air balloon, moving very slowly, peering over the side of the basket at the newly incorporated town of a few hundred inhabitants. When a citizen thought of the previous war, it would have been the Civil War, a conflict that had been over for less than thirty years. We can see the occasional horse and buggy meandering along the dirt streets. The first appearance of the motor car in Ayden was several years away. It was owned by John E. Hart from Kinston. He drove the car into a tobacco warehouse and charged ten cents for the curiosity seekers to sit behind the wheel of the new-fangled contraption.

There would have been no airplanes in the sky to interfere with our balloon ride, no telephones on which to catch up on local gossip, and no *Ed Sullivan Show* on television to view Elvis' scandalous display of swinging hips. Gathering around the radio to hear President Roosevelt's fireside chats during the Great Depression was still four decades away.

That same year, 1891, the first electric lights were installed in the White House. President Harrison's family was afraid to turn the new devices on and off for fear of receiving a shock. As a result, the staff turned the electricity on at night and off in the morning. At the time, virtually all of Ayden's citizens could have traveled north to participate in our nation's centennial in 1876. For them, a trip to Philadelphia would have taken several days rather than a few hours. Just a year ago in 1890 the Census Bureau had declared that the frontier was over. Our country's greatest man-made spectacle to that point, the Chicago World's Fair, would have been two years in the future.

Over the years, conflicting renditions of how Ayden got its name have appeared in the oral and recorded histories of the community. Sifting through the various versions and settling on only one of them would be sure to get an author on Ayden's 10 Most Wanted list. One story that used to appear on the town brochure stated that the little village was first known as Otter Town, named for Otter Dennis, a man who seemed to stay in trouble with the law because he "loved to fight." Apparently, Mr. Dennis attracted others of like persuasion; so much so that the area became known as "a den" of misfits and criminals. "A den" became Aden. During that time, the center of town was located in the vicinity of today's Farmer's Funeral Home.

In 1929, Bonnie Ruth Tripp described a bar where the men would go each night until their wives became angry. "When asked where their husbands were, wives would say 'at the den' for that is what they called the barroom." The town was temporarily named Aden. Ms. Tripp stated that some of the local business men were responsible for placing the "y" in the name.

Additional versions of how the town was named have become intermingled with how the hamlet actually got started. All agree on at least one thing: Ayden grew up around the railroad. The owners of the Wilmington-Weldon Railroad, later known as the Atlantic Coastline Railroad, made a decision to extend its tracks from Scotland Neck to Kinston. William Henry Harris, who had visions of a town being located on his farmland, was successful in persuading the railroad to build its tracks through his property. When the railway depot was built, the middle of town shifted to the railroad tracks, and 2$^{nd}$ Street became the community's main street.

Published dates vary, but most likely in 1889 the first postmaster, Alf Harrington, was asked by the U.S. Post Office to provide a name for the town, a requirement as part of the application for the town to be awarded a post office. He could have chosen Harrisville, Harriston, or Harristown – three different names that appear in the descriptions of that era. Daddy always claimed that this was the true version of the origination of his home town. In addition, he was sure that Mr. Alf was part of the Harrington family and that he initially named the town after himself. I cannot vouch for the authenticity of this story. I can assure you, however, that his story was consistent. Maybe I should call Mr. Alf, "Uncle Alf." Daddy called him one of those two names. It appears more likely that the town was named after William Henry Harris, the man who sold his property to the railroad. If Daddy were here today, he may be persuaded that it was Uncle Harris and not Uncle Alf who deserves credit for Ayden's first name. And then again ....

On one occasion, I arrived in Ayden to visit my parents and discovered that Daddy was unhappy about an article that had appeared in the latest version of *The Times-Leader*. The reporter quoted the town manager's account of Ayden's beginning. He grabbed his cane from behind the door, drove to the Town of Ayden office, and demanded to see the manager. He was never afforded the opportunity. Let's just say that my Daddy was sometimes incapable of applying the skills of diplomacy. More than likely, his reputation arrived before he did.

No one knows why Uncle Alf chose Aden unless the postmaster had knowledge of Otter Dennis and his "den" of cutthroats. Some say he simply searched a map of the world and settled on the Gulf of Aden, an extension of the Indian Ocean located between Asia and Africa. When the name, Aden, was submitted to the U.S. Post Office, the agency asked that a "y" be inserted. Another version claims that our representative in Washington, D.C., Congressman Small, suggested to Mr. Harrington that a "y" be placed after the "A" to "dignify the name."

Like the uncertainty of how Ayden got its name, the precise date of its official "naming" has also been elusive. At least as early as 1889, there was an *Ayden Reflector* newspaper, so the small cluster of houses, businesses, and churches had become Ayden at least that early. Another account indicated that the first newspaper appeared between 1890 and 1900. The *Ayden Journal* was published and edited by A.L. "Trump" Harrington. I assume this Mr. Harrington was the same Alf Harrington, the postmaster.

Before the North Carolina legislature provided Ayden with its incorporation papers in 1891, people came from far and wide in their spring-wagons, buggies and surries to see the first train on its inaugural run between Kinston and Weldon. Few people of the horse and buggy community, who gathered in large crowds to gaze at the huge black iron huffing and puffing locomotive and its procession of cars, could have imagined the new-fangled contrivances that awaited them and their children and grandchildren in the upcoming century.

In the late 1890s and early 1900s, after William Henry Harris laid out the first streets and sold some more of his property for building, Ayden became home to "two growing colleges, five churches, a fifty-room hotel, three tobacco warehouses, a municipal swimming pool, and doctors, lawyers and druggists in abundance."

A.W. Sawyer, my Granddaddy, remembered watching the first noisy automobiles ramble down an unpaved street, the first airplane flying overhead, and the first time he clicked on a radio. I recollect turning the knob to a large console radio that stood between Grandmamma's chair and the oil circulator stove in their living room. A large green light appeared on the dial, a prelude to the actual radio broadcast that finally came on after the tubes had time to warm up. Together, Granddaddy and I watched our first television programs. Sitting on my grandparents' couch next to Granddaddy in his easy chair, we were watching a program when he exclaimed, "William, look at those women." Even at an early age, I didn't need to be prompted to view the little black and white screen that was filled with dancing girls. I really didn't know what he was getting at until he explained, "I didn't see your grandmother's ankles until after we were married."

A few years later in 1969 when Granddaddy was 77 years old, I asked him what he thought about a man setting foot on the moon.

"Oh, I don't believe it," he exclaimed.

"But Granddaddy, we saw it on television."

"They were somewhere down there in the Everglades." A man who remembered gazing at his first flying machine couldn't believe that astronauts had really walked around on that big white ball in the sky.

After several additional successes by America's space program, I asked Granddaddy the same question again. "I guess those damned fools have put somebody up there," he answered. His biggest question then became, "Why would anybody want to do such a thing?"

To resurrect Ayden's early history, I've relied on word-of-mouth accounts, unpublished papers, and *The Ayden Dispatch*. From time to time an article referring to those times would appear in the newspapers of the 1920s and 1930s. The February 25, 1937 publication of a four-section special edition of *The Ayden Dispatch* represents the most informative single-source of Ayden's history that I've been able to recover.

The first residence erected on Lee Street, the home of Mr. and Mrs. J. R. Smith. The family, including little May, now Mrs. P. R. Taylor, is shown in the picture, which was made in 1898.

**The first residence on Lee Street, Ayden, N.C.** *(Scan of Unknown Newspaper Clipping)*

## Early Ayden

1908: Whiskey is sold by the Town of Ayden. Profits = $1,713.43. A year later, a referendum passed outlawing the sale of hard liquor.

1912: *Ayden Dispatch's* first edition; contest held to name the paper; Vida B. McLawhorn wins $10.00 prize.

1926: Cost for storing a bale of cotton in warehouse, 35 cents per month.

1926: Buy your new Whippet at Turnage Motor Co. for $695.

1927: Mr. and Mrs. M.C. Moye are the new managers of the Hotel Beverly.

1927: City life tending to wipe out sex lives; making women masculine and men feminine.

1928: When the post office is closed, go to John Burgess for postage stamps.

1929: Town employees take 25% cut in salaries.

1929: Veneer Plant closes after thirteen years.

1929: Stub Johnson and his orchestra will play at the Princess Theater.

1929: Crime will be reduced to a minimum by the super-microscope.

1929: Get America's favorite drink, an ice cream soda, at Edwards Pharmacy.

1929: Warning = Do not drop cigars or cigarettes from airplane.

1929: Midway Service Station officially appointed as testing station for headlights.

1929: Auto Polo to be played at fair.

1929: Filling station owner outraged by price of a gallon of gasoline, 21 cents.

1929: Mr. Charles McGlohon trades his house and lot on Park Lane to Mr. J.A. Collins for a small farm out on the western skirts of the city.

1929: Ayden Rotary Club's 64 consecutive meetings of 100% attendance broken when one of members gets married and forgets about the meeting.

1930: Wanted – A good looking, home-loving, sweet, tender woman, to become the wife of a good looking man; state age in first letter.

1932: Cost of portable typewriter = $34.75; it writes small letters as well as capitals.

1933: Meeting of Eastern Carolina Chamber of Commerce to hear about President Roosevelt's "New Deal."

1933: Child Labor Law: prohibits regular employment of children under 16; farm children excepted.

1934: Deposits at First National Bank increase by 650% over last year.

1935: Woman's Club sets out cedar trees on drive to cemetery.

1935: New law requires dogs to be vaccinated for rabies.

1935: Of the 140 privies in Ayden, only 3% comply with state law.

1935: Warning not to lift new telephone while it is ringing; may cause mechanical problem.

1935: Community Building formally opens in December; J.R. Turnage presiding and Miss Virginia Belle Cooper in charge of music.

1936: Helen Joyce Whitehurst wins the Shirley Temple contest at Amateur Night.

1936: By a 6-3 vote, the United States Supreme Court rules President Roosevelt's "New Deal" unconstitutional.

1936: East Carolina Teachers College; largest enrollment in school's history = 1,077.

1936: S.F. Peterson announces rat eradication campaign; order for bait will be sent in on Wednesday.

1936: Social security spreading throughout states; now in 21 states and District of Columbia.

1936: On May 21 Spring Festival to be held in Ayden; expected to surpass anything ever undertaken in the community.

1936: Highway patrolmen will not accept applications for driver's licenses from anyone who has the slightest odor of alcohol on their breath.

1938: Princess Theater to show local movies; contact W.C. Ormond, Manager, with suggestions.

1938: Suggestion at Rotary Club meeting to re-open old swimming pool; money from WPA could be used.

1938: Ayden Symphonic Chorus, as part of eastern North Carolina Symphonic Coral Association, invited to sing at World's Fair in New York.

1938: Miss Frances Tripp wins trip to Charlotte to see Gene Autry in person; had several conversations with Autry and will talk of experiences during next week's 5-year celebration of Princess Theater's re-opening.

1939: Ayden Bowling Alley opens next door to J.E. Cannon's Store.

1939: John Burgess advertises Coca Cola in bottles.

1939: Attorney Robert Booth opens office over Edwards Pharmacy.

1939: France's army of 6,000,000 men looked on as one of greatest armies in world.

1939: Al Capone will receive a government bill of $350,000 for past income taxes from 1924-1929 when he is freed from Federal Prison.

**1894 Ayden Railroad Depot** *(Scan of Unknown Newspaper Clipping)*

Andrea (Harris) Norris ('61) has compiled a storehouse of published and unpublished materials which often provided me with information that was unavailable elsewhere. The Town of Ayden office also maintains a collection of the minutes of board meetings starting over 100 years ago.

The oldest known record of the Ayden Board of Commissioners, called the Planning Board at the time, was dated May 9, 1907. During the board meetings that year, one of the most contentious issues pertained to the cattle and hogs that often roamed through the streets and yards. The citizens complained to the board members, and an ordinance was passed to build fences to keep the livestock outside the town limit. Ordinance 53 "made it unlawful for any person or persons to injure, impair or leave open or for a child or children to swing on any of the gates belonging to the town under penalty of $10 and repair damage to said gate or gates." As a young boy, Daddy remembered standing next to the fences on the roads leading into town in hopes that someone would come along and flip him a nickel to open the gate.

Twenty years later, the problem had not been completely resolved. The March 24, 1927 issue of *The Ayden Dispatch* carried the following message from the mayor: "Mayor K.A. Pittman requests us to call to the attention of our citizens the ordinance prohibiting chickens running at large within the town limits." Another plea would be forthcoming a year later; A.W. Sawyer, as manager of the town office, was charged by the board with asking the Chief of Police to enforce the ordinance disallowing chickens to run free. Once again in 1940, Mayor W.C. Ormond admonished Ayden's citizens for not following the law and warned them "to keep [your] chickens at home." Over the decades, the chickens lost their battle for liberty entirely; a 2005 local law prohibited chickens within Ayden's town limit. I assumed that my research into Ayden's chicken conundrum had been settled. Not so. Yes, the chickens had lost the battle, but – as it turns out – not the war. Recently, the eternal question arose again. This time, the battle cry appearing on the Commissioners' agenda was "bring back the chickens." Finally on a 4-1 vote during a February 10, 2014 meeting, the governing board once again provided the chickens with their freedom – at least for now.

The early 20th century "animal problem" continued into 1908. When some townspeople complained of the odor, an ordinance was passed prohibiting the building of a hog pen within one-hundred feet of an occupied dwelling. A stock pound was built to hold any pigs that were confiscated under the new law. At the following board meeting, the Chief of Police, C.G. "Church" Moore, reported that citizens living near the stock pound had also complained of the odor. At the next meeting, board members appropriated $1.25 to build a new stock pound at another location.

Ordinance 58, passed into law on April 2, 1912, "declared that all drivers of automobiles are required to drive on the right side of the road and are forbidden to drive at a speed of over 10 miles an hour. They must also give a signal at all street crossings or turnings on street corners." The fine for each offense was $5.00.

On February 4, 1913, the minutes of the board reflected the authorization to purchase a horse and cart for use by the Town of Ayden. The cart cost $20.40 and the horse cost $250.00. The following year the street committee made it easier for the town's horse and cart and the automobiles in town to navigate the streets of Ayden by passing a motion to remove all electric light and phone poles from the middle of the streets. The Town of Ayden also hired "the county road machine and other equipment" to improve the town's roads. During a two-year period from approximately 1920 to 1922, the streets were paved for the first time with the support of a $225,000 bond issue.

*Still floating along in our balloon, I'm looking for the Chamber of Commerce office. There it is ... right over there. I understand that they've just published a booklet that tells all about Ayden. I'll bet Mr. W.E. Hooks, the Secretary, or the President, Reverend Samuel B. Waggoner, will give us a copy.*

*Seems strange to call Ayden a little city, but that's what it is called throughout the publication, which is undated. Judging by the amenities that are described, I'm gonna give it a 1916 release date.*

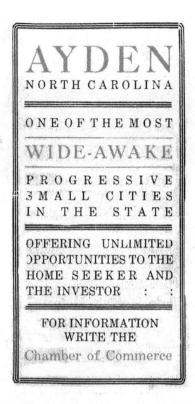

**1916 Ayden Chamber of Commerce Booklet** *(Courtesy, Elaine McLawhorn Dail)*

The 1916 print date means it is one of the oldest documents of Ayden in existence. Only the 1907 board meeting minutes, archived at the Town of Ayden office, are older. The narrative is interspersed with pictures of the churches, banks, businesses, and noted citizens' homes in the community. The Bank of Ayden and the Farmers and Merchants Bank are across the street from each other. The Methodist Church is still on the corner of Lee Street and 3rd Street. The Chamber brags about the newly built 50-room hotel with telephones in each room: "The town now has a beautiful twenty-five thousand dollar hotel, which is classed as one of the finest and most pretentious structures to be found in this section of the State." The Sauls' Drug Store ad emphasizes that its "prescriptions receive our most careful attention, and are compounded by thoroughly experienced druggists." I assume prescriptions were written by the

doctors whose names grace the pages of the booklet: W. Harvey Dixon
and M.T. Frizzelle.

L. C. TURNAGE HARDWARE COMPANY,
SECOND STREET, AYDEN, N. C.

FARMERS & MERCHANTS BANK, AND
J. J. EDWARDS & SON'S STORE, CORNER
LEE AND SECOND STREETS, AYDEN,
NORTH CAROLINA.

BANK OF AYDEN, CORNER LEE AND
SECOND STREETS, AYDEN, N. C.

HOME OF MR. W. E. HOOKS, SECRE-
TARY OF THE AYDEN CHAMBER OF
COMMERCE.

HOME OF MR. R. W. SMITH, VICE-
PRESIDENT OF AYDEN CHAMBER OF
COMMERCE.

**Photos from 1916 Ayden Chamber of Commerce Booklet** *(Courtesy, Elaine McLawhorn
Dail)*

CHRISTIAN CHURCH, SECOND STREET, AYDEN, N. C.

INTERIOR VIEW OF HARDWARE DE-PARTMENT OF J. R. SMITH & BRO'S. STORE, SECOND STREET, AYDEN, N. C.

NEW AYDEN HOTEL, SECOND STREET, AYDEN, N. C.

METHODIST CHURCH, CORNER LEE AND THIRD STREETS, AYDEN, N. C.

**Photos from 1916 Ayden Chamber of Commerce Booklet** *(Courtesy, Elaine McLawhorn Dail)*

Gazing through this public relations booklet is like peeping into Ayden's first chapter – maybe it's the second chapter when the 25 year old village developed into a little city. I can see the early beginnings of the thriving community it became. It may have been called a little city, but farming was its centerpiece, its economic underwriter. The dry goods stores, grocery stores, clothing stores, and all the businesses were able to flourish primarily because tobacco and other crops provided the cash to grease the wheels of progress.

There are so many business leaders of the early Ayden community to be celebrated. The aforementioned 1937 four-section edition of *The Ayden Dispatch* offered pictures and narratives of most of them. Distinguished leader after leader helped build the town into what it is today. I wish I could cover them all, but it would require another book to tell their stories. I will mention one of Ayden's finest, a man I knew from my childhood.

George Grady Dixon attended the Medical College of Virginia and graduated in 1915. Bill Norris and I remembered him in the same way – a man with a gravelly voice and a big heart. Dr. Grady loved Ayden: "I have traveled about the world a great deal in the past 35 years and I never yet have found a place to compare with Ayden in friendliness and living appeal." A stranger in town would have questioned the physician's statement if he'd heard how Dr. Grady spoke to my paternal grandmother when she visited his office once: "Hey Lou, what in the hell's wrong with you?" Dr. Grady and his family lived two houses from us on Snow Hill Street, but I never saw him at home. He was always taking care of people at his office or at their home. Dr. Grady died much too soon – at the age of 64. Bill Norris remembered that Saturday in May of 1958: "He had a heart seizure and turned to his wife and said, 'This is it.'" Bill was 17 years old at the time.

*Let's hover for a few minutes over the marshes in the Swift Creek area before we set her down in a place that's special to me.*

Years before the polio epidemic was brought under control by the Salk vaccine and decades before the scourge of the HIV virus, malaria presented a significant health problem in the Swift Creek area near Ayden. By researching the medical records of local physicians, the U.S. Public Health Service "... estimated that 25 per cent of their practice on the Swift Creek water-shed was for malaria. In the survey, out of 500 citizens interviewed, 58.8 per cent gave a history of 'chills and fever.'" By 1937 the drainage of the Swift Creek marshes had been completed. This endeavor brought to an end what Dr. N. Thomas Ennett, Pitt County Health Officer, described as the "greatest health project ever undertaken in Pitt County."

On this significant accomplishment, I suggest that our history balloon touch down in a spot of your choice, inside or outside of the town limit. You imagine when and where; could be at your current address, could be on the day you first traveled to Ayden, could be on the street or the farm where you grew up, could be anywhere you desire. For me, I believe I'll land in Momma and Daddy's back yard. I want to admire Bill Harrington's garden again. One more time, I want to taste Momma's fried chicken and cornbread accompanied by fresh butter beans and tomatoes from his garden. I don't know about you, but I've timed my visit to coincide with the first harvest of Daddy's little strawberry patch. As I walk through the back door, Momma is whipping *real* whip cream to go on the strawberries and little Merita cakes she just purchased from Louise Moseley's grocery store.

I wish I could personalize a balloon trip for everyone who journeys through this chapter – especially if you grew up in Ayden. I'll gladly loan you the balloon if you want to climb into the basket and linger over a place that's special to you.

### Start-ups in Early Ayden

(Ayden census: **557** in 1900; **990** in 1910; **1,673** in 1920; **1,750** in 1937)

1900: **Tripp Brothers Garage**

1901: **Sauls' Drug Store**

1904: **Turnage Brothers Company**

1906: **Ayden Loan and Insurance Company**

1906: **Spear Jewelry Company**

1907: **J.B. Pierce Company**

1912: **Ayden Dispatch**

1914: **Edwards Pharmacy**

1916: **Ayden Tailoring Company**

1916: **Veneer Plant**

1916: **Hotel Beverly**

1917: **J.E. Jones, Plumbing and Electrical Contractor**

1919: **Mumford's Sanitary Market**

1919: **Tyndall-Boyd-Stroud Company**

1920: **P.R. Taylor and Company**

1920: **J.J. McClees Company**

1922: **Building and Loan Association**

1923: **Ayden Free Will Baptist Press**

1924: **Ayden Rotary Club**

1925: **Midway Service Station**

1925: **Ayden Woman's Club**

1926: **Serv-U Battery Company**

1926: **Roy L. Turnage Department Store**

1926: **Ayden Ice Company**

1927: **Light and Water Office (Town of Ayden)**

# Chapter 2
## Ayden, the Education Town

**1914 Ayden Graded School in 1916 Ayden Chamber of Commerce Booklet** *(Courtesy, Elaine McLawhorn Dail)*

If I were to describe progress in the 20th century to someone who knew little about America, at some point in my explanation I would have to tell the story of public school education: from one-room schools to the world's premier higher education system. The single most important decision that I ever made was to go to college – not for the dollars and cents reasons politicians always crow about, but because of what it did for me as a person. Sure, matriculation helped me climb the socio-economic ladder. However, attending college did something that money cannot buy. It became the focal point of my self-esteem and led to a lifetime of learning.

*Climb in, I'm gonna drive through the neighborhood near 515 Snow Hill Street where I grew up. Let's keep the top down because nobody will recognize me in the Thunderbird unless they can see my face. Let's say it's sometime in the 1950s. But, remember in our magic car, we'll be able to look backwards as well as forwards. My neighbors would recognize me if I were driving one of my father's Chevrolets. He didn't like Fords; thought they were inferior vehicles. I'm sure he's turned over in his grave with all these accolades I've been attributing to the Ford Motor Company's Thunderbird.*

You might say that I was surrounded by "education." Faust Johnson, the only principal I ever had, lived near my boyhood home. Uncle Frank, the Agricultural and Industrial Arts teacher at AHS for over 30 years, Aunt Edna, and Frankie Lou occupied the house directly in front of ours. Another teacher, Mary Sumrell, lived next door to my aunt and uncle. My high school English teacher, Louise Little, resided three houses down from them, and next to Mrs. Little another teacher spent her formative years. Several other teachers and school administrators and their families also lived close by. If I were to total up all the years my neighbors spent in the education field, it would be about 300 years. They spanned the instructional continuum – from a pre-school teacher to elementary, secondary and college teachers. Two Ayden athletes from the neighborhood would go on to become college presidents. That's what I mean when I say I was surrounded by education.

My family on my mother's side had a relative in Wilson, N.C. Cousin Mary, as we called her, lived across the street from Atlantic Christian College. I remember visiting her when I still needed Granddaddy to accompany me as I played around the campus. Visiting relatives when I was a teenager was not exactly the coolest thing to do; nonetheless, I always liked Cousin Mary and her neighborhood of big white houses, majestic oaks, and tall green Magnolia trees. A college campus is still one of the most beautiful places in America to me. It could be that Atlantic Christian College provided me with my first "taste" of that beauty.

Atlantic Christian College became Barton College in September 1990. One of those college presidents I just cited grew up around the corner from the Harringtons. His mom, Mavis "Bo-Parts" Parker ('28), and my dad graduated from high school together. Incidentally, one of the teachers I just mentioned – Louise "Squeeze-her" Prescott ('28) – also graduated with dad from high school. Of course, those were their maiden names and their nicknames as they appeared in Ayden High School's first annual published by their senior class. After marrying, they became Mavis Hemby and Louise Little.

At that time, married women were often called by their husband's names – especially if their names appeared in the newspaper or some other pubic document. Mrs. Louise Little was Mrs. C.C. Little. My Sunday school teacher, who I always referred to as Mrs. Stroud, was Mrs. O.C. Stroud. To this day, I did not know Mrs. Stroud's first name until her daughter-in-law, Helen Joyce Stroud ('49), told me it was Annie. This may not seem fair today, but another version of this practice did assist us in addressing the two Mary Sumrells who lived nearby. One was called Mary "Dalton" and the other was Mary "Stancil." In this case, the first names of their husbands were used to eliminate any confusion.

You can bet that I had no chance of getting away with anything in Ayden, especially in the few blocks surrounding my house. Of course, that did not deter me from trying. The time or two that I was bad, my mother knew about it before I reached home. Daddy was at work where I hoped he'd stay forever. I sometimes lobbied Momma not to tell Daddy of my transgressions. Sometimes I won, but not often. The enforcer always seemed to appear at about the same time every day. The dragnet of friendly spies extended well beyond the town limit. After graduation and under the cover of darkness, Richard McLawhorn ('61) threw a party for us in one of his family's tenant houses on their farm. Champagne was the drink of choice. The next morning, Momma asked me how I enjoyed the party last night.

Back to my neighborhood. One of the college presidents was James Hemby ('51), Mavis' son. In October 1983, he spent his first day as president of Atlantic Christian College. James grew up on Park Avenue. When James was dodging the trees and bushes while playing football in the McGlohon's side yard across 4th Street, I'm sure he had no idea that he would someday be leading the college that originated a few blocks from his boyhood home.

The Town of Ayden offered $100 in cash and five acres of land donated by William Henry Harris and J.S. Hines to the Disciples of Christ, known later as the Christian Church. The trustees of Carolina Christian College voted to accept the town's incentives. With seventeen students, the new school opened on September 18, 1893 on property located on the north side of Cannon Street between East College and West College Streets. By 1902, Carolina Christian College had enrolled 160 students. In that year, the Disciples of Christ denomination made the decision to merge several of their existing schools into one college located in Wilson, N.C. In 1905, Carolina Christian College in Ayden moved to Wilson as part of the consolidation. The new school was named Atlantic Christian College. The property in Ayden was sold the following year to the county school system. Until the beginning of World War I, the classroom building was used as a graded school. The building was demolished in the 1920s.

In 1898, five years after the forerunner of Barton College opened its doors, the Free Will Baptist denomination constructed a building to house a theological seminary on the corner of Lee Street and 6th Street. (In 1929, Ayden High School would open on the same property. Currently, the building is the home of the Ayden Arts and Recreation Center.) The two-story frame structure included classrooms, a library, and a society hall. Within the next several years, the building was expanded by adding an auditorium.

The primary objective of the Free Will Baptist Seminary was the training of ministers to meet a demand that had been expressed by leading members of the church. The college eventually expanded its mission and offered junior college level work. By the end of the school year in 1925, the Board of Directors authorized the president to offer the first year of a Bachelor of Arts degree; freshman college courses were offered at the beginning of the next school year. Those courses were added to the curriculum, which had previously included regular high school work, music, commercial work, and Bible courses.

In 1926, the school's name was changed to Eureka College and moved to Boulevard Street where it intersected with East College Street, an area of town known as Sunrise Park. The campus eventually included a two-story brick classroom and dormitory building, athletic fields, and tennis courts. The high school tuition was $5.00 per month and the college tuition was $6.00 each month. For music majors, an additional 75 cents was charged.

Toward the end of World War I, a general consensus arose among the Board of Trustees: the institution may have to close unless the curriculum was expanded to include college work toward a four-year degree. This started the effort to keep the doors of the college open and led to the expansion of the curriculum. After years of financial problems, Eureka College closed in 1931.

In 1951, the college reopened in Mt. Olive, N.C. The University of Mt. Olive currently has off-campus programs in six locales around the state: Jacksonville, New Bern, Research Triangle Park, Smithfield, Washington, and Wilmington.

Before I entered the first grade, I knew where I'd be going to school: four years in the "little red brick building" on the playground two blocks from my house and eight years in the high school building. I never gave any thought to doing it any other way. One-room schools were things that I read about in books and saw on *Gunsmoke* and other television shows. Also called rural free schools, those schools were scattered throughout the rural areas around Ayden. They were too numerous to mention them all. One was built by the Spring Branch Free Will Baptist Church; another was called the Garris School originally located near Elm Grove Free Will Baptist Church. The Oak Ridge School was built across the road from what would become Ayden-Grifton High School.

Unlike the huge multi-room, multi-winged monstrosities built today, a rural school lived up to its other name – one-room schoolhouse. To construct these modern buildings, bond issues have to be passed, government regulatory boards need to be satisfied, and blueprints approved. For the sake of brevity, I've left out many steps. When I asked my first cousin, Sammy Anson Pierce, about the history of the Pierce Community Center a few miles east of Ayden on State Highway 102, his description scarcely resembles the brick and mortar giants. It was built by Sammy Anson's great-great grandfather, John Pierce (1839-1907), and his wife, Elizabeth Ann McLawhorn (1843-1916), as a one-room school *for the extended family*. It became known later as the Pierce Fellowship Hall and was used for family reunions and social events. By the time Sammy Anson's dad, Sammy Pierce ('38), retired and returned to Ayden, the building was deteriorating. The elder Pierce converted the building into the Ayden VFW, and their meetings were held there for several years. Next up, the little white wooden building became a church when a rift occurred in Sammy Anson's dad's church. The congregation met there until Sammy's death. Last up, the former one-room school became home to American Legion Post 289.

**Pierce Community Center located west of Ayden on NC Highway 102.** *(Photo by Mitchell Oakley)*

In the mid-1980s, a retired teacher was interviewed for an unpublished paper that summarized part of the history of education in Ayden. At the age of eighteen, this anonymous interviewee launched her career in one of the one-room schools. For her monthly salary of $65.00, she taught grades four through seven, a class totaling 22 students. One of her initial qualifications was a high school diploma, to which she added two summer sessions at East Carolina Teacher's College, a few miles away in Greenville, N.C. The curriculum she taught consisted of the three r's, history, geography, music, art, and drama. The school day began at 9:00 in the morning with the Pledge of Allegiance, singing, a Bible story, and the Lord's Prayer. Since a library was not available to the school, books were rented from the North Carolina Library Commission. The school day ended at 4:00.

At times, hot cocoa would be made to go along with the bagged lunches brought from home. The water to make the cocoa was collected from an outside hand pump. When a student asked the inevitable question, "May I go to the bathroom," he or she had the choice of dual outhouses in the woods behind the building.

Once the currently named Barton College moved to Wilson, the vacated buildings were purchased by the Town of Ayden for use as a graded school. When those structures became inadequate, a new graded school was completed and opened in 1914. The two-story brick building was the building where Daddy graduated from high school and where I attended grades one through four. It was located diagonally across the block from the tennis courts in Veteran's Memorial Park facing Snow Hill Street and near the corner of Washington Street and 3$^{rd}$ Street.

After several years of lobbying by local citizens and school officials, work started on a high school building on May 1, 1929 – giving the builders four months to complete the structure before school opened. To be located on Lee Street on the "old site of the Free Will Baptist Seminary," the building and equipment were to cost $100,000. Delayed construction postponed the opening; the school year started on September 23, 1929 rather than the planned date of September 16. The new building included a "gym for boys and girls" and a 900-seat auditorium. I attended grades five through twelve in that building at the corner of Lee Street and 6$^{th}$ Street.

During the latter part of the 19$^{th}$ century and the first three decades of the 20$^{th}$ century, one-room schools, a graded school, and the two colleges existed simultaneously for the youngsters of Ayden. A woman born in 1913 preferred to remain anonymous when she told her story to the local newspaper. She attended grades one and two at Hardee School (one-room school); started Corey School (one-room school) in the 3$^{rd}$ grade, and, in the 6$^{th}$ grade, attended Ayden Grammar School (graded school) while her brother attended the Free Will Baptist Seminary. Her freshman year was spent at the Free Will Baptist Seminary and her junior year at the new Ayden High School. Finally, she graduated from Ayden High School, a member of the class of 1931.

**1929 Ayden High School (***Photo Courtesy of Andrea Norris***)**

The configuration of education buildings – the grammar school on Snow Hill Street and the high school building on Lee Street – remained essentially the same from 1929 until the Ayden Elementary School opened in the fall of 1957. Tommy Craft, the school's first principal, remembered working during the summer to prepare for the fall opening: "I can recall spending many hours painting the old lunchroom tables." At that time, he was a building principal who carried a full-time teaching load:

"Office work and records were completed after the regular school day. The school secretary was located at the high school building (several blocks away). Letters and reports were sent or delivered to the high school at the end of the day. Lunchroom receipts were given to the school secretary after the lunch break. The secretary came over for lunch as well as the high school students.

Only one lunchroom was operated and the students in grades eight through twelve were transported by bus to the elementary building for lunch break."

In March 1984, I remember news reports of a tornado that plowed through Ayden. I felt compelled to drive to my home town to see the destruction first-hand. Beginning on Snow Hill Street Extension in the country, I drove toward Ayden and followed the path of the twister through town. The weather reports of tornadoes and their immense power had always been something I'd seen on TV. All of what I'd seen became very real: trees twisted like match sticks, a row of houses with one house destroyed and the others untouched, apartments near the elementary school damaged, and Farmer's Funeral Home destroyed. Mr. Craft, now superintendent of the Pitt County Schools, summarized the damage and subsequent chaos caused by the storm:

"On March 28, 1984, the Ayden community experienced a devastating tornado. The tornado struck Ayden at night while the building was vacant. The timing of the storm may have sparred many injuries as well as lives. Ayden Elementary School had to close its doors. The students were transferred to nearby Grifton for the remainder of the school term. Students, parents, and citizens of each community worked very cooperatively in successfully accomplishing the tremendous task of keeping the school operating for the remaining three months of the school year. Meanwhile, the task of rebuilding and renovating the Ayden School began. After many hours of hard work, on September 4, 1984, the doors of the Ayden Elementary School were once again opened with a "new look" and with great excitement on the part of the students, faculty and staff. A new year began!"

*Now, it's time to visit Ayden High School's first football team. To accomplish this, we'll need to rocket back to a time before the Great Depression. After we get some gasoline at Robert Johnson's Midway Service Station (where Guns Unlimited, Inc. is now located), you and I are gonna drive to Williamston for a historic event on a Friday afternoon in October 1926.*

## Early Education in Ayden

*One room rural schools with one or two teachers, two colleges (currently Barton College and Mt. Olive University), and the graded school existed simultaneously in Ayden during the first three decades of the 20th century.*

1914: First graded school – built for that purpose – opens on corner of Washington & 3rd Streets (now Veterans Memorial Park). First graded schools prior to 1914 were located in buildings designed for other purposes.

1921: Temporary wooden building erected on graded school property (where tennis courts are today) to accommodate overflow of students.

1924: First president of the new Parent Teachers Association, Mrs. O.C. Stroud.

1924: High school graduation exercises, nine girls and two boys.

1926: Cost to build new Eureka College auditorium, $5,000.

1927: Eureka College dining room and kitchen destroyed by fire.

1927: Ayden public school enrollment; elementary = 425; high school = 142.

1929: Mrs. Grimes works with several boys to plant hedges at new school to hide fence.

1929: New seats at Ayden High School auditorium delivered and installed, 900 seats at $3.45 each.

1929: Ayden High School building opens; eight month school year replaces six. Opening hymn was "Onward Christian Soldiers" led by

Miss Sara Brown Braxton with Miss Virginia Belle Cooper, accompanist.

1929: High school enrollment = 159.

1929: Physical education starts.

1930: Ten year comparison: # of years of college training for Ayden public school teachers in 1919-1920 = 1.8; 1929-1930 = 3.4.

1931: Remainder of Eureka College destroyed by fire; not used for college for two years; was being used as church.

1931: Consolidation of schools, Ayden to get 125 more students.

1931: Pitt County has a mixture of 6-month, 8-month, and 9-month schools.

1933: Woman's Club opens first public library in rear of John Burgess' drug store. Open Tuesday 7 – 9 and Friday 3 – 6.

1933: For last two years Ayden schools did not know if enough funds were available to complete school year. Each year, combination of citizens and government officials worked together to raise enough money to finish year.

1933: Opening of school year = total of 680 students in Ayden public schools.

1934: Old frame building on campus of grammar school to be torn down. Timber will be used in the construction of the Community Building and to repair a portion of the gym at the high school.

1934: Loonis Reeves McGlohon, at twelve years of age, makes the highest score in the the state on the 7th grade achievement tests.

1934: Gladys Best Tripp wins all-summer pass to the Princess Theater after being chosen the best all-round student at Ayden High School.

1935: Town library to be moved to Community Building; please return all books.

1935: Law requires that all children from 7-14 years of age are required to attend school.

1935: $600 will be awarded to family for every child killed on a school bus.

1936: 35 AHS students go on Washington, D.C. trip.

1936: 7th graders take trip to Raleigh to see the penitentiary and Dix Hill.

1938: Ayden School Board passes resolution for North Carolina to have 12th grade.

1939: Ayden High School graduating class = 17 boys and 17 girls.

1939: Faust Johnson resigns his position at First National Bank in Ayden to accept post of Athletic Director at Bethel High School.

1939: Band concerts to be held in front of AHS building by high school band during summers.

# Friendly Ghosts

## Chapter 3
### The First Football Season

Once upon a time when we ran onto the football field or the basketball court or the baseball diamond, many of us stepped into the shoes of our favorite player – the person we looked up to at Ayden High School. Was there someone you admired, someone who was bigger than life – someone you wanted to emulate? Maybe your hero was an older brother or sister. On the other hand, the person you wanted to model yourself after may not have been a player at all; he could have been Coach Stuart Tripp ('40) or Coach Tommy Lewis or Coach Tommy Craft. Maybe you played for your parents and the other fans in the bleachers and those scurrying along the sidelines. Perhaps you weren't taking part in athletics with anyone else in mind; for me, participating in sports was part of being a Harrington, part of growing up in Ayden – one of the rites of passage on my way from being a child to becoming an adult. I wanted to be as tough as R.L. Collins ('57) and a gifted three-sport athlete like Tommy Edwards ('58). Somehow I knew before my first game that I wasn't going to be that good, but I also knew that I would be on the team and, if I worked hard, maybe I could get better and play more. Ikey Baldree ('57) put it this way: "It was Teedy Bullock and Tommy Bullock, the Troy Jacksons and Mac Whitehursts, and Ham Langs … people like that who went before you and you wanted to be like 'em." Playing was the thing to do; it seemed to be built into the fabric of the community.

It is impossible to say just when this tradition started or, for that matter, how it began. I just know it ran onto the football field with me; it was right there next to me when I drove in for my first layup during warmup, and it strolled up to bat with me when I took my first turn at home plate. Even though I played much more baseball, football was my favorite. I can still hear the cleats making their familiar sound on the floor of the dressing room and the thundering of our blockers leading the way on the first "fullback around end" play of the game. There was also a smell that permeated the cool Friday night air. Could this tradition have started with the very first team?

The football players of the inaugural season of 1926-1927 could take their girlfriends to the movies in style when the Princess Theatre advertised the following modern convenience: "Management of the Princess Theatre wishes to announce that it is now possible to warm the building and make it comfortable for its patrons."

### Princess Theater
*Birth of a Nation* at Princess Theater
Matinee – 25 cents
Night – 50 cents

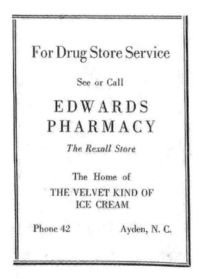

For Drug Store Service

See or Call

**EDWARDS PHARMACY**

*The Rexall Store*

The Home of
THE VELVET KIND OF
ICE CREAM

Phone 42          Ayden, N. C.

**1928 Edwards Pharmacy Ad** *(The Wheel, Vol. 1)*

Local citizens and students alike waited with anticipation for Edwards Pharmacy to advertise its latest shipment of what must have been a coveted item: "Johnston's Candy: Fresh shipment just received." Tripp

Brothers Garage advertised "car washing 75 cents to $1.25 according to condition of car." Turnage Motor Company ran an ad offering new cars at a reduced rate, ranging from $685 to $975. A high-torque engine was promoted and touted to reach the breathtaking speed of "5 mph to 40 mph in 21 seconds."

## TRIPP BROTHERS GARAGE

N. C. TRIPP, *Manager*

### AUTOMOBILE ACCESSORIES AND REPAIRING

OILS AND GREASES

AYDEN, N. C.

**1928 Tripp Brothers Ad** *(The Wheel, Vol. 1)*

Support of the school and athletics by local businessmen started early. They bought uniforms and equipment and ads for the premier issue of *The Wheel* in 1928. Bill Harrington remembered: "At first we had to go around to the merchants in Ayden and try to get them to donate money for our uniforms. The high school could not afford to buy them. Almost to a person, they gave us money." Once the players became business owners later in life, they returned the favor – over and over.

WILLYS KNIGHT                          WHIPPET

NASH

## TURNAGE MOTOR COMPANY

AYDEN, N. C.

**1928 Turnage Motor Co Ad** *(The Wheel, Vol. 1)*

The fall of 1926 marked the beginning of football at Ayden High School. For decades to come, the local print media would cover football in more detail than any other sport. First, *The Ayden Dispatch* and then *The Daily Reflector* in Greenville were my most dependable sources of information. Because this season was the Tornadoes' first, I've decided to duplicate the write-ups just as they appeared in the Ayden newspaper. There are some misspellings, run-on sentences, and other grammatical errors, but I want to provide you with the "flavor" of the reporting during that time period – especially prior to World War II. Once my research took me to the years after the war, the written commentary became more sophisticated; thus, providing us with more pertinent detailed coverage.

It is relatively safe to state that Ayden's first offensive formation was the single wing. Glenn "Pop" Warner invented the attack he referred to as the Carlisle formation because he was the head football coach of the Carlisle Indian Industrial School (1893-1917) when he first introduced it in 1907. Up to that time the team simply formed a wedge with the ball carrier in the middle and powered ahead. Warner's team not only lined up in an odd way in the backfield, but his team also ran from an unbalanced line. In what must have been baffling to the opposition, for the first time the plays were designed to be deceptive.

**The 1930-31 Ayden High School Starting Eleven**
This team defeated Chapel Hill, 12-0, on Thanksgiving Day, 1930. Members of the team in the double wing formation include (l-r): 'Undy' Dunn, Poss Sumrell, Bill Moore, Boots Mumford, Randolph 'Gorilla' Cannon, Bink Cox, and Andy Noe. Second row: W.O. Jolly, Boyd Cox, Russell Britt and Ed Hooks. (*Photo Courtesy Rudolph Cannon*)

The backfield position names are familiar to us; however, the quarterback, halfback, fullback, and tailback had different responsibilities. The quarterback was actually a blocker on most plays and the tailback was a triple-threat player: runner, passer, and punter.

The double wing was a version of the single wing. The picture of an early 1930s Ayden football team seems to be lined up in a double wing formation. Throughout the next several decades several innovations were introduced until the 1950s when the quarterback "moved underneath the center."

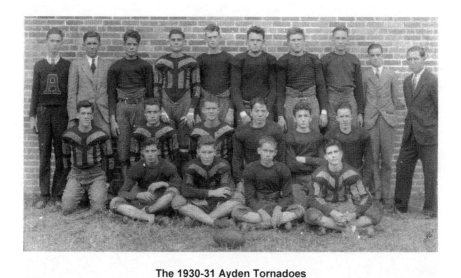

**The 1930-31 Ayden Tornadoes**
Members of the team include: (first row l-r): Unknown, C.O. Armstrong, Edward Harrington, and Edward Hooks. Second row: "Undy" Dunn, William Oscar Jolly, Russell Britt, Randolph 'Gorilla' Cannon, 'Boots' Mumford, and J.R. Taylor. Third row: Corey Stokes, Frank Pierce, Mark Tripp, Boyd Cox, "Poss" Sumrell, William Moore, Milton Cox, Andy Noe, C.L. Cannon and Ralph Coggins (Coach). (*Photo Courtesy of Bill Norris*)

On the Friday afternoon of October 8, 1926 in Williamston, N.C., the first football team representing Ayden High School played Williamston High School to a 0-0 tie.

### Ayden Plays Williamston to Scoreless Tie
(*Ayden Dispatch*: Thursday October 14, 1926)

*Last Friday afternoon at Williamston the first football team representing Ayden High School went into action. During the first few minutes of play the Williamston boys seemed to be headed for a touchdown, but at this juncture the Ayden defense stiffened and Williamston was forced to kick. During the remainder of the game the ball see-sawed back and forth with both teams fighting for the advantage.*

*The bright side of Williamston's play was their interference. The forward passing of Baldree with McLawhorn, Barwick, Smith and Edwards on the receiving end was the feature for Ayden. Six passes were attempted, five of which were completed for a gain of sixty five yards. The last whistle found Williamston in possession of the ball near the middle of the field.*

The second game of the season – the first ever played by an Ayden High School team on its home field – proved disastrous. Greenville won, 35-0. Tickets for the Friday afternoon game were 25 cents for all school children and 35 cents for adults.

### The Foot Ball Game, Were You There?
(*Ayden Dispatch*: Thursday October 21, 1926)

*Friday afternoon, October 15, the first football game ever played in Ayden took place between the two challenging teams – Greenville and Ayden. The Score being 35 to 0 in favor of Greenville. Those playing in the line up of Ayden were Kitchen McLawhorn, L.E.; Howard Sumrell, L.T.; Graves Mumford, L.G.; Elmer Tripp, C; Larry Tripp, R.G.; Mac Harrington, R.T.; Foy Barwick, R.E.; A.T. Baldree, Q.B.; Gene Smith, H.B.; Edwards H.B.; and Worthington, F.B.*

On Friday October 22, 1926, Ayden High School won its first football game by defeating La Grange High School.

### Ayden Wins
(*Ayden Dispatch*: Thursday October 28, 1926)

*Last Friday was a red letter day in the history of athletics in the Ayden High School. It was on this day that the football team won its first victory. The game was played at La Grange against the LeGrange High School. There was nothing freakish about the outcome, the victory was clean-cut and well earned. The team came back after its defeat at the hands of Greenville and played the best brand of ball yet displayed. It would not be hard to mention outstanding players in this game but it would be unjust to say that anyone man won the victory. The team played as a unit, the back field and line showing up equally well. LaGrange made many assaults on Ayden's line but in most every case the line held like a brick wall, and on several occasions the line opened up great holes in LaGrange's defense.*

*In the backfield Baldree at quarter ran the team like an old timer. The winning touchdown came in the last quarter as the result of a fake play around left end, Edwards going over for the only score. McLawhorn playing his first game at center showed up well. On the defense the tackling of Baldree and Smith was of a high order, many times they broke through to spill the LaGrange backs for losses. Ayden's gains came mostly as the result of end-runs and forward passes. Five times Baldree sailed the pigskin far over the LaGrange line and four times for substantial gains. Smith, Edwards and Barwick were on the receiving ends. LaGrange also attempted five passes, one of which was completed for a gain of two yards. Two of these attempts were intercepted, one by Baldree and the other by Worthington, another was grounded by Edwards.*

*While there were certain outstanding players every man on the team did his best, and the team as a unit feels that it is beginning to feel sure of itself.*

*The team is expecting a hard fight in the game here on Friday afternoon. Injuries have not kept any of the men out of the games so far, but accidents outside may hurt us Friday. Elmer Tripp, center, has been out for a week because of a burned hand, Harrington, Tackle, stuck a nail in his foot, Larry Tripp, guard, may be out of the game on account of boils. In spite of this the boys are determined to take LaGrange into camp again. Several new plays and formations have been worked out since last Friday and it is thought they will be used to advantage.*

The next game was also played against La Grange.

## Ayden Defeats LaGrange
(*Ayden Dispatch*: Thursday November 4, 1926)

*Bam! The LaGrange kicker socks his foot into the ball and the game is on. Howard Sumrell received the kick-off and was tackled almost in his tracks.*

*Ayden tried two plays and made a small gain. It was then that Captain Baldree made a touchdown by a fake play.*

*It was a hard fought game from then on. Sometimes LaGrange gained and sometimes lost. It was in the second quarter that Hal Edwards made a touchdown by an end run. From then on no score was made. Three minutes before time for the game to close, the LaGrange coach called his men from the field. The total score was 12 to 0 in favor of Ayden.*

## Ayden Defeats Robersonville
(*Ayden Dispatch*: Thursday November 18, 1926)

*One of the best foot ball games of the season was played on Tuesday afternoon, when Ayden met Robersonville on the home field. It was a hard fought game from the beginning and both teams played a clean game. Fine sportsmanship was shown on both sides. In the first quarter Hal Edwards make his third touchdown of the season. This made the score 7 to 0 in favor of Ayden and no other score was made.*

*The pet play of Robersonville was a line plunge but our famous guard Larry Tripp stood his ground like a brick wall. Robersonville has the material to make a fine team. The game was the most enjoyable of the season to both players and spectators.*

*The officials were: Mr. Worsley of Grifton, referee, Mr. Case of Eureka College, umpire, and Jamie Prescott, head linesman.*

*The local club will play Williamston here tomorrow afternoon (Friday). They have played Williamston once before this season and the game went for a scoreless tie. Come out and help the boys win.*

## Ayden Defeats Williamston
(*Ayden Dispatch*: Thursday November 25, 1926)

*The Ayden boys defeated Williamston in football game on Friday afternoon, November 19. The score was 6 to 0.*

*It was in this game that Hal Edwards made his fourth touchdown of the season. Hal caught the ball on the thirty yard line and ran seventy yards for a touchdown. His interference was perfect. Mack Harrington dipped three men, Gene Smith three, Howard Sumrell two, A.T. Baldree one and Hal stiff armed two.*

*Clean sportsmanship was shown on both sides. Many spectators declared this to be the best game of the season.*

## Ayden Wins Again
(*Ayden Dispatch*: Thursday December 2, 1926)

*Ayden defeated Tarboro in a hard fought game on Wednesday afternoon, November 24 by the score of 3 to 0, Captain Baldree making a successful place kick in the third quarter.*

*This was the last and best game of the season. Clean sportsmanship was shown on both sides and everyone enjoyed the game. Tarboro had made a record in football but Ayden defeated them.*

*The crowd was larger at this game than ever before. The cheering from the side lines was very good. Two cheering squads gave yells for Ayden. Everyone seemed to be happy to see the Ayden boys play so well.*

*The officials were: Mr. Worsley of Grifton, referee, Mr. J. H. Coward of Ayden, umpire, and Mr. Hearn from Tarboro acted as head-linesman.*

Out of the seven games played during the first season, Greenville was the only team that scored.

## 1926-1927: Ayden High School's First Football Season
### (5-1-1)

| | | | | |
|---|---|---|---|---|
| 10-8-26 | Ayden | 0 | Williamston | 0 |
| 10-15-26 | Ayden | 0 | Greenville | 35 |
| 10-22-26 | Ayden | 6* | La Grange | 0 |
| 10-29-26 | Ayden | 12 | La Grange | 0 |
| 11-16-26 | Ayden | 7 | Robersonville | 0 |
| 11-19-26 | Ayden | 6 | Williamston | 0 |
| 11-24-26 | Ayden | 3 | Tarboro | 0 |

*Final score not provided; assume 6 points

The first victory was over La Grange on the opponent's home field. Although the actual result was not reported, the final score was probably 6-0 since only one score was reported and no extra point was mentioned.

The last four opponents – La Grange and Williamston each for the second time, Robersonville, and Tarboro – were held scoreless. Hal Edwards scored four out of the five touchdowns scored during the season.

The final game of the season was played on Ayden's home field on Wednesday November 24, 1926. Tarboro was defeated on a field goal by Captain A.T. Baldree, the only score of the game. The team was assisted in its win by a challenge provided in the second quarter by H.G. Mumford. Mr. Mumford told the team that he would treat them to an oyster roast if they won the game.

## Mr. H. G. Mumford Entertains Foot Ball Squad At An Oyster Roast
### (*Ayden Dispatch*: Thursday December 9, 1926)

*Mr. H.G. Mumford entertained the foot ball squad at an Oyster roast on Friday evening, December 3, at the power plant. The roast was proposed during the second quarter of the last foot ball game of the season which was fought between Tarboro and the home team. No one had scored so Mr. Mumford promised the boys an Oyster roast if they would Win the game. True to his promise Mr. Mumford made a trip to New Bern for the oysters and procured five barrels for, as he said, he wanted everybody to get their fill. The squad with the faculty and a few of the town girls for their guests fell in line around the table of steaming Oysters which disappeared rapidly at the onslaught. The foot ball squad never attacked any team in any more earnest then they attacked those Oysters. Parts of the Farmville and Eureka College basket ball teams were also guests of the squad.*

After starting 0-1-1 in its first two games, the Tornadoes won all five of their remaining games to finish, 5-1-1 – a firm foundation for its second season. For the first two seasons, the players attended the school that faced Snow Hill Street. Eventually, the two-story red brick structure would be called the grammar school and would house grades one through four. The high school building on Lee Street would not open until 1929, AHS's third year of football.

The Tornadoes' second season coincided with the publication, by the senior class of 1928, of volume #1 of *The Wheel*, Ayden High School's annual. *The Wheel's* editorial staff chose the following quote to summarize the football season: "Too much praise cannot be bestowed upon Coach Fouts and Captain Baldree for the most successful season any athletic team has ever experienced for Ayden High."

1927-28 Ayden High School Second Football Team.
Members are sitting: (Mascot) Pee Wee Stallings. Front Row: Mumford, M. Harrington, Buck, Britt, Collins, Hart, McClees, Second Row: Coach Fouts, Pierce, Fouts, Durham, (Capt.) Baldree, B. Harrington, Edwards, Worthington, (Sponsor) G.H. Sumrell, (Mgr.) Worthington. Back row: W. Jolly, Stocks, H. Jolly. *(The Wheel, Vol. 1)*

## 1927-1928: Ayden High School's Second Football Season
### (6-1-2)

| Ayden | 6  | Kinston       | 6  |
|-------|----|---------------|----|
| Ayden | 20 | La Grange     | 0  |
| Ayden | 12 | Robersonville | 0  |
| Ayden | 49 | Farmville     | 0  |
| Ayden | 0  | Wilson        | 0  |
| Ayden | 6  | Kinston       | 2  |
| Ayden | 18 | Robersonville | 0  |
| Ayden | 12 | Morehead City | 0  |
| Ayden | 7  | Washington    | 13 |

In the most talked about game of the season, Ayden fought Wilson to a 0-0 tie. Shortly before the game that was reported to be "the greatest in the history of Ayden football," the local school board voted to change the school colors from blue and white to maroon and white. At the time, Wilson High School was a powerhouse in football and a much larger school. One of the members of that AHS team, Bill Harrington, remembered the game: "I remember Wilson had a big fullback – at least big for those times. They drove to our goal line and our defense held on downs inside the one-foot line." For my father, the Wilson game must have been a significant memory. He told the same story over and over in the same way – with one exception; the fullback increased in size over the years. I once reminded him of that fact: "Daddy, if that fullback keeps getting bigger and bigger and you live to be an old man, he'll be as big as a World War II tank." He just looked at me with his piercing blue eyes and smiled. And, to show me who was boss, not too long before he died at the age of 93 he claimed to have made all four tackles on that goal-line stand from his linebacker position. No matter how hard I tried, Daddy always got in the last word.

Daddy reiterated another story pertaining to the Wilson game so often that I have been able to tell it almost verbatim. "Hal Edwards was the best punter I ever saw – in the pros, college – at any level. He could punt a football farther than anybody. You know back then, there was no television; no radio broadcasts of the games, and the newspapers didn't write up our games like they do now. So, our opponents didn't know how far Hal could punt a ball. I never saw a punt returned against us. When Hal punted it, the ball would always go over the head of the deep man. I don't remember a single runback. It was in the Wilson game that it happened. After we held on downs, we tried to run the ball and hardly got anywhere. On fourth down, Hal dropped back into his own end zone and punted the ball out of sight. It rolled out on the six yard line." Instead of a fullback that eventually became as big as a tank, the number in Daddy's last sentence kept getting *smaller*. If he had lived past his 93 years, Daddy would eventually have run out of real estate. The "94 yard punt story" may very well have become the "end zone to end zone punt story."

In reality, I do not know the size of the Wilson fullback or the actual distance of Hal Edwards' punt. On the other hand, I was witness to an event that made me a believer for one of Daddy's stories. One night at football practice when I was in high school, Mr. Edwards came out to the field. He had on his suit, white shirt and tie, and his wingtip shoes. Someone tossed him the ball and asked him to kick it. I don't know how far it went, but it was a long way. Even his son, William Edwards ('62) was impressed.

The 1928 team finished 7-3 and the 1929 team completed its season with an 8-2-1 record. The first four football teams during the last years of the 1920s compiled a record of 26-7-4, a 79% winning percentage (excluding the ties). In the first 37 games played by an Ayden High football team, 25 of the opponents were held scoreless.

Let's take one more look at an elusive topic.

Ever since Daddy told me tales about Babe Ruth and Lou Gehrig, I've been a New York Yankees fan. As I've watched player after player don those familiar pinstripes over the decades, I've often wondered how many games the Bronx Bombers have won because of tradition. Tradition doesn't enable the batter to hit the ball any harder or to speed up the ball on a throw from center field to cut down the runner at the plate. Or, does it? Whatever this thing called tradition is, I believe each one of us, who played for Ayden High School, put it on every time we suited up for a game. Every Ayden High School player owns a tiny bit of that tradition. Like a 500-piece jigsaw puzzle, every part is important; the puzzle cannot be complete without all of its pieces.

I could feel the tradition. My brother, Joe, knew what "it" was during a football regional final. "At the half Windsor was leading us 21-7. Coach Lewis asked us, 'Are you boys gonna quit on me?' Assistant Coach Tommy Craft was the first to speak up, 'Coach, Ayden boys don't quit.' Joe concluded, "We still lost 28-27, but we didn't quit."

During the 1926-1927 and 1927-1928 school years, the first two years of football at Ayden High School, the two teams shut out 12 of their first 16 opponents. How was it possible that first-time players were able to be so good on defense? Sports programs that have tradition, win. However, tradition evolves over time. Yet, those first-time players got something from somewhere. We'll never actually know for sure what it was or where it came from.

We can be sure that there's a lot more to a winning tradition than the won-lost record, so this book is not only about what happened on the field or on the court, it is also about the school and the community – the people from outside and inside the town limit, the school administrators, and the teachers who supported the players and coaches at Ayden High School.

Before moving further, I want to refer you to Appendix 2: Ayden High School Football Scores and Season Records from 1926-1971." Mitchell and I have been able to recreate the individual game scores of nearly every football season from the first game in 1926 to the final football game in 1970. We knew some scores, even full seasons, would be impossible to unearth, but we've come close. To complete the reconstruction, the two of us have had to engage in some guesswork. Rather than go into detail here, the explanations for the conclusions are also included in the appendix.

## Advertisements in *The Ayden Dispatch*: Late 1920s, Early 1930s

### Home Furniture Company – Greenville

| | |
|---|---|
| Cook Stove | $11.89 |
| Wood Heater | $39.67 |
| Mattress | $6.89 |
| Dining Room Suite | $124.69 |

\*\*\*

### Announcement – All Barber Shops in Ayden

| | |
|---|---|
| Shaves | 20 cents |
| Neck Shave & Cup | 5 cents |

(All other prices are to remain the same)

\*\*\*

### Turnage Brothers Company, Inc. – Ayden

YOUNG MULES: Carload of young mules. Well broken and ready to work.

\*\*\*

### Black Draught Liver Medicine

25 cents

\*\*\*

## Mr. and Mrs. Moye

New Managers of Beverly Hotel on June 1

\*\*\*

## 666

A prescription for colds, grippe, flu, dengue, bilious fever and malaria.

\*\*\*

## Paul Waner

Voted MVP in 1927 National League says "Lucky Strikes do not affect his wind."

\*\*\*

## North Carolina Nursery
## (Opposite Beverly Hotel)

Opening March 15$^{th}$
Strawberries will be served free to everybody
Come and bring your friends

\*\*\*

## Edwards Pharmacy

Favorite national drink, ice cream soda, available at Edwards Pharmacy

\*\*\*

## Roy L. Turnage Store

Men's Suits: $5.00 to $13.00
Neckties: 5 Cent and Up

Prices Lowest Since 1913

## Sports and Other Notations from *The Ayden Dispatch*: Late 1920s, Early 1930s

1926: Ayden High School's first football team.

1926: "While football isn't altogether a safe game now, it doesn't crowd the hospitals as formerly."

1926: World Series games were shown on outside scoreboard (later called playographs) erected between the post office and Edward's Pharmacy.

1927: Immediate need for new high school stressed by J.E. Sawyer, Superintendent; enrollment: elementary = 425 and high school = 142.

1927: Princess Theater: "Box office being moved so that the ticket seller can pass out tickets to both white and colored without both races coming in contact with each other."

1927: Light and Water Superintendent, A.W. Sawyer, advertises the Universal Electric Range to be sold by the Town of Ayden: equipped with an oven heat control that automatically controls the cooking operation.

1927: *Ayden Dispatch* headline: "Prominent Colored Man Dies Almost Suddenly;" Sam L. Blount operated a pressing club and store in the rear of the newspaper's office.

1928: *Ayden Dispatch*: "Now His Hat Fits; Dr. Royal De Rohan Baronides, member of the United States Medical Corps during the World War, had been carrying around a piece of German shrapnel in his scalp for the past ten years. It worked its way over his right ear, and prevented his hat from sitting properly. So that his hat would fit, he has had it ejected."

1928: Coach Leary (Ayden High School football coach) to introduce KNUTE ROCKNE style of play. "The Notre Dame system is very complicated and requires time as well as work."

1929: *Ayden Dispatch*: "Need of High School Gym; Ayden has use of a warehouse many blocks from school; not made for basketball. Rafters are low; no equipment, no bath facilities. [Players] have to dress several blocks away and are liable to catch cold going from one building to another. Warehouse leaks as witnessed last Friday; caused many men to slip down [because of the] wet spots.

But we are hoping that next year will not only bring us a new school building, but a new gym also."

1929: Princess Theater installs sound.

1929: J.K Long acknowledged as the "pioneer of athletics."

1929: First game played at Ayden High School gym; girls of the Christian Sunday School defeated the fat men, 20-19; 150 fans witnessed the game.

1930: Training in grammar grades begins in basketball, coached by high school players.

1930: First year that football schedule established before start of season.

1930: Chapel Hill High School to play at Ayden; opponent's average linemen, 160 lbs.; average backfield, 140 lbs.

1931: 35 report for football.

1931: Ayden wins first boys' basketball game after losing 23 straight games over two years; Ayden 32, Fountain 12.

## Chapter 4
### Boys' Basketball

During my high school years of the late '50s and early '60s, I remember distinctly the spotless shining gym floor at the beginning of each basketball season – like it was covered with a thin layer of glistening ice. There wasn't a blemish in sight. It didn't take long before the constant stampede of players converted the immaculate surface into its late season form. No matter how great the floor looked, the place always smelled the same – like, well, an old gym. We dressed for each game in the auditorium because the dressing rooms had deteriorated over the years. They were not renovated until a few years later. We threw our street clothes over the backs of the first few rows of seats. As seniors, we'd be sitting in those same seats – with our clothes on of course – several days later for "chapel."

In contrast to my father's time on the Tornadoes' basketball court, my experiences were comparable to the Waldorf Astoria. Growing up in Ayden, I'd heard stories of playing basketball in a warehouse and of playing outside before the gym was completed in 1929. I've never known enough specifics to put together the full picture, so I needed to dig deeper.

Researching the past often turns up questions that lead to further investigations. Playing Sherlock Holmes is part of the fun. Unfortunately, there are questions that cannot be answered. To do so would require the ability to talk to several 100+ year old persons. I kept hoping that a ghost or two would pop out of the woodwork so that I could converse with someone who had played sports during the first three decades of the 20<sup>th</sup> century. Barring an apparition or some other vision, you and I will be left with several mysteries. On occasion I have been able to unearth some clues and, like Sherlock, I've attempted to solve the whodunit.

One of these mysteries pertains to basketball and baseball at Ayden High School. When did the first Tornado basketball team take the court? Where and against whom was that game played? Same for baseball. Unlike football, the records for the first basketball and baseball teams have been lost.

**The 1927-1928 Ayden High School Boys Basketball Team**
Members of the team include: Front Row (l-r): Fouts, Durham, (Capt.) Harrington, Edwards, and McClees. Second row: (Coach) Fouts, (Sponsor) G.H. Sumrell, McKinney, Cox, Worthington, McLawhorn, (Mgr.) Worthington, and Mascot Pee Wee Stallings. *(The Wheel, Vol. 1)*

The first basketball season for which there is a full season's evidence was played during the 1927-1928 school year, the same year that produced the first yearbook. Quoting from *The Wheel, Volume I*, the 10-7 season appeared to be one of the Tornadoes' best. "Our Basketball Team has had one of the most successful seasons in the history of the school, being characterized by the remarkable recovery from a slump in mid-season. The showing made can be attributed to the cool-headed captain,

Bill Harrington, and Coach Fouts, who not only proved worthy of their titles in developing a great team, but also in instilling a great appreciation of clean sportsmanship in every player." This quote obviously indicates that basketball had been played at AHS previously, but I do not know for how long. If we choose to, an assumption that we may want to garner from this message is that the previous seasons had not been outstanding. In other words if a 10-7 record was in reality "one of the most successful seasons in the history of the school," that would imply that the prior records had not been stellar.

### 1927-1928: Ayden High School Basketball Season (10-7)

| Ayden | 33 | Kinston | 11 |
|-------|-----|---------|-----|
| Ayden | 19 | Winterville | 16 |
| Ayden | 16 | W. C. I.* | 18 |
| Ayden | 32 | Kinston | 11 |
| Ayden | 19 | W. C. I. | 35 |
| Ayden | 14 | Everetts | 27 |
| Ayden | 19 | Belhaven | 12 |
| Ayden | 11 | Everetts | 16 |
| Ayden | 28 | Winterville | 10 |
| Ayden | 30 | Maysville | 45 |
| Ayden | 9 | Williamston | 19 |
| Ayden | 10 | Fremont | 49 |
| Ayden | 29 | Robersonville | 20 |
| Ayden | 48 | Belhaven | 21 |
| Ayden | 52 | Fountain | 13 |
| Ayden | 47 | Robersonville | 23 |
| Ayden | 19 | Williamston | 16 |

*Washington Collegiate Institute

Before the gym at Ayden High School was completed in 1929, the games were played in a tobacco warehouse. Had I been working at Daddy's ice plant in the 1920s instead of the 1950s and 1960s, I would have been able to walk across the street and into the rear door of the building next to J.P. Sumrell and Company's cotton gin. The structure's front entrance faced 2$^{nd}$ Street. Today, the block that was home to Tornado basketball is bordered by Martin Luther King, Jr. Street (formerly Venters Avenue) and Snow Hill Street. Duplexes and single family houses now cover the foundation.

If the ball was passed too high or if the trajectory of a shot had too much of an arc, it would hit one of the rafters. Reports vary on the playing surface; some say that the players competed on a dirt floor; others say that the team practiced on a dirt floor and played on a more substantial surface in the warehouse. It would not have been farfetched to have played on a dirt floor. Other schools played on dirt floors into the 1930s. In 1935, Winterville and its opponents played on a dirt floor. In 1936, Ayden's basketball team defeated Grimesland, 21-17. The dirt surface on Grimesland's court contained a section of sand. That made it impossible to dribble on that part of the court, so passing the ball became a necessity. When local students and officials in Ayden were lobbying for a gym to be a part of the new high school building, one critique of the current court stated that the roof of the warehouse leaked, causing the players to slip down on the wet spots. No mention was made of mopping up the floor to make it safer. If the floor was dirt, then wiping up the water would have been impossible. In one game in February 1929, Ayden defeated Vanceboro 14 to 7. In his report of the game, the journalist indicated that the game was low scoring because the cold temperature led to numerous ball handling mistakes.

No bath facilities, little or no heat, and muddy spots. Playing a basketball game in Ayden's warehouse on a wet, freezing winter night in the 1920s must have been an adventure. No locker rooms in the warehouse necessitated dressing elsewhere. Getting to the "elsewhere" in one's sweaty suit after the game was probably like I've heard citizens of Chicago describe a cold blustery day in the Windy City. The number of years the Tornadoes spent in the warehouse is not known. Could it be that the team played outside before the warehouse became available? Or, did the Tornadoes always play inside? I have also read one account of three tobacco warehouses in Ayden. It is undoubtedly possible that I've chosen the wrong pre-1929 basketball arena.

Even after the team started playing in the new gym in December 1929, it still could have lacked central heating. The basketball games during the last week in January 1936 were called off because of the cold weather. Bear Baldree ('48) remembered the pot-bellied stove that was the only source of heat in Bethel's gym in the late 1940s. Sue Sutton ('57) also told me of playing in Winterville's gym when a pot-bellied stove was used for heat in the mid-50s.

Following the 10-7 season on March 1, 1928, the basketball team left for Raleigh to enter the State Class B championships at the Frank Thompson Gym on State College's campus. The first game was played against Haw River High School. The only source of information, *The Ayden Dispatch*, would often neglect to report the results of a game when the team lost. The assumption must be made that Ayden High lost to Haw River in the first game. The only mention of basketball in the following weeks was the announcement that the basketball season was over.

For the three major sports in the 1920s, the schedules were put together as the season progressed. During the 1925-1926 basketball season, four players were dropped from the team "because we chose to schedule high school games for ourselves without the knowledge or consent of the high school basketball coach." The first preseason football schedule did not appear in the local newspaper until 1930. Although football was the last of the three sports to get started, the games on the gridiron were covered by *The Ayden Dispatch* in a relatively comprehensive way. In contrast, basketball games were reported sporadically. For example, only one basketball score appeared in the local newspaper for the 1925-1926 and 1926-1927 school years. In future years, one or two scores would appear, and then the entire remainder of the season would disappear from the radar screen. On other occasions, a write-up of a game would occur with a reminder of "everybody come out and support the team next Friday," but the report of the next game would never be forthcoming. Suddenly a game would appear out of nowhere only to have the rest of the season evaporate.

Since *The Ayden Dispatch* was virtually the only source of information for the 1920s and 1930s, the irregular – almost random –

availability of the local sporting news will leave Ayden High School's historic jigsaw puzzle without some of its most important pieces. I'm afraid Father Time has disappeared with many of the cookies in the cookie jar.

As might be expected, the early winning teams received better coverage than the teams that weren't performing as well. That was what happened during the 1930-1931 school year. Interestingly, Coach Coggins' Ayden High School basketball team played in two conferences at once. The first two games ended in defeat: Kinston 24, Ayden 7 and New Bern 27, Ayden 9. Future reporting for that year was totally absent, probably because the 1931 team finished 0-19. The following year, 1931-1932, Ayden defeated Fountain, 32 to 12, in the fifth game of the season, the school's first victory in 23 games. This was Ayden High School's longest *recorded* losing streak in any sport. I have italicized the word "recorded" to make a point; making a statement like this one with such certainty means "to the best of my knowledge, from my sources ..." It would be redundant to say this over and over. (See "Appendix 4: Notes on the Writing of *Ayden, the Sports Town*" for a more detailed explanation.)

The following year's basketball team was undefeated through its first ten games before losing to Hertford, 23-21. In a state playoff that was termed the Championship Series, Ayden won its first game against Beulaville, 52-25. While awaiting the next game in the playoffs, Ayden defeated Plymouth, 31-29 and Grimesland, 24-14. These two games were not part of the playoffs. Ayden played Jonesville for the Eastern North Carolina Class B championship; the score was Jonesville 68, Ayden 18. Jonesville played the winner of the Western North Carolina final for the state championship. Two additional games were played after the loss to Jonesville. The 1933 team finished 15-4-1, the Tornadoes' best record in basketball so far.

The 1934-1935 Ayden High School Tornadoes played a total of 33 games, completing their season, 25-8 – more than likely the most victories up to that time. Ayden played in three tournaments. Ayden lost to Bethel in the championship game of the Pitt County Elimination

Series, a tournament held at the beginning of the season. Ayden was runner-up to Rose Hill in the Kinston Invitational, losing 27-26 in the championship game. Ayden also played in the East Carolina Teachers College Invitational, losing to Dover, 32-13. (E.C.T.C. was the forerunner of East Carolina College and East Carolina University.) The team managed some stingy statistics on defense; six of the opponents were held to single digits and four were held to 10 points. There was no mention of a playoff. Even so, an eastern champion and state champion could have been crowned and not reported.

The next year, 1936, Ayden again lost to Bethel, 25-11, in the championship game of the Pitt County Tournament. The records for the 1937 calendar year have been lost.

After a losing season in 1938 (5-9) and another year of lost records in 1939, the 1939-1940 school year brought the best season yet for the basketball Tornadoes. After playing a total of four football games and going 1 and 3 at the start of the 1939-1940 school year, the basketball team got off to a great start. Although the game was Bethel's sixth of the year and Ayden's first, Coach Ridenhour's Ayden team won, 18-16, the only game scheduled in December. In January, the team followed up with wins over Grifton, Chicod, and Bethel again. In the Chicod game, Ayden led at halftime, 20-0; the final score was 43-10. The regular season ended with a 16-1 record. The only stumbling block occurred in the first meeting with Farmville. Ayden won the second round against Farmville, 29-16.

Twelve teams competed in the Pitt County Tournament at E.C.T.C.'s gym. In the championship game, the Ayden team defeated Farmville, 31-13. To this point, the 19-1 record was the best ever for an Ayden High School basketball team. The victory in the final game represented Ayden's first tournament championship and its first Pitt County Tournament championship. The player's names most often mentioned in the local newspaper were Hamilton, Nobles, Fleming, G. Tripp, Kinlaw, and a young man named Stuart Tripp. Most likely, Charlie Hamilton was the team's leading scorer.

Like so often during the two decades prior to World War II, putting the '39-'40 basketball season together necessitates guess work. The first question that comes to mind is, how did AHS do in the playoffs? I do not believe there were any playoffs that year. As strange as it may sound, the playoff system came and went. If no games beyond the regular season were reported, I assume that no such tournament existed after the regular season. There's another possibility; Ayden could have lost in the first round and the local newspaper could have continued its tradition of not reporting the Tornadoes' losses. But I believe this is unlikely because *The Ayden Dispatch* would have included a story on an upcoming playoff game in the hopes of getting the fans to turn out for the contest.

The 1939-1940 basketball season was AHS's last until near the end of World War II.

*Let's take a break from boys' basketball until after the war. We're gonna turn the time machine dial on the dashboard of the Thunderbird to long-ago baseball. I wish we could stop along the way at the high school to watch the Ayden Wildcats play. I want to see Coach Ridenhour, Stuart Tripp, and Garland Little ('41). I hear the Coach hit a home run. But, that's really all we know about the game. The Wildcats were probably a town team made up of anyone who was good enough to play. Based on what I heard the old-timers say, Stuart Tripp and Garland Little were beyond good enough – Tripp with the bat and Little, the left hander, on the mound.*

# Chapter 5
## Baseball

When the Tornado football team was running its first plays during its opening season in 1926, the most popular sports in America were baseball, boxing, and horse racing. Although this would obviously change, I assume Ayden's preferences mirrored the national favorites. So many times, I've heard, "Every crossroads had a baseball team." At the same time, the widespread interest in baseball was not reflected in coverage of high school baseball in the local newspaper; for example, only one high school score was provided in 1927: Ayden 15, Winterville 14. The Eureka College team received better coverage than the AHS team. In March of 1928, an appeal was made: "The High School team is having hard workouts and also some hard problems in finding the best material for the position. There are several positions that are not filled and Coach Fouts wants every boy to come out, who is interested."

In comparison to football and basketball, Ayden High School's early baseball history was even sketchier. One of the reasons may have been the availability of other baseball teams in the area. Teams came and went – the Ayden Aces, the Ayden Boll Weevils, the Ayden All-Stars, the Ayden Wildcats, the Ayden Town Team, and teams that were simply called Ayden. In the late '30s, a team named Ayden beat the Durham Luckies, 6-5. No mention in the newspaper story was made of the constitution of either team. Including Pitt and the surrounding counties, the names of the various alliances reflected the area: Tobacco County League, Bright Leaf League, Pitt-Greene League, Coastal Amateur League, and the Goober Belt Baseball League.

An important consideration was also the timing of the high school baseball season. The season usually started in March and ran through part of May, an important time for students to help their families on the farm. If a conflict arose between baseball and farm chores, fathers saw to it that the family's livelihood won out. This dilemma did not disappear with the 1930s. Thomas Heath ('54) and his dad faced this problem in the 1950s. Thomas once disobeyed his dad to play baseball "in town" and lived to regret it. Playing high school baseball was possible only when it did not interfere with work.

I'm going to take us through the 1930s. During this time period, major league baseball, Eureka College baseball (at least for a short period of time), the Cotton Belt League, the Coastal Plain League, Ayden town teams, business and industrial teams, and "every crossroads had a baseball team" were all in competition for the fans' and players' attention.

One of the most anticipated events of the year for sports fans was the World Series. For the first three decades of the 20th century, few followers of the "nation's pastime" had a radio. This brand-new way of keeping up with one's favorite team was available, but few could afford to purchase a "wireless." Just like the introduction of television in the 1940s and 1950s, radios gradually appeared in almost every home. Before that time, novel ways of "broadcasting" baseball and boxing events were introduced in saloons and billiard halls. Telegraph messages were sent directly from the game to saloon owners who would pass the news along to their patrons.

Starting in the late 1800s, thousands of fans congregated in "theaters, armories, saloons, fairs, dancehalls, and outside of newspaper offices" to view mechanical and electronic devices eventually called playographs. The big boards ranged from simple baseball diamonds with light bulbs to larger and more complicated apparatuses that displayed seven inch wooden figures with movable arms and legs. Hypothetically, when the operator received a message that the batter had hit a line drive between first and second, the batter, with arms and legs flailing, would run to first base. The wooden figure "players" were manipulated by an operator from behind the board.

**1914 Playograph**
**This Playograph depicts the 1914 World Series game between the Boston Braves and the Philadelphia Athletics.** *(Photo Courtesy of the National Baseball Hall of Fame, Cooperstown, NY)*

In September 1926, Ayden's version of the playograph was erected between the post office and Edwards Pharmacy. "Every strike, foul ball, hit, etc. is indicated by electric lights." The board was paid for by Dr. G.H. Sumrell and Mr. S.M. Edwards. The newspaper article made clear that there would be no cost to fans.

The following winter on March 3, 1927, *The Ayden Dispatch* reported that 16 inches of snow had fallen on the previous Wednesday. Daddy had always told me that the biggest snow fall in Ayden occurred in 1927. However, he claimed that 27 inches had fallen. Long before my research started on this book, I learned of this snowfall from reading about it in a publication other than *The Ayden Dispatch.* I couldn't wait to announce my findings to Daddy. For once, I had proof that he had greatly stretched the truth. His immediate response, "It might have been 16 inches where they were, but it was 27 inches where I was." How could I argue with that?

At about the same time that Mrs. Grimes was working with several boys to plant hedges on the site of the new Ayden High School building, Coach Leary's 1929 baseball team played a practice game, defeating Winterville, 16-2. At the time, Clayton was a powerhouse in high school baseball. They had twice been Eastern Champions and twice been runners-up. Ayden and Clayton split their two games. After Ayden defeated the Vanceboro Cornhuskers, 13-1, it was announced that the first string players would be academically ineligible. Players had to pass three-fourths of their courses to play. To the list of aforementioned obstacles to fielding a competitive high school baseball team, I am forced to add another.

It is unclear as to whether or not the *entire* first team was unable to play. In any event, the remaining players again defeated Vanceboro; this time, 17-1. Another game was played against New Bern, but the winner was not reported.

The narrations available for the 1929 and 1930 seasons were typical of the times; individual player statistics and even team records were excluded. Year by year, I found it impossible to discern when the season started and when it ended.

Coach Coggins did not appear to be very optimistic about the 1931 team. "Ayden won't have a super team, but it will do its best." Since only two scores were made available, his forecast must have been accurate.

At about the same time that AHS's players were pulling out their baseball gloves to start practice for the 1932 season, a question arose: Would the Ayden schools have enough funds to complete the last two months of the eight-month school year? Because of the Depression, the same dilemma occurred and was subsequently resolved during the previous year, 1931. This time the situation seemed more serious. The responsibility for the solution was divided three ways. The county offered $1,946; the state would come up with $1,100 – if the Ayden public schools could raise the remaining $700. The grade mothers representing each of the eleven grades were given the responsibility to raise Ayden's part. The schools continued as solicitations were made. At one point, $531.35 was in the bank. The name of each gift giver and the amount of each contribution were published; the cash donations ranged from 25 cents to 15 dollars; the single in-kind gift was a country ham. The final totals were not reported. At any rate, the school year was completed, so we can assume that the remainder of the $700 was raised. Someone must have had the foresight to save money for the Junior-Senior prom. The theme for the 1932 affair was Hawaii. For 1933 the same funding problem was repeated. That time, all Pitt County Schools were asked to cut expenses by 20%.

After the 1932 school year ended, a league called the Cotton Belt League was organized. The Ayden Boll Weevils played in a four-team configuration; the other teams were La Grange, Tarboro, and Vanceboro. I am unaware of any remaining records of this league with the exception of the written accounts of the few games that were covered in *The Ayden Dispatch*. Usually referred to as "town teams," these clubs were composed of amateur players who were competing for the fun of it. I suspect that high school players could have played. However, the teams were composed of anyone who could make the team.

The Boll Weevils played teams outside of their respective league as well, but those games did not count in the regular standings. The "outside" teams were Grimesland, Macclesfield, Godwin, Snow Hill, and Williamston. The final standings:

### 1932: The Cotton Belt League Final Regular Season Standings

| | |
|---|---|
| Tarboro | 15-2 |
| Ayden | 9-8 |
| Vanceboro | 7-10 |
| La Grange | 3-14 |

Once the dust had settled on the 1932 season, for some unknown reason, Tarboro refused to play Ayden in the planned seven-game series for the championship. The first and second place teams were supposed to play for the trophy. By default the Ayden Boll Weevils became the champions. Tarboro and the third place team, Vanceboro, decided to play a best of seven game series. The results of that series remain unknown.

For the first time, season tickets costing $1.50 for the upcoming 1933 high school season went on sale. AHS's opening game was played a few days after the first public library was opened on March 17, 1933 by the Ayden Woman's Club. The library was located in a room in the back of John Burgess' Drug Store, and it opened one afternoon and one night each week. In the meantime, the baseball team finished with a .500 record.

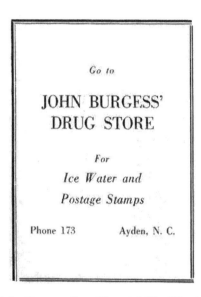

Go to

### JOHN BURGESS' DRUG STORE

*For*

*Ice Water and*

*Postage Stamps*

Phone 173          Ayden, N. C.

**1928 John Burgess Drug Store Ad** *(The Wheel, Vol. 1)*

When Daddy and I first started watching professional baseball on television, the networks offered only one "game of the week." I was often working at the ice plant during the summer when this one and only opportunity appeared on our little black and white set – one chance to see my idol, Mickey Mantle, hit a home run. Daddy was often someplace else in the plant working on a job that he thought only he could do. This meant, of course, that I was left to wait on the customers. If I positioned myself just right on the steps leading up to the office, I could watch the game and keep an eye out for a customer at the same time. Numerous times, I wished that no one would show up during the game. Certainly I did not want to get so busy that I would miss the game altogether. I prayed for rain in Ayden but not in Yankee Stadium. The more rain, the fewer the patrons.

As more baseball games were offered, Daddy and I got to watch together. At least a zillion times I heard him exclaim, "There's a right way and a wrong way to play baseball." He considered the "right way" to be the only way. The "wrong way" was considered a sin. Under certain circumstances, for instance, the batter was supposed to "lay down a bunt" instead of attempting to hit the ball. In addition to absorbing the nuances of the competition, I grew to love "America's pastime."

Likewise, the Ayden townspeople must have loved the game. A few conversations between friends, and a game would materialize; for example, a team comprised of Ayden high school players and old-timers defeated a Hookerton team of like membership, 8-5, in July 1930.

An Ayden town team would often be assembled to play the high school team; in May 1932 the AHS high school team was defeated, 10-9. The high school team then played the Kinston Salvation Army team and lost, 12-5. The school team decided to join with the town team when the Kinston Salvation Army baseballers came to Ayden. This action suggests that the AHS team did not wish to lose again to the same team. The answer: combine the efforts of the two Ayden teams. Today, we would call these players "ringers." At that time, apparently, the practice was not frowned upon. Just the same, to persons like us – over eighty years later – it is impossible to tell if there were real boundaries between the high school team and the other teams competing for ballplayers in the area.

Reading the old records leads one to believe that not only did every town and every crossroads have a team, but every business must have as well. Many of the teams would be unrecognizable today, as illustrated by a May 1933 game: AHS 7, Greenville Water and Light Department 3. On occasion, a score without a narrative would be given: Ayden 6, Durham Luckies 5. The players representing Ayden in this contest could have been from the high school team, or the town team, or a group of citizens could have gotten together spontaneously to play the Luckies.

Through most of the 1930s, baseball games were played during the day. If the sun went down before the game was completed, the umpire called it off "on account of darkness." This practice explains the reason for the tie scores that were included in the final records of various teams. Many Ayden citizens saw their first night game in 1939 when they attended a game at the new Guy Smith Stadium in Greenville – the score: Kinston 1, Greenville 0. Ayden townspeople were issued a special invitation by Greenville officials "to express appreciation to the people of Ayden for their support."

An alliance called the Coastal Amateur League was started in the summer of 1942. Ayden fielded a team in that league, but nothing is known about the other teams comprising the league or of the season that transpired. The player make-up of the teams is also a mystery. A couple of tidbits of the summer's activity appeared in the local newspaper; the Ayden Aces finished 31-6, and Crack Rogerson pitched the final game.

The three sports at Ayden High School were de-emphasized or discontinued during World War II. The teams that did play were coached by volunteers, and there are no signs of organized league play. The war couldn't smother the will to play ball entirely, however. An article in a London newspaper in 1943 reported that Sargent Joe Sumrell ('36) had scored the first run in a game in the London International Baseball League. A few months later this same soldier received the Good Conduct Medal and the Baseball Medallion.

Using the word "jack ass" during a baseball game didn't always pertain to the umpire. Donkey baseball came to town occasionally to stimulate everyone's sense of humor. One of the civic clubs would sponsor and coordinate preparations for the game. The advertisements asked that the men chosen to play for each team should know "donkey psychology," a brand of the social sciences with which I am unfamiliar. The game in the late summer of 1939 was played under giant flood lights. Dr. Rand Smith was captain of the Rotary Club team and Bill Harrington was the skipper of the Jesters Club team. Once the ball was hit, the runner had to hop on the back of a donkey and round the bases. The jenny named "Mae West" was noted to be in particularly good shape. The final score sounded like a pitcher's duel, Jesters Club 2, Rotary Club 1. On behalf of the Jesters Club, Hal Edwards scored the first run and Earl Hart scored the second. Roy Turnage, Jr. scored the lone run for the Rotary Club. For the run to count, Mae West or one of the other donkeys had to be ridden all the way around the bases. Frank Peterson was scheduled to be the umpire, but some unknown circumstance must have prevented him from completing his duty, so "Foot" Holton called the game.

For several years and as the 1930s came to a close, the evidence for AHS baseball became sparse and finally vanished. It is possible that baseball was discontinued during this time period. I know that it was finally dropped near the beginning of World War II or soon after our country entered the war; I just don't know precisely when. A few years before the diamond Tornadoes disappeared, the Coastal Plain League was created. Baseball was played in a myriad of formats from as far back as the records can take us – from spontaneous games amongst friends, to town teams that made up their schedules as they moved along, to industrial teams, to the organized league play that encompassed several towns. The granddaddy of them all was the Coastal Plain League.

## Advertisements in *The Ayden Dispatch*: 1930s

### LLOYD E. TURNAGE

Farm Implements – Automobiles
Phone 96
Ayden, N. C.

\*\*\*

### PITTMAN & EURE

ATTORNEYS AT LAW
Office Next Door To Post Office
Ayden N. C.

\*\*\*

### M. B. PRESCOTT

ATTORNEY AT LAW
First National Bank Building
Ayden, N. C.

\*\*\*

### Dr. Grady Dixon

General Practitioner
Ayden, N.C.

# Chapter 6
## The Coastal Plain League

If we were able to magically query every Ayden High School athlete and sports fan who lived in the 1930s and beyond, it may very well be impossible to pinpoint a person who'd never heard about the old Coastal Plain League. The word *old* always preceded the league's name. Those four words were uttered with reverence. I never really understood what it was all about; to be sure, I knew that Daddy and his friends had experienced something that was special. But then I read a book entitled *We Could Have Played Forever: The Story of the Coastal Plain Baseball League* by Dr. Robert H. Gaunt. On occasion, when accomplishing research for a writing project, an author runs across a treasure. I struck gold when I discovered Dr. Gaunt's book. Now I get the picture.

When Daddy spoke of the "good old days" of the Coastal Plain League, I've come to believe that those really were the grand old days of baseball. Mixing steroids, lots of money, and millions of television sets together in the same broth has somehow produced a soup that has too many lumps in it. But I'm still hooked. On a recent trip, I had the pleasure of visiting Cooperstown, the museum of baseball. I spent almost the entire time in the pre-1950s section. I don't fully comprehend my nostalgic feelings about those times, but I believe it has something to do with why they played the game. I do recognize that my heroes, Mickey Mantle, Yogi Berra, "Moose" Skowron, Bobby Richardson, and a few more, played when the game was different – more importantly, when I was growing up. My favorite ballplayers from those times won't change.

Just as I cannot turn my internal timepiece backwards, the baseball clock only runs one way.

African-American baseball players and any league affiliations they might have created were not mentioned by the local written press. The South Ayden Eagles never fielded a baseball team. I'm sure, however, that there were black teams in and around Ayden that played America's pastime, but I'm equally aware that the opportunities for black players had to be "manufactured" by the black community.

That state of affairs would have mirrored the country-wide discrimination that prompted the development of the Negro Leagues. Interestingly, black players did populate baseball teams before the 1890s. Toward the end of the 19$^{th}$ century, what is sometimes described as a "gentlemen's agreement" shut the door on African-American participation in the minor and major leagues of the day. The Negro Leagues sprang up during the early 1900s. "Giants" was a favorite name: the Chicago Giants, the Cuban Giants, and the St. Louis Giants. After the depression shut down some of the franchises, Gus Greenlee started the Negro National League in 1933. He vowed to put together the best baseball teams in the nation. Some believe he did. The roster of the Pittsburg Crawfords included five future Hall of Famers: Cool Papa Bell, Oscar Charleston, Josh Gibson, Judy Johnson, and Satchel Paige. Once Jackie Robinson broke the color barrier in 1947, the Negro Leagues began to lose their best talent to the major leagues, and they eventually went out of business in the early 1960s.

One notable story did make the Ayden newspaper in the late 1930s. The headline read: "Negro Clouts Seven Homers in Row." A hitter from Clayroot named Ratclife James supposedly hit six of his long balls in a creek 350 feet from home plate and the seventh landed in a tree.

Dr. Gaunt's book on the Coastal Plain League aptly describes eastern North Carolina baseball at the time:

"One could build a convincing case that there are very few places where baseball was more warmly embraced than Carolina's Coastal Plain. Old timers remember when it was possible to crank up one's old Ford for a Sunday afternoon drive through the countryside, and every place where two roads crossed, you'd see a baseball game. And there'd be a couple of hundred people watching."

The Coastal Plain League was born in Ayden in 1933 with the following basic rule: "no professional ball player who has played ball for the past three years will be eligible for the league." This meant essentially that the four-team alliance would be an independent league. There would be no formal relationship with professional baseball – no part of the major league farm system. The league's first president was J. Bruce Eure. Mr. Eure accepted the job after he'd been practicing law in Ayden for 10 years. During his tenure as head of the Coastal Plain League, Mr. Eure was also president of the Ayden Rotary Club, the Community Chest, and the Parent-Teachers Association. In addition, he was Vice President of the Chamber of Commerce, Mayor of Ayden, and Judge of the Municipal Recorder's Court.

Playing three games each week between Wednesday June 7 and Saturday August 26, Ayden, Greenville, Kinston, and Snow Hill were the charter members. Faust Johnson and others arrived in town to play for the Ayden Aces. I've always been told that Mr. Johnson moved to Ayden for the sole purpose of playing baseball. I'll bet he had no idea that he'd eventually become a principal and coach in the school across the street from the Aces' field.

Team members already residing in Ayden or the surrounding countryside were Preston Dunn, Doug Johnson, Ander Mumford, and Claxton "Crack" Rogerson. During one of the early games of the season, a special ceremony was held in Mr. Johnson's honor. To commemorate his graduation from Wake Forest College, he was awarded a fountain pen and a wallet. The observance was the fans' way of showing their appreciation for Johnson's decision to play in their town.

The final standings:

## 1933: Inaugural Year of the Coastal Plain League
### Final Regular Season Standings

| | |
|---|---|
| Greenville | 24-16 |
| Ayden | 24-17 |
| Kinston | 21-20 |
| Snow Hill | 12-28 |

The overall team batting average for the Ayden Aces was .288 for the regular season. Ayden's leading hitter for the first year was Crack Rogerson with a .390 average. Greenville won the best of seven playoff series over the Aces, 4 games to 0.

I put on my Sherlock Holmes hat again and began to hunt for the book's author, Dr. Gaunt. I wanted to ask him a few questions. To my surprise I easily located him in Zeeland, Michigan. We talked for an hour. When I was finally able to hang up, I turned to my wife and said, "I didn't think I'd ever be able to get off the phone with that character." I'll bet he shared the same sentiments. Dr. Gaunt is a true connoisseur of the game. His love – his devotion to the game – couldn't be matched by many.

I asked him why he picked the Coastal Plain League. He told me, "I sorted through the Class D leagues. I wanted one of quality. I thought that it would be hard to beat the Coastal Plain League." From 1993 to the publication date, 1997, Dr. Gaunt made his headquarters in Wilson. He spent three consecutive months on one occasion and five straight weeks on another in that town. When he found out I was from Ayden, he told me, "Yeah, Ayden, when I was in Ayden I went to that place out on the highway."

"You mean The Skylight Inn," I said.

"That place with the great barbecue." Dr. Gaunt went on to tell me how much he enjoyed eastern North Carolina barbecue and "how these people up here don't know how to make real barbecue." He had the same sentiments for the hotdogs in Wilson. It was obviously more than baseball that attracted Dr. Gaunt to the coastal plains of North Carolina.

The Coastal Plain League was enlarged for the second season, 1934. New Bern and Tarboro were added to the four charter members. At first, Ayden seemed to be the class of the league. The Aces started 11-1. One of the team's outfielders, Worlise Knowles, had a game to remember on July 13. He went 4-for-4 with a double and three home runs. That day the final score, thanks to Knowles' production, was 17-6 in favor of the Ayden team.

At one time or another, at least ten sets of brothers played in the league. By far the most intriguing group of siblings played for the New Bern Bears; five men from the same family were on the roster. When Bill Ferebee was pitching, he and his brothers would have made up more than half the players on the field. Smoky Ferebee was a star shortstop and quarterback for the University of North Carolina Tar Heels.

Rules were made up as the season progressed. Halfway through the second campaign, Tarboro's record was 4-26. Nothing they attempted seemed to help, so team officials made a plea to the league. They urged the decision makers to split the season into first and second halves, thereby providing the Tarboro players encouragement to play harder. The league directors were not enamored with the proposal and offered one of their own. The team's record would be adjusted. Adding eleven wins to Tarboro's record would bump them up to a tie with fifth place New Bern. In an amicable reply, the representatives from Tarboro turned the offer down.

With the exception of Tarboro, the final standings were close. Ayden faded after a great start and ended up in fourth place with a record of 32 and 29, five games back in the loss column. The playoffs featured the season's winners, Kinston, against second place, Greenville. The Kinston Eagles won the first two games, but the Greenville Greenies earned the playoff trophy by winning the next four.

As I traveled from ballpark to ballpark in the summer of 2011 on a major league baseball tour, the glitz of the huge video boards, the fireworks, and the dozens of restaurants and kiosks was dazzling. I had attended previous games in Atlanta, Washington, and Seattle, but had never been on a multi-park, multi-city tour like that. The new Yankee Stadium turned out to be a small city. The trip was so much fun that I repeated it two summers later. Those memories reappear when I think of the Coastal Plain League. At this point in its evolution (after the 2nd season), none of the fields had lights; the fireworks would have been confined to the diamond; and I doubt the word kiosk had been invented yet. Something else was missing. Where were the nicknames? My guess is that the players of the Coastal Plain League wore their designated tags with pride: Uriah "Swamp" Norwood, D.C. "Peahead" Walker, Alfred L. "Chubby" Dean, Woodrow "Lefty" Upchurch, Ernest "Mule" Shirley, Bruce "Hack" Gaylord, Horace "Horse" Mewborn, Fred "Snake" Henry, Art "Pappy" Diem, Owen "Ace" Elliott, Charlie "Holy Cow" Gadd, Elzer "Slats" Marx, and Vern "Preacher" Mustian. I could go on and on. There were more players named "Lefty," and a few "Reds" and a "Shorty" or two, I'm sure. Even the umpires had nicknames; one of the most prominent was Roy "Never Wrong" Greene.

The 1935 schedule was expanded from 60 to 72 games, and the Goldsboro Goldbugs and the Williamston Martins were added. Ayden had experienced attendance problems in 1934. After grappling with the decision, Ayden decided to field a team and paid its $500 fee. Dr. Gaunt reported that the rest of the league did not consider Ayden's dilemma to be an irreconcilable problem. Several towns professed an interest in buying into the league. There were two ways of fielding a new team in the league. One was to purchase an existing team's franchise when the town dropped out. The second was to be voted in by the governing board when the league expanded.

The league adopted a schedule that eliminated overnight travel and allowed the players "to sleep in their own beds following each contest." The home and home format was played on successive days. Ayden and Snow Hill began a two-game series when the Billies visited the Ayden Aces on June 28. The teams managed to amass a total of forty hits. The final score – Snow Hill, 15 Ayden 13 – after eleven innings. Traveling to Snow Hill the next day for game two, someone must have inadvertently soaked Ayden's bats in ice water. The Billies' pitcher, Chan Parmalee, tossed a no-hitter; Snow Hill won 1-0. The Aces' pitcher, Coon Weldon, allowed only two hits. Back to back doubles produced the only run of the game.

Memorable pitching and hitting performances abounded throughout the season. Worlise Knowles put on another hitting spectacle in the latter part of the summer. The Ayden outfielder hit eight homeruns in five games. Red Sivley, pitching for Snow Hill, won both games of a double header; he defeated the New Bern Bears 5-2 and 9-3. Snow Hill scored thirteen runs in one inning against the Goldsboro Goldbugs; final score: Snow Hill 18, Goldsboro 8.

Not all of the fun came about during the actual games. In route to play Snow Hill on July 16, New Bern encountered a heavy downpour that lasted for two hours. The foul weather did not deter the Bears, however. Maybe the game could still be played. Once they arrived, the team knew playing would not be possible. Snow Hill's park was located in the low grounds between the banks of a creek that wound completely around the field. The playing surface was not only too wet to play, it was engulfed in water. Even so, the diamond was being put to good use. A bunch of little kids who'd forgotten to put on their swim suits were having a great time. The New Bern "spectators" were told that yes Snow Hill had a swimming pool, but the water at the ball park was deeper. The show's finale took place near second base; three 10-year olds mooned the out-of-town guests as they were exiting the field.

In the 1935 playoffs, the four highest finishing teams played a best of five-game series. League regular season champion, Greenville, was bested by the fourth place team, Ayden, 3 games to 2. In the other semifinals, Kinston defeated Snow Hill in three games. In the best of seven series, Kinston conquered Ayden, 4 games to 1.

In 1936, Ayden experienced the same financial issues as the year before: Could the team be financed for a fourth year or would the town have to give up its franchise? Goldsboro faced the same uncertainty. A last minute fund-raising effort enabled the Goldbugs to fly for another season. Similarly, the Aces came up with the $500 fee just when it appeared that the franchise would be placed on the market.

For the small towns like Ayden, money was always the bugaboo. The expenses went well beyond the entry fee – salaries for the manager and players, funding for the players' temporary living expenses, and someone or some entity had to pay for the upkeep of the fields. At its annual meeting for the fourth season, the league's officials set limits on club salaries: $450 for each team per week. It may come as no surprise that a pot of money was needed to "supplement" individual player salaries. The phrases that the author used were "unofficial" and "under the table," terms with which we are all familiar. If the town wanted to field a competitive team, behind-the-scenes cash was a necessity. Along with good pitching and timely hitting, it was just part of the formula.

When I asked Dr. Gaunt about this routine procedure, he provided me with a simple hypothetical. One of the officials of the local team would visit one of the bankers and they'd work out a deal. The player or players who were receiving a "supplement" would visit the bank and be given an envelope.

Once the money and the players were in place, the curtain was raised on the first game. The Assistant Baseball Coach at the University of Alabama, Tilden "Happy" Campbell was hired as a player-manager with the Ayden Aces. The season looked promising: the bat of Worlise Knowles was back, and Woody Upchurch was expected to carry a heavy load as pitcher. A future major leaguer, Jim Tabor, was the third baseman. He spent seven years with the Boston Red Sox and Philadelphia Phillies. Tabor played third base for both teams and finished with a .270 lifetime batting average.

On August 12 and 13, the stadium would not have required any of today's fireworks. Jim Whatley, the Aces first baseman, supplied all the Roman Candles that would have been necessary. In a 7-3 win over the Kinston Eagles, he hit three home runs in his last three times at bat. The next day Whatley smacked three more pitches over the fence in his first three turns at bat. Ayden won, 5-3. Not many players would ever enjoy such a feat – home runs in six consecutive times at bat.

Whatley had followed his coach from the University of Alabama. One of the most notable sportsman to suit up for the Aces, he had earned All-American honors as a football tackle in 1935. The big guy at first base lettered in four sports for the Crimson Tide, an accomplishment that's unheard of in today's collegiate world. After his playing days, Whatley went on to a distinguished career in coaching. After a stint at the University of Mississippi, he became the head basketball and baseball coach at the University of Georgia.

Ayden finished third in the final standings with a .597 winning percentage, two games in the loss column behind first place, Williamston. The first and fourth place teams and the second and third place teams played a best of five game series in the semifinals. The Williamston-Kinston series went the full five games. The finals turned out to be a slugfest. The fourth place Eagles built up what appeared to be an insurmountable lead, 12-4. The regular season champs came roaring back to tie the game at 12, but Kinston pulled it out with a late inning run, 13-12.

Jim Whatley put on another show in Ayden's fourth game of the other best of five semifinals. He went 4 for 4; however, the MVP honors belonged to Lefty Upchurch, the Aces' pitcher who shut out Greenville, 13-0, and blasted a two-run homerun. Ayden won the series, 3-1.

Ayden and Kinston squared off for the championship. Playing in the Aces ballpark before a crowd of 2,500 fans, Kinston won the first game in the best of seven series, 3-1. The Aces mustered only six hits off Cecil Longest. Charlie Keller, the future New York Yankee star, hit a homerun in inning number eight for the Eagles. Ayden came back to win the next four games. Harry Brownlee pitched a shutout in the final game, winning 4-0. Babe Bost, a collegiate player attending Duke University, hit a home run and laid down a squeeze bunt to account for three runs, all the tallies his team needed.

The Ayden Aces had won their only Coastal Plain League playoff championship. The Aces never finished number one during the regular season. The Aces' fans would have almost a year to celebrate before Class D minor league baseball came to town. Leaving the status of semipro to become affiliated with the major league farm system had its advantages, but the new classification eliminated a particular type of player from the league's rosters.

# Chapter 7
## Class D Baseball Comes to Town

Up to 1937, the Coastal Plain League had been operating in what was termed semiprofessional baseball, an independent configuration of teams bound together by a set of "legislative" policies that were sometimes made up as the season progressed. This meant that the Coastal Plain League was not formally associated with the major leagues; in other words, the league was not a part of the major league's minor league system. The minor league classifications ranged from the highest, AA, to the lowest, D.

At that time, the prevailing viewpoint was that Class D leagues were a step above independent baseball like the Coastal Plain League. Dr. Gault didn't think that viewpoint was necessarily accurate. Nonetheless, the owners believed in that notion when they assembled to discuss the upcoming season. That belief probably encouraged their decision-making, but the primary consideration was survival. The escalating costs had to be brought under control.

Dan Hill, who was the president of the Class B Piedmont League, attended the January meeting at the Central Fire House in New Bern. He had been sent as a representative of the National Association of Professional Baseball Leagues to provide answers to the owners' questions. Hill made a revealing point; he believed that the Coastal Plain League had cost more money than the Class B league, of which he was chief. Class D baseball had limits. Each team was restricted to thirteen players and a manager. This lineup had to be supported with $1,000 per month per team. Hill proposed two more weighty benefits for the group's consideration. It was possible that cash would be paid to the various teams when a player was summoned to a higher-standing league. And, major league teams may send players to the Coastal Plain League at no cost to the receiving team.

A change that would be difficult to swallow pertained to many of the fans' favorite players; Class D rules prohibited collegiate athletes from participation. The meeting in New Bern was concluded without a resolution, but a subsequent owner gathering yielded an affirmative vote. The Coastal Plain League had become a Class D enterprise – starting in the summer of 1937.

Unlike the year before, the Ayden ownership was enthusiastic about the upcoming summer. Three of last years' towns weren't so sure; Goldsboro, Tarboro, and Snow Hill apparently had to engage in lots of soul-searching before finally signing on for 1937. As in previous years, the league's board had a contingency plan. The backup blueprint was different this time, however. If all three teams had backed out, Smithfield-Selma was the only team set to buy in, thus forming a six-team rather than an eight-team league.

The Ayden High School baseball field as it appears today was the former home of the Ayden Aces baseball team, an entry in the Coastal Plain League. *(Photo by Mitchell Oakley)*

Opening day for the 1937 season was May 6. The season kicked off with band music and political speeches in Ayden, Goldsboro, Kinston, and Williamston. Accounts of that day celebrated "good turnouts." The Aces of Ayden were known for their diminutive ball park and short left-field fence. Many homeruns cleared that fence. Over twenty years later when I was playing for the Tornadoes, Coach Tripp used to take his turn when we'd finished batting practice. He'd say, "Put it right here," as he held his hand slightly above his belt. Provided the pitcher could put it where he wanted it, Coach would hit a few that would sail over the fence and land near the large oak tree that used to be across Venters Street (now, Martin Luther King, Jr. Street).

I have often wondered how many baseball and softball games have been played on the field that I've always referred to as the high school field. I played little league, junior league, and high school baseball there. Let's not forget the donkeys that scampered around the bases on occasion. Details of the infield, outfield, dugouts, backstop and bleachers light up in vivid color as I think about my playing days there.

*Walk with me down the left field line until we get to the H-shaped silver goalposts and I'll give you a late 1950s perspective of the diamond and outfield. Since this historic excursion is make-believe, let's hop up on the crossbar to get a better view. You can see that the hard-surfaced infield encroaches slightly onto one corner of the football field near the goalposts where we're sitting. To our left is the famous short left field fence. When someone got one of those cheap home runs in the Coastal Plain League, he had to hit it down the line. You can see how the fence runs parallel to the street so that there would be no easy way to hit it out of the park in center field. See how the cyclone fence (chain-link fencing) runs down behind those green bleachers. That's the Agriculture Building down the right field line. I remember Donald Carmon hitting one off of that building to win a game for us. I've also heard of balls being hit over that building. You can see if a batter could hit a ball past the center fielder or right fielder, he'd get an inside-the-park home run.*

Tommy Riley, a very good athlete who played basketball and baseball for Grifton High School, hit the longest home run I've ever seen on this field. But the umpire ruled it a double because he thought it had bounced over the fence. I don't remember Grifton's coach or his player arguing the call. From my vantage point at first base, I saw the ball clear the green bleachers in center field, soar over the fence, and bounce in the street. The paved street caused the ball to bounce very high. That fact alone should have convinced the umpire that the hit was a home run. So, the longest home run I ever saw in this ballpark was a double. Those bleachers were very nearly in straight-away centerfield. I believe that ball would have cleared the centerfield fence in any major league ballpark – maybe even the centerfield fence in the old Yankee Stadium.

There was no other fence except the cyclone fence. Enclosing the ballpark with a permanent fence would have been impossible because of the football field. During the summer in the 1950s, a temporarily fence was erected for little league and junior league. The Agriculture Building was eventually abandoned and moved across the street. It was then converted into dressing rooms for the home and visiting football teams.

Back to the Coastal Plain League. By far, the most unusual owner-player relationship existed in New Bern. The Bears were owned by the New Bern volunteer fire department. The organization also collected dues from the fire fighters rather than pay them a salary, a one-of-a-kind practice. The fire department focused on the betterment of the community; it "served as a center for local social activities, and supported many worthwhile civic projects." Because of this association, the Bears' ball players continued to hang out at the fire station long after private ownership took over the franchise.

Ayden struggled to finish in fifth place during the '37 season, completing the year one game over .500. The Snow Hill Billies had a banner year and ended up on top of the regular season standings. The team had a 62-36 record, a .633 winning percentage. As in all seasons, the Aces registered some high points. For example, Faust Johnson batted .296 and hit 11 homers while playing every game in the outfield. The catcher, John McCormack, hit 23 home runs, but his .226 average showed inconsistency.

The major problem was weak pitching. The game to remember took place on May 12. Ayden defeated Tarboro, 17-15. The Tarboro starter was Walter Johnson, Jr., son of one of the greatest pitchers to ever toe the rubber. He didn't fair nearly as well as his famous father. Johnson walked four batters and never made it through the first inning. The string of pitchers that followed gave up 16 walks, hit a batter, and allowed 12 hits. The hitting star of the afternoon played for the losing team. Tarboro's second baseman must have liked the now famous short left field fence. He had a single, double, and belted three home runs in his six trips to the plate.

A game that could only be described as bizarre was played over a two day period. On August 10, a contest between Ayden and New Bern ended in a 3-3 tie after ten innings. The contest was called because of impending darkness and resumed the next day. The two teams played another fourteen innings before New Bern claimed the victory, 11-10.

There was "no joy in Mudville;" Ayden missed the playoffs. The Aces finished only one game behind the fourth place team, New Bern. That meant that New Bern played the first place Snow Hill team. The second and third place teams, Williamston and Tarboro respectively, played in the other semifinal series.

Tarboro held the record for the most name changes. The franchise was called the Combs, the Serpents, the Cubs, the Orioles, the Tars, and the Athletics. In 1937 they started out as the Combs, a name drawn from its county of Edgecombe. The moniker didn't last the full season. Tarboro was renamed the Serpents. Interestingly, the Tarboro Serpents' first baseman was "Snake" Henry.

Snow Hill and Tarboro ended up in the best of seven championship series. Both towns had reason to be enthusiastic. The Billies installed 1,000 additional seats to bring the park's capacity to between 3,500 and 4,000. The Serpents had swept four games from Williamston and were on a 12-game winning streak. For various reasons, several of the players had to exit early and were unavailable to play for the trophy. The injury bug had bitten two of the league's home run hitters, one from Snow Hill and one from Tarboro. A forthcoming household name to Aydenites and to University of North Carolina Tar Heel fans, Jim Tatum, had to leave prematurely after the first game to become assistant football coach at Cornell under the head coach, Carl Snavely. Tatum had been Tarboro's catcher. Both Tatum and Snavely were destined to become head coaches for the Tar Heels. The locals could not claim Tatum as a hometown boy, but his wife was from Ayden.

In the deciding game, Cecil Longest, another player with University of North Carolina connections, pitched the Snow Hill Billies to victory, 7-2. Thus, the smallest town in the Coastal Plain League had won both the regular season and playoff championships. That happened only three times during the years of the league.

Tarboro's disappointment in the finals was tempered by their excitement for the upcoming year. The Serpent followers thought that they could have won "had Jim Tatum been available and had George Rimmer not been injured for three of the games." This speculation was probably true. In the semifinals, Tarboro had hit .413 as a team and had, inexplicably, dipped to a dismal .173 against Snow Hill.

The Coastal Plain League's first Class D season had gotten off to a great start. In spite of the optimism that prevailed in Ayden for the 1938 season, the team fought all season to stay out of last place in the standings. There were individual performances to celebrate, however. Outfielder Phil Morris led the league with a .377 average. Some considered Bill Herring to be the best pitcher in the league. Ayden's ace finished 18-11. Herring pitched 249 innings, more than any other hurler that summer. As an outfielder, he also belted nine home runs and hit .332.

Because of the previous summer's success, Tarboro's fans were very high on their team's upcoming year. The Tarboro Serpents were good in 1938 but not quite good enough – depending on which of the final regular season standings the fans chose to honor, the official revised standings or the non-revised unofficial standings. Tarboro was on top in the former; New Bern was on top in the latter. Provided we could have overheard a couple of sports fans discussing that season after the playoffs, most likely they would have used words like eligibility, controversy, crazy, one-to-remember and a few that it would be best for me not to mention.

The culprit – eligibility. The controversy began forty games into the season. The Williamston Martins were using a veteran player, Hans "Dutch" Stanley. There was a limit on the number of veteran players per franchise, so the team listed him as a rookie and changed his name to cover up the misdeed. As reported in Dr. Gault's book, the rules of the league in respect to veterans were somewhat vague. I suspect that his sources were incomplete; that is, the specific definition was not included in the documents to which he had access. Even the interviewees were probably unfamiliar with these regulations after so many years. I know that each club was limited to the number of veterans it could carry on its roster. All the other players had to be rookies. More than likely, a rookie was a player who had never played in the minor leagues. In any event, there was never any indication that the rules were unclear to the owners and managers. Substituting a veteran for a rookie was undoubtedly a violation.

Ayden reported the infraction to the president of the league. Accusations of corruption began flying between the eight towns. Based on the various reports of the allegations, no franchise was left unscathed with the exception of Tarboro. One of the major issues applied to the playoffs; if the punishment for the guilty would mean missing the postseason, some of the teams threatened to leave the league.

Guy Smith, president of the Greenville Greenies, saved the day and, consequently, saved the alliance. His prescription called for a complex solution. "Violators would be relegated to lower spots in the standings. It would be fair, Smith maintained, if all the teams were afforded a chance to earn a playoff spot. In addition to taking victories from offending teams, Smith proposed that victories be awarded to the franchises who would otherwise be out of contention after penalties were imposed." Becoming a Class D league had obviously not altered the practice of making up the rules as the season progressed.

Previously in fourth place with a .575 winning percentage, Williamston's record was "amended." The team with the most egregious infractions landed in fifth place with a .519 winning percentage. The teams benefitting the most were the clubs near the bottom of the standings. For example, Greenville, a team floundering in last place with a 21-60 record before Smith's miracle cure, suddenly enjoyed a 41-38 record. At 25-55 and in seventh place before the alterations, Ayden found itself tied with Greenville with a 41-38 record. After the dust had settled, Ayden, Goldsboro, Greenville, and Williamston were all tied for fifth place in the eight-team configuration. The only teams that did not change positions in the standings were first-place Tarboro and second-place New Bern. Every team had an opportunity to make the playoffs.

Ending a season that their fans thought would turn out much better, Tarboro lost to Snow Hill in the semifinals. New Bern swept their semifinal series with Kinston. At the end of what must have been one of the weirdest seasons in baseball history, it was the New Bern Bears versus the Snow Hill Billies. Great joy abounded at the fire station on the city next to the Neuse River; New Bern swept their opponents and won the playoff championship.

The crazy 1938 season was Ayden's last in the Coastal Plain League. The Aces finally succumbed to the financial problems that had plagued the team for most of their six years in the league. The cost of the 1937 season had been $7,000, and the funds could not be raised for the upcoming summer. There was also talk of night baseball. Several towns including Kinston, New Bern, and Tarboro were already mounting lights on the tall poles that were soon to grace ball parks throughout the league. The Ayden Board of Directors voted to sell the franchise to Wilson.

The Wilson Tobacconists had a successful tradition of minor league baseball. From 1908-1911, they had been in the Eastern Carolina League, and later from 1920 to 1927 the town had supported a team in the Class B Virginia League. The team's nickname soon became too much to pronounce and even harder to spell, and the team was soon known as the Wilson "Tobs."

Here is where the Ayden Aces get off the train – at the railway terminal in Wilson. The league voted to halt operations in 1943, 1944, and 1945. The summer of 1946 again came alive with the sounds of minor league ballplayers in eastern North Carolina. The Coastal Plain League continued through the 1952 season before shutting down for good after a total of seventeen years.

I have made extensive use of Dr. Gaunt's book. The extent of research and effort that went into this book was remarkable. If he had not written *We Would Have Played Forever*, so much of this colorful era in eastern North Carolina, when the game was still played for fun, would have been lost forever.

*This finishes up baseball until after World War II. The red time machine and I have got a lot of roads to travel before we get back to the diamond. Next stop: the Lady Tornadoes of Ayden High School.*

## Morsels of Information from *We Would Have Played Forever* by Robert Gaunt

Prior to 1937, the year the Coastal Plain League became affiliated with major league baseball as a Class D franchise, team and individual player statistics were seldom available. Beginning with the Class D designation, each team was required to keep such numbers. All of the statistics in the book's extensive appendices started with 1937.

1933: Dr. Gault reported that the Coastal Plain League's first year was 1934. In reality, the inaugural year was 1933. *The Ayden Dispatch* reported the events of that year throughout the summer. When I brought this up to Dr. Gault, he indicated how difficult it was to amass information on the league before 1937. He was simply unaware of this fact.

1933: Crack Rogerson led the Ayden Aces with a .390 batting average. This was the highest batting average ever published for the league. An Ayden player won the batting crown in 1937 (Monk Joyner, .380) and 1938 (Phil Morris, .377). No Ayden player ever led the league in home runs.

1937: Most hits by Ayden player: Monk Joyner, 136. (Remember, this statistic not available before 1937.)

1937: Most home runs in Ayden uniform by Monk Joyner: 24.

1938: Most innings pitched by Ayden pitcher: Bill Herring, 249. The following year pitching for Kinston, Herring pitched 291 innings. Bill Herring held the all-time CPL record for number of pitching appearances, 221. During his tenure, he pitched for five teams. He also held the CPL record for most career wins, 118.

## (Info specific to Ayden)

Charter member, 1933. The first president of the league was an Ayden attorney, J. Bruce Eure.

Prominent local CPL management figures: J.D. Cannon and A.W. Sawyer.

The Ayden Aces' final game in the Coastal Plain League: September 2, 1938. Ayden 9, New Bern 7.

Franchise sold to Wilson on January 19, 1939.

**Lady Tornadoes**

## Chapter 8
### The Golden Age of Girls' Basketball

The first recorded account of a girls' basketball game occurred in February 1926: Ayden 12, Winterville 9. The other game of the evening featured the boys' team: Winterville 35, Ayden 12. There would be exceptions, but playing the girls' and boys' games on the same night against the same school continued for the life of Ayden High School. The scores of those two games were representative of the final scores during that time. The girls' teams averaged fewer points than the boys' teams. In 1928 the Ayden girls lost to Robersonville 30-1, to Belhaven, 10-3, and to Fountain, 12-6.

There were numerous games in which one of the teams would score in single digits and occasional shutouts in girls' basketball. In January 1934, the Lady Tornadoes held Bethel scoreless, 16-0. In their next game, Grimesland got the best of the Ayden's girls, 48-2. Although not as often, single digit team scoring also occurred in boys games. Later that same season, the Ayden boys were defeated by South River, 20-8 and by Vanceboro, 33-7. Without knowing the time of year, it would sometimes have been challenging to tell the basketball scores from the football scores.

"Playing second fiddle" to the boys' basketball team started early in the history of the girls' game. In AHS's first annual in 1928, individual game scores and a photo of the boys' team were included, but only a picture of the Lady Tornadoes and the following caption appeared: "The team this year was composed of girls inexperienced in the game. They went in with spirit and determination. Although they did not win every game, they came to the front. Our sister Tornadoes fought beside their brother Tornadoes bravely. We hope for them the best of success in the coming years." Even after the local newspaper reporting improved in the late 1940s, on a given night the commentary of the preliminary Lady Tornado's game and the second boys' game followed the same format: the article started out with a brief running account of the boys' game and then an even briefer account of the girls' game. Sometimes "brief account" is not an adequate portrayal of the actual words. For instance, in a 1958 game the following one-sentence description appeared: "The Belvoir-Falkland girls took a 47-45 win in the other game." Occasionally, the girls' write-up would be placed first when the contest was a particularly important tilt.

Prior to World War II, my primary source was *The Ayden Dispatch* supplemented with interview accounts and my memory of stories from those times. *The Daily Reflector* did not begin its coverage of Ayden sports until the late 1940s. Luckily, the Greenville paper's coverage started at about the same time as the Ayden newspaper accounts became unavailable. Later print-editions of the newspaper that was serving the Ayden community were not transferred to microfilm. Over time, starting with early 20th century editions, Ayden archived newspapers were obliterated by fire more than once. A later flood destroyed the Ayden papers in the latter part of the century. This is what I mean when I use the term "unavailable." Mitchell and I have been able to locate individual Ayden High School graduates who kept scrapbooks, and these albums contained newspaper write-ups that were no longer in print.

Even with the available sources, documenting basic information such as a team's final record proved a challenge. In the final analysis, the Sherlock Holmes method was employed; that meant assembling all the available clues from all the sources I could muster. Then, I usually did one of two things; I solved the mystery or I provided the reader with clues and left the final "whatdoneit" decision up to you. (For a more detailed account of decisions and source materials, please see Appendix 4: Notes on the Writing of *Ayden, the Sports Town*.)

**1927-28 Ayden High School Girls' Basketball Team**
Members of the team include (l-r): Dot Dinkins (Captain), Hazel McKinney (Manager),
Margaret Edwards, Geneva Dail, Pat Turnage, Katherine Flaugher, Hortense Mozingo
(Coach), Hazel Ruth Turnage, Mary Alice Bullock, Ruth Moore, Gertrude Coward,
Bruce Little, Myrtle Gray Hodges. *(The Wheel, Vol 1)*

It has been impossible to re-construct even one season of individual game scores for girls' basketball before the war. Likewise, not one season's overall record was ever reported. There is no reason to believe that an Ayden girls' team had an outstanding season until after World War II. Of course, this statement is my best guess. I am assuming that an exceptional season would have generated more interest and, hence, better coverage in the local newspaper.

The nearly non-existent attention to the Lady Tornadoes would change in 1946 – mirroring the overall improved coverage for all sports in both the Ayden and Greenville newspapers. For the first time, game statistics were available, and individual Pitt County school stars received press attention. During a period of several years in the 1950s in *The Daily Reflector*, a headline reading "Pitt County Games" would be followed with several box scores of the basketball games played on a Tuesday or Friday night. For weeks no narrative would appear for either the boys or girls games unless an unusual event occurred; a player with a high point total was the favorite topic. At periodic intervals the conference standings were printed. I'm sorry to say that the individual school records were not always reported accurately. At one point, the AHS girls' team was 5-2 in conference play and four days later the record had taken a detour to 4-4. An explanation for this miraculous deterioration was not forthcoming in later additions. Rarely would the overall records (including non-conference games) of conference teams be included in the standings. Starting in the mid-50s, the only source of information on girls and boys basketball was *The Daily Reflector* in Greenville. The coverage grew in both quality and quantity throughout the late 50s and early 60s and then took a pronounced turn for the better in the mid-60s.

Tournament time in February and March signified a transformation in press coverage. Boys and girls brackets would appear a day before or on the day of the tournament's first night of play. Occasionally, the sports reporters for *The Daily Reflector* would get into predictions of tourney winners and losers. Game pictures showed up from the previous night's action, and box scores of each game were accompanied by a narrative of the contest. A picture of the girls and boys tournament champs highlighted the next edition after the two championship games. These team photos were always the same: the winning team's trophy proudly displayed in the forefront of a bunch of smiling faces.

The Golden Age of Girls' Basketball occurred from 1946 through 1952. The records for each of those years are as follows:

### 1946-1952: The Golden Age of Girls' Basketball at Ayden High School: Overall Season Records

| | |
|---|---|
| 1946-1947 | 14-7-2 |
| 1947-1948 | 20-2 |
| 1948-1949 | 19-4 |
| 1949-1950 | 27-2-1 |
| 1950-1951 | 22-6 |
| 1951-1952 | 20-5 |

Winners of 82% of their games (excluding the three ties), the combined record of 122-26-3 for the six years following the war would never be duplicated. Identifying this period as the "golden age" is my idea. Summing up the numbers for the remaining 19 years of girls' basketball at Ayden High provided me with the basis for my designation. Between 1953 and 1971, the Lady Tornadoes' record was 139-200. These totals represent estimations of season records; nevertheless, the figures are pretty close to reality.

Faust Johnson was both the principal and girls' basketball coach throughout this era. I remember many of the girls who played in the later 40s and early 50s. Many would go on to become some of Ayden's finest citizens. Mr. Johnson arrived in Ayden in the early 1930s to play in the Coastal Plain Baseball League. Fortunately for the community, he stuck around for a long time.

Girls' basketball rules allowed three forwards on offense and three guards on defense. None of the six players was allowed over the center court line. These rules plus the allowance of only two dribbles per player partially accounts for the low scoring games. More specifically, if a team could not field three guards capable of getting the ball to mid-court and into the hands of their forwards, the opponent's three forwards could take the ball away and virtually score at will. This predicament must have occurred more frequently in the 1920s when there were fewer skilled girls playing the game. I'm obviously assuming that the girls' teams of the teens and twenties played by the half court rules. It could be that at first in the teens and 20s the same rule book governed both girls' and boys' basketball, and the girls' half court rules came into being at a later date. It is certain that after World War II the half-court rules were in effect. In the 1960s, the rules changed to include more dribbles and the "rover" position, and, in the early 1970s, the girls started played "like the boys" – five on five and full court.

The 1946-1947 team kicked off the successful run with its 14-7-2 record. The starters were as follows:

Forwards: Martha Fleming ('47), Janice Turnage ('49), and Helen Joyce Whitehurst ('49)

Guards: Hannah Heath ('48), Patricia Jackson ('48), and Evonne McLawhorn ('48)

Captain: Janice Turnage

Coach: Faust Johnson

*Captain*

Janice Turnage

The girls' basketball team under the direction of *Coach* E. F. Johnson has enjoyed a very good season this year.

The forwards: Martha Fleming, Helen Joyce Whitehurst, and Janice Turnage have been ringing up the points. The guards: Patricia Jackson, Hannah Heath, and Evonne McLawhorn have been doing excellent work. The other players are Betty Lou Worthington, Marion Skinner, Mary Grace Holland, Peggy Hart, Barbara Little, Shirley Kinlaw, Margaret C. Andrews, Delma Worthington, Margie Davenport, June Stokes, and Louise McLawhorn.

The girls' basketball team and the school wish to thank *Coach* Johnson for giving his energy and time to the team.

| | | | | | | |
|---|---|---|---|---|---|---|
| Ayden | 19 | Grimesland 19 | Ayden | 10 | Winterville | 24 |
| Ayden | 42 | Snow Hill 11 | Ayden | 26 | Chicod | 14 |
| Ayden | 35 | Grifton 13 | Ayden | 33 | Stokes | 22 |
| Ayden | 38 | Snow Hill 14 | Ayden | 21 | Grifton | 14 |
| Ayden | 17 | Stokes 5 | Ayden | 23 | Bethel | 5 |
| Ayden | 23 | Bethel 9 | Ayden | 14 | Farmville | 17 |
| Ayden | 17 | Winterville 23 | Ayden | 26 | La Grange | 17 |
| Ayden | 27 | Grimesland 17 | Ayden | 23 | Chicod | 37 |
| Ayden | 23 | Farmville 25 | Ayden | 24 | La Grange | 27 |
| Ayden | 12 | Maury 12 | Ayden | 28 | Grifton | 13 |
| Ayden | 32 | Bel Arthur 29 | Ayden | 19 | Grimesland | 26 |
| Ayden | 28 | Belvoir 23 | | | | |

**1946-47 Ayden High School girls' basketball team.** *(The Wheel)*

The following year's team, 1947-1948, finished the regular season 18-1. The only loss was to Arthur, 30-26. The leading scorer was Helen Joyce Whitehurst, 14.7 points per game. The guards in girls' basketball never got their due. They were not allowed to shoot and, consequently, their point totals never showed up in the newspapers. Their sisters on offense received most of the credit. The defenders on the '48 version of the Lady Tornadoes must have been special. At a time when single digit point totals were disappearing, three opponents were held under ten points: Ayden 55, Stokes-Pactolus 4; Ayden 34, Winterville 9; Ayden 23, Chicod 6.

**HELEN JOYCE WHITEHURST**
*Captain*

The Ayden High School Girls' Basketball team enjoyed one of their most successful years in history, under the direction of their able coach, E. F. Johnson.

Helen Joyce Whitehurst, Janice Turnage, Patricia Jackson (forwards); Evonne McLawhorn, Hannah Heath, and Betty Lou Worthington (guards), composed the starting team. The other players were Margaret Andrews, Louise McLawhorn, Sue Jackson, Elaine Hatch, Phyllis McLawhorn, And Marjorie Craft (forwards); Barbara Little, Lois Jolly, Ramona Taylor, Marion Skinner, and Marjorie Davenport (guards).

High scorer for the season was Helen Joyce Whitehurst, who scored 235 points in 16 games, followed by Janice Turnage and Patricia Jackson, with 150 and 111, respectively.

| | | | |
|---|---|---|---|
| Ayden | 19 | Grimesland | 12 |
| Ayden | 48 | Snow Hill | 15 |
| Ayden | 28 | Belvoir | 11 |
| Ayden | 40 | Snow Hill | 17 |
| Ayden | 55 | Stokes | 4 |
| Ayden | 30 | Grifton | 21 |
| Ayden | 34 | Winterville | 9 |
| Ayden | 22 | Grimesland | 15 |
| Ayden | 25 | Farmville | 14 |
| Ayden | 23 | Chicod | 6 |
| Ayden | 30 | Bethel | 22 |
| Ayden | 26 | Arthur | 30 |
| Ayden | 25 | Winterville | 11 |
| Ayden | 32 | Mt. Olive | 12 |
| Ayden | 22 | Arthur | 20 |
| Ayden | 26 | Grifton | 18 |
| Ayden | 33 | Mt. Olive | 19 |

**1947-48 Ayden High School girls' basketball team.** *(The Wheel)*

In the Pitt County Conference Tournament, Ayden was seeded 1$^{st}$, Authur 2$^{nd}$, and Farmville 3$^{rd}$. In the semifinals, Farmville upset the favored Ayden team by the score of 23 to 16. Farmville won the trophy by defeating Grimesland, 17-12. AHS finished the season 20-2, the best won-loss record up to that time.

The starters for the '47-'48 team were as follows:

Forwards: Patricia Jackson ('48), Janice Turnage ('49), and Helen Joyce Whitehurst ('49)

Guards: Hannah Heath ('48), Evonne McLawhorn ('48), and Betty Lou Worthington ('48)

Captain: Helen Joyce Whitehurst

Coach: Faust Johnson


I phoned the captain of the '48 team, Helen Joyce (Whitehurst) Stroud, to set up a time for an interview. When I asked to speak to Helen Joyce, she knew someone from her hometown was on the line. Her friends now call her Joyce. I've always referred to her as Helen Joyce. I decided to store away her "new name" of Joyce for a later date. Like me, Helen Joyce lives in a retirement community. I drove to Raleigh wondering if I'd recognize her after all of these years. I didn't know whether to wave hello, shake her hand, or hug her neck. Helen Joyce solved that dilemma promptly; I got a long "we're both from Ayden" hug. In case you're wondering, I didn't recognize her and she didn't recognize me. I suspect the last time we saw each other was in the mid to late 50s.

Helen Joyce has a miniature trunk full of Ayden memorabilia. I didn't get to see the letters from her high school sweetheart, Bill Stroud ('45), but she shared some interesting keepsakes from her and her husband's days in Ayden. Bill had kept two copies of *Aydenites*, the newspaper that his class published during his high school days. Bill graduated in 1945 when there were 11 grades and Helen Joyce graduated in 1949 when there were 12 grades. Bill, the advertising manager, must have given his girlfriend a copy of *Aydenite* to read. I turned to the back of the issue and found a handwritten note:

*JOYCE*
*Joyce – finish cleaning your room if you have time. You all can eat when you want to – cabbage and spareribs are on the table, get some bread and open some peaches.*

*MOTHER*
*[PS] Take in clothes off line.*

I guess since Mrs. Whitehurst called her daughter Joyce, I should also. I like the note. Mothers always had ways of hinting at things they wanted you to do: clean your room, take in the clothes from the clothesline, and if you have any time left over, eat.

The 1948-1949 team made history; for the first time a girls' team representing Ayden High School won a tournament. AHS defeated Arthur 43 to 25 in the championship game of the Pitt County Conference Tournament. The team finished with a 19-4 record.

Forwards: Unreported
Guards: Unreported
Co-captains: Barbara Little ('49) and Janice Turnage ('49)
Coach: Faust Johnson
Team members: Helen Joyce Whitehurst, Janice Turnage, Katherine Wooten, Alice Jean Cox, Annie Mae Cox, Phyllis McLohon, Louise McLawhorn, Sue Jackson, Margaret Joyner, Margaret Andrews, Elaine Hatch, and Barbara Little.

Janice Turnage          Barbara Little

Co-Captains

The Girls' Basketball Team under the superb guidance of Mr. E. F. Johnson enjoyed one of their best seasons in the history of A. H. S. The girls won 19 games while losing only 4.

Those who composed the Girls' Team were: Helen Joyce Whitehurst, Janice Turnage, Katherine Wooten, Alice Jean Cox, Annie Mae Cox, Phylis McLohon, Louise McLawhorn, Sue Jackson, Margaret Joyner, Margaret Andrews, Elaine Hatch, and Barbara Little.

These girls ended the season by winning the Pitt County tournament, with a 43 to 25 victory over Arthur.

| Ayden | 33 | Snow Hill | 15 | Ayden | 23 | Grifton | 20 |
|-------|----|-----------|----|-------|----|---------|----|
| Ayden | 31 | Grimesland | 36 | Ayden | 41 | Belvoir | 11 |
| Ayden | 44 | Stokes | 9 | Ayden | 26 | Chicod | 23 |
| Ayden | 29 | Stokes | 18 | Ayden | 25 | Vanceboro | 17 |
| Ayden | 43 | Belvoir | 9 | Ayden | 33 | Bethel | 25 |
| Ayden | 31 | Vanceboro | 18 | Ayden | 38 | Grifton | 39 |
| Ayden | 32 | Winterville | 17 | Ayden | 32 | Walstonburg | 16 |
| Ayden | 13 | Walstonburg | 19 | Ayden | 36 | Grimesland | 18 |
| Ayden | 20 | Farmville | 19 | Ayden | 25 | Farmville | 10 |
| Ayden | 29 | Winterville | 20 | Ayden | 42 | Chicod | 21 |
| Ayden | 24 | Arthur | 29 | Ayden | 27 | Farmville | 21 |
|  |  | Ayden 40 |  | Arthur 25 |  |  |  |

**1948-49 Ayden High School girls' basketball team.** *(The Wheel)*

# Chapter 9
## "Buggy" and Mae

**Alice Jean "Buggy" Cox (on the left) & Annie Mae Cox (on the right) in 1949.** *(The Wheel)*

Soon after embarking on my research and interviews, I started hearing about this very good girls' basketball player who played sometime in the 40s or 50s. No one seemed to know precisely when. One person told me that she was "the best girls' basketball player Ayden ever had."

I arrived at Alice Jean (Cox) Smith's ('52) house in "The Circle" on a warm summer's day. Visiting that neighborhood is always nostalgic. Several of my friends and their families lived there, and Daddy enjoyed telling stories about the old race track. He told me about the auto races and before that the horse races that he used to sneak into as a boy. Alice Jean ushered me into the den where she sat in her favorite chair and I sat across from the brick fireplace on the couch. On the mantel over the fireplace and over the TV were pictures of children and grandchildren.

I had a 1952 newspaper clipping with the headline, "Ayden Will Miss Buggy." I wondered if she had discarded that nickname. As it turns out, everyone still calls her by the name she got from her family as a little girl. Alice Jean and her brothers and sisters decided one day that they would give each other nicknames. Buggy's the only one that stuck.

1952 *The Daily Reflector* clipping photo captioned, "Ayden Will Miss Buggy."
*(Courtesy of Tina Smith Hardee)*

After graduating from high school, Buggy went to work at DuPont. As supervisor, one of her jobs was inspecting the Dacron. The rolls of yarn that passed went into shipping boxes, and the "rejects" went onto a buggy. Right away, Buggy was told that "the name everyone called me" could not be used because of the confusion that would ensue. So, Buggy became Jean at DuPont.

Alice Jean Cox married Bill Smith between her junior and senior years in high school much to the dismay of her parents. As Buggy put it, "We musta done something right. We've been married for 63 years." However, Buggy did not want her two daughters to duplicate her feat, so she told them that she was 21 years old when she was married. After a few math classes, they realized that the numbers didn't add up and their mom had been 17 on that matrimonial occasion.

For her outstanding personal attributes as well as her prowess on the basketball court, Alice Jean Smith was awarded the 2016 Legend Award at the annual Alumni Golf Tournament by the Community Foundation, Inc., a non-profit that supports athletes at Ayden-Grifton High School.

Before moving on, I feel that I must make an important point – a detail that will be obvious to my female friends: when recreating the interviews of the female players I mention their husbands and then don't mention the wives when writing about the male athletes. Why is this? The answer; the women always talked about their husbands and the men never spoke of their wives. There is also a more practical reason; the women's last names were changed once they were married.

After Buggy's interview, my brother Bob and I had lunch. He asked if Buggy's husband, Bill Smith, was the same Bill Smith who umpired little league games. When he told me that the ump used to say "yes, it's in there" when he called a strike, it all fell into place. I remembered that distinctive call. A phone call to Buggy confirmed our memories.

Annie Mae Cox ('50), Buggy's older sister, was a guard. Defensive sports stars have never received the credit they deserve. The goalies in soccer and hockey may be an exception. I used to think the players who received the least amount of newspaper ink were the defensive linemen in football. On the other hand, this distinction maybe should go to the offensive linemen. In any event, the players who score touchdowns, make the most points, and hit home runs get the headlines. I can now add the guards in girls' basketball to my list of unsung heroes. I refer to this period of girls' basketball as the half-court era. Another name given to these years is the 6 on 6 era. Even when the defensive player was fouled, the referee tossed the ball to a designated shooter at the "offensive" end for the foul shot. In the newspaper box scores of girls' basketball games, the three starting forwards would be listed first. The three starting guards were listed next. Of course, none of the guards had point totals next to their names. At the end of the article, the defensive standouts would sometimes be credited with outstanding games. The sting of "playing behind the scenes" was lessened a tad when the all-conference teams were announced at the end of the year. Unlike the boys' team, the all-conference girls' team was divided between the best forwards and best guards.

There was one obstacle that the girls had to endure that did not befall the boys. I remember watching a girls' game during high school when one of our players exited the game hurriedly and disappeared into the dressing room. She was back in a flash. I had no idea what had happened; the "ways of the world" were still a mystery to me. After the game, I listened intently to someone explain the equipment failure that had prompted my friend's hasty departure: a bra strap had malfunctioned.

Another quirk of half-court girls' basketball was the ignoring of the all-around competitor – the player who was skilled both offensively and defensively. It must have been extremely frustrating to stand at one end of the court without being able to participate at the other end. I remember watching girls stand with their hands on their hips – spectators in their own games. The best defensive player may have been on the offensive side of the court. Likewise, one of the team's best shooters may have had to play on the defensive half of the court. The sexism that was built into the 6 on 6 game ignored the multi-skilled female players of the day.

Years later in the mid-1960s, Suzanne (Wilson) Gray ('66) remembered that basketball was the only sport available to girls. "It was cheerleading or basketball." Another hurdle that girls often had to overcome was pressure from within their family. Suzanne's father "didn't want his girls playing sports." He told her that she'd have to make all "As" before he would let her participate. When Suzanne brought home a report card with an "A" on every subject, he still said no. Luckily for Ayden High School, Mr. Wilson finally acquiesced, and the future all-conference team member got to play a game she loved.

Mae was one of those unsung heroes. Anne Mae (Cox) Eichorn currently resides in Greenville. When I contacted her, we decided to do a phone interview, so I sat in my "office away from home" at Bum's Restaurant and talked to the defensive standout. As I'm writing these words, I can't help but think of how long ago Mae played basketball – nearly 60 years ago; for me it's been over 50 years. Another time and another chapter in our lives. Mae explained that her family lived in the country and had one car. "It was an effort to get to practice." She went on to say, "It was a blessing to be on the team and play. I enjoyed every minute of it."

Together, Buggy and Mae played on some of Ayden's best girls' teams – ever. Mae remembered throwing the basketball all the way to Buggy at half court when she took the ball out of bounds after a made basketball – a sort of girls-style fast break of the times. The girls who'd grown up and worked on the farm together got to star on the basketball court together.

One of Buggy's teammates was Katherine (Wooten) Bright ('52), a lifelong friend. They used to play basketball on a goal on the Cox family farm. Sometimes they'd borrow the key to Ayden High's gym and play there. "I loved to play basketball more than I loved to eat," Buggy told me.

Love of the game leads to confidence. Buggy remembered the waning seconds of one game in a conference tournament on East Carolina College's campus when she stood at the foul line after time had expired in the first overtime. Hit the shot and Ayden wins; a miss would mean a $2^{nd}$ overtime. She could not remember the circumstances surrounding the game but knew that it was in the college's gym. I did a little more snooping in my files, and Buggy's story matches the ending of a game against Farmville in the finals of the Pitt County Conference Tournament during the 1949-1950 school year: "Alice Jean Cox, the Tornado forward who this year has been the mainstay in placing Ayden at the top of the heap in the county, was the heroine of the game Saturday night as she clinched victory for the girls on a free throw in the last four seconds."

The games against Farmville that year were tenacious. Ayden handed Farmville its first defeat on the Red Devils' home court after the two teams had fought to a 29-29 tie on the Tornadoes' home floor. A late foul call and a made free shot led to Ayden's victory, 21-20. The referees took such verbal abuse from the stands that they refused to call the second game. Two referees from Wilson were summoned, and the boys' game started at 10:30.

I cannot assure you that this was the best of the six teams. I can, however, state that they finished with the best regular season and overall season record during this period. Additionally, the 1950 Lady Tornadoes were the first and *only* Ayden girls' team to play in the state playoffs. That year marked the first year of the state playoff system for girls' basketball.

**1949-50 Ayden High School Girls' Basketball Team**
**Members of the team are First row (l-r): Elaine Hatch, Jean Rouse, Charlene Smith, Unknown, and Joanne Padley. Back row: Bertie Lee Thomas, Annie Mae Cox, Katherine Wooten, Coach Faust Johnson, Alice Jean "Buggy" Smith, and Unknown.**
*(The Wheel)*

Before dropping in on the six-team state tournament in Southern Pines, let's take a look at a remarkable season. No amount of impersonating Sherlock could uncover all of the individual game scores of that year. After a loss to Chicod before Christmas, the Tornado sextet went on a winning streak. (Since the girls' game required six players, reporters often referred to the team as a sextet.)

Ayden finished on top of the Coastal Conference regular season standings:

## 1949-1950: Coastal Conference Regular Season Girls' Basketball Standings

| | |
|---|---|
| Ayden | 6-0-1 |
| Farmville | 6-1-1 |
| Vanceboro | 3-4 |
| South Edgecombe | 0-7 |

The team went on to win the Coastal Conference Tournament with a semifinal victory over Vanceboro, 40-24. In the championship game, they defeated Farmville, 36-32.

Ayden played in two conferences. For the second consecutive year, the girls' team won the Pitt County Conference Tournament: Ayden 57, Belvoir 29; Ayden 45, Arthur 19; Ayden 27, Farmville 26 in the championship game. The only regular season loss was to Chicod. Buggy was the leading scorer with an 18 point per game average.

Sporting a 26-1-1 record, AHS was invited to the first Girls' State Championship Tournament in Southern Pines. Ayden won its first game in the six-team tournament, besting Fairmont, 37-30. In the team's second contest, the eventual state champion, Cool Springs, defeated the Lady Tornadoes, 48-36. The final 27-2-1 record would never be equaled.

Alice Jean Cox received an honorable mention for the All-State Team. Alice Jean and Annie Mae were both placed on the All-Pitt County and All-Coastal Conference teams.

The 1950-1951 team competed in three tournaments, finishing with a 22-6 overall record.

### Coastal Conference Tournament

| | |
|---|---|
| Ayden 44 | Robersonville 18 |
| Ayden 53 | Farmville 49 |

### Gold Medal Tournament

| | |
|---|---|
| Ayden 46 | South Edgecombe 42 |
| Ayden 51 | Farmville 52 |

### Pitt County Conference Tournament

| Ayden 36 | Bethel 32 |
|----------|-----------|
| Ayden 52 | Grifton 38 |
| Ayden 48 | Belvoir 49 |

The 1951-1952 team was the 6th year of this successful period. This was Buggy's and her best friend's senior campaign; Katherine and Buggy traded single-game scoring honors throughout the year.

The season started with a 51-33 victory over Grimesland; Katherine was high scorer with 19 with Buggy close behind at 18. The Tornadoes ran into a buzz saw in the second game. Winterville won 63-40. Ann Speir bucketed 27 points and her teammate, Jean Liverman, scored 21; these two forwards would go on to have a stellar year in conference play. Buggy was switched to defense in an effort to thwart Speir's scoring. That meant, of course, that Buggy could not play offense. Katherine took up part of the slack by scoring 27 points. Winterville duplicated the win two weeks later: Winterville 60, Ayden 45. Spier again scored 27 points and Liverman added 22.

Ayden got back on the winning track by defeating Bethel 45-37. In the 11th game of the season – a 59-40 win over Robersonville – Katherine hit for 41 points, 20-30 from the field and 1-4 on the foul line. *The Daily Reflector* stated that the point total "set an unofficial school record for the most points scored by a single player." Based on my research, this statement is accurate. At this point, the Tornadoes' record was 8-3.

The injury bug hit Katherine, and Ayden lost to South Edgecombe 38-36. Once the star forward returned, Ayden got back to their winning ways and handed Belvoir-Falkland its first loss in conference play by the score of 40-37. In the return game against South Edgecombe, Buggy and Katherine outscored the other team with 27 and 18 points respectively: Ayden 62, South Edgecombe 36.

Winterville did not play in the Coastal Conference. The final standings were:

## 1951-1952: Coastal Conference Regular Season Girls' Basketball Standings

| | |
|---|---|
| Ayden | 7-1 |
| Vanceboro | 5-3 |
| Robersonville | 4-3 |
| Farmville | 2-5 |
| South Edgecombe | 1-7 |

Going into the tournament, the Ayden girls' and boys' teams had identical records of 7-1. Both had won the Coastal Conference Tournament the year before and were favorites to win again. In the semifinals, Ayden beat Farmville 76-55 and Buggy recorded 45 points on 20 field goals and five foul shots. Up to this time, I believe this point total to be the most ever scored by a female player at Ayden High School. Play in the tournament was suspended for two weeks because of the Tornado boys' entrance into the state playoffs. Once the tournament resumed, Buggy again led the way with 26 points in a 60-45 victory over Vanceboro – Ayden's third straight Coastal Conference trophy. Buggy often played facing the basket, just like a guard would do in the boys' game; in this game she opened up the inside "by hitting consistently on set shots from outside the circle." Ayden's guards were lauded for their defensive efforts: Peggy Conway, Betty Jean Padley ('53), and Wilma Stocks ('54).

The '52 Pitt County Conference Tournament proved to be a tough assignment. In the Lady Tornadoes' first game, Ayden defeated Chicod 61-42. In the semifinals, Ayden upset Belvoir-Falkland for the second time, 66-49. In the championship game, the Ayden lassies encountered the buzz saw that had chewed them up twice before: Winterville 68, Ayden 62. The game stats revealed four outstanding offensive performances: for the winners; Ann Spier (31), Jean Liverman (27) and for the losers; Alice Jean Cox (33), Katherine Wooten (20).

This game completed the careers for Buggy and Katherine – the two best friends who had spent so much time shooting hoops on the farm and in the gym; so much time doing more than their part to defeat the other team. Coach Faust Johnson had this to say about Buggy: "She is probably the best player I have ever coached. It will be hard to replace her." Alice Jean Cox finished her career with the second highest point total in history, 1,615 points. Katherine completed her career with the highest number of points, 1,624. Coach Johnson stated that Buggy's 17.4 average per game for her four years was the highest ever for a girls' player at AHS. Up to that time, her 22.4 average for her senior year must have been the highest for a single season.

Buggy was sometimes switched to guard in an effort to stymie the high scorer for the other team. This meant that she couldn't score points at the other end of the court on offense. Wonder what Buggy and Katherine could have accomplished had they been able to play full court? To play both offense and defense? To dribble more than two times? We'll never know, of course. What we do know is ... the friends were two of the best to ever wear maroon and white.

You will learn in the next chapter that Sue Sutton in 1957 and Andrea Harris in 1961 averaged 25+ points per game during their senior years. Sue and Andrea take the prize for the highest point averages during a given season. Katherine Wooten holds the record for the most points in a career. For a high school career that spanned four years, I suspect that Buggy's 17.4 per game average was the highest. And, Alice Jean Cox would get my vote for the best overall player.

An 82% winning percentage for six years is difficult to continue. Could the Lady Tornadoes find enough points to continue such a high level on the basketball court?

## Chapter 10
### Frustrating Times

After six years of "stepping in high cotton," the girls' teams over the next four years struggled to win games – finishing in the bottom echelon of both the Coastal Conference and Pitt County Conference. By my best estimate, the average number of wins in each of the four years was less than five. One of the high points of the '52-'53 season took place three miles away in Winterville: Jean Liverman, now without her sidekick Ann Spier, scored 65 points in a 109-44 victory over Walstonburg.

During the mid-'50s, a question concerning the two conferences arose: When did the Coastal Conference go out of business? The answer – it depends on the sport. For now, I will focus on girls' basketball. Some of the pieces of the puzzle are missing; nonetheless, I'm going to take a shot at creating the parts that aren't there. The Ayden girls played in the Coastal Conference through the 1956-1957 regular season. However, for the first time, there was no conference tournament for girls. The Farmville girls were crowned as regular season champs. As usual, a boys' tourney was held; the Ayden boys were unable to participate in the tournament because they were involved in the state playoffs. The following year, 1957-1958, marked the first year that no Coastal Conference regular season or tournament was held for the boys and girls basketball teams. The two Ayden teams continued to play their former Coastal Conference foes as non-conference opponents.

After going 20-5 in '51-'52, it wasn't until the 1956-1957 school year that the Lady Tornadoes finally had something to crow about. Sue Sutton

('57), Ann Long ('57), and Carolyn Sumrell ('58) led the way on offense, and Sandra Basden ('57), Bonny Rutledge ('57), and Barbara Worthington ('58) handled the defensive chores. With four seniors and two juniors, the starting six had weathered the hard times and were primed to have a good year. Without published stats to go by and without write-ups of all games, season records have to be approximations. I feel comfortable in saying that Sue Sutton averaged over 25 points per game during the regular season. Carolyn scored in double figures in most games, and Ann had the third highest scoring average. One journalist paid tribute to Ayden's defenders: "Basden, Worthington, and Rutledge are among the best defensive players in the league."

The Pitt County Conference was competitive all year. Stokes-Pactolus completed the season on top with an 11-3 record; Winterville was 12-4; Grifton was 11-4, and Ayden was fourth at 9-4. In a sense, the conference foes had "beaten each other up" during the season.  For instance, the Lady Tornadoes defeated the regular season champ, Stokes-Pactolus 63-46 but lost 52-38 to Farmville, a lower echelon team that year. Later on, the Ayden players redeemed themselves against Farmville, defeated Bethel twice, and then lost to Grifton by one point.

The sports writers chose Stokes-Pactolus to win the Pitt County Conference Tournament. The six-day playoff opened with nine girls and nine boys teams vying for the title. The boys and girls alternated nights with the boys playing two games and the girls playing one; the next night the girls played two and the boys played one.

Since Ayden and Farmville had split during the regular season, Ayden's first game was a toss-up. The Tornadoes won a close one, 40-38. In an upset, Ayden won the next game over the tourney favorite: Ayden 53, Stokes-Pactolus 37. Next up was nemesis Winterville. In another surprise, Ayden won the championship game, 52-43. Sue Sutton had a great tournament, averaging 26 points per game. Carolyn Sumrell averaged 15 and Ann Long 7. Overall, the Lady Tornadoes completed the season with a record of 16-6. Sue Sutton made All Conference at forward and Bonny Rutledge received the honor at guard.

I often relied on Mitchell to track down former players whom I wanted to interview. Like other AHS alumni, I'd lost track of Sue Sutton. Much to my surprise, I received an email from my co-author saying, "I believe you may know her husband." Sue had married Rob Roy Turnage ('61), one of my Ayden High classmates. During the ensuing phone call to Carolina Beach, one of Ayden's best basketball players was too modest to talk about her exploits on the hardwood. Instead, she heaped praise on two of her opponents: Jean Liverman of Winterville and Dawn Smith of Grifton. Sue was surprised to learn that I'd determined she and Andrea Harris ('61) were the two highest scorers in AHS girls' basketball history. Sue immediately suggested that Buggy must have gained that distinction a few years before in the earlier part of the decade. "No," I said, "you and Andrea averaged more points." These stats pertain to Sue and Andrea's per game average for their senior years.

**Sue Sutton (1957) and Andrea Harris (1961) were scoring machines for Ayden High School girls' basketball.** *(The Wheel)*

The next year ('57-'58) the Lady Tornadoes struggled during league play and lost their first game in the Pitt County Conference Tournament to Farmville, 48-38. This was my freshman year, and I remember Carolyn Sumrell's distinctive shot from the left side of the basket. It was sort of a combination hook and jump shot. Once she got the ball in the "right" spot, Carolyn was unstoppable. For her efforts, Carolyn Sumrell was named to the All-Conference team.

The following year in 1958-1959, the team continued its downturn course and finished with a 2-9 record in the conference. Ayden, the 7th seed, drew the 2nd seeded Winterville (12-4) girls in their first tournament matchup. Winterville pulled ahead 21-18 at half, and then Ayden won the game 41-33. Dawne Rouse ('60) scored 21 points, Carol Braxton ('60) got 12, and Barbara Yorke ('62) netted 8. The Tornadoes made it close but lost to Grimesland in the next game by the score of 45-44. Braxton scored 29 points. At forward, Carol Braxton carried the offensive load and made All-Conference. Barbara Gagnon ('59) made the All-Conference team as a guard.

In 1959-1960, the three starting forwards and the number one sub returned: Carol Braxton, Dawne Rouse, Barbara Yorke, and Andrea Harris. The first two games were not confidence builders. In the opener, Grifton defeated the Tornadoes 73-39 and, in the second game, Grimesland's forward, Mabel Singleton, scored 51 points and the opponents won handily, 90-60. Carol Braxton scored 25, Dawne Rouse 17, Barbara Yorke 2, and Andrea Harris came off the bench to get 14 against Grimesland.

One of the most hotly contested evenings of the year occurred just before Christmas. Ayden's arch rival, Bethel, came to town. The Ayden girls won in overtime, 48-45 in the first game, and the boys won the second contest in double overtime, 65-61. The Lady Tornadoes finished 1959 with a win over Chicod 71-44 and started '60 with another win over the same team, 51-39. Things were looking up until a non-conference loss to Robersonville, 49-30 followed by a conference loss to Belvoir-Falkland, 71-63. The highlight of the early season was the emergence of Andrea as a scorer. She bucketed 12 and 15 points in two games against Chicod, 27 against Grimesland, and 28 against Stokes-Pactolus.

The Tornadoes final overall regular season record was 8-10. In the Pitt County Conference Tournament, Ayden's fortunes looked bleak in the first game. Grimesland had won the first meeting by 30 points and the second game by nine points. However, the girls continued a tradition of playing well in the first game of the tourney even when the season's record had been less than .500. Grimesland was defeated 56-34. Braxton scored 27 points, Harris 15, Rouse 8, and Yorke 2. Sue Fort came off the bench to get 4 points. Stokes-Pactolus stopped Ayden from pulling another upset when they won 46-42 in Ayden's second game of the tournament. The high spot of the tournament occurred in the finals; Grifton defeated Stokes-Pactolus 72-60, thus ending the Blue Jays' 46 game winning streak in conference play.

Carol Braxton again made the All-Conference team at forward. Ann Willis ('60) was placed on the All-Conference team at guard.

The Lady Tornadoes' season again took a nose dive in 1960-1961, my senior year. The highlight of the year was the offensive prowess of forward Andrea (Harris) Norris. Andrea's season reminded me of Sue Sutton's senior campaign in 1957 – both could be counted on to score 25+ points nearly every night.

As had happened twice in recent years, Ayden was an upset winner in the first game of the Pitt County Conference Tournament. Ayden defeated Grifton but then lost to Bethel, 48-40. Andrea scored 30 points in the final game of her career.

Andrea Harris made All-County at the forward position and Billie Thompson ('62) was presented with the honor as a guard. Andrea averaged 25.4 points per game her senior year. Her highest point total was 41 points against the Bethel Indians.

After a disappointing year in '61-'62, the 1962-1963 team became the first of three straight winning seasons. There would be reason to celebrate if not for a trend that started in the '63 conference tournament. In the recent past, Ayden's less than .500 record teams had started the conference tourney with an upset win. Contrastingly, in the near future, winning seasons would be followed by a loss in the first game of the Pitt County Conference Tournament. Prior to the tournament pairings, Ayden was second in the conference standings with an 11-5 record; the Farmville Red Devils were 15-1 and in first place. Ayden drew the Stokes-Pactolus Blue Jays in the tournament, a team that the Lady Tornadoes had beaten twice during the league's regular season. The Blue Jays, with a 6-10 conference record, upset the Tornadoes 40-38. Farmville would go on to win the title. The final record was in the neighborhood of 12-6.

Ayden's Nancy Stokes ('63) took home All-Conference honors.

The '62-'63 school year was notable for an innovation in the girls' game. Suzanne (Wilson) Gray ('66) remembered that she and a teammate were the first "rovers" to play. A rover was a player who could play both offense and defense – the first female athletes to play full court. When she first heard about the rover position, Suzanne knew immediately that she wanted to play there. At about this same time – maybe to coincide with the creation of the rover – girls were allowed to dribble three times rather than two. The evolution would continue until the girls' game became like the boys in the early 70s.

The '63-'64 team improved on the previous year's regular season mark and then fared better in the end-of-the-year tourney. The Lady Tornadoes moved quickly out of the gate by winning 10 of their first 11 games. Going down the home stretch, however, Ayden lost 3 of its last 5 to finish with a 12-4 conference record.

In the first game of the Pitt County Conference Tournament, Ayden defeated Stokes-Pactolus handily, 41-24. In the second contest, the Tornadoes eked out a 36-34 victory over Winterville to gain a shot against Farmville in the finals. The Lady Red Devils had won the two previous encounters and made it 3-0 over the Tornadoes with a score of 56-28. Pat Pridgen ('64) was a unanimous All-Conference selection at forward, the only girl to receive all of the coach's votes for that honor. LaRue Willis ('64) made All-Conference at guard.

For the third straight year, the Lady Tornadoes finished the season with a winning record, but the 1964-1965 girls lost their first game in the Pitt County Conference tournament: Chicod 27, Ayden 15. Dottie Harris ('66), Suzanne Murphrey ('65), and Suzanne Wilson traded scoring honors during the season. Suzanne Wilson ('66) made All-Conference at forward. The team's final overall record was 11-6.

Over the next two years – '65-'66 and '66-'67, the Lady Tornadoes finished below .500. Both teams lost to Winterville in the first game of the Pitt County Conference Tournament. In 1966, Suzanne Wilson repeated as an All-Conference forward. Kay Williams ('66) received the honor as a guard. In 1967, Kay Kite ('69) and Judy Corbett ("68) made the All-Conference team.

In 1967-1968, the Lady Tornadoes had one of their best years – finishing tied for first place with Bethel in the regular season Pitt County Conference standings. It is often impossible to be sure of the final overall records of Ayden's girls' teams. The records in the conference were given periodically, but the overall records that would have included non-conference games were often ignored. Counting the victories and losses would not have provided someone with a true picture because all the games were not covered in the newspapers – after nearly 50 years, the only source of game summaries.

**1967-68 Ayden High School Girls' Basketball Team**
Members of the team include: First row (l-r): Iris Carraway, Cathy Booth, Linda Stox, Judy Corbett, Louise Mumford, Jennie Lou Oakley, Kathy Manning and Kay Kite. Second row: Janie McLawhorn, Kathy Wilson, Diane Brown, Kathy Worthington, Kathy Wheless, Cheryl Claybrook, and Ann Miller. Third row: Christine Mumford, Frankie Pierce, Nancy McLawhorn, Jane Garris, Jackie Dail, and Patricia Hill. *(The Wheel)*

Ayden won its first three games before bowing to Chicod in overtime, 37-35. After beating Stokes by 21 points, Ayden arrived in Bethel hoping to move into first place. The Tornadoes could not overcome a six point halftime deficit and returned home with a loss, 36-30. After stumbling in

Indian territory, it appears that Ayden won eight straight games before losing to Belvoir-Falkland in its final game before tourney time. The final win in the victory string came at home over Bethel, 26-21. This game was dominated by the defensive guards, or maybe both clubs had an off-shooting night. In an unusual twist, neither team scored in double figures in any of the four quarters and no forward in the game got into double figures. The Tornadoes owned first place with 2 losses; the Indians had 3. The loss to Belvoir-Falkland denied the Tornadoes a regular season crown. Bethel and Ayden finished 9-3. Ayden was seeded first (I must guess that the two teams were seeded based on a coin flip since they each had won one game apiece in their home and home series.)

No matter how good a team is in basketball, there's usually at least one game that is decided by a wide margin. In other words, a championship team – at least once – is "blown out" by an opponent. This season, the AHS girls were "in every game." A basket here and another one there, coupled with a few additional defensive stops, and a truly great season could have unfolded. The joy of being a number one seed ended abruptly. The bug that had triggered the recent "first game loss syndrome" in the Pitt County Conference Tournament also stung this team; the season ended with an upset loss to Grifton, 26-19. Bethel took the tournament trophy home with a resounding victory over Grifton in the finals, 41-18.

The scoring was "balanced" all year with four forwards carrying the load. It was not unusual for 3 forwards to finish in double figures – even in a low scoring game. In a 40-31 victory over Winterville, for instance, Kay Kite ('69) scored 13 points, Frankie Pierce ('68) got 12, and Jackie Dail (A-G) hit 10. (A-G means that Jackie graduated from the consolidated Ayden-Grifton High School.) Christine Mumford chipped in with 5 points. Three of those forwards received post season recognition: Kay Kite and Frankie Pierce were placed on the All-Conference team and Kay Kite and Christine Mumford ('69) made the All-County team. The Lady Tornadoes final record was 12-4.

The 1968-1969 team completed the year 12-8. Senior Kay Kite gained momentum on offense as the season progressed. The forward scored in double figures over the first third of the season and then seemed to hit her stride just before the halfway mark. Against Charles B. Aycock, she scored 24 points to help avenge an earlier loss. Kay brought her shooting touch to her hometown gym when the Chicod Hornets rolled into Ayden. Her 34 points led to a 62-21 drubbing of the visitors. Cheryl Claybrook ('70) contributed 10 points as a total of 7 Lady Tornadoes got into the scoring column.

The Bethel Indians girls' team was referred to as the Squaws, but I cannot bring myself to use that term (I don't know which female team would get my vote for most derogatory name – the Bethel *Squaws* or the name the reporters gave to the Winterville *Wolf Gals*!) Admittedly, my knowledge of Bethel's girls' basketball is limited; however, the 1969 team must have been one of the school's best. In the early February league standings, the Indians were 9-0; Belvior-Falkland was 2 ½ games back at 7-3; and Ayden was 6-3, another half-game behind the leaders. At this point, an interesting set of statistics emerged: all three of the Bethel forwards were in the top ten in individual conference scoring. Setting the pace was Faye Everett of Winterville at 12.7 points per game; followed by Kay Kite of Ayden at 12.6 and Marion McLawhorn of Grifton at 12.5. The Bethel players' averages ranged from 10 to 12 points.

The first matchup against Bethel on Ayden's home floor had been a close one; the Indians won, 46-39. The two teams squared off in Bethel a couple of weeks before tournament time. The contest was nip and tuck during the first half. As the clock wound down to intermission, Kay scored 6 of her 16 points; each time the Indians got close, the forward hit a timely basket. Ayden led the undefeated Bethel girls at the half 22-20. The out-of-towners were ahead by one at the end of three quarters. In the decisive 4th quarter, the home team pulled away for their 22nd win of the year. The final score was 42-34. The Bethel girls would go on to finish 12-0 in the conference.

In their first Pitt County Conference tournament game, Ayden had little trouble with Chicod – winning 37-20. The win pitted the Lady Tornadoes against the Belvior-Falkland Eagles in the semifinals. The two teams had divided their home and home series. Neither team had a good shooting night, but Ayden did just enough to win, 42-36. Kite managed only 5 points. Ann Miller ('69) hit for 12 and Jackie Dail got 11. Sheryl Claybrook ('70) scored 7.

Next up, Bethel, in the championship game. The Tornado girls could not make it close as they had done on the Indians' home court. After leading 19 to 5 at half, Bethel won the trophy 35-22. Bethel finished the season with a 26-0 record.

Kay Kite ('69) at rover and Janie McLawhorn ('69) at guard were named to the All-Conference team.

The following year's team (1969-1970) experienced difficulty in putting points on the scoreboard. In a 37-25 loss to Grifton, AHS had no one in double figures. Likewise, in an unusually low scoring game in January 1970, Farmville defeated Ayden 18-16, and no Lady Tornado scored in double figures. In the Pitt County Conference Tournament, Ayden won its first game against Chicod, 43-37. Judy Dail (A-G) scored 11 and Kathy Manning ('70) netted 10. The Lady Tornadoes' season ended in the next tourney game. Cathy Booth ('71) and Cheryl Claybrook made All-Conference.

The difficulty in putting the ball in the basket also plagued Ayden's last pre-consolidation team in '70-'71. In a weird game against Oak City, Ayden lost by the score of 22-6. The high scorers for AHS were three players with 2 points each. Ayden lost its first game in the Pitt County Conference Tournament to Grifton, 34-19. A team that finished with a less than .500 record (probably 6-10) placed three on the All-Conference team: Lynn Langston (A-G), Patsy Loftin (A-G), and Kathy Wheless ('71).

## Unbelievable Numbers during Six on Six Girls' Basketball Era

During the age of girls' basketball that I refer to as "half-court," some refer to as the 6 on 6 era. This appears to me to be a misnomer; it was not actually 6 on 6 but 3 on 3 on one end of the court and 3 on 3 at the other end. I must admit that 6 on 6 sounds better.

Mitchell has the knack of finding things in cyberspace that I wouldn't even know how to begin looking for. Must be all those years of searching for numbers to support his rationale for the thousands of editorials he's published. He sent me the website below. I refer you to that web address for more info on this topic.

**(www.luckyshow.org/basketball/NC6hiscores.htm)**

In the historical first girls' state tournament in the '49-'50 school year, Ayden lost to Cool Springs, the eventual state champion. The Tornado defense could not stop Martha Stroud who scored 27 points. I don't know if Stroud was the first or just one in a series of star forwards in Cool Springs' history. Succeeding her was a scoring machine named Susie Warren. It was not unusual for her to score 40+ points per game. During the 1951 and 1952 seasons, Warren scored 47 points on four occasions and 50 points three times. The same two years of her career, Warren amassed the following single-game point totals: 56, 58, 60, 65, 68, 73, 74, 81, and 86. In the 1952 Valdese Gold Medal Tournament, the Cool Springs' star forward scored 124 points in two games. In an odd "twist of fate," Susie Warren once scored all of her team's 73 points only to lose the game to Goldston High, 76-73.

Even more astonishingly, in the game in which Warren scored 81 points, she wasn't the high scorer. A forward for the other team scored 88 points! This other scoring marvel was Joan Gilbreth. The final score was Cool Springs 96, Hiddenite High 90. This website does not tell us whether or not these opponents were in the same conference. In another match involving the same schools, each of the two scoring machines netted 86 points: Hiddenite High 100, Cool Springs 95.

In 1953, Joan Gilbreth scored 102 points in a win over Mt. Ullna, 106-65. Her season averages were 58.9 points as a sophomore, 52.1 as a junior, and 64.6 points per game as a senior.

According to this website, here are the three highest per game point totals in the history of 6 on 6 girls' basketball in North Carolina:

**107 points**                                    **Beulah Thompson**
    (1954: New Hope 120, Mt. Olive 111)

**107 points**                                    **Martha Ann Bowers**
    (1955: Norlina 112, Wm R. Davis 34)

**106 points**                                    **Judy Vaughn**
    (1961: Westfield 132, Shoals 60)

**104 points**                                    **Kay Wilson**
    (1963: Talorsville 132, Marion 32)

In the 1961 game, Judy Vaughn hit 40 field goals and 26 foul tosses in 30 minutes. And, in the 1963 contest, Kay Wilson scored 39 points in one quarter and had 68 points at half.

**Two Aydens**

## Chapter 11
### Growing Up White during Jim Crow

A day or two before Christmas around 1955, Daddy, Joe, Bob, and I climbed into the family's Chevrolet and drove to Sarah's house, immediately across the street from the silver goalposts at the south end of the football field where I later played football and baseball. The goalposts were down the same left field line that was so famous for the "cheap" homeruns in the Coastal Plain League. Sarah had helped raise my brothers and me, and we had a gift for her. Someone came out of the house to give us the bad news: Sarah Shepard had died. My family had no idea. There were separate funeral homes in town, one for white people and one for black patrons. That surprise was one of my first recollections of what "separate" could actually mean. Even our grief had to be endured separately.

To a young teenager, the whole world was lily-white. When I picked up a magazine, all the advertisements were inhabited by white people, and the products they were trying to sell seemed to be aimed at my kind. *The Ayden Dispatch*, *The Daily Reflector*, and *The News and Observer* were filled with white news and white ads. The customers of the restaurants I entered were white. The bank president and his tellers were white. My school was white; my church was white; my little league team was white. All white.

Sarah's house on 6th Street and my house on Snow Hill Street were less than three small town blocks from each other. As Daddy turned left onto 6th Street, we passed my principal's house; Mr. Johnson and his family lived on the corner of 6th and Snow Hill Streets. Once we passed

Park Avenue and a large ditch that eventually ran behind Mrs. Phillips' apple orchard where I'd been admonished for performing my civic duty, the community's social, economic, and cultural landscape changed – white folks to our left and black folks to our right. The street on which we were driving was the same street I would walk to school on in grades five through twelve. We arrived at Sarah's house.

I don't really know when I started to climb out of the quicksand of my confusion surrounding racism. From very early in life, I remember attempting to reconcile the ongoing paradox of beliefs I often encountered. Black people were supposed to "know their place." What place was that? Why did the *Bible* verses from the *New Testament* become meaningless when I walked down the steep steps of the Methodist Church after Sunday services? Wasn't God a benevolent being who loved *everybody*? Why did Sarah and later on Daisy, the two black women who cooked and cleaned for Momma when my brothers and I were young, have to ride in the backseat? My family could eat their great Southern cooking, but Sarah and Daisy had to experience the indignity of "going to the back of the bus." Daisy cooked the best biscuits I'd ever tasted – small crusty morsels of goodness with a doughy inside. I once entered a contest with Uncle Sammy to see who could eat the highest number of her biscuits. He edged me out by the "football score" of 13-12.

The members of my family were Dr. Jekyll and Mr. Hyde. The kind and considerate Dr. Jekyll was the one I loved and understood. When the conversation turned to Dr. Martin Luther King, Jr. and the civil rights movement, Mr. Hyde appeared. At that moment, the people I loved and who loved me suddenly changed into something I didn't recognize. And something that became more and more incomprehensible.

My maternal grandmother thought my endless questions and subsequent attitudinal change resulted from my attendance at East Carolina College. She once scolded me by saying, "William, the more education you get, the crazier you get." I still loved her and she still loved me. Nothing could have changed those feelings. Nevertheless, the world of my parents and grandparents – a world that seemed so clear from the front seat of the predictable past – was quickly disappearing into the rearview mirror. The Supreme Court was making strange decisions, and Congress was passing heretofore forbidden laws. In reality, Grandmamma had it wrong. Ways of thinking about my African American neighbors in South Ayden – about race and ethnicity – started changing for me before high school. I've spent the rest of my life trying to understand my transformation, to understand bigotry itself, and to understand how it can be overcome.

The *Brown vs. Board of Education* case had been just a blur until I rediscovered it in my history and political science classes at East Carolina College. The 9-0 decision could not have been clearer. Why in the early 1960s did the Ayden schools remain separate and unequal? There were two separate bus systems furnishing transportation to the different black and white schools. It had felt weird over the last several years watching the orange school buses pass each other on their respective routes.

I had not attended a class with a black student until I was a sophomore at ECC. It was during that same year that I had a memorable experience. The event occurred at a movie theater in Greenville, the home of ECC. I decided to get some refreshments for my friends and me and retreated to the concession stand. Ordering his treats next to me was a young man of about my same age. When I returned to my seat, it suddenly occurred to me that he was a person of color, my first colorblind experience.

The concession stand event could not have happened ten miles away in Ayden when my Western heroes were galloping across the silver screen. In the 1950s the Myers Theater had been segregated, with black customers relegated to the balcony while white patrons got the choice seats downstairs. The two races were not allowed to mix when purchasing goodies from the concession stand or even when buying a ticket. The black movie goers had a separate entrance. Sometimes I would peep over the shoulder of the lady selling tickets to see a face in the dark, a face "from the other side of the tracks," the face of a person I never recognized. At least in that small theater, the patrons in the balcony were able to exact some small degree of revenge for the blatant racism they were facing. On occasion a paper cup with leftover bits of ice would "accidentally" be knocked off the balcony railing to shower the patrons below.

**Myers Theatre in the 1960s.** *(Photo Courtesy of Larry Dennis)*

I started to marvel at the African Americans who "made it" – the people who refused to "know their places." I asked myself: "In the face of so much adversity, how was it possible to succeed?" As a small boy, I once asked Sarah why she was black and the palms of her hands and the soles of her feet were white. "When the good Lord was painting me black, I was standing on my hands and knees." Her answer demonstrated the humor that I've never forgotten. How could a repressed person have such a great sense of humor?

I should have known better. Just a glimmer of hope goes a long way. I paid attention to the stories of black people who overcame poverty and racism to move into the mainstream. I still recollect my relatives making statements like, "When the going gets rough, he'll fold." But, Jackie Robinson didn't fold; number 42 ran just as fast and played just as hard when it counted the most. Bill Russell led the Boston Celtics to championship after championship. He didn't just excel, Russell set the standard for the professional basketball "big men" that followed him. Sunday afternoons were never the same after Jim Brown put on a Cleveland Browns' football uniform. He was simply the best. I danced to my favorite black recording artists, cheered for my favorite ball players, and laughed at my favorite comedians. Although I may never fully understand how I overcame the "built-in" bigotry around me, I do know that black athletes played a key role.

Back to Ayden. During the first half of the 20th century, the black and white populations of the community crisscrossed in a number of ways, sometimes under unusual circumstances. During the 1930s when he was in his twenties, Daddy refereed high school basketball games. On one occasion when a player on a girls' team called him a pug-nosed son of a bitch, she had to take an early shower. We Harringtons are known for our pug noses. Daddy apparently did not like to be reminded of that particular feature. But, that's another story. The one that fits in here is more complicated.

One day Daddy received an unexpected visitor. The basketball coach from the South Ayden High School Eagles stopped by the ice plant to ask a favor: "Mr. Bill, would you be willing to referee a basketball game between South Ayden and Pantego?"

Daddy was surprised and curious about the coach's request. Pantego High School had a basketball player that, as the coach put it, "can do so much with the ball that our referees and coaches don't know whether he's breaking the rules or not." He explained that the player could dribble behind his back and between his legs. The coach continued by saying that the player had caused quite a controversy and asked again if Daddy would call the game. At that time, only one referee officiated basketball games, so no other person was needed.

In the 1930s, basketball was a different game than it is today; it was never played above the rim. No player ever left his feet to shoot the ball, only for a jump ball or to retrieve a rebound. The game was essentially played flat-footed. Observing a player who could dribble behind his back and between his legs was unique.

When I first started hearing this story in the 1950s, my obvious question was why. During Jim Crow, why would an African American coach want a white man to referee one of his basketball games? Maybe Daddy was trusted because he believed so vehemently in honesty. Daddy's actions in respect to African Americans were paradoxical. He believed in the biased viewpoints of his day, but held a steadfast belief in fairness. I did not know until Daddy passed away that he used to "sell" ice and coal to townspeople who he knew could not pay him. Maybe this is why he was asked to officiate the contest. I'll never really know for sure. I do know that Bill Harrington agreed to referee the game.

The game started normally, but it didn't take long before the Pantego acrobat started showing off his skills. Daddy had never seen anything like it. He did a wise thing; Daddy called time out and brought the two coaches together and said to them: "I don't know whether he's traveling (i.e. breaking the rules) or not. Let's talk about it and I'll go by what we decide." The two black coaches and the only white person in the gymtorium decided that the player's maneuverings were legal and the game should continue. The game ended without incident.

Black shoppers' money was welcomed in the town's main business district, but they weren't. Sarah and Daisy could buy their clothes at P.R. Taylor and Company's Department Store. They could go to Mumford's Market and J. J. McClees' grocery stores. They could pay their electric and water bills in person at the Ayden Town Office where Granddaddy and Miss Laura Mae traded their money for receipts. In spite of the importance of "black money" in the white business district, there was nowhere for "colored people" to go to the bathroom. I remember one of my white friends exclaiming, "Another n***** got arrested for pissing in the alley." I asked, "Where else are they supposed to pee?" That type of question often got me into trouble. I wasn't supposed to ask such questions – especially the unanswerable kind.

**Former offices of the Ayden Fire Department and the Ayden Town Hall prior to 1971.**
*(Photo Courtesy of Bill Norris)*

Granddaddy ran the Town of Ayden office. When I was very small, I was allowed to visit him and to roam around the building. I remember being fascinated by the dark jail with its freshly painted silver metal enclosures and especially the fire trucks. My favorite fire truck was an old red one with a hand-cranked siren. I loved winding the worn handle around and around.

During the summer ice season and the winter coal and fuel oil business, Daddy hired several African American men to work for him. Likewise, several black men were employed by the town. One thing I noticed early on was that black people were not introduced in the same way as whites were. Often, people of color were not introduced at all and, when they were, only first names were used. Consequently, I knew the workforce of the two establishments by first names. At the plant, I got to know Fernie, Henry, C.T., and Semmie. At the Town Office, Oscar and Tom laughed at my jokes. The longer I knew the men the more likely I was to learn their last names.

All around town – at least in the white section of Ayden – black men and women held secondary jobs, never managerial positions. On no occasion did I experience an incident of disrespect toward me, and I always treated my co-workers and Granddaddy's workmen with respect. Of course, I *was* the son and grandson of the two bosses. Communications between the people I loved and their subordinates and between blacks and whites in general occurred all around me. Those interactions became the food of my ravenous appetite for trying to understand. Added to those experiences, I have participated in zillions of conversations, read non-fiction and fiction books, attended seminars, and completed college course work. Somewhere along the way, I realized that the journey had no destination – that there would be no final answer – only the continued pursuit of why prejudice still plays such an important role in human affairs.

**The Eagle, mascot of South Ayden High School.** *(From South Ayden High School History and Memories, Courtesy of Charles Becton)*

# Chapter 12
## South Ayden School

That narrow black strip of asphalt named 6<sup>th</sup> Street might as well have been the Atlantic Ocean. I know so little about the part of town that I refer to as South Ayden. In this chapter, we are going to take a closer look.

*Let's return to our mythical convertible. It's a hot summer's day, so we'll put the top down. Let's follow the route to Sarah's house and past Ayden High School. Then, we'll take a right and head south, down Lee Street. Remember, Lee Street is Ayden's main street.*

Let's say it's the mid to late '50s. The difference between the two Aydens is stark: paved streets on one side and dirt streets on the other; street lights and sidewalks on one side and almost none on the other; and more modern houses surrounding the white business district and older, often dilapidated structures surrounding the smaller black business section.

As we drive down the length of 6<sup>th</sup> Street with the top down, we can see people on both sides, going about their daily lives. There are children laughing and playing on both sides. There are mothers and fathers working on both sides. There are churches on both sides. I can hear laughter and crying and singing and talking and arguments about politics and bitching about taxes and musings about the future – on both sides.

*Wait! What's that smell? Collards and fried chicken for supper. Can't tell from which side of the street, but someone's gonna eat good tonight.*

*I'm turning right onto Lee Street now between Louise Mosely's grocery store and Johnnie Ray Craft's little store where I used to buy myself a Pepsi and honey bun at recess. Oh, this brings back memories. There's Jenkins Motor Company and Lutz and Schramm and ...*

*What's that? You wanta know what Lutz and Schramm is. That's the pickle plant. Those big round things are where the pickles are made. Lots of people had jobs there, and my friends worked there during the summers when I was working at the ice plant. Now, we're getting to a part of town that I don't know much about. I didn't know the names of these businesses until I looked at the advertisements in the back of the 1955 yearbook edition of* The Eagle.

**People working at Lutz & Schramn (in top photo) and pickle vats (in below photo) at the Ayden business.** *(Photos Courtesy of ECU Joyner Library, Reflector Collection)*

*Here we are. This is South Ayden School. I passed by here many times on the way to and from Grifton, three miles to the south – before the bypass was built. I've never been inside, though. I remember the building. I believe those four brick columns are new.*

*I have asked Charles Becton if he would meet us here. By the way, did you read that book I loaned you last night? Good. Mr. Becton wrote that book. He's a 1962 graduate of South Ayden High School.*

**South Ayden School** *(From South Ayden High School History and Memories, Courtesy of Charles Becton)*

*We'll have a little time before Charles is due to meet us at the school, so take a look at the three annuals that I've borrowed.* The Eagle *was published three times in the history of South Ayden School – in 1955, 1966, and 1970.*

*Charles will recognize some of the businesses that advertised in the '55 yearbook. There's Mr. Norcott's funeral home and C.C. Flemings Café. I always like to look at the ads in past annuals because they bring back memories. This annual in the mid-50s had an ad from Worthington's 5 cents to $5.00 dollar store. I always called it Worthington's 5 and 10 cents store. You could actually buy something for 5 and 10 cents. Daddy's ad listed his phone number at the ice plant,*

*3431. Interesting to see the numbers without their three-digit prefixes or area codes.*

*Turn over to the basketball teams. We don't have many pictures of those teams.*

**1954-55 South Ayden High School boys' basketball team.** *(The Eagle)*

**1954-55 South Ayden High School girls' basketball team.** *(The Eagle)*

*Now, turn to the page I have marked in the 1966 annual. There's a picture of the South Ayden Band. I remember how great they were in the Christmas parades I watched when I was a boy.*

**1965-66 South Ayden High School band.** *(The Eagle)*

*Charles won't know it and I'm not gonna tell him that the annual for the 1969-1970 school will be his school's last yearbook publication. The following year, '70-'71, will be South Ayden School's final year before consolidation.*

**Three editions of the South Ayden High School yearbook, The Eagle: 1955, 1966, 1970.** *(Photo by Mitchell Oakley)*

I received one of the first editions of the *Ayden Magazine*, and on the cover was someone I did not recognize – a person from my hometown, a man about my same age, a black man with a distinguished career in the judiciary. In the article about him, I learned that he had authored a book in 2007: *South Ayden School: History and Memories*. While taking the book's trip down memory lane, I didn't have to climb into a make-believe car to revisit my past. Again, the "split mind" of Ayden returned. How little I knew about a community so close yet so far away.

Between 1937 and 1971, a total of 1,256 students graduated from South Ayden School. As occurred in many parts of North Carolina in the years after the *Brown vs. Board of Education* court ruling, the school was closed in 1971, and no use was made of the existing buildings on campus. Instead, all of the buildings were demolished. A marker near the front entrance to the school is the lone reminder of its existence.

Becton's quote of Governor Charles B. Aycock's statement in the early part of the 20th century depicts the attitude toward the education of black children:

"The civilization of the state was based on an ultra-individualism, and thousands of citizens, conscientious, intelligent, patriotic, honestly could not understand why they should pay taxes to educate other people's children. Other thousands were willing to support schools for white children, but stood steadfastly and doggedly against the education of the Negro … these people appear to have been willing to deny education to white children in order that they might keep the Negro in ignorance."


The construction of the South Ayden School building replaced a frame building that had one teacher – much like the rural one-room school houses scattered throughout the countryside. It is possible that this original building was the Ayden Institute erected by the Baptists after the Civil War.

The president of Sears, Roebuck and Company, Julius Rosenwald, established a fund that eventually built 5,300 schools in the South between 1915 and 1932. The Ayden Colored School initially cost $27,250; public funds provided the bulk of the money, $23,650. The African American community contributed $1,500, the Rosenwald fund donated $2,100, and the white community offered none.

So much of Becton's book magnified my ignorance of Ayden's black community. I was surprised to learn that several buildings graced the school's property: "the 1920s Rosenwald-designed ten-classroom brick building, the 1951 and 1958 classroom additions, a Vocational Agriculture building, a Home Economics building, a Gymnasium, a

Lunchroom, and a Band room." And I never considered where the "feeder" schools were located.

### South Ayden Buildings and Feeder Schools

**South Ayden School Buildings & Feeder Schools.** *(From South Ayden High School History and Memories, Courtesy of Charles Becton)*

*South Ayden School: History and Memories* is brimming over with attempts to overcome inadequate resources. Principals, teachers, and townspeople struggled to raise funds to acquire more books, more classroom space, and more teachers – more of everything to improve the instructional program. For example in 1937, the Board of Education received a request by "a delegation of negroes, [and] patrons from the Ayden and Winterville Districts" to procure money for the purchase of a bus. The Board suggested "for each district to buy its own bus and this would be only for the transportation of high school children." The Board also required that the bus would have to be "entirely new, both body and chassis, equipped according to rules and regulations as set forth by the State School Commission." Finally, the Board's decision included the following stipulation: "The Board would not assume any liability for the operation of the bus but would supervise only its routing and maintenance should the State School Commission see fit to pay all the costs thereof." The Ayden Colored School's first bus was a 1938 Chevrolet procured with funds raised by the P.T.A. of Ayden High School. Students were picked up from Grifton, Haddocks, Pleasant Plain, Rogers, and Shiloh.

During the same decade that saw the purchase of the school's first bus, the Ayden Colored School's lab equipment was valued at $27.00. The library consisted of 200 books and two magazines housed in an 11 X 19 room. In grades 8-10, one teacher made $652.80 per year during the 1935-1936 school term and the other two teachers made $460.80 for the same time period.

Most of the book's information on teacher names, number of graduates, student-teacher ratios, and physical plant was gleaned from principal reports that were required by the state. The number of graduates varied greatly from six in 1937 to 78 in 1967. Strangely, there were no graduates in 1946, probably because of World War II. In 1952, the graduating class numbered 36; 44% attended a four-year college, the biggest proportion to attend college in the school's history. The numbers pertaining to books, classrooms, and overall resources increased over the decades. As one would surmise, these figures never matched the higher numbers at the white Ayden High School. In 1938 when Ayden Colored School was accredited, Ayden High School had a lunchroom, a gymnasium, superior lab equipment, and far better library facilities. The school only a few blocks south on Lee Street had no teacher restrooms, no lunchroom, no gymnasium, and no separate library. Basketball was the only sport offered at Ayden Colored School. The unequal expenditure gap persisted into the 50s and 60s, although black school enrollment outnumbered the white enrollment. The contrast in the actual financial receipts and reimbursements was drastic: "the fiscal year ending June 30, 1955 shows Ayden High with total receipts of $43, 681.77 and disbursements of $34,374.10 whereas South Ayden School had total receipts of $11,708.91 and disbursements of $11,417.48."

In various reports and minutes since the 1930s, the school's name was recorded as Ayden Graded School, Ayden Colored School, Ayden Colored High School, Ayden Special Colored School, and Ayden Negro School. During the 1953-1954 school year, the name was officially changed to South Ayden School.

*Just past Lutz and Schramm and where Venters Street (renamed Martin Luther King, Jr. Street) intersects with Lee Street, I turn right onto the circle drive and pull up to the front door of South Ayden School. Don't forget: our make-believe Thunderbird has taken us back to ... let's say1959. If that were really the case, Charles Becton and I would be teenagers of about the same age. Here he comes now ... running across the street from 105 Ormond Street and jumping the ditch to meet us here. Charles was born in Morehead City and moved to Ayden to live with his aunt while attending South Ayden School.*

I knew that I wanted to interview Charles Becton for this book, so I arranged with Mitchell to meet him at the 2014 Ayden Golf Tournament where he would be presented with the Legend Award by the Community Foundation, Inc. Since I don't play golf, I happened to arrive just in time for Bum's barbecue and fried chicken. I don't know if this built-in GPS for fabulous barbecue is genetic or maybe it was learned while growing up in Ayden. Really, it doesn't matter. What I know is that the smell of eastern North Carolina barbecue triggers an automatic hunger response topped by nothing else.

I learned quickly after moving away that I could anticipate with great exuberance a BBQ dinner for the two or three hour trip to Ayden. It has occurred to me that on some future occasion that Bum may show up with hotdogs and hamburgers. I'm afraid I'd have to vacate the premises and travel to Bum's Restaurant.

I didn't know whether to call the guest of honor Judge Becton or Chancellor Becton – Judge Becton for his long and distinguished career in the judiciary; Chancellor Becton for his recent position as Interim Chancellor at North Carolina Central University in Durham and the more recent Interim Chancellor at Elizabeth City State University. He eventually asked me to call him Becton. I decided not to pull out my recorder for an "official" interview. I wanted to get to know him better – besides, the Bum's barbecue feast on my mind had temporally chased away all the topics I'd thought to cover in the interview. Had I not known who Becton was, I would have been able to guess that he was from "barbecue country" by the way he attacked the morsels on his plate.

While waiting for the golfers to complete the course, I learned that Becton and I live in the same neighborhood in Durham. I knew that he had been a board member of the retirement community in which I currently live, but I did not know that he literally lives across the street. I went on the mapquest.com website; time of travel = *28 seconds*. Two men who grew up in Ayden in two different worlds now reside 28 seconds apart.

*I ask Becton to show us around the campus. First of all, the three of us walk out to Lee Street to gain a better view of where the campus is situated.*

*We face the school and Becton points to his right and says: "That's Venters Street, the same street that runs past Ayden High School's football field. Next to Venters is West Barwick Street that runs on the right of the school and Ormond Street ... where I live ... is on the left of the school's property. A couple of streets over to our left is Pete's Barbecue."*

*Still standing and facing the front of the main building with our backs to the street, Becton points to the small window on the far right: 'That's the principal's office, and on the far left is Mrs. Brown's room, my fifth grade teacher. The building is shaped sort of like an "H" with classrooms on either side of the auditorium in the middle. Following*

*Becton, we walk toward the little building next to Venters Street. Would you like to have a little refreshment?' he asks.*

*Never one to turn down such an offer, we enter the Soda Shop just off campus at the intersection of Venters and Lee Streets. While sipping on my milkshake with a cherry on top, I want to know about the new gym.*

*"Yeah," he said, "we just got a new gym behind the main building ... last year in '58. When we walk through the building, I'll show you where our basketball teams used to play."*

*We leave the Soda Shop behind and walk across campus. Becton points toward the door nearest us and suggests that we go inside for the rest of the tour.*

*"This is Mr. Ormond's office right here, and the auditorium is down the hall on our left. Before the new gym was built, this is where we used to play. You had to be careful when the chairs were removed from the auditorium and it became the gymtorium. If you were running too fast toward the basket on your right ... on that end, you may have ended up on the stage behind the backboard. And, the floor's slanted a little bit toward the stage. Sometimes, an outside shot had to be aimed so that it didn't hit the ceiling."*

*Becton led us around the edge of the auditorium to the back of the building.*

*"Right here we have a classroom out in the hall 'cause we don't have enough rooms."*

*"Becton ... is that the chorus I hear?"*

*"Yes, they're singing our school song."*

Dear South Ayden, we love you
for what we are today.
Your honor we never can repay.
With joy we shall lift up our
banners in the sky. We love you,
Our Dear South Ayden High.
South Ayden, South Ayden,
to thee be true, be true
Our trophies we'll spread
just for you. With joy

we shall lift up our banners
in the sky. We love you,
Dear South Ayden High.

(Composed by Daniel Brown, Class of '62)

*"What are all those buildings behind this building?" I ask.*

*"The elementary wing was added in 1952, and that building over there is now the bandroom. It used to be a cannery. That little building is the first grade building where I attended first grade. Grifton has an elementary school – grades one through eight, and then the students come to our school here in the ninth grade."*

*"Becton, I have another question or two. Let's walk back toward the front of the building."*

*Walking through the front door, I notice that it's beginning to get dark outside.*

*"What does the future hold for you?" I ask.*

*"I want to play basketball here at South Ayden High and go to college when I graduate"*

*"Yeah, I'd like to do the same."*

*"Becton, why is it so dark around here?" I asked.*

*"Oh, that's because we don't have all the street lights that you white folks have in your part of town."*

*I shake Becton's hand, thank him for his time, and drive toward Lee Street.*

*My last thoughts were – I hope I didn't offend him with that last question. And, I hope someday I will see him again.*

### Additional Information from *South Ayden School: History and Memories*
### by Charles Becton

Survey information on North Carolina schools serving black school age children from early 1900s: (The following are quotes cited by Charles Becton in the book from a publication named *Some Facts About the Education of Negroes in North Carolina, 1921-60* by G.H. Ferguson.)

- Less than one-half of the children who should have been attending public schools were enrolled.
- The average daily attendance was less than 50% of the enrollment and was particularly poor during the opening and closing months.
- More than half of the children, especially in the rural schools, were enrolled in the first grade – ranging in age from 5 years to 15 years or more.
- Only seven high schools were accredited, and four of those were attached to the four Negro State Colleges operating at the time.
- More than 50% of schools were of the one teacher type.
- A large number of the rural schools had negligible furnishings and the buildings were in deplorable conditions. As was said of one of these schools you could study animal science through the cracks in the floor, plant life through openings in the walls, and astronomy through the holes in the roof.

Many pages of the book are adorned by the rhymes of the poet, Charles Becton. Here are a few of the verses:

We remember
Trudging 'cross campus in total darkness
'Cause all streets south of Barwick were lampless
When the school lay outside city limit
And blacken'd clouds did not moonlight admit.

How darker clouds – separate but UNEQUAL –
Took their toll long past *Brown* and its sequel
And now, despite all, we overcame.
Thank you South Ayden, you name we proclaim.

We remember
The Cannery built long before the school
Doubling as bandroom and baptismal pool,
Band practice and the dancing majorettes;
The sometimes shriek of sax and clarinets.

We remember
Sardines, crackers, that banana sandwich
That caused the squeamish to quiver and twitch.
Though peanut butter and jelly was their fare
Of loom'd irony they were unaware.
4 cent cartons of milk and ice cream cup
Sold whenever that freezer wasn't locked up.
Ginger snap cookies, two for a penny
But nickel-less we could not buy many.

We remember
The coaches: Mebane, Lowry, and Wilson,
Malloy, Brown, Haselrig, Davis, Ebron,
Grade school teachers who stayed 15 plus years
Who, like natural moms, removed our fears.
Murphy, Moore, Hall, M.B. Burney, Jackson,
Warren, Cox, Brown, Lowry and Albritton
Are our heroes and heroines unsung.

The few white teachers bold enough to come
To help us be all that we have become.
'Course we taught them too – a "Win-Win" for all
Lane, King, Wilson, Stancil, Hughes, LaRoque, Ball.

The fiat that caused each seventh grade class

To be moved to white Ayden School en masse
When no whites were assigned to our school
"Twas a failed one-way integration tool.

Black/white students meeting in '69
At the Holiday Inn, with hope, they dined
To discuss the consolidated school,
Its mascot, colors … coexistence rule.

Charles Becton's final tribute from the school song…

South Ayden, we love you
For what we are today
Your honor we never can repay
With joy we shall lift up
Our banners in the sky
We love you
Our dear South Ayden High

## Chapter 13
### South Ayden Eagle Football

A few days after the golf tournament, Becton and I met for an interview. I asked him if he had anything to say about his early school life. He said, "All the teachers cared." This statement was followed with example after example of teachers and students who excelled at their crafts – from the teachers who made sure their students got to summer camp to students who sang, played musical instruments, and were exceptional athletes.

Since *Ayden, the Sports Town* is a book about athletes, the word opportunity and lack thereof kept surfacing in my mind as Becton described his classmates. There was no track team, no baseball team, no tennis team, no golf team, no swimming team, and, until 1965, no football team. Becton put it succinctly in a brief note he wrote on my questionnaire. There are "four things I remember often: caring teachers, great scholars, super athletes, few options." The first three he remembers fondly, and the last one, few options, Becton specified as having only one sport and few educational opportunities. I asked Huey Lawrence about the class of 1962; the social studies teacher, band leader, and assistant football coach remembered the 1962 class as one of the most talented in his 20+ year career at South Ayden School. Then, Huey told me just how much Charles Becton was respected and looked up to by his classmates.

Football arrived on campus late in the history of South Ayden School. The Eagles fielded a team for 5 years – from the school year of

1965-1966 through 1969-1970. The sport was discontinued one year prior to consolidation in 1970-71.

With Becton and his friends' assistance, the inaugural season was kicked off in the fall of 1965. During the summer, Becton and four other alumni returned from college to assist the first-year players in the fundamentals of the game. Gathering the students together to practice meant driving through the country to pick up players. Becton arrived to talk to someone who he described as big and strong. On that day, the potential player was in a "discussion" in the tobacco field. The mule wanted to go one way and Charlie Williams forced him to go another. "Man ... you're gonna play football." Becton and his buddies had located the Eagles' fullback. The novice players had a tough time blocking; nevertheless, giving the ball to the fullback often meant at least a three yard gain – sometimes after being hit multiple times in the backfield. The rookie fullback also played in the line on defense. "Nobody could move him," Becton remembered.

The Eagles played their first game on Saturday, September 7, 1965 against Queen Street High School in Beaufort, an experienced football program. Queen Street kicked off first, and the Eagles' player caught the ball on the fly at about the 20-yard line and started up the field. Suddenly at the 40-yard line, he saw all the Queen Street players bearing down on him. The kick returner reversed his field in an attempt to "run around" the hoard of humanity rushing at him. He was soon tackled on his 20-yard line – the very place from whence he started.

Bernard Haselrig was interviewed by the Sports Editor of *The Daily Reflector* as part of Woody Peele's beginning-of-the-year series with area head coaches. The coach was realistic about the Eagles' first season on the gridiron. He talked about the newness of his team to the game of football and the difficulty in getting all of the 28 players together for practice. Coach Haselrig listed his starters. On the offensive line, the expected starters were Robert Williams and Donald Gaskins at ends, Willie Holloway and probably Arthur King at tackles, Curtis Joyner and Willie Suggs at guard, and Herbert Suggs at center. The backfield makeup would be either Henry Clay Davis or James "Butch" Lowry at quarterback, John Hooks and Donald Anderson at halfback, and Charlie Williams at fullback. The defensive starters were going to be Robert

Williams and Linwood Best at end, Willie Holloway and Willie Suggs at tackle, Herbert Suggs at middle guard, Charlie Williams and Henry Clay Davis at linebacker, Donald Anderson and Eddie Smith at cornerback, and Junior Ormond and Willie Garris at safety.

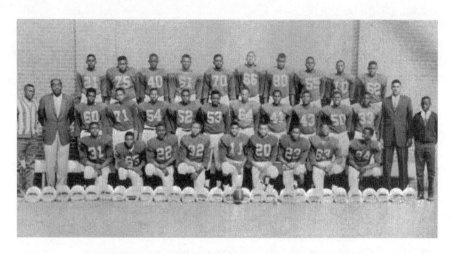

**1965-66 South Ayden High School First Football Team**
Members of the team (in no particular order) include: 1st Trainer Samuel Holloway, Asst. Coach H. L. Lawrence, Kenneth Jones, David Gilbert, George Carr, Donald Anderson, James Lowry, John Ormond, Willie Garris, William Harp, Eddie Smith, Head Coach B.R. Haselrig; Asst. Trainer Robert Jones, Curtis Joyner, Manuel Elmore, Bobby Gilbert, Gleen Whitehurst, Henry Davis, Melvin Williams, Donald Gaskins, John Hooks, Arthur King, Willie Holloway, Robert Garrett, Hubert Suggs, Curtis Williams, Louis T. Williams, Jasper Woods, Linwood Best, Robert Wiliams, Charlie Williams, Jimmy Whitehurst, and Willie Suggs. *(The Eagle)*

Queen Street went into the dressing room at halftime with a 26-0 lead and eventually won the game, 48-0. The winners rushed for 261 yards and held South Ayden to 50 yards on the ground.

Next up was the Adkin High School Pirates of Kinston, another experienced football program that played its home games at Grainger Stadium. Four hundred fans braved a soaking rain to watch the game: Adkin High 48, South Ayden 0. All of the Pirates scores came on the ground with the exception of one. The outmanned Eagles never threatened.

For the following two weeks, South Ayden met the same opponent: Georgetown High School of Jacksonville. SAH won the school's first victory in football by the score of 18-0. The following Saturday's game was closer; on the first play of the game after the kickoff, South Ayden's fullback, Henry Davis, galloped off-tackle for 40 yards and the game's only score. The extra point failed, but the 6-0 lead held up. The Eagles were now 2-2.

South Ayden would be unable to schedule another football game with Georgetown High School. In the wee hours of the morning a few months later, the Jacksonville high school was burned to the ground. A car carrying "four or five white men" was seen leaving the scene of the huge fire. Stuart Albright, the major editor of *Ayden, the Sports Town*, chronicled the details of this story in his 2009 publication, *Sidelines: A North Carolina Story of Community, Race, and High School Football*. Over the next few years as the state's public schools were integrated, more incidents would occur. The major thrust of Stuart's book paints a more positive picture; it is filled with great tales of legendary coaches and their high school football programs in North Carolina.

Hoping to make it three in a row, South Ayden High hosted South Greene High School of Snow Hill. The visiting Tigers left happy: South Greene 34, South Ayden 8. The Eagles crossed the goal line in the 2$^{nd}$ quarter and must have provided the young players with some optimism. That TD closed the gap to 12-8. Just before the half, however, Alex Dixon scampered 70 yards with his team's 3$^{rd}$ touchdown. The Tigers were ahead 18-8 at half and won going away.

The 2-3 Eagles played Farmville's Sugg High School Lions in Ayden. SAH managed only 36 yards of total offense. The big story of the night belonged to William Barnes, the Lions senior halfback who had accepted an offer to play for North Carolina College (currently North Carolina Central University) in Durham. The Lions' co-captain rushed for 149 yards on 11 carries and caught four passes for 96 yards. Barnes also intercepted a pass and returned it 94 yards for a touchdown. In the 44-0 loss, Coach Haselrig lauded the play of Charlie Williams, a star for the night on both sides of the ball.

Against the Eppes High School Bulldogs of Greenville, there was reason for optimism when South Ayden scored first to take a 6-0 lead. In the second period, Elmer Floyd of Eppes returned an intercepted pass 75 yards to make it 6-6 at halftime. It was all Bulldogs in the second half; the final score, Eppes 46, South Ayden 6. South Ayden's only score occurred when halfback Curtis Lowry went over from one yard out. The Eagles had an open date the following week.

After losing to W.A. Patillo High School of Tarboro 44-0, South Ayden played the J.T. Barber High School Warriors in New Bern. Like in several of the first-year team's previous games, the Eagles' opponent roared to what must have seemed an insurmountable lead at half, 24-0. But South Ayden didn't give up. In the 3$^{rd}$ period, Charlie Williams, SAH's junior fullback, hit pay dirt and ran over for the two-point conversation. Donald Anderson's rushing touchdown and subsequent two-pointer made the score 24-16. The home standing Warriors then put the game away in the 4$^{th}$ quarter; final score: 32-16. The South Ayden Eagles finished their first year of football with a record of 2-7.

South Ayden's first game of year number two was against Carver High School of Mt. Olive, a team that had been playing football for three years. The reporter gave the edge to the more experienced football program. Coach Haselrig's players must not have read the paper on the morning of the game. Carver failed to pick up even one first down and lost 7 fumbles on their way to recording 92 yards of total offense. SAH never punted while generating nearly 300 yards of offense. Henry Davis scored four touchdowns as the Eagles romped over Carver, 58-0.

The following week at Sampson High School in Clinton, South Ayden was defeated in a low scoring contest, 6-0. All zeroes dotted the scoreboard until the final quarter. Sampson High's Arthur Mathis intercepted a James Lowry pass and returned it 25 yards for the only score of the game. I'm sure Coach Haselrig was proud of the Eagles' defense. On the other hand, it was a frustrating night on offense. SAH managed to drive inside of Carver's 20 yard line on three occasions in the 4$^{th}$ quarter but couldn't push the ball into the end zone.

For the third game, South Ayden traveled to Farmville to play H.B. Sugg High School, the Eagles' arch rival on the basketball court. The Eagles had a game that the players probably wanted to forget; 10 turnovers led to a 20-6 victory for the home team. The only SAH highlight for the evening occurred when David Gilbert intercepted a pass and returned it 70 yards for his team's only score.

One week after the Sugg's game, the Eagles lost to Patillo of Tarboro 12-6. Once again, David Gilbert scored the only touchdown. This made it three losses in a row. The next Friday Harnett High School of Dunn came to town. The first touchdown of the game belonged to the visitors. In the initial quarter, Dunn's punt receiver hauled in a South Ayden punt on his own 40-yard line and ran it back all-the-way. Leading 6-0, Harnett High called a pass play on the Eagles' one yard line. Bad idea. SAH's linebacker, Eddie Smith, intercepted the pass. South Ayden then marched 99 yards and tied the game when junior fullback Melvin Williams scored from one yard out. David Gilbert did it again. From his safety position, he picked off a pass and returned it 50 yards for the decisive touchdown: South Ayden 14, Dunn 6.

After the game against Harnett, David Gilbert repeated his feat of scoring the Eagles only touchdown – this time on a pass from James Lowry. It was the only TD to celebrate in a 48-6 drubbing by Eppes High. The Eagles' fullback, Melvin Williams, and end, Donald Gaskins, received accolades for the contest.

South Ayden High School journeyed to Rose Hill to play the Charity High School Yellow Jackets and returned home with a 3-4 record. However, the Eagles almost didn't make the game because of trouble with the bus. Since they arrived late, the game was shortened to eight minute quarters. South Ayden's initial score occurred in the 1st period when William Harp ran 20 yards to complete a 60-yard drive. David Gilbert and Melvin Williams scored the second and third touchdowns respectively and South Ayden won, 24-0. The Eagles' defense played one of its best games of the season – allowing only one first down in the first half. The following defensive players were singled out for their play: Curtis Joyner, Willis Suggs, and Glenn Whitehurst.

The defense also came to play in the next game; South Ayden defeated R.B. Harrison High School of Selma, 14-0. Curtis Williams intercepted a pass and Willie Suggs recovered a fumble. Other standouts on defense were Curtis Joyner, George Preyer, and Robert Williams. Offensively, South Ayden made 10 first downs, rushed for 186 yards, and James Lowry hit 4 of 5 passes for 20 yards.

South Ayden High's last two games were away. In Trenton, the undefeated Jones High School Blue Devils walloped their visitors, 42-0.

The Eagles managed less than 115 yards of total offense while Jones High rolled to 388 yards on the ground and 65 yards through the air.

In the last game of the season, South Ayden High bested Dubois High School of Wake Forest, 8-6. For the year, no one was selected from the Eagles for All-Conference honors. SAH's record of 5-5 in its second season would turn out to be its best.

Bernard Haselrig was again interviewed by Woody Peele of *The Daily Reflector* at the beginning of the '67 season. He emphasized that he was counting on speed to offset his light line. Haselrig also echoed a familiar concern voiced by coaches in tobacco country: "We haven't been getting boys out for practice and that could kill us. It's hard to do anything until school starts since so many boys are working." As the Pitt County Board grappled with plans for the new Ayden-Grifton High School, South Ayden High launched its third season on the gridiron.

The archives were not good to me for year three; for some reason, the results of only five games appeared in print. In what was most likely the first game of the season, South Ayden defeated the P.S. Jones Yellow Jackets in every category but where it counted; the scoreboard read 7-6 when time ran out. The Eagles scored first via a seven yard run by John Parker to make it 6-0. In the 3$^{rd}$ quarter, South Ayden's punter backed up near his goal line. The ball was snapped over his head and into the end zone. The Yellow Jackets recovered the ball for a touchdown. The extra point was good and the 7-6 score stood up.

South Ayden put no points on the board in three games: Clinton Sampson 25, South Ayden 0; Sugg 20, South Ayden 0; and Eppes 25, South Ayden 0.

In the game against Sugg High School in Ayden, the Eagles were able to muster only 98 yards of total offense – 38 rushing and 60 passing. The Lions lost three fumbles and were penalized 115 yards, but the visitors' defense played an outstanding game. Two blocked punts for touchdowns were followed by a 60-yard drive for the final tally.

The Eppes High School Bulldogs held South Ayden to 107 yards of total offense in gaining their first victory of the year, 25-0. All of the scoring came through the air: 218 yards on 8-17 passing without an interception.

South Ayden played powerhouse Jones High School next. After receiving the opening kickoff, the Eagles' touchdown drive covered 80 yards, and they led 7-0 at the end of the 1st quarter. Then the Blue Devils' Carlton Ward went to work. He duplicated his 4-touchdown night the game before and helped carry his team to a 34-7 victory. He was helped along by Franklin Brown's 99-yard TD with the kickoff to open the 2nd half. SAH could not match Jones High's 21 first downs and 300 yards rushing.

It would be easy to place the responsibility for such meager coverage on the backs of the local newspaper staffs. In fact, the shoe may be on the other foot. I'm sure there were not enough reporters for "live" coverage of every football game in the area. The print media must have relied on a school-based reporter to call in the results of each game. No call-in meant no article in tomorrow's newspaper. Having a good team would increase the probability of their games appearing as write-ups in a forthcoming edition. Throughout the book, this may explain why teams suddenly disappeared from the radar. Under these circumstances if I were a betting man, I'd put my cash on the following supposition: an unreported game = a loss. Without some proof, however, it would be unfair to translate my thesis into actual numbers. The reported games gave South Ayden High an 0-5 record and indicate problems in the scoring department. It is safe to assume that the 1967 football team completed its season with a less than .500 record.

In the opening game of the 1968-1969 school year for both teams, The South Ayden Eagles played the H.B. Sugg Lions of Farmville. Sugg blocked a punt that turned into a safety; the 2-0 lead held up until the 3rd quarter when SAH went ahead. Leon Mayo passed 10 yards to David Gilbert to give the Eagles a 6-2 lead. The two teams had trouble generating offense: South Ayden's total yardage was 78 and Sugg's final total was 119. The Lions put things together in the closing minutes of the game to win 9-6.

The next game of the young season was against W.A. Patillo High School of Tarboro. As Yogi would say, it was "deja vu all over again." SAH had trouble sustaining offensive drives and lost 5 fumbles en route to 161 total yards. The final score was Patillo 32, South Ayden 0.

The following week, the Eagles got their first win: South Ayden 19, Mt. Olive Carver 16. The contest turned into an aerial rodeo; both teams had more yards passing than rushing. Leon Mayo passed for all 3 touchdowns. SAH went ahead in the 3$^{rd}$ quarter on a 51-yard pass play from Mayo to Charlie Grimes. Except for a safety on a blocked punt, South Ayden held Carver scoreless for the rest of the game.

Against Sampson High in Clinton, South Ayden generated 243 yards on the ground but could not muster any points. The Eagles' passing attack couldn't match its running game: 2-17 for 34 yards. The visitors' first drive of the game died on Clinton's one foot line. Two bad snaps led to two of Sampson High's TDs. South Ayden's ground game was paced by David Gilbert and Glenn Williams. Curtis Joyner led the Eagles on defense. Final Score: Sampson High 25, South Ayden 0.

Yogi's quote would again be appropriate for game number five: Eppes of Greenville 25, South Ayden 0. The Eagles lost 5 fumbles and could manage only 63 total yards. For the winners, the game could have been called "the Johnny Smith Show." In the 1$^{st}$ quarter, Smith ran 22 yards for his first TD. Next quarter, he intercepted a pass and took it in from 15 yards out. In the 4$^{th}$ quarter, Smith found yet another way to cross the goal line; he scored on a 65 yard pass play.

South Ayden pitched a 12-0 shutout against Snow Hill. Both touchdowns were through the air. The 1$^{st}$ quarter was scoreless. In the 2$^{nd}$ stanza, Leon Mayo hit Jesse Woods with a 7-yard TD pass. In the 3$^{rd}$ quarter, it was Mayo to Charlie Grimes on a 25 yard pass play. Mayo completed 8 of 15 passes for 101 yards. The South Ayden coaches lauded their outstanding defensive stars: Buck Cox, John Prayer, and Hub Wilson. The Eagles were 2-4 on the season.

Up next was a trip to Wake Forest to play unbeaten Dubois High School. South Ayden tallied first on a 30-yard pass from Leon Mayo to halfback David Gilbert. That was all of the scoring the Eagles offense could muster. The final score was 25-6. Mistakes were the difference in the game; three of the visitors' touchdowns came after high hikes on punts gave Dubois good field position. Coach Haselrig had special praise for two of his defenders: end Manual Elmore and middle linebacker Glenn Williams.

Rose Hill's Friday night visit to Ayden was a big disappointment: South Ayden 42, Rose Hill 0. This game against Charity High School was the Eagles most complete game of the '68 campaign. SAH came out of the gate in full force in the 1st quarter; Leon Mayo passed to Jesse Woods for the first TD, and David Gilbert ran 23 yards for the second score. The winners added two more touchdowns in the 2nd quarter and two more in the 3rd frame. The defense played another stellar game, holding Rose Hill to three first downs and -18 yards rushing. South Ayden was 3-5 after their win.

South Ayden's woes on offense came back to haunt them against Johnson Central High School in a game played in Smithfield. Johnson Central gave the visitors a solid thumping by the score of 38-7. The winners put 25 points on the scoreboard in the first half. SAH's passing attack was stymied by the defenders. Mayo was 4-10 for a total of 73 yards. He threw one interception and the Eagles lost two fumbles. The record: 3-6.

In the final game of the season, South Ayden traveled to Farmville to meet Sugg for the second time. Neither team had had a winning season, but I'll bet that didn't matter to the two old rivals. Sugg scored in the 1st quarter on a 15-yard pass to take a 6-0 lead. South Ayden came back in the next stanza when Leon Mayo completed a 62-yard pass to one of his favorite targets, Charlie Grimes. Glenn Williams ran for the extra point and SAH was ahead 7-6. In the same quarter, the Eagles' Leon Mayo connected with Alonza Cox on a 19-yard scoring strike to make the score 13-6 at the half. With less than a minute to play and Sugg on their opponent's side of the field, it looked as if South Ayden was going to win its fourth game. The Lions weren't through, however. Sugg's quarterback dropped back and hit William Jones on a 66-yard bomb with only 40 seconds left. Jones also ran for the extra point to tie the game at 13. South Ayden season's record: 3-6-1.

A coaching change highlighted the early part of the 1969-1970 season, the final year of football for the South Ayden Eagles. Johnny Davis took over for Coach Bernard Haselrig when the four-year head gridiron coach took a position as assistant principal at Bethel Union High School. By this time the transition to a fully integrated and consolidated

Ayden-Grifton High School was well under way. As I have heard it explained, the multitude of changes is like trying to unravel the lights from a Christmas tree – knotty but not impossible. I'm not going to untangle all of the lights, but I'll identify the ones which relate to our story.

Coach Davis had been hired the year before ('68-'69) as a teacher at SAH, as head basketball coach, and as Coach Haselrig's assistant in football. When Mitchell and I met the retired teacher and coach for lunch, Johnny described himself as a "green" football coach. He had lots of help from his two assistants: Huey Lawrence mentored the linemen on offense and defense and James "Shorty" Wilkes directed the offense. Shorty's "day job" was 6th grade teacher at South Ayden. He'd been a running back at Eppes High School in Greenville, one of his employer's rivals in football and basketball. Wilkes was a graduate of Elizabeth City State University where he'd also played in the backfield. Huey Lawrence had distinguished himself as a B-1 bandsman in World War II, had played fullback at North Carolina A&T State College in Greensboro and, most importantly for the new coach, introduced him to his future wife.

The Eagles opened in New Bern against J.T. Barber High School. Barber struck first to take an 8-0 lead, the score at halftime. Leon Mayo got on track in the 3rd period, hitting Charlie Grimes on a 40-yard pass and then again on a 9 yarder to take the lead at 12-8. The celebration was short-lived. On the kickoff after the Eagles' score, Carl Smith of Carver ran 65 yards to pay dirt. Time expired with South Ayden on Barber's 3-yard line. An upset had been narrowly averted by the 4-A school; final score: Barber 14, South Ayden 12. The Eagles' fullback, Glenn Williams, rushed for 81 yards on 18 carries, and Charlie Grimes caught 6 passes for 77 yards. On defense for SAH, honors went to tackles, Walter Gardner and Alton Wilson, and to end, Lee Ruth. South Ayden was scheduled to play its home opener against Morrison Training School on the following Friday.

**The 1969-70 Final South Ayden High School Football Team**
Members of the team include: First row (l-r): Leon Mayo, Nathan Cannon, Glen Williams, Ned Garris, Ricky Allen and Carlton McCarter. Second row: Jessie Moore, H.L. Lawrence, Line Coach; Jesse Guion, Ivory Phillips, Donald Smith, Lester Darden, Mark Smith, Alton Wilson, and Johnny Davis, Head Coach. Third row: Charlie Grimes, Issac Prayer, Lee Thomas Ruth, Kelvin King, Walter Gardner, Derander Holton, Terry Carmon, Alton Ellis and Jerry Bizzell. *(The Eagle)*

Leon Mayo again brought his "A" passing game to his home field against Morrison. He hit on 9 of 18 attempts for 157 yards and a 24-0 victory. The Eagles also ground out 96 yards rushing to make them 1-1 for the year.

Next, South Ayden High traveled to Tarboro to play W.A. Patillo High School. Patillo displayed a potent ground attack – grinding out 254 yards. To complement their rushing game, the Tarboro club hit on 5 of 8 passing for 142 yards. They never punted and experienced no turnovers. The home team won handily, 32-6. The only score that SAH was able to marshal occurred in the 2nd quarter – a Mayo to Grimes pass for 16 yards.

After starting 1-2 for the season, Coach Johnny Davis was interviewed by Woody Peele, *The Daily Reflector's* sports editor. Coach Davis began the interview by emphasizing how close his team was to being 2-1. He remembered being on the 3-yard line when the game ended in New Bern. Out of a roster of 33 players, Davis stated that about 15 would play regularly. "If we can stay well, we'll give anybody we play a good game." The veteran team returned 11 starters from last year's 3-6-1 team.

On offense, the coach singled out Glenn Williams' rushing prowess – almost 200 yards so far in the season. Coach Davis also complemented Leon Mayo for his passing ability in the three games: 28 out of 53 attempts for 241 yards and 5 touchdowns. He'd been intercepted only once. Charlie Grimes was the #1 receiver with 15 catches for 3 TDs.

From last year's team the following four starters were lost: David Gilbert, halfback; Curtis Joyner, guard; Troy Mabery, tackle; and Manuel Elmore, tackle. The returning starters were Jesse Moore, guard; Jesse Woods, end; Alvin Wilson, center; Walter Gardner, tackle; Lee Ruth, end; Charlie Grimes, end; Leon Mayo, quarterback; Glenn Williams, fullback; Alonza Cox, halfback, Eddie Brown, halfback; and Kelvin King, end.

Coach Davis told the reporter that the Eagles ran from a Wing T, pro-set and from two defensive alignments: a 6-3-2 and a 5-4-2. The conference was the North Carolina High School Athletic Conference.

The following Friday's game did not take place because of problems with the lights on Brawley High School's field in Scotland Neck. The next night the South Ayden Eagles gained their third win by the score of 20-0. After a scoreless first quarter, Brawley punted to the visitors. Quarterback Leon Mayo guided his team to their first score on a 50-yard drive. A pass from Mayo to his halfback, Kelvin King, covered the final five yards. South Ayden's second score of the 2$^{nd}$ quarter came after Walter Gardner recovered a Brawley fumble on the opponent's 35-yard line. Fullback Glenn Williams took it in from 10 yards out to make the score 14-0 at the half. In the 4$^{th}$ period, Jesse Woods intercepted a pass and returned it 15 yards to make it 20-0, the final score.

The next game was against Carver High School in Mt. Olive. South Ayden jumped out to a 14-0 lead before Carver scored in the 2$^{nd}$ quarter to make it 14-6. Glenn Williams rambled in from the 4-yard line for the first TD and Mayo connected with Charlie Grimes for the second. In the 3$^{rd}$ period, Carver intercepted a Mayo pass and returned it 16 yards for the home team's second touchdown. The two-point conversion made it 14-14. In the final stanza, South Ayden reached Carver's 20 yard line when the drive was stymied by penalties. The game ended in a tie.

Against Sugg High School of Farmville, Glenn Williams had one of his best games; the workhorse rushed for 134 yards on 15 carries. Sugg hit paydirt first on a 64-yard run in the 2$^{nd}$ quarter. Then, Williams made the score 6-6 on a 6-yard TD run. Williams did it again in the 3$^{rd}$ period scoring on runs of 15 and 40 yards. Leon Mayo passed to Kelvin King for 40 yards and a touchdown for SAH's final score to make it 24-6. Sugg stormed back in the final stanza with 14 points but it wasn't enough. South Ayden won 24-20.

The seventh game of the season required the South Ayden Eagles to travel 20 miles to Grainger Stadium in Kinston. The Adkin High School Pirates won their fifth game, 47-6. Fullback Melvin Fields ran 70 yards on the Pirates' first play from scrimmage. He and his teammates rushed for 436 yards and passed for 105 yards in accumulating 20 first downs.

The season's second meeting between South Ayden and the Sugg Lions ended in a 14-14 deadlock. The Eagles scored first to take an 8-0 lead. Leon Mayo passed to Charlie Grimes for 17 yards and the score. Glenn Williams rushed for over 100 yards again: 101 yards on 16 carries. Mayo was tackled in his own end zone for a safety, making the score 8-2 at the end of the 1$^{st}$ quarter. Sugg then crossed the goal line twice in the 2$^{nd}$ stanza to go into the dressing room with a 14-8 lead. In the final period, Williams scored on an 8-yard run to tie the game at 14.

In a game that turned out to be the South Ayden Eagles' last on the gridiron, Jordan-Sellars High School of Burlington routed the fifth-year team 84-12. Quarterback Leon Mayo passed for South Ayden's two scores. In the 2$^{nd}$ quarter, he hit Charlie Grimes on an 81-yarder for the Eagles' first touchdown. And, in the 4$^{th}$ period, Mayo threw 12 yards to Eddie Brown for his team's final tally. Interviewed after the game, Coach Davis was gracious in defeat: "They were unbelievable. They were a real solid team and very strong. They were 8-1-1 and had tied Patillo and beat Wilson Darden." The coach went on to say, "they blocked our first two punts for two quick scores. They were so big we couldn't move against them." South Ayden's final season ended with a record of 3-4-2.

The following year in 1970-1971, Coach Johnny Davis moved to Ayden High School as teacher and assistant football coach. The players who donned the maroon and gray for SAH had the option of playing for the maroon and white Tornadoes while continuing their classes at South

Ayden High. In the late 60s, the 8th graders at South Ayden School were integrated with that same class at Ayden High School. In the near future, that meant that some African American students played for the Tornadoes while some of their older classmates played for the Eagles. In another interesting set of circumstances, the year that Johnny Davis was a teacher and an assistant football coach at Ayden High, he was head basketball coach at South Ayden High.

## Chapter 14
South Ayden Eagle Basketball

Becton's made-up wish to play basketball came true in a big way at South Ayden School and at Howard University, where he played for four years. The 1961-1962 Eagle basketballers, during Becton's senior year, had one of their best teams ever. They were undefeated during conference play with a record of 8-0.

**1961-1962: South Ayden Final Regular Season Basketball Standings (8-0)**

**Boys***

| | |
|---|---|
| South Ayden | 8-0 |
| H.B. Sugg | 5-2 |
| Pitt Co. Training School (Grimesland) | 3-4 |
| Bethel Union | 2-4 |

**Girls**

| | |
|---|---|
| Robinson Union | 7-1 |
| H.B. Sugg | 6-1 |
| Pitt Co. Training School (Grimesland) | 3-4 |
| South Ayden | 3-5 |
| Bethel Union | 0-6 |

*The Robinson Union boys were inadvertently left out of the standings.

SAH's number one finish did not come easily. With one victory over its arch rival, South Ayden traveled to H.B. Sugg for their final regular season meeting. The Eagles pulled it out by the score of 57-52. Jimmie Brown bucketed 27 points. The final conference game of the season was against Pitt County Training School of Grimesland; South Ayden won 61-48. Three SAH players scored in double figures: Jimmie Brown, 29 points, Wilbert Kilpatrick, 16, and Charles Becton, 10.

Up next was the Pitt County Interscholastic Athletic Association tournament. In addition to the conference record of 8-0, the Eagles' overall record was 13-4. In their first game, South Ayden was matched up against Robinson Union of Winterville. The Eagles led by 17 points at the end of the 1$^{st}$ period. The regular season winner continued its torrid pace and won by the score of 79-33. Jimmie Brown led the scoring with 39 points and Charles Becton scored 21.

For the third time, South Ayden played H.B. Sugg; this time for the tourney championship. Like the game against Robinson, the Eagles moved ahead quickly with a 29-21 lead at the end of the 1$^{st}$ quarter. The lead was increased in the 2$^{nd}$ half and SAH won 54-43. South Ayden's coach, Bernard Haselrig was named Coach of the Year.

The South Ayden girls' team also won the PCIAA title by defeating Robinson 25-14. During the regular season, the girls' team had won only three of its eight conference games while Robinson had finished on top with a 7-1 mark.

During the presentation of the tournament trophies, the All-County teams were announced. The two South Ayden winners were Jimmie Brown and Faye Woods.

The district tournament was held in La Grange. The first and second place finishers from the PCIAA were included. In the opener for the fourth time, it was South Ayden versus H.B. Sugg. I don't know which to credit – great defense or a night when a lid covered the basket – SAH could not make it four straight over their rivals. Sugg won 44-33. The usual high scorers could not get into double figures. South Ayden's Eddie McCarter was high scorer with 11 points.

Simple math gives the South Ayden Eagles a 15-5 record. However, over two weeks elapsed between the final game of the conference tournament and the first game of the district playoffs, so it is possible that additional games were played.

South Ayden lost to Frink High School of La Grange twice during the regular season in 1962. The Frink Wildcats defeated the Eagles 69-57 in November 1961 after Frink had its 22 game winning streak snapped the game before. Charles Becton and Jimmie Brown tied for the losers' top scoring honors with 17 points apiece. In the second meeting, Frink again bested South Ayden 72-55. For the Wildcats and for the game, Ellsworth Joyner was high scorer with 28 points. Two of Joyner's teammates picked up double-doubles: Murthis Wooten got 13 points to go along with his 19 rebounds, and Jimmy Williams scored 12 points and pulled down 10 rebounds. South Ayden's Wilbert Kilpatrick netted 22 points and Charles Becton scored 20. Becton bemoaned the fact that he and his teammates could not stop Ellsworth Joyner; the Frink High player matriculated at Shaw University in Raleigh and set the school's scoring record that lasted for two decades.

During this same school year, the Ayden High School Tornadoes had one of their best records in school history – losing only one regular season game in basketball. Becton remembers his coach, Bernard Haselrig, commenting on the possibility of playing AHS in basketball. It isn't known if Coach Haselrig attempted to arrange a game. If played, the contest would have been analogous to a game played under the cover of darkness between Duke University and North Carolina Central University (named North Carolina College at the time) in Durham in 1944. Like the DU-NCC game, an AHS-SAH game would have had to be played secretly on the African American campus – in the gym at South Ayden High School. The historic game didn't take place – then. In December 1970, Coach Haselrig's wish came true; the year before consolidation marked the first meeting between the two schools on Lee Street.

Attempting to put together the various South Ayden School basketball seasons is similar to the struggles I've faced in doing the same for baseball and girls' basketball at Ayden High School prior to World War II. During the almost 20 years of *The Ayden Dispatch* that I researched, the black community received virtually no coverage. It was as if the

African American community was invisible. In the 1937 special historical edition of the Ayden newspaper, there was one article authored by J.W. Ormond, Principal of South Ayden School. The short piece entitled "Ayden Colored High School" had the following to say about basketball: "In the field of athletics, our high school is most outstanding in basketball. The teams have played eleven games, nine of which were Conference games. Out of the nine Conference games they have lost one. Out of all games played they have lost only two." It's instructive that Mr. Ormond used the plural "teams" and the word "they" to describe basketball. He may have been describing the boys' and girls' teams simultaneously.

For his book, Becton interviewed Ms. Carrie Belle Payton Nino, a 1940 graduate of South Ayden High School. After describing "how students were warmed by the potbellied stoves that were in each classroom," she talked to him about having "to go uphill to one basket and downhill to the other basket." Ms. Nino remembered that "Coach Annie Wilson put her in only one game in four years, and then only when the team was up by about 50 points." She went on to say that "many parents did not want their daughters to play basketball and that, therefore, two boys from the elementary school played on the girls' team for the first two years she was on the team." Girls' basketball started in the 1930s and was discontinued around 1965. In the archives available to me, I was unable to put together even one season. The closest I came was the aforementioned 1962 season.

Information related to South Ayden School sports was gleaned from the following: *The Daily Reflector* (Greenville), *The Kinston Daily Free Press*, *South Ayden School: History and Memories* by Charles Becton, and interviews. (For a more detailed description of these sources, please see Appendix 4: Notes on the Writing of *Ayden, the Sports Town.*)

From basketball in '61-'62, we're gonna accelerate to '65-'66. Terms with unfamiliar meanings have been gradually added to everyday speech; segregation, de-segregation, integration, reassignment, and freedom of choice were but a few of the words that were not fast enough for some and too fast for others.

After a down year in 1964-1965, the South Ayden Eagles finished the 1965-1966 season around .500. One of the high marks of the latter season had to wait until the conference tournament. After losing to W.H. Robinson by wide margins in their home and home series, SAH defeated their rival, 99-96 in two overtimes, in the semifinals of the Pitt County Interscholastic Athletic Association tournament. SAH's James Vines was high scorer with 39 points; Donald Gaskins scored 16 and Linwood Best got 15. Playing on their home floor, Bethel Union High School won the tournament trophy over South Ayden by the score of 68-53. In what was a sign of the future, the South Ayden JVs took the tourney crown over Bethel Union, 36-32.

**1965-66 South Ayden Eagles Varsity Basketball Team**
Members of the team include: First row (l-r): Melvin Pollard, Jimmy Whitehurst, Donald Gaskins, Wilbur "Nunney" Garris, Lindwood Best, and Steven Little. Second row: Head Coach B.R. Haselrig, Charlie Ruth, Charlie Williams, Robert Williams, and Ruby Walston. Third row: Robert West, James Vines, Jessie Collins, Donald Anderson and Jasper Woods. *(The Eagle)*

**1965-66 South Ayden Eagles Junior Varsity Basketball Team**
Members of the team include: First row (l-r): Head Coach B.R. Haselrig, James
Lowry, Leo Cox, David Gilbert, John Roundtree, Clarence Farrell, and William Harp.
Second row: Samuel Holloway, Curtis Williams, Dennis Harp, Louis Williams, Melvin
Williams, and Carlton West. *(The Eagle)*

The 1966-1967 Eagles again completed their season with a .500
record. When time for the Pitt Interscholastic Tournament arrived, South
Ayden High did not play like a team that had won half of its games. In
the semifinals, the Eagles defeated Bethel Union, 48-41. Up next was
Robinson, the regular season conference champion. South Ayden led
throughout the first half and took a 32-26 lead into the locker room. In
the 3rd quarter, Robinson pulled to within one point and tied the score at
50 at game's end. South Ayden pulled the game out, 58-56, in overtime.
South Ayden's high scorer for the evening was James Lowry with 13
points. Jimmy Whitehurst had 12 and Clarence Farrell had 11. The All-
County team was announced after the game; James Lowry received the
honor for the Eagles. The celebration was short-lived, however. This
same Robinson team came back to defeat South Ayden 77-66 in the first
game of the District Tournament.

Five seniors were in the starting lineup for the first game of the young
1967-1968 season: Dennis Harp, William Harp, James Lowry, Curtis
Williams, and Melvin Williams. All of the starters had been members of
the '65-'66 junior varsity team that had won the jv tournament over
Bethel Union. Moreover, seven of the first eight players were seniors.

SAH was anticipating an even better team than the year before when they won the tourney championship and then lost their first game in the District Tourney. Coach Haselrig was optimistic when he was interviewed by Sonny McLawhorn ('65) for the Greenville paper. I wonder if the coach dreamed of just how good his Eagles would be.

"Everybody loves a winner," so the *recorded* game summaries were more numerous than in the past. In *The Daily Reflector*, for instance, 16 games were chronicled. At first, things didn't look as bright as anticipated when the Eagles lost one of their first games to Eppes High School of Greenville, 78-76. In a return match, South Ayden defeated their rivals, 56-54. As forecast, however, South Ayden won eight straight before losing in a close one (45-42) to Woodington High School in a mid-season game.   Getting back on the winning track didn't take long; SAH won its final five games, thus qualifying for the state playoffs. Again, these games are recorded games and do not necessarily reflect real numbers. In fact, I am quite sure that the newspaper missed some victories and some defeats along the way.

In the District AA Tournament held in Woodington, South Ayden won its first game easily over Hargrave, 61-34. Next in the semifinals, the Eagles defeated Central, 66-51. In the finals, SAH squared off against a familiar foe, the Woodington High School Longhorns. Could they avenge an earlier season loss? Things didn't look good at half for the Eagles; Woodington led 36-28. South Ayden outscored the home team by eight points in the $3^{rd}$ quarter to tie the game at 45. In the closing seconds, Melvin Williams hit a free throw to tie the game at 54. With 12 seconds left on the clock, Williams was fouled again and made a free throw to put the Eagles on top by one. Woodington would have the final shot to win the game. Then, the inbounds pass was stolen by Curtis Williams, and South Ayden managed to hold the ball until time expired. The senior-laden Eagles were headed to the eight-team state tournament. The scoring leaders for the winners were Melvin Williams with 25 points and James Lowry with 15.

South Ayden played R.B. Deans High School in the state tournament held at Darden High School of Wilson. James Lowry turned his scoring game up a notch by burning the nets for 32 points. Melvin Williams added 15. In all, nine players got into the scoring column for the Eagles as they easily defeated Deans, 80-48.

In the semifinals, South Ayden shellacked Lincolnton Newbold High School by the score of 85-61. Once again, James Lowry brought his "A" game by scoring 30 points. Melvin Williams got 19 and John Roundtree added 15.

The team that was called the Cinderella team of the tournament had won the right to play for the state championship, a first in school history. The Whiteville Central High School Hornets had finished undefeated and won the title the year before. On the Hornets' home floor, James Lowry had another great game with 24 points, but it wasn't nearly enough.

Whiteville won 102-62 and again completed their season 20-0. For the champs, Reggie "Tree" Royals scored 31 points and blocked 12 of the Eagles' shots. The 6-10 Royals matriculated at Florida State University and became one of their all-time best players. He led the Seminoles to the 1972 NCAA championship game while scoring over 500 points that year. In his career, Royals scored 1,402 points and pulled down over 1,000 rebounds. At the time, I'm sure that the season's record of 21-6 was little consolation; nonetheless, one of South Ayden High School's best basketball teams – maybe *the* best – had earned the bragging rights for the only Eagles squad to reach the state championship game.

Curtis Williams and Melvin Williams were named to *The Daily Reflector* All-County team.


South Ayden High School's trophy case now contained the runner-up award in the state championship. It was going to be difficult to do better in 1968-1969, Johnny Davis' first year as head basketball coach. In the first game or two, SAH defeated Eppes of Greenville 69-68 in overtime. Soon after, the Eagles got by Goldsboro, 66-63, for their third win. Another one point victory over Douglas of Warsaw and the team was 4-1. As so often happens, the games that are lost do not appear in print. This makes the loss side of the end-of-season record more suspicious than the win column. So, we don't know anything about the game that produced the one loss. After a loss to Eppes High School, the reporter announced that SAH was 4-3. At this point, two out of the three losses had not been reported.

The Pitt County Interscholastic Athletic Association conference race was close all year. Going into a late season game, South Ayden and the Bethel Union Bears were tied atop the league. On their home floor, Bethel moved ahead at the end of the 1$^{st}$ quarter, 22-16. The '68-'69 Eagles were a resilient team. They put on a rally in period two to take a 31-30 lead into the dressing room at halftime. The contest couldn't be decided in regulation. Bethel took a 68-66 lead as the clock wound down in the first overtime. Charlie Grimes made sure of a second overtime period when he made a field goal with 12 seconds left. Bethel again gained a two point lead as the clock ticked off the final few seconds of overtime number two. David Gilbert hit two free throws to knot it at 75 and send the game into a third overtime. Finally, South Ayden won 85-82 to clinch a tie for first place. Charlie Grimes topped all scorers with 29 points; Jesse Woods hit for 25, and Leon Mayo got 12.

The rematch with Bethel Union occurred during the same week; this time the game was played in Ayden. Maybe the home court gave the Eagles an edge. The contest was close, with South Ayden taking a 43-37 lead at halftime. In the 2$^{nd}$ half, the Eagles edged further ahead of the Bears and won 91-82. South Ayden scoring: Leon Mayo, 25; Charlie Grimes, 24; John Roundtree, 20; Jesse Woods, 13. High scorer for the game was Bethel Union's Richard Roberson with 29 points. This win brought the Eagles' league mark to 8-1 and awarded them the regular season championship. The conference tournament was next.

The PCIAA conference tournament was played in Winterville in mid-February. South Ayden was seeded first and Bethel Union was third. Bethel was upset in its first game. In the semifinals, the Eagles defeated G.R. Whitfield High School 84-74. Charlie Grimes had another stellar night bucketing 33 points on 11 field goals and 11 free throws. Robinson beat Sugg 67-52. South Ayden and W.H. Robinson High School of Winterville played for the tourney championship.

South Ayden High brought its scoring shoes to the finals. The 1$^{st}$ quarter was close, but Robinson fell further behind as the game progressed. The final score was 98-67. Three Eagles hit in double figures: Charlie Grimes, 26; Jesse Woods, 25; and John Roundtree, 21.

The tournament trophy won the team a spot in the 3-A District Tournament in Goldsboro.

The first game pitted South Ayden against Douglass High School of Warsaw. Behind by two at the end of the 1st quarter, the Eagles had a torrid 2nd stanza and led at intermission, 38-32. In the 2nd half, SAH added to its lead and won by a score of 83-72. Out of the 10 players who saw action, seven got into the scoring column. Charlie Grimes led all scorers with 22 points.

South Ayden faced a familiar foe in the semifinals. Pamlico Central High School had won the first matchup, 85-82 and South Ayden won the second, 78-76 in overtime. Again, the contest was close; the score at half was 46-46. Pamlico surged ahead in the 3rd quarter and won in another close game, 91-86. Kenny Credle led all scorers with 33 points for the winners. Leon Mayo led South Ayden's scoring with 24 points and Charlie Grimes was second with 18. John Roundtree got 13 and Jesse Woods hit 11.

South Ayden High completed its season with a 15-4 record.

South Ayden Eagles basketball struggled to win games during the school's last two years before consolidation. The '69-'70 team completed the season with a record in the neighborhood of .500. The highpoint of the year may have been the two out of three wins over W.H. Robinson (Winterville). Early in the season, SAH won in a high scoring contest: South Ayden 114, Robinson 99. In the second meeting, Robinson won 54-46, and in the third meeting it was SAH 69, Robinson 52. For his senior year, Leon Mayo led all area basketball players with a 19.9 scoring average. Charlie Grimes and Leon Mayo were voted to the All-Conference team.

I don't believe any of my classmates, who walked down the aisle to *Pomp and Circumstance*, imagined that Ayden High School would be disappearing in 10 years. I doubt that the seniors of 1961 at South Ayden High School would have predicted the demise of their school. These two schools and Grifton High School, just three miles away, were consolidated in the fall of 1971. This meant, of course, that the 1970-

1971 school year would be the last for the athletic programs at the three respective schools.

The South Ayden High players struggled to win games in their final year as Eagles. The 17 games which made *The Daily Reflector* featured only two wins. This year was the continuation of a modified "freedom of choice" plan before full integration in the fall. The '70-'71 "transition" year led to several "firsts." In Pitt County, schools that were "down the block" or across town or possibly across the county from each other engaged in a basketball game for the first time. As a case in point, the white Ayden High School met the African American South Ayden High School on the basketball court. AHS won the first encounter 61-49 and the second, 48-32. Ten years after Coach Haselrig's idea, a game between the Eagles and the Tornadoes had come to fruition.

As the season progressed, H.B. Sugg of Farmville, a traditionally black school, became the team to beat that year. Sugg had defeated both Ayden teams and was sporting a 15-0 record when they came to town to play Ayden High in early February. After beating the Tornadoes by 21 points in Farmville, Sugg left town with its first loss, 68-67. The Eagles could only watch as their old rival and their future schoolmates battled each other in the conference tournament. H.B. Sugg and Ayden High both made it into the state playoffs.

All-Conference and All-Area teams were announced at the end of the basketball campaign. South Ayden High did not place anyone on the All-Area team, but three players were named All-Conference: Robert Gaskins, Sam Holton, and John Ormond.

I wish I could go back before the 1960s to tell the stories of the African American basketball players at South Ayden High School. I chose to start with that decade because I realized that attempting to drive my Thunderbird to those times would be virtually impossible. There would be no written documentation and my memory would be useless.

I've decided to close this section of the book with the following excerpt from my communications with Charles Becton: "I'm [Charles Becton] told that Simon Reeves, who for many years ran the only shoe repair business in Ayden, was a great basketball player in the 30s and that William Jones, Luby Gardner, and Bert Whitehurst were great basketball players in the 40s. Bert Whitehurst became a professional boxer who defeated Hurricane Jackson in 1953 and later fought Archie Moore and Sonny Liston. I know that Tedock Bell, Harold Newkirk, and Charles Cannon were great basketball players in the 50s. Tedock Bell had a tryout with the Harlem Globetrotters and is the grandfather, I believe, of Alico Dunk, former Ayden-Grifton standout."

South Ayden School, the school that had meant so much to so many, closed in 1971, and by 1981 all the buildings on campus had been torn down. All that's left is a marker next to Lee Street. The blood, sweat, and tears that had gone into putting together the community's school – book by book, building by building – vanished. Charles Becton's book celebrates the memories of all who graced its halls and cheered for the South Ayden Eagles.

**Current South Ayden High School Marker**
Willard Earl Grimsley, Patricia Ann Grimsley, Helen G. Davis and Harold Davis purchased the school property July 30, 1975 from the Pitt County Board of Education. The purchasing parties sold the 9.157-acre school site to the Town of Ayden December 22, 1980, per deeds recorded with the Pitt County Register of Deeds. The buildings on the site were demolished and replaced with public housing. *(Photo by Mitchell Oakley)*

# The Great Depression

## Chapter 15
Two of the Best Football Teams Ever
(And then, the Mystery of Mysteries)

Prior presidents had used the term "depression" to describe economic downturns. President Herbert Hoover spoke of "a great depression," but referring to the 1929 economic crisis as The Great Depression with a capital "G" and a capital "D" did not make it into the lexicon until later. Some historians have given credit to Lionel Robbins, a British economist, for actually coining the phrase we use today. His book called *The Great Depression* was published in 1934.

Governor O. Max Gardner initiated a program he called "the live-at-home campaign" in 1929. The purpose was to make North Carolina self-supporting by encouraging farmers to plant as much of their land in food crops as possible. Part of the program was an urging by state government for the people of the state to "buy local." The governor also proposed a 10% reduction in salaries for all state, county, and city employees, a much more controversial recommendation. At that time, the average urban teacher's salary was $75.00 per month and the average rural teacher's salary was $60.00 per month.

In 1931, Ellen McGlohon made the following public announcement in an attempt to increase the turnout for the upcoming Ayden-Greenville basketball game: "We realize the financial depression upon the people of Ayden; therefore we are charging only small admission fees, that everybody can afford."

In October, A.W. Sawyer, the tax collector and treasurer for the Town of Ayden, listed in *The Ayden Dispatch*, the personal and business property taxes that had to be paid by November 2, 1931. The two lists were divided according to race: "205 white properties and 106 colored properties." If not paid by that date, the properties would be sold at auction.

In November 1931, the bad luck in Ayden continued when Eureka College was destroyed by fire. The structures had not been used as a school for two years; however, the main building was being used as a church. When the firemen arrived it was obvious that nothing could be done to save the former institution.

Amid all the anguish and following Ayden's first losing campaign in football in 1930 when the team went 4-5, the Tornadoes experienced one of their most dominant seasons ever.

### 1931-1932: Ayden High School Football Season
### (10-1-1)

| Ayden | 12 | Aulander | 0 |
|-------|-----|----------------|----|
| Ayden | 0 | Elizabeth City | 32 |
| Ayden | 3 | Washington | 0 |
| Ayden | 21 | Beaufort | 0 |
| Ayden | 0 | Washington | 0 |
| Ayden | 25 | New Bern | 0 |
| Ayden | 35 | Farmville | 0 |
| Ayden | 80 | Clayton | 0 |
| Ayden | 18 | Rich Square | 0 |
| Ayden | 6 | Plymouth | 0 |
| Ayden | 73 | Roper High | 0 |
| Ayden | 31 | Smithfield | 7 |

Initially, I thought the games against Clayton and Roper High must be newspaper typos. Scoring that many points in a football game in the 1930s when there were still 0-0 and 6-0 games seemed unbelievable. Then, I did the math, matched the totals with another source, and it all added up: Ayden High School outscored its opponents 304 to 39, a per game average of 25 points to 3 for their opponents. Ten out of the twelve opponents were held scoreless. The only blemish came against Elizabeth City, 32-0.

Hal Edwards, by then an Ayden High School alumnus, played for two quarters in the first game of the season against the Aulander Blue Jackets. Ayden's first year coach, Coach McBane, was allowed to play Edwards because the Aulander eleven was made up mostly of high school graduates, the only way they could field a team.

After their 10-1-1 season, the following season in 1932 Ayden High School finished with an 8-1-1 record. Not since the first four seasons from 1926-1929 when Ayden High School won nearly 80% of its games had Tornado teams been so dominant. The combined records of 18-2-2 would turn out to be the best two-year period for some time to come. Eliminating one game when the final score was unknown, the defense shut out 17 of its 21 opponents. The only two loses were both to Elizabeth City.

Tornado football would go on to receive accolades for their accomplishments in the 50s and 60s. When sports fans think about and sometimes vote on their favorite teams and players, it is not surprising that the most recent almost always win out. I hope this book will encourage fans not to forget the great teams that took the field before many of us were born. During the late 20s and early 30s with less than 200 students in the top four grades, the Tornadoes defeated schools with larger student bodies.

In the early 1930s, what other kinds of entertainment were available during those years of economic depression? Music lovers had several choices. One could tune into a CBS network radio broadcast of Bing Crosby, advertised as an original crooner. WABC was a coast-to-coast station that aired two daily shows each evening. One's preference may have been to tune into a station with entertainment from a "little closer to home." Miss Virginia Belle Cooper and Mrs. Sam Pierce could be heard on WPTF. For those families that could afford to eat out, the Hotel Beverly served a family-style meal for Sunday dinner, a specialty of the house. The cost was 50 cents per person. Patrons were encouraged to phone for reservations no later than Saturday night.

If an Aydenite could find transportation to Kinston, the 10-county fair offered an opportunity to win a prize in the jousting contest. The rewards ranged from $25 to a $150 diamond ring. Spears had to be flung through rings that were suspended over the track. The knight's charger was not required to be of any particular bloodline; he could ride an "Arabian stallion or a North Carolina plow horse."

The Princess Theatre always attempted to keep up with the times by offering up-to-date movies: "Lon Chaney talks in *The Unholy Three*" – a Metro-Goldwyn-Mayer all talking movie. Lon Chaney had started his career during the silent film era. His son, Lon Chaney, Jr. would follow his dad into the movie business soon after the talkies debuted.

Residents made up their own entertainment. The Ladies Sunday School Class of the Christian Church created the henpecked husband contest. The final results were never published, probably because everybody knew who would win. At one point before all the ballots were cast, Mr. Mike Moye was running away with the victory: Mike Moye (425 votes), W.W. Salisbury (276 votes), and John Burgess (228 votes). I hope Mr. Moye enjoyed his prize, a cake baked by the Sunday School Class.

The most original recreational activity was indicated by the following page one headline: "A Hoover Cart Parade in Ayden Next Saturday." The definition of a Hoover Cart was "a horse or mule drawn vehicle, which is made of a set of automobile wheels to which are attached shafts and a seat of one sort of another. There are literally scores of these odd-looking vehicles in the Eastern part of the state." No two of the carts were alike. Some of the seats were made of wood, and others were removed from the cabs of cars. Since money was scarce, the owners built their carts out of old car parts. Obviously, the "motor" had to be fed, but no gasoline was necessary. No license was required. The parade started in Ayden on Saturday morning, continued through Winterville and Greenville, and returned to Ayden by late afternoon – a distance of about 20 miles.

Running a close second in originality to Hoover Carts was the "Win a Baby Contest." Directors of the Robeson County Fair "announced that a white baby, complete with adoption papers, would be given away on the final night of the fair." The largest crowd in the fair's history showed up for the drawing. The winner was presented with a squealing white pig.

**Hoover Cart, 1951** *(Photos Courtesy of ECU Joyner Library, Reflector Collection)*

The following football season in 1933, the team finished 1-6; and in 1934, 6-3-1. During the 1934 season, Ayden defeated Snow Hill, 88-0, a game in which the opponents recorded no first downs. To my knowledge this game represents the widest margin of victory and the most points scored in the football program's history.

During the 1935 season, the mystery of mysteries occurred. The season started out with a bang; the high school crafted the biggest push ever to start the football season. In a special four-page supplement published by *The Ayden Dispatch*, Coach Faust Johnson made a public plea for "all boys to be in school and come out for football." The players' heights and weights were published: the heights ranged from 5"4' to 6"0', the weights from 104 to 190 pounds. New equipment and uniforms were purchased. The home schedule was potentially the best ever with games against Tarboro, Kinston, Williamston, Windsor, Washington, Farmville, and Greenville.

After starting the season 3-1-1, the Tornadoes next game was to be an away contest. After the encouragement to attend the game at Vanceboro

– *nothing*. There are no reports of another game in the local paper. It is unlikely that all of the remaining games were lost since the team had experienced early success with victories over Mt. Olive, Tarboro, and Ahoskie. The lone loss had been in the first game against Beaufort by the score of 7 to 6. After a 0-0 tie with Morehead City, the Vanceboro game was next. We could blame the depression, but that's also doubtful. The school had purchased new equipment and uniforms, so a financial problem was probably not the culprit.

At first, I thought the seven game home schedule must have been a misprint, but the 3-1-1 record came against five opponents that were *not* listed in that newspaper account. And, Ayden had played 12-game schedules in recent years. Consequently, I tend to believe that it was accurate.

As I plowed through the old newspapers, I couldn't wait to get to the next year in hopes that I could uncover a clue to ascertain "whodunit." Or maybe, "whatdunit." Had the previous season actually been halted after five games? Why spend money on new gear and outfits and then cancel the season? What I found was more baffling.

The won-loss record for 1936 was 0-1; New Bern 19, Ayden 0. The boys going out for football were divided into four teams – two junior teams and two varsity teams. The teams scrimmaged against each other – playing essentially an intramural package. "Later in the year there will be one big team and maybe this team will play other schools."

Ayden played their only football game against New Bern in mid-November, and the basketball season started the following month in December. The next year, 1937, all sports records have been lost with the exception of a special edition of *The Ayden Dispatch* composed to celebrate the 20-year anniversary of its publisher. In that newspaper, Faust Johnson contributed an article in the school section. "In the beginning of the 1936-1937 school term we decided to change our athletic program. There are several reasons back of this change. Our biggest reason was to build up the strength of our teams for the future. Interest in the high school athletics was declining both in the older people and in the school students and where interest is lacking spirit is lacking." In another part of the article, the principal had some harsh words for Ayden's citizens: "I think that our people had forgotten our boys and girls and had all their interest directed to the college sports. Do you think it fair to allow your own boys and girls to suffer because you are taking more interest in others? I wish you could think of it in that light." Johnson continued by stating that the new effort was paying off. "If you have attended one of our basketball games you have noticed a great difference in interest and spirit."

Johnson's comments did not offer any information pertinent to the 1935-1936 season *per se* when it appeared that the season had been called off at the halfway point. I've tried just about everything except a Ouija board and a séance to ferret out the details, but without success. It is safe to say that local support – from both the citizenry and the student body – had faded to the point that school officials thought it best to de-emphasize sports. Often pointing to one reason for such a change oversimplifies the true picture. Attempting to construct the full picture would be only speculative at best.

Perhaps the de-emphasis pertained to football mostly or to football only. Some support for this conjecture would appear reasonable in view of what happened during the last two years of the 1930s. (Remember; the records for 1937 have been lost.) The 1938 Tornadoes' record was 3-3-1, followed by a 1-3 record in 1939 – a total of eleven games played in two years. Football was discontinued after the 1939 season, even more evidence to boost our supposition. Further speculation will have to wait until after World War II.

# Chapter 16
## *The Wheel*

From the time of my high school graduation, I've hauled the four annuals of my high school days around with me – from job to job, from town to town, and from marriage to marriage. Losing one would have been like leaving a friend behind. I was honored to MC my class's 50th anniversary reunion in 2011. To put myself in the proper frame of mind, I pulled out the old yearbooks, "studied" each one, and read all the autographs one by one.

**The Wheel, Ayden High School Yearbook** *(Photo by Mitchell Oakley)*

I also read a fifth annual. Since Daddy's class of '28 had produced volume one, his copy had been a part of my family forever. I've always known that I wanted to include a chapter about *The Wheel* in our book. Starting in 1928, I assumed that yearbooks had been published every year throughout AHS's history. That supposition turned out to be false.

With nicknames like Bo-Parts, Mouse-head, Big Jim, Squeeze-her, John Boy, and Cat, the first annual was published one year before the stock market crash. No yearbook was published the following year, Hal Edwards' senior year. His youngest of four sons, Tommy Edwards ('58) and William Edwards ('62), recalled no annual from their dad's class of 1929. Tommy remembered pictures from the 1928 annual. More than likely, the inability to produce volume number two was a consequence of the depression. Publication of the yearbook would have necessitated the selling of ads, support that the merchants of the community would have found difficult to muster during the economic woes of the late 20s and early 30s.

Those circumstances bring up an obvious question: when was volume two published? Before I bring out Sherlock's spyglass again, let's take a closer look at Ayden High's first annual.

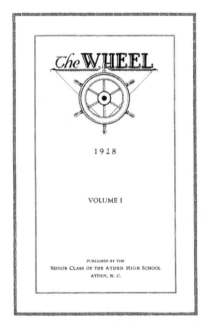

**1928 The Wheel, Vol. 1**

As compared to future versions, *The Wheel, Volume I*, had fewer pictures – all in black and white – but more narratives by the class members. Classmates took turns writing poetry and jokes as well as testimonials and tributes entitled "High School Memories," "Prophecy," "Last Will and Testament of the Class of '28," and "Who's Who." In addition, a student representing each high school class composed a poem or narrative describing the current sentiments and future desires of his/her respective classmates. Some of these compositions were serious, but most were humorous, tongue-in-cheek accounts of students' years at Ayden High School.

*Dedication*

*To our fathers and mothers, who guide and provide for us; to our faculty members, whose interest and helpfulness have been invaluable; and, to the business men of Ayden, whose financial aid has been essential – this, the first volume of THE WHEEL is lovingly and respectively dedicated.*

**1928 The Wheel Staff**

<u>Staff</u>. Hazel McKinney ('28), Editor in Chief, and her four-member staff with the support of their Faculty Adviser, Miss Daisy C. Chapman, worked to publish the first volume.

**1928 The Wheel Faculty**

Representing the seniors, Mavis Kinlaw ('28) composed an eleven-stanza poem with the final verse summing up the class's journey:

We've worked hard to gain this summit,
Sometimes in tears, then in smile
The tasks were hard, but we tackled the job
And we're here! We've won the first mile.

A chart listed the "Statistics for Class of '28." The chart included each senior's name, height, weight, shoe size, hat size, and hobby. The height/weight numbers ranged from Marie Spear at 4 feet 5 inches tall and 92 pounds to Walter Scott Buck at 5 feet 10 inches and 193 pounds. Totals were provided at the bottom of the chart: total height of the class, 128 feet and total weight, 2,738 pounds. Hobbies included hiking, chewing gum, football, baseball, breaking promises, talking, pleasant pastimes, and riding in Pontiacs.

## THE  WHEEL                                    1928

Douglass Sumrell
*Class Mascot*

WILLIAM HARRINGTON........................................*Senior Class President*
CATHERINE FLAUGHER........................................*Vice President*
DOROTHY DINKINS...........................................*Secretary*
HEBER CANNON.............................................*Treasurer*

"Conquer"
CLASS COLORS: *Green and White*
CLASS FLOWER: *White Rose*

**1928 The Wheel Class Mascot**

# 1928                              THE WHEEL

## Seniors

### WALTER SCOTT BUCK
"Scott"                       *Pest*

*"It is not birth, nor rank, nor state,*
*Tis "get-up and git" that makes men great."*

O'Henry Society, Critic '28; Debater '28; Football '28; Senior Play '28; Assistant Business Manager o WHEEL '28.

A stork on an unexpected visit to Ayden one night left little Walter Scott. This little babe has grown to be a great imitator of Patrick Henry. Not only being a second Patrick Henry, he is a second Babe Ruth.

### HEBER CANNON
"Hebe"                     *Reserve*

*Honest, hard-working, and true,*
*No better boy one ever knew.*

Athenian Society '28; Treasurer of Senior Class '28; Declamation '28.

"Hebe" is a small, clean-cut boy and has come through high school with flying colors. His chosen vocation is to be a preacher. Some think Heber to be bashful but give him a chance and he will show you that he knows his ground among the opposite sex.

### GERTRUDE COWARD
"Gert"                      *Sweet*

*Always sweet, always true,*
*Hair of gold, eyes of blue.*

O. Henry Society, Secretary '28; Glee Club '28; Associate Editor of WHEEL '28.

Everybody knows Gertie, and everybody loves her too. She has great originality in all her thoughts, but very few know of her jolly disposition. This year Gertie made the basketball team and has proven her control over the English language.

### GENEVA DAIL
"Tite"                    *Dependable*

*"Not too sober, not too gay,*
*But a true blue girl in every way."*

O. Henry Society '28; Basketball '28.

"Tite" may be the least in the room in weight but no in intellect. Temper is an immortal being that belongs to every one. Some have this being caged; Geneva has hers caged, but sometimes the door comes open and it escapes only to be recaptured in a few minutes.

### DOROTHY DINKINS
"Dot"                    *Sporty*

*"No better than you should be."*

Senior Play '28; O. Henry Society '28; Cheer Leader '28; Basketball, Captain '28; Joke Editor of WHEEL '28; Advertising Manager of WHEEL '28.

Things in life always go from bad to good and from good to bad, still Dot is always on the job. Dot is the captain of the basketball team and a great worker for the Annual this year.

# THE WHEEL                                1928

### MAVIS PARKER

*"Bo-Parts"*                                                    *Neat*

*"Some say the world is made for fun and frolic, and so do I."*

O. Henry Society '28; Senior Play '28.

Tell me, dear world, how could the class get along without Mavis and her jokes? It seems that every night "Bo-parts" must go out on a long pilgrimage to Jokeland for "era" day she has a joke for every one. But what is the use of living without a little fun?

### GRAVES MUMFORD

*"Mouse-head"*                                          *Instructor*

*"Ever-ready to do what there is to be done."*

Athenian Society '28; Basketball Team '28; Football Team '28; Senior Play '28.

In the midst of the Senior room "Mouse-head" rules over his zoo when it comes to geometry. He is able to prove any proposition Cat can mention or any other one of his domestic mates. "Mouse-head" seems always willing to help his pals when anything comes up, and due to this fact of his ability to act promptly he has been made assistant editor of the WHEEL.

### SALLIE MOORE

*"Sal"*                                                         *Lovable*

*"Not too serious, not too gay, But altogether a jolly good fellow."*

O. Henry Society, Reporter '28; Glee Club '28.

Here is a real true "Green and White" girl. Sallie is an efficient senior. To her a job is a job, to be done well, whether it be for class, society, or friend. Her personality radiates sunshine, her actions prove her unselfishness, and her thoughts express wholesomeness.

### HAZEL McKINNEY

*"Miss Boston"*                                            *Charm*

*"Much may be said on both sides."*

Editor-in-Chief of WHEEL '28; Basketball, Manager '28; Senior Play '28; Glee Club '28; Athletic Reporter '28.

Last summer Hazel spent some time in Boston when she returned it was—"Aw! Gee, kid, Bos-ton is great!" "Miss Boston" is our Editor-in-Chief this year and has the ability to fill such a responsible position. For six years she has led her grade and this year made the basketball team.

### ESTHER McLAWHORN

*"Es"*                                                            *Calm*

*"Of manners gentle, of affections mild."*

O. Henry Society '28.

Esther is not a girl to talk all of the time and on all occasions. She is so quiet that we do not know that she is with us until we see her. Esther is a girl that lets her conscience be her guide. Before her Esther has a good future.

# 1928     THE WHEEL

### BRUCE LITTLE

"*Big Jim*"     *Quick*

"*The way to have a friend is to be one.*"

Athenian Society '28; Basketball '28; Cheer Leader
'28; Glee Club '28.

Bruce is very odd, being the only member of the
Senior class of '28 with "r-e-d" hair. She lights the
pathway to all good deeds of the class. When love-
ships go wrong—Bruce patches them. Emotional in
all; she is a friend to all.

### MAVIS KINLAW

"*Mavis*"     *Cheerfulness*

"*A cheerful disposition is a fund of ready capital.*"

Athenian Society, Reporter '28; Senior Play '28;
Glee Club '28.

She loves and is loved by all! What more need we
say about Mavis? She means a great deal to all with
whom she comes in contact, and proves a friend—real,
true, and lasting.

### RAY JOHNSON

"*Silly*"     *Sheik*

"*He is a jolly good sport
With a mind of rare sort.*"

Athenian Society '28; Track '28.

Every class must have its "sheiks" and "shebas."
Ray has adopted the role of Sheik and has played it
well. To match this Sheik there is a little Sheba in the
Junior class and I think she would be foolish to turn
Ray down because he has a great future before him.

### RUTH JACKSON

"*Ruthie*"     *Right There*

"*Love conquers all.*"

Athenian Society '28.

All day long Ruth is there, but seldom does she
express her opinion. She is not bashful—but, being a
woman her opinion often changes and she hates to dispute her "own" word. Triangles in geometry and
triangles in love are different, Ruthie, but all of us wish
you luck in getting both kinds solved.

### RUBY LEE HART

"*Ole Ruby Lee*"     *Gentle*

"*Take things as they be.*"

O. Henry Society '28.

One has seen the bay at calm when the moonlight was
softly casting its shadows all about—this is the kind of
"atmosphere" that Ruby Lee seems to live in. She
is just a tiny slip of a girl but Gee! isn't she some heart
breaker.

# THE  WHEEL                          1928

### LEVI WORTHINGTON

*"Lev"*                                                     *Worthy*

*"There is no wisdom like frankness."*

O. Henry Society '28.

Levi is another quiet member of our class. He is seldom heard in the Senior class but on the playground he is as lively as can be. It seems that Levi has learned that it is best to be seen and not heard in the classroom unless he is spoken to. All through high school he has been with us and is a good sport in helping the Seniors put across their jokes.

### PATTIE MAE TURNAGE

*"Pat"*                                                     *Daring*

*"Seldom serious, often gay
But a jolly good sport in every way."*

Athenian Society '28; Glee Club '28; Senior Play '28; Basketball '28.

Dare is only a four-letter word to most people, but to Pat it means all. Pat never dares to hand in a paper without a trial, never gets a ball she doesn't dare to dribble it, and never does she take a bet without a dare — for she is unlucky when it comes to betting. In all Pat is good and is one of the few who know that the happy days of school life are at an end but still dares to finish her work.

### MARIE SPEAR

*"Charlie"*                                                 *Sincere*

*"The most precious goods oft comes wrapped in smallest packages."*

Athenian Society '28.

Those who are not so well acquainted with "Charlie" think that she is a quiet, meek, studious person. It is true that she can be all of these; but, on the other hand she's as good a "sport" as you can find anywhere. She has a wonderful habit of laughing which adds cheerfulness to all of her classmates.

### JOHN WILLIAM SAWYER

*"John Boy"*                                                *Mischievous*

*"For if he will, he will, you may depend on't;
And if he won't, he won't, so there's an end on't."*

Athenian Society '28; Assistant Business Manager of WHEEL '28; Senior Play '28.

Not only is John Boy blessed with sun-kist hair, beautiful brown eyes with china doll eyelashes but with an art of wooing. Not a girl in the class has missed his long glances, for he has paid them all his share of attention. But alas he has been captured and inspired. I wonder who?

### LOUISE PRESCOTT

*"Squeeze-her"*                                             *Never Still*

*"Talking, she knew not why, and cared not what."*

Athenian Society '28; Glee Club '28.

Always like a babbling brook Louise goes day in and day out. It is often said that great talkers say nothing and little talkers say everything. But this does not hold true with Louise for "ole Squeeze-her" often has a wise word of counsel for her friends. She is the kind of girl that we all like—sincere and faithful.

# 1928                          THE WHEEL

### WILLIAM HARRINGTON

*"Bill"*                                *Athletic Ability*

*"A calm manner is an asset."*

President of Senior Class '28; Basketball Team, Captain '28; Football Team '28; Athenian Society '28.

"Bill," president of our class, is a member we are proud to own. Bill is the kind of boy that is always happy. He has won the name of being the best athlete in the Senior class. He was one of the eleven in football and captain of the basketball team.

### HARVEY HARDEE

*"'Twas-it"*                                *Funny*

*"It isn't any trouble just to giggle-ee."*

Athenian Society '28; Senior Play '28.

Introducing Mr. Harvey Hardee, the second Will Rogers! Days may come and go still "Twas-it" never seems to take note of the passing time. Twice does he think before he speaks.

### CATHERINE FLAUGHER

*"Cat"*                                *Cute*

*"Variety is the very spice of life."*

Athenian Society '28; Debater '28; Vice President of Class '28; Basketball Team '28.

Some people have a "rep" for being a smarty, but Cat has a "rep" for being "cute," not with a crazy sense but with common sense. On the basketball team, on the class day team, and on the team of life Cat shows her "variety" in taste from a stick of chewing gum to a perfect paper in geometry.

*Organizations*. A group picture of each organization was taken on the steps of the school: the O. Henry Literary Society, the Athenian Literary Society, and the Glee Club.

*Advertisements*. Businesses from Ayden, Greenville, Kinston, Charlotte, and even Louisville, Kentucky supported *The Wheel* by purchasing advertisements. Some of the Ayden businesses continued to be familiar names in the decades to come: Tyndall, Boyd and Stroud; Roy L. Turnage; Edwards Pharmacy; Midway Service Station; Mumford's Market; Tripp Brothers Garage; Free Will Baptist Press; M. M. Sauls' Drug Store, and J.J. McClees and Co.

To Those Who Advertised:

*Just a line or two to say*
*How much we thank you for your aid*
*In helping us to make this book,*
*A volume that will tell to all*
*The progress that our school has made.*
*You've shown your interest, and friendships, too.*
*In all the work we're trying to do.*
*May health and wealth your comrades be,*
*And bring you all prosperity.*

JUNIOR CLASS

1928       THE WHEEL

## Junior Class

Roy McClees...................................................*President*
Brownie Wingate...............................................*Vice President*
Smith Hooker.................................................*Secretary-Treasurer*

Motto: *B²*

Colors: *Blue and Gold*         Flowers: *Sweet Pea*

### MEMBERS

| | |
|---|---|
| Marvin Baldree | Estelle Lyon |
| James Cannon | Estelle McClees |
| Sally Dale | Roy McClees |
| Jetta Maud Dail | Lourenia McLawhorn |
| Alda Rena Davis | Maidline McLawhorn |
| Hal Edwards | Julius McLawhorn |
| Warren Finch | Georgia Moore |
| Lillian Mae Hardee | C. L. Patrick |
| Mac Harrington | Blanche Peede |
| Floyd Harris | Sadie Stokes |
| Raymond Hart | Dalton Sumrell |
| Smith Hooker | Brownie Wingate |
| Ada Bett Joyner | Mary Worthington |
| Pearl Little | R. H. Worthington |

Stamey Worthington

Evelyn Lyon, *Mascot*

SOPHOMORE CLASS

1928          THE WHEEL

## Sophomore Class

EDNA SULLIVAN . . . . . . . . . . . . . . . . . . . . . . . . . . . . . . . . . . . . . . . . . . . . . . . . . . . . . . . . . . . . . . . *President*
BLANTON FOUTS . . . . . . . . . . . . . . . . . . . . . . . . . . . . . . . . . . . . . . . . . . . . . . . . . . . . . . . . . . . *Vice President*
DEE DURHAM . . . . . . . . . . . . . . . . . . . . . . . . . . . . . . . . . . . . . . . . . . . . . . . . . . . . . . . . . . . . . . . . . *Secretary*
EMMETT EDWARDS . . . . . . . . . . . . . . . . . . . . . . . . . . . . . . . . . . . . . . . . . . . . . . . . . . . . . . . . . . . . . *Treasurer*

MOTTO: *Still Climbing*

COLORS: *Purple and Gold*                                      FLOWER: *Pansy*

### MEMBERS

| | |
|---|---|
| MARY ALICE BULLOCK | WALDO MCGLOHON |
| WILLIAM BULLOCK | ROBERT MCKINNEY |
| BOYD COX | RUTH MOORE |
| JAMES DAIL | FRANK PIERCE |
| REDDIN DAIL | ASHLEY PIERCE |
| DEE DURHAM | KATIE PIERCE |
| EMMETT EDWARDS | HAZEL PHILLIPS |
| BLANTON FOUTS | BEVERLEY SAULS |
| LAURA MAE GRIFFIN | HULDAH SMITH |
| BEATRICE HARDEE | LINDSEY STALLINGS |
| MARGARET HIGHSMITH | EDNA SULLIVAN |
| MYRTIE GREY HODGES | HAZEL RUTH TURNAGE |
| MILLIE HOOKER | ELIZABETH TRIPP |
| MILDRED JACKSON | FRANK TYSON |

MILTON WORTHINGTON

FRESHMAN CLASS

**1928**     THE WHEEL

## Freshman Class

| | |
|---|---|
| Ellen McGlohon | President |
| Harry Dail | Vice President |
| Louise Tripp | Secretary |
| Edwin Harrington | Treasurer |

Motto: *Striving onward*

Colors: *White and Green*       Flower: *White Rose*

### MEMBERS

| | |
|---|---|
| C. O. Armstrong | Neva Kinlaw |
| Wilson Ballinger | Ellen McGlohon |
| Albert Bateman | Luby McLawhorn |
| Ruby Boyd | Renno McGlohon |
| Russell Britt | Ruby Moore |
| Vernon Cannon | Blanche Moore |
| Cassie Lee Cannon | Earle Moore |
| Jack Collins | Willis Moseley |
| John Coward | Helen Padley |
| Alex Cuthrell | Genevieve Prescott |
| Albert Dail | Paul Smith |
| Harry Dail | Wesley Smith |
| Preston Dunn | Alton Speir |
| Louie Dell Hardee | William Stocks |
| Vera Belle Hardee | Corey Stokes |
| Allie Harrington | Pierce Sumrell |
| Edwin Harrington | Louise Tripp |
| Velma Hart | Bonnie Ruth Tripp |
| Chester Hart | Ben Tucker Tripp |
| Robert Harris | Virginia Turnage |
| Burley Highsmith | Cassie Lou Williams |
| Donnie Mae Hurst | Ethel Lee Williams |
| Hubert Jolly | Clarence Wilson |
| William Jolly | Tom Worthington |

Heber Cannon ('28) was called on to write the "Last Will and Testament of the Class of '28," a mostly humorous but sometimes serious two-page composition organized to look like a will. The following are excerpts:

*Article I. For the love and esteem we hold for the Dear A. H. S. we will and bequeath our one hundred and thirty dollar stock in the Bank of Ayden, requesting that they use this in the future High School building.*

*Article III. To our superintendent, Mr. J. E. Sawyer, we bequeath his same position in the new high school building which is prophesied to be here in less than a year.*

*Article IV. To Mr. Fouts, the principal, we leave the job to see that all baseball, basketball, and football uniforms are washed and packed away not with baseballs, however, but with moth balls.*

*Article XII. We, as individual Seniors, wish to make certain bequests to some of the Juniors, hoping that they will use them to the best of their advantages.*

*Pattie Mae Turnage wills her great admiration for eighth grade boys to Estelle Lyo.*

*Dorothy Dinkins wills her ability to flirt with any boy in high school to Sallie Bett Dail, since Sallie has less distance to reach this ability than any other Junior.*

*Sallie Moore wills and bequeaths twenty pounds of her weight to Jetta Maude Dail; provided, that in the taking she let not one drop of blood be spilled.*

*Walter Scott Buck wills and bequeaths to Dalton Sumrell two inches from the length of each of his feet and a quarter of an inch from each side. He explains that he has a plenty remaining for himself, then, with extra. He leaves also, a big piece of cheese to the high school since members of his class call him "the whole cheese."*

*Ruby Lee Hart wills her ability to blush on all occasions to Sadie Stokes.*

*Graves Mumford wills and bequeaths to Hal Edwards his nickname, "Mouse-head," together with his mischievous habits. He, also, wills to Hal his ability to work geometry.*

*John William Sawyer wills and bequeaths his membership in the "Know Nothing Party" together with his saying on class, "I forgot and left it home," to Stancil Sumrell.*

*On this, the 17th day of May, nineteen hundred and twenty-eight, the class of '28 of Ayden High School do gather together and sign this, our Last Will and Testament.*

In search of volume two, I continued to look, listen, and write – moving chronologically from year to year through the 1930s. At last, a hint appeared in October 1938 in the form of a statement in the local newspaper. It was reported that nine years had passed since AHS had published an annual, and the class of 1939 wished to re-start what the class of 1928 must have hoped would become a tradition. To complicate my investigation, I was unable to verify if the class of '39 was successful in publishing the second edition of *The Wheel*. Furthermore, simple subtraction implies that an annual was issued in 1930. I am not convinced, however. Attempting to turn newspaper numbers into proof – especially prior to WW II – is an "iffy" proposition.

I had Daddy's annual and the one published by the class of 1945, a gap of 17 years. Like the '28 edition, *The Wheel* of '45 was a softback version. Bill Stroud ('45) was the senior class president, and his future bride, Helen Joyce Whitehurst ('49), was the annual queen. Tommy Edwards ('58) in his Sunday best and Peggy Wood ('59) in her tutu were pictured as the mascots.

Class historian, Jo Ella Sawyer ('45), paid tribute to the 75 "bright-eyed youngsters" who entered the first grade together in 1934. This means that the seniors of '45 were born prior to the "crash of '29," experienced their preschool years during the depression, and their high school years in World War II. Within weeks after they walked through the doors of AHS for the first time as high schoolers, the attack was made on Pearl Harbor. In the 10th grade ('42-'43), all of the extracurricular activities were canceled. In place of those endeavors, Jo Ella spelled out what students did. "We put our shoulders to the wheel, to help win the war by devoting all our efforts toward doing what we could; such as, collecting paper, iron, tin cans, and buying war bonds and stamps."

The class of '45 was the last class to graduate in 11 years. In 1946 there was no senior class and, therefore, no annual.

Was I to assume that volume two had actually been published in 1939? I continued to plunge through AHS's history lesson with that question in mind. Then, I opened the 1946-1947 version of *The Wheel* and on the cover sheet under the black and white picture of Ayden High School was Volume III. I hurriedly picked up the following class's yearbook: *The Wheel, Volume IV*. Starting with the class of 1949, the Roman numerals disappeared.   We are left with two conceivable possibilities. The most plausible seems to be that volume one was published in 1928, volume two in 1945, and volume three in 1947. This scenario assumes that a yearbook was not published in 1939. It could be that the class of '39 did produce an annual that year and it was considered to be volume one.

I began to wonder, did the classes substitute some form of periodical when no annual was viable? Over a cup of coffee brewed by Loys Sumrell ('38), I was able to add a little more evidence. As an English project, her senior class produced a mimeographed booklet of their high school days for each student. Mrs. Sumrell thought this format was followed for the last two years of her high school experience. In that way no advertisements had to be sold.

During the early to mid-1940s, classes published what they termed a "school newspaper" called *Aydenites*. Joyce Stroud has kept two copies of Bill Stroud's newspapers. When Loys Sumrell described the mimeographed publications that her class produced in the mid-1930s, I assumed that no ads were sold. This may have been an incorrect assumption. The school newspapers in the 1940s were funded by the sale of ads that were hand-drawn. The merchants must have paid a nominal amount as compared to the ads they'd buy when the annuals were restarted.

The *Aydenites* were 8 ½ x 11 inch mimeographed booklets. As near as I can decipher, they were published quarterly. Two members of the faculty advised about 12 students who enjoyed titles like editor, advertising manager, gossip editor, joke editor, and typist. There were actually two gossip editors; this should give you a clue as to the content of the newspaper. A section called "Chuckles" was filled with jokes and witty accounts of various students' activities. Making students laugh was obviously one of the *Aydenites'* objectives, but not all of the content was humorous. The times were too serious. Fellow students were encouraged to participate in an upcoming Red Cross Blood Drive and to buy war bonds and stamps. It must have worked. Ayden High School won a flag from the United States Treasury Department "for having ninety per cent of the students buying stamps and bonds each week." For the presentation, the student body gathered on the front lawn for the celebratory flag-raising.

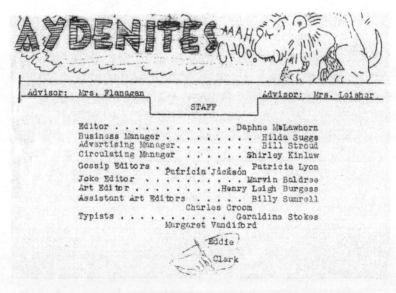

**1944 Aydenites school newspaper** *(Courtesy of Helen Joyce Whitehurst Stroud)*

**1944 Aydenites school newspaper** (Courtesy of Helen Joyce Whitehurst Stroud)

In an article in one of the newspapers, the students asked the principal, Faust Johnson, to increase the time they were given for lunch. That worked too. Mr. Johnson increased lunchtime from 45 to 55 minutes. There was a catch, however: five minutes were appropriated from recess. The principal needed five more minutes, so the teachers lost the other five minutes off of second period. The final decree was official: Mr. Johnson signed and dated his decision, 2-28-44, in the *Aydenites*.

Another section called "Did You Know?" pertained to Ayden's past. For instance, one of the historical facts was pertinent to sports: "on March 23, 1909 a committee was appointed to inspect streets and clayholes near the tobacco warehouse which was on second street." I believe this is the warehouse where Ayden High School eventually played basketball. It is also interesting to note that a bad spot in the street was called a clayhole. Second Street would not be paved for another ten years. I wonder when the term pothole became part of the vernacular.

Starting in 1945 and excluding 1946 when there was no senior class to put out an edition of *The Wheel*, yearbooks were published every year except 1950. When I asked Elmer Tripp ('50) if he knew why, he speculated that maybe it was because the class was so small.

All of the yearbooks were named *The Wheel* until 1966. The senior class of 1960 tried to make a change, and then a few years later in 1966 one succeeded. During my junior year at AHS, a controversy arose over re-naming the yearly publication. There was a movement to rename the book, *Wipe Out*. To resolve the dispute, a debate featuring the "modernists" versus the "traditionalists" was held in the auditorium. The student body voted, and *The Wheel* was retained as the name. I remember being vehemently opposed to the change because my Daddy's senior class had named the original.

The class of 1966 was successful in its attempts to call their annual *Wipe Out*. During this time period surf boards were popular on the beaches of North Carolina. A surfer who "wiped out" would come crashing down into the waves as his board slipped out from under him. The yearbook of the following senior class, 1967, returned to the traditional name.

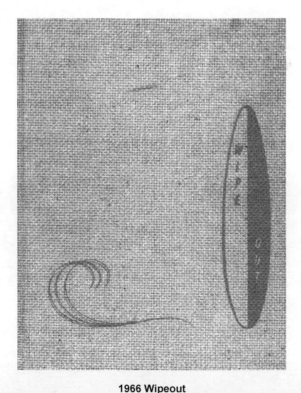

**1966 Wipeout**
The cover of this Ayden High School yearbook was unique because its name was changed from "The Wheel" to "Wipeout" in 1966, the only time the yearbook named differed in the history of the school. *(Photo by Mitchell Oakley)*

It is unfortunate that copies of Ayden High School's yearbooks are not kept in one location. Mitchell and I had to borrow numerous annuals from AHS graduates. On the other hand, thank goodness for the hard work of all the faculty and student staff who worked to preserve the stories of Ayden High School.

*The Wheel* was published through the '70-'71 school year, after which a new name needed to be created for Ayden-Grifton High School's history book.

**1928: Selected Advertisements:** *The Wheel, Volume I*

**Tyndall, Boyd, Stroud Company, Inc.**

Whole Groceries and Drugs
Ayden, N.C.

\*\*\*

**Publishers**
**Printers**
**Book Dealers**

*Your Business Solicited*
*and Apppreciated*

**F. W. B. Press**
Ayden, N.C.

\*\*\*

IF YOU WANT GOOD EATS
Buy Your Meats
at
**Mumford's Market**
Phone 35
FREE DELIVERY

\*\*\*

**M. M. SAULS' DRUG STORE**
Everything in Drugs
Full Line Druggist Sundries
PRESCRIPTION WORK OUR SPECIALITY
Waterman Fountain Pens, School Supplies, Purest Fountain Drinks

Fresh Box Candy, Smokes
*We Invite Your Patronage*
Phone 80
Ayden, N.C.

\*\*\*

## MIDWAY
## SERVICE STATION

AYDEN, N. C.

*Gas, Oils and Accessories*
*General Tires*
*a Specialty*

Robt. Johnson, Prop.

\*\*\*

## THE FIRST NATIONAL BANK
## OF AYDEN

solicits your cooperation
in helping to make this a
safer and better community

**Ayden Goes To War**

## Chapter 17
## December 7, 1941

We've made it through the 1930s. As we turn the corner into the 1940s, one of the most horrid times in our history awaits us; World War II will prove that World War I was not the war fought to end all wars. By 1939, Germany's tanks have already rolled into Poland and Adolf Hitler is planning to take over the world.

Back home, Ayden's citizens are trying to live their lives without interference, but conditions in Europe continue to deteriorate. The news will only get worse.

In 1942, *The Ayden Dispatch* reprinted an article from *The Chapel Hill Weekly*. Dr. Charles Maddry, a minister in Orange County and Foreign Mission Secretary for the Southern Baptist Convention, was in Honolulu preparing to start his day. He thought he'd heard a terrific thunderstorm. "At exactly 7:55 am Sunday morning the treacherous and murderous attack began." From his hotel window, Dr. Maddry looked toward Pearl Harbor at the same moment that an airplane was crashing to the ground. It was after he turned on his radio that he realized the parachuting pilot was Japanese. Instead of laying the cornerstone of a new church as planned, Dr. Maddry and his missionaries were forced to take a flight back to the mainland.

I've listened to numerous presidents' speeches. President Roosevelt's appearance before Congress and his "shall live in infamy" line has had the greatest personal impact. I am not sure why. It's probably because Daddy was a Motor Machinist Mate in the Navy and Uncle Sammy Pierce ('38) was an Air Force fighter pilot in the southwest Pacific.

Unlike many who served their country during World War II, my father and uncle did not share the well-known "code of silence." Conversely, the opposite was true. I spent numerous family gatherings listening to these two men talking about the war – sometimes their stories went on and on. Uncle Sammy was one of the few men who could out-talk my dad. I'm afraid there's something in the genetic makeup of our family that lends itself to these kinds of "discussions." Of course, this observation does not pertain to every member of the family.

I have attended numerous seminars conducted by Dr. Gerhard Weinberg, one of the world's foremost experts on World War II. Dr. Weinberg experienced the war like few did. He and his family were forced to flee Nazi Germany. They reached England just in time to experience the bombs raining down on London. Eventually, Dr. Weinberg came to America and became an internationally recognized scholar. The book to read is *The World at Arms* by Gerhard L. Weinberg. When he speaks, Dr. Weinberg always makes a simple but nevertheless constantly overlooked point. "If we really want to understand history, we must look at it from the perspective of the times." In other words, to understand what Ayden was like during the early 1940s, we need to wear the glasses of that time period.

I'm reluctant to tell Uncle Sammy Pierce's story. I do not want *Ayden, the Sports Town* to read like Ayden, the Harrington and Pierce Town. At the same time, the Harrington and Pierce clans must be related to everyone who was born in Ayden before and during the decades covered by this book.

I am relatively sure that Lt. Col. Sammy Pierce was Ayden's highest decorated soldier in World War II. He was featured in the fourth edition of *The Ayden Magazine* in 2006 soon after receiving Ayden's Highest Hero award, an honor given each year by the Chamber of Commerce. I will not expound on his 15 medals here; instead, I refer you to the list provided in the '06 magazine article. I will mention one: Sammy received the Distinguished Service Cross, a medal that is second only to the Medal of Honor.

Sammy's second marriage was to my mother's younger sister. Aunt Frances and Uncle Sammy had six children. It seemed that during Sammy's 23 years in the Air Force and in subsequent jobs that also took him around the world, he and my aunt would have another baby whenever they returned home for a visit. Since I was the oldest in the family, I got to hold each of the babies on their trips to Ayden. Their oldest son, Sammy Anson, was nicknamed "Jughead" by his father. I don't know that he would want this to get out, so I hope you will join me in keeping it a secret. Sammy Anson is the genealogist and historian of the family and has supplied me with lots of historical information on his dad. Since Sammy and his relatives go far back in Ayden's history, I've been able to use Sammy Anson's knowledge in other parts of the book as well.

After my maternal grandparents, A.W. and Rena Sawyer, passed away, Sammy and Frances retired to their house on Lee Street. On the wall behind his desk, Sammy had a picture of a skinny little kid standing next to a propeller-driven aircraft. This was the first time I'd seen the old photograph, and I recall vividly wondering who that was. Almost immediately, I knew who it had to be; it was Sammy, of course. I will never forget that experience. When the saber-rattling heats up around the world, I've often thought of the "little boy" who went off to war in the big airplane.

Sammy returned home. So many others did not.

Yes, Sammy Pierce is a hero; there's no doubt. Another reason I was reluctant to tell one soldier's story is it leaves out the heroes who did not return to Ayden. In a sense, these soldiers and their families are the real heroes of the war.

**Veterans Memorial Park dedicated Nov. 11, 2000.** *(Photo by Mitchell Oakley)*

In 1959, after their dad had been assigned to a base in Colorado Springs, Sammy Anson and his brother, Rick, were unpacking the moving boxes and burning the wrapping paper in an incinerator. Sammy Anson pulled out an old ratty-looking green baseball cap with a big white "A" on it. There were holes cut on each side that would have been just above the ears. He started to toss it in the fire when "something told him not to." Sammy Anson thought he'd better ask his mom. The cap turned out to be his dad's "good luck piece" on his 279 flying missions as a P-38 and P-40 pilot. He had seven confirmed and five probable "kills." For this Sammy received the designation of ace.

**Sammy Pierce with his lucky Ayden baseball cap.** *(Photo Courtesy of Sammy Anson Pierce)*

Sammy was an athlete during his days at Ayden High School; he played football, baseball, and boxed while in high school during the mid-1930s. The cap, however, was from his semi-pro baseball days. The Pierces and I have been unable to locate any confirmation of the team he played on. It's conceivable that he played for the Ayden Aces during their years in the Coastal Plain League. With the proliferation of baseball teams in the area during those years, he could have played for a number of different teams. Wherever the cap came from, there was one situation where it may have played a role in saving his life – at least Sammy thought it did.

After the boxes had been unpacked, Sammy told his oldest son that the holes in the baseball cap over the ears were for flaps and an oxygen mask. He wore the hat instead of the leather flying helmet. There was one situation when he was afraid he'd lost it when he bailed out over New Guinea in 1943.

Sammy was flying in a four-ship of P-40s when he and his fellow pilots ran low on gas and headed home. The convoy was composed of one American destroyer, ten PT boats, and several supply ships. The captain of the destroyer asked the flight lead to remain a little longer because he was concerned that Japanese aircraft would eventually attack. The P-40s had no instruments, so they were supposed to be flown only during daylight hours and in clear weather; however, the decision to stay was made. They stayed too long. When they did start back to base, dusk and a thunderstorm made flying impossible. Sammy crash-landed on an island about ¼ of a mile from the Japanese army. He was so close that he could hear the enemy talking.

I've heard Sammy tell this story. He used to describe in stark detail every inch he walked and crawled across the island until he reached friendly forces, an Australian patrol. Even then Sammy wasn't safe. One of the Aussie soldiers shot at him since he was walking from the enemy's direction. Later on, the soldier told him how lucky he'd been. The Aussie's gun was on single-shot rather than multiple shot. Once again, the baseball cap with the big white "A" had done its job.

I asked Sammy Anson for more details: "Before bailing out, Dad removed his oxygen mask, put the baseball cap inside his jacket, opened his canopy, and held the stick full aft, while applying full nose-down trim. When he released the stick, the aircraft nosed over and tossed him out. He said the Japanese shot at him as he was descending, but it was dark enough that he thought they could not see him and were shooting at the white parachute."

As soon as he was safe, Sammy reached into his jacket and pulled out the Ayden baseball hat. The good luck piece had been more than just an accessory to his flying suit. The green cap with the big "A" above the bill remains an important heirloom in the Pierce family.

Huey Lawrence was a hero of a different kind. He and his colleagues formed the B-1 band, the first African Americans in the Navy above the rank of a messman. The trumpet player graduated from North Carolina A&T State College in Greensboro and took his first job in 1949 at South Ayden School as a social studies teacher. He was soon asked to start the band and later was assistant coach of the Eagles' football team.

Mitchell Oakley, Johnny Davis, and I arrived at Huey's house in Ayden on a beautiful day in August. Johnny was the first to tell me about the man who was his assistant football coach when he stepped into the head coaching job at South Ayden High in 1969. The 92 year old veteran of World War II told us that he was recruited by A&T to play football. He traveled from his home in Pittsburg, Pennsylvania where he'd attended integrated schools to the south where he would enter a different world – where he'd attend a segregated college. At the time, Greensboro, the home of North Carolina A&T, was known as a musician's paradise between New York and Atlanta.

Lawrence told me about a book: *The Forgotten First: B-1 and the Integration of the Modern Navy* by Alex Albright, a retired East Carolina University professor. Much of the story I will be telling is from this 2013 publication. Like I indicated on the book written about the Coastal Plain League, had it not been for Professor Albright, these valuable stories would never have been preserved.

Huey Lawrence was "the man with the horn." He and his trumpet traveled to Norfolk, Virginia for basic training. Then, the B-1 band members were sent to Chapel Hill, North Carolina in 1942 where they were assigned to the Navy Pre-flight School. This school became famous for its trainees; George H.W. Bush, Gerald Ford, and Ted Williams trained there. Chapel Hill was anything but the sanctuary of liberalism for which it is known today. Most of the campus and town were off-limits to the bandsmen. The men knew they were still under the thumb of Jim Crow, but they also knew that what they were doing was a step away from the oppressive past.

For this reason, James Parsons, the band's leader, wanted the musicians for whom he was responsible to be perfect. When the Naval officials in Chapel Hill offered to provide transportation for the three miles to campus, he turned it down. Each morning, the band marched to campus to play for the raising of the flag. After their first job of the day, Parsons' men marched over to the Tin Can where they had formal drill practice. Another job was playing for the cadets to march to and from classes. When they were not carrying out specific duties, Parsons' men were practicing, practicing, and practicing, some more.

The bandsmen had most of their nights free. They formed dance bands, "taught music to local children, performed at local churches, dated and in several cases married local women." In addition, B-1 performed at officers' parties and socials in Woolen Gymnasium.

For the most part, the men were careful and stayed out of trouble, an incredible feat given the discrimination that they faced from the local all-white police department. Officers apparently were under orders to keep an eye on B-1; for example, Huey Lawrence remembered witnessing squad cars suddenly appearing when a local minister accompanied white students to the band's barracks. Incidents did occur. None escalated out of control, but one came close. Parsons said that some of the musicians "were accused of accosting while on liberty some white girls." Officers from the Chapel Hill Police Department, the police chief, and the sheriff showed up after dark and tried to talk Parsons into a lineup. The band leader asked them to wait outside while he got his men together. Parsons went downstairs and phoned Navy headquarters on campus. Parsons said "it seemed like the Marines had arrived." The soldiers entered through the rear of the barracks, charged through the building, and seized the officers. All of the men – including the police chief and the sheriff – were hauled off and incarcerated in the brig. Within 24 hours, the governor and the university president arrived on the scene to help remedy "the problem." All charges were dismissed.

After being told that they'd spend the duration of the war in Chapel Hill, the men of B-1 were ordered to Hawaii in 1944. The band's playing repertoire increased; they performed at "reviews, football and baseball games, wrestling and boxing matches, parades, bond rallies and concerts, sometimes with a portion of the show featuring one of the two swing bands formed from B-1 in Hawaii." As quoted by Albright in his book, Huey Lawrence stated that "playing for the servicemen on the ships was the best part of Hawaii."

As I read the book on B-1, out of nowhere I recognized a name: Ensign Talmadge Neece was the personnel officer responsible for scheduling the band. Talmadge and his wife, Edith, and Maija and I live in the same retirement community in Durham. Talmadge told author Albright that "they had a reputation when I got there as being the sharpest outfit on the island." The cliché "it's truly a small world" is certainly appropriate here.

On September 1, 2007, B-1 was invited to Chapel Hill for a long overdue ceremony. A plaque was positioned above the fireplace in the reception room of the band's old barracks – currently known as Hargraves Center. After 65 years, Chancellor James Moeser said, "I think this if the first time that we have welcomed you on this campus, and it is very, very, very late, but it is never too late. I only regret that we didn't do this many, many, many years ago when we could have had the entire band on campus." Several local Chapel Hillians spoke of how much their lives had been enhanced by the bandsmen of B-1. In Kenan Stadium at the half of the game against James Madison University, the band from so long ago was made honorary members of the Marching Tar Heels.

I'm sure you're asking yourself the same question I had; what was the meaning of the name, B-1? Nobody really knows for certain. The moniker could have come from the fact that it was the first band of its kind. Maybe the Navy actually meant that the players constituted the first "colored" band. I like to think – whether official or unofficial – that B One stood for the best.

Mitchell, Johnny, and I hung around for a few minutes in Huey's front yard to talk about the time we'd spent with him. If Johnny and Mitchell hadn't told me that Huey was blind, I would not have known it – probably until he asked me to retrieve the B-1 book from his bookshelf. I have learned way too many times that "life ain't fair." The man that meant so much to so many for so long had not been able to see for so long. Veteran Lawrence received the Asiatic-Pacific Campaign Medal, a Good Conduct Medal, and the World War II Victory Medal. Before long,

I heard a few notes coming from the living room. The man with the horn was blowing his trumpet.

On December 7, 1941, Ayden became a different place. Every life was changed. The boys, who had played so hard for fun, were asked to become soldiers or local volunteers. In comparison, sports must have seemed trivial. Ayden's citizens prayed for peace, watched the skies for enemy aircraft, conducted scrap drives, and purchased war bonds.

*Prayer vigils.* January 1, 1942 was proclaimed by President Roosevelt as a "National Day of Prayer." Beginning in April 1942, the town board asked all citizens to pause for prayer: "Surely with the world at war we can give one minute each day in prayer." The fire whistle gave one blast at 6:00 pm each day to signal the time. A "World Day of Prayer" was declared for Friday March 12, 1943 and observed at the Episcopal Church in Ayden.

*Defense Aircraft Observers.* Hal Edwards, a halfback on Ayden's first football team, became one of the leaders of the local aircraft observers. Soon after Pearl Harbor and continuing until October 13, 1943, volunteers from Ayden watched the skies for enemy aircraft. After perusing the Observation Schedule that appeared in *The Ayden Dispatch* each week, teams searched the skies at all hours, every day. A vacant lot owned by Frank Peterson, the high school's vocational agricultural teacher, was used by the two-person teams.

*Civil Defense.* Eugene Smith was Civil Defense Warden. He worked with town officials to develop a plan to warn citizens of an enemy attack. The fire whistle was blown in a certain way for a blackout; it meant go inside and pull down the shades and turn out the lights.

*Atlantic Coast Line Railroad.* The railroad around which Ayden had grown for fifty years ordered 2,000 new freight cars to meet the requirements of the war. Although the planning had started before the United States entered World War II, passenger train service between Kinston and Rocky Mount was discontinued on April 25, 1942. The depots of the railroads in North Carolina became collection stations for scrap metal drives. Eventually, President Roosevelt placed the entire railroad system under army control.

Railroad service from Ayden to the surrounding towns was taken for granted during the first half of the 20th century. Helen Joyce (Whitehurst) Stroud remembered being in Miss Stokes' second grade class when the students took the train to Winterville. She wasn't sure how they got back home. We can guess that she and her classmates were picked up by parents and neighbors. Helen Joyce also caught the same train when she was 12 years old to visit her second cousin near Bethel. The stop was at Whitehurst Station, a railroad stop named for her extended family. After a week, the little girl took the train back to the depot in her hometown.

I was fascinated by trains when I was a boy. I remember the locomotive service when I was very young. It was a really big deal when the long sleek diesel "Streamliner" took the place of the engine (or one like it) on which Helen Joyce traveled to Bethel. One day I happened to be uptown in the vicinity of Sauls' Drug Store when the crew from the Streamliner stopped on the tracks and walked across the street to have lunch at the drug store. I saw my opportunity; I asked one of the men if he would let me ride on the train. I sat up in the cab of a "real train" and rode up and down the tracks for a few minutes.

*Rationing.* The rationing of tires started on January 5, 1942. New tires were reserved for essential professions such as doctors, nurses and veterinarians. Farm equipment could be outfitted with new tires. Trucks hauling such commodities as ice, fuel, and construction materials were also exempt from the new rules. Everyone else was expected to purchase retreads. Fatal automobile accidents caused by faulty tires increased by 250% from June 1941 to June 1942. This prompted the Office of Price Administration (OPA) to order an inspection of all auto tires between December 1, 1942 and January 31, 1943. Beginning in February 1943, tires would be inspected at periodic intervals. Of course, not everyone complied, so the OPA came out with a ruling: "no gasoline or tire ration books will be issued to a motorist who fails to have their tires inspected." The rationing of food began in February 1943.

*War bonds.* "Help defeat the aggressors by putting your savings – regularly – in U.S. Defense Bonds." The Princess Theater sold $2,000 worth of war bonds in the first week of sales and $10,000 worth in its first month. During September 1942, a war bonds dance was proclaimed a huge success when it was announced that $1,900 had been collected.

A bond auction was held a few days before Thanksgiving in 1942 between the First National Bank and Welcome Service Station. Group singing was directed by Roy L. Turnage, and Wilbur Ormond played the accordion. A Winterville citizen, Ray Oglesby, a locally famous tobacco auctioneer, conducted the auction. A total of $16,500 was paid for the donated goods. The item that brought the highest price was a country ham, purchased for a bid of $2,000.

*Scrap drives*. By July 3, 1942, the rubber salvage drive had reached 834,293 tons in the United States. In Ayden, the service stations were collections hosts. The collection of scrap metal rivaled the purchase of war bonds in terms of volunteer hours expended.

Ayden school students were asked to collect scrap metal. On Wednesday November 4, 1942, the schools proclaimed a "scrap holiday" and closed for a half day. The Princess Theater offered a challenge; every student who turned in five pounds of metal would be admitted free for the upcoming Saturday matinee. As part of the school activities, a Scrap Carnival was proclaimed. There would be apple bobbing, bingo, penny pitching, fortune telling, and weight guessing. The school had already collected 14,000 pounds before the carnival. The first prize for most pounds went to a 5$^{th}$ grader, Donald McLawhorn. For collecting 1,525 pounds, Donald won $1.00 worth of defense stamps.

Tin can drives were separated from the overall scrap metal drive. During the 1943 school year a "Tin Can Week" was held. The first year principal of the Ayden Schools, Faust Johnson, asked citizens to phone him and he would see that all tin cans would be picked up. In addition to the school's participation, Pitt County housewives were told that they could "save enough steel for 1,258 machine guns simply by replacing one can of fruits or vegetables a week during the coming year with fresh or home-packed produce."

*Ayden schools*. In September 1942, the high school student body numbered 135, down 20% from the previous year. Near the beginning of that school year, the Pitt County schools started closing at noon to permit the students an opportunity to work on the farms. The initiative was continued the following year; by mid-October 1943, students had worked a total of 1,308 hours in the cotton, peanut, and sweet potato fields. Air Raid drills started in September 1942. Eight Pitt County schools collected a total of 24,000 pounds of paper in 1942. School commencements were to be streamlined to save gasoline. At the beginning of the 1943 school year, it was announced that the first six week's school hours would be 8:30-1:00. Students would go to school every 5<sup>th</sup> Saturday. School would close by May 10 in 1944.

*Women in war.* Women dedicated an uncountable number of volunteer hours while their loved ones were fighting in some far off place – often a tiny island in the Pacific that no one had ever heard of. For example, a call for assistance announced the following: "2,000 quarts of soup mixture must be canned this summer in order for the elementary school lunch room to continue its operation for the school year 1943-44." The Navy asked for 3,000 women to enlist in the Waves, the female version of the soldiers at sea. By the spring of 1943, a WAAC recruiting campaign was started. The Cadet Nurse Corps advertised the need for 65,000 new student nurses.

The nation's clothing dealers made the decision to discontinue putting cuffs on men's trousers to save cloth. Every little bit helped.


Clearly, history never stops, but it does on occasion take a drastic turn. The early to mid-1940s in Ayden obviously qualified as one of those events. The farmers, business owners, housewives, teachers, and students had no choice but to take the detour – no matter what it meant to them personally. I'd taken history courses in college, paid attention to my family's stories, and attended dozens of seminars on World War II (and other wars); however, I had little knowledge of the sacrifices endured by my relatives and their friends back home in Ayden.

I was examining anecdotes for a book about sports and suddenly none of that mattered anymore. Day to day life changed for nearly everyone.

Finally, it was all over.

# Chapter 18
## The View From Ayden Around 1946

Let's pause, look back for a moment, and steal a glance ahead. Ayden turned 50 years old during 1941, the same year as the attack on Pearl Harbor. Since its birth, the houses, businesses and churches that were nestled around shiny new railroad tracks and pitch black crossties had lived through two world wars and a depression. Now, it's 1946. The world looks different; North Carolina looks different; Ayden looks different. About ten years after Ayden was born, the director of the United States Patent Office advised Congress to abolish his position because everything that could possibly be invented had been invented. I don't know which was more astonishing – that a governmental official would suggest the elimination of his position or his actual belief that America's resourcefulness had run its course. Ten or so years before, while commenting on the 1890 census, an official proclaimed that the rush to conquer the frontier was over. No doubt, the oodles of Americans who had headed west with little more than a dream in their pockets had slowed. Their legacy had not.

In reality, our country's pioneering spirit and inventiveness had just begun. Peeping at us from around the corner were the 1950s and 1960s, decades of unprecedented economic growth and social change. Before and after World War II, contrasts were all around. The differences were astonishing.

Citizens of Ayden could start their automobiles from the inside. The driver and the passengers were enclosed in a cab, something that the early "horseless carriage" drivers would not have recognized. Cars had heaters on the inside. Electrical and phone lines abounded, but they were no longer strung on poles in the middle of the street. Lights and modern electric stoves could be operated all day, rather than only at night.

Ayden's incorporation in 1891 came at a time called the Nineties, the 1890s. Numerous new products came on the scene and were marketed not so much in a new way as in a greatly enhanced way. Lavish claims, comical to us today, were made; for example, Post Toasties, the first breakfast cereal, was advertised as a cure for appendicitis. One's back pain could be alleviated by a thing consisting of a bunch of crisscrossing wires that were supposed to produce some kind of "healing" electricity. Products that took years and sometimes decades before being recognized as everyday items were first manufactured around the turn of the century: cars, bathtubs (with hot and cold running water), refrigerators, bicycles, central heating systems, coffee vending machines, contact lenses, motion pictures, jukeboxes, ice cream cones, automatic pistols, and many, many others. The first electric chair was installed during that time period; by the time I made my 7th grade trip to Central Prison in Raleigh, the device had been changed to the gas chamber – a more humane machine that made a graphic, lasting impact on my pliable young mind.

One of the biggest changes over the first 50 years of the 20th century had been in public education. The one-room school houses had given way to two graded school buildings in Ayden, the smaller at the corner of Washington Street and 3rd Street and the high school building at the corner of Lee Street and 6th Street. The school year had evolved from six to eight to nine months, and the seniors now graduated from the 12th instead of the 11th grade.

The athletic facilities had kept pace with the overall advances in education. Although still a few years off, the football field next to the high school building would soon have lights. Now the company bringing the Donkey baseball games to the hardball diamond at one end of the gridiron field would not have to supply their own flood lights. When the games started at night, more fans were able to attend after their work days. The largest crowd ever in the gymnasium experienced the luxury of central heat and a floor without muddy wet spots. Lindy Dunn's ('57) arching two-handed set shots didn't come close to the rafters that used to obstruct the flight of the round ball in the tobacco warehouse that was home to Ayden High School basketball prior to 1929.

The year of the Axis defeat, 1945, would be celebrated by millions around the world. The most destructive war in history was finally over. The end of the war signified a rebirth – and a renewal of the football program, dormant since the 1939 season. The available records are clear; the white yard markers on the field across the street from the AHS gymnasium were unneeded for six years. Trying to ascertain the fate of the basketball and baseball programs during the war years has been more complex. Only meager published and unpublished accounts – mere bits and pieces – of the actual history remain.

After the football team finished 1-3 in 1939, Coach Ridenhour's 1939-1940 boys' basketball team finished 19-1 and won AHS's first tournament title ever. After that season, the evidence practically disappeared. After losing an exhibition game to the faculty, 38-17, the prospects for the 1940-1941 season must not have been encouraging. The first game of the regular season: Stokes 17, Ayden 8. The following season, 1941-1942, started out much like the preceding one with a loss; this time to Fountain, 19-12. At some point during the war, the high school either lost its ability or chose not to hire a coach. Local citizens volunteered to coach teams that I assume were not members of an organized league. In December 1944, the basketball program was revived with a victory over Winterville, 13-11. The game was refereed by Stuart Tripp. Volunteer coaches continued to coach the basketball team until a full-time coach was hired in 1946. Two names that appear as volunteer coaches in various reports were Leslie Stocks and Till Chauncey.

With only one short sentence to go by in the local paper, it appears that high school baseball had been discontinued for several years by the spring of 1942. In the summer of 1942, Ayden placed a team in the Coastal Amateur League. The Ayden Aces finished 31-6 with Crack Rogerson pitching the final game in September. AHS baseball was re-started in the spring of 1946, probably with a volunteer coach. At the same time, the Ayden Aces, often described as the town team, began their schedule. The coach and one of the starting pitchers for the Aces was Faust Johnson.

So far, I've been reluctant to focus undue attention on any one citizen, any one player or coach or teacher. The reason: heaping praise on one individual would invariably leave others out. Applying the same rationalization, I was even wary of listing Ayden's early businesses and civic clubs. But then, I couldn't fathom a history of Ayden without including the business community. Ayden wouldn't be Ayden without them.

Before launching into the post-war era beginning in 1946, we need to do a bit of analysis. Over the two decades of sports from the mid-twenties to the mid-forties, a couple of unfortunate trends emerged. The first concerned student and citizen support. The merchants and civic club members of the town were great supporters of athletics. Regrettably, the overall fan support was lacking. It was obviously present, but its numbers were too small. Secondly, lack of good sportsmanship became a concern. It is unclear if this tendency was due to the players or the fans. It's possible that both shared part of the responsibility. For Ayden High School's athletic program to become something special, those two problems had to be solved.

Prompted by Faust Johnson, AHS principal; Dr. Grady Dixon, physician; Alton Rowe, banker; and others, the Rotary Club kicked off a fundraising drive to hire a football coach and purchase equipment for the upcoming school year, 1946-1947. Mr. Johnson suggested that a supplement of $50.00 per month, in addition to his teacher's salary, would be needed. A young man who had played in Ayden High School's last football game prior to World War II was coaching in Roxboro. Would a hometown boy return to his roots in the fall of 1946 to coach a bunch of kids, some of whom had never even seen a football game?

**A New Beginning**

## Chapter 19
### Friday Night Lights

Stuart Tripp was hired in 1946 to coach football, basketball, and baseball. The principal, Faust Johnson, the same outfielder who had arrived in Ayden to play during the first season of the Coastal Plain League in 1933, would coach girls' basketball.

So many people deserved credit for kicking off the post-war era of sports at Ayden High School. Faust Johnson and Coach Tripp have earned the right to be ranked at the top. It was not easy. As late as 1949, the president of the student body, Mary Alice Brown Davenport ('49) made the following appeal for the fans to employ good sportsmanship: "But how can we have clean outstanding athletics if the students and fans will not back us with a spirit of good sportsmanship?" A few months later, Coach Tripp and Faust Johnson penned an article that deplored the "abuse of the referees" after a football game with Greenville. They were blunt: "This needs to change." Over the years, they stated, several players had been expelled from Ayden's teams. At the time, Tripp was president of the Pitt County Athletic Association and Johnson was president of the Coastal Conference Athletic Association. "Someday we want Ayden boys to get scholarships at colleges – sportsmanship will be part of that." The demands began to pay off; the boys' and girls' basketball teams won sportsmanship trophies during the 1953-1954 school year.

I don't remember the word sportsmanship being spoken when I played for Coach Tripp. It didn't have to be; it was built-in. Treating other players and coaches with respect was integrated into the game he taught. With an occasional snafu along the way, AHS's coach and principal employed the blueprint that would become as much of a tradition as solid defense in football. George Bryant, sports editor for Greenville's *Daily Reflector*, captured this fact when he congratulated the Ayden players and fans during the Class A basketball tournament in Durham in 1962: "They demonstrated to people all over the state that Pitt County can produce good teams and that the players are capable of doing an excellent job of representing the area."

Gate receipts had to increase. Time after time, the merchants and civic clubs of the community had raised money to keep athletics going. In 1934, drop boxes into which a citizen could drop change were set up at Edwards Pharmacy and Burgess' Drug Store. "The athletic program is not breaking even so we must have your help if we [are going to] have a team." Income from paying customers had not kept pace. Just before Christmas in 1949, the largest crowd to witness a basketball game in the AHS gym, 431 paid fans, had lots to cheer about, Ayden 45, Winterville 25. One year later in 1950, the largest crowd ever to watch a football game, witnessed the Tornadoes win their second straight conference championship. The increase in numbers must have been contagious; 4,000 people turned out for Ayden's first Santa Claus parade. That total nearly doubled the official Ayden census count for that year. I was probably watching as the old man with the white beard and red suit exchanged his sleigh for a ride in the town's new fire truck. That year or at a future parade, I remember trying to catch little bags of candy when St. Nicholas threw them down from that same shiny red fire truck.

To supplement improved sportsmanship and increased attendance, another ingredient needed to be added to the mix: winning teams. Earlier in our story, we've already traveled to Southern Pines to watch Coach Johnson and his team play in North Carolina's first state tournament for girls. The 1950 team won 93% of its games. For a period of six years from 1946 to 1952, the female version of the Tornadoes won 122 of 148 games (excluding three ties).

Now, it is time to turn to football's first season in six years. At the same time the Rotary Club was searching for a coach for the upcoming 1946 football season, it had to raise money to supplement his salary and to purchase new equipment. At a club meeting in May 1946, Faust Johnson announced that $790 had been procured so far. Mr. Johnson provided the membership with the total cost of "putting a football team on the field." At a later meeting, Corey Stokes announced that a Chevrolet would be raffled off at Thanksgiving with the proceeds going to the athletic program. The Rotary Club voted to hold a series of square dances in the AHS gym to help fund the upcoming season.

**1946-47 Ayden's First Football Team After World War II**
Members of the team include (not in any particular order): Hilliard Kinlaw, Richard Cannon, Lloyd Wilson, L.L. Kittrell, John C. Andrews, Frank Harrington, John Clark Noble, Douglas Stocks, J.W. Stocks, Allen Ormond, Sydney Ormond, Charles Croom, R.H. Mason, Bob Holland, Bill McLawhorn, Tommy Bullock, Leonard Bullock, Gene Harris, Gene Baldree, Marvin Baldree, Reginald Worthington, Conrad Cannon, Jimmy McCormick, John Cheek, Jack Sugg, Mark Manning, and Walter Lee Williams. *(The Wheel)*

To start the 1946 season, Bear Baldree ('48) remembered getting discarded helmets from East Carolina College. "We could almost fold them up and put them in our pockets. The girls from the home economics class sewed the numbers and letters on our jerseys just in time for the game." Officials at ECC also donated football shoes and pants. "Some shoes didn't have cleats." The players' vision was not hampered by face guards, except under unusual circumstances. Bear remembered one of his teammates wearing a special football hat. A single steel bar welded to each side of his helmet was designed to protect his broken nose. Like Bear, Elmer Tripp remembered that the "old" AHS football equipment had been stored in the projection room in the rear of the high school auditorium. Once the various pieces of football paraphernalia had all been assembled in one place, Ayden High School was ready for its first football season after the war.

"Ringers," players not in high school, occasionally played in football games as late as the 1940s. Bear recalled a game against Columbia High School: "Their team was made up of men whose children were running along the sidelines cheering for their dads." Bear went on to describe that game: "I played only when we were so far behind or so far ahead that I couldn't affect the outcome of the game. Coach asked me if I wanted to go in." Bear replied, "No, I think I'll pass. They were bringing our boys off the field in pairs." The Columbia team was composed of more physically mature men who had returned from serving in the war. More than likely they were students participating in a special Federal program that was similar to the GI Bill. It was designed to pay for returning soldiers to take high school courses in an effort to assist them in returning to the workforce.

Gene Tripp and James Ray McLawhorn were two of the Ayden graduates who suited up and entered the game. "They played, but it didn't help. There weren't enough of them," Bear said. Coach Tripp was getting ready to suit up, but his boss, Mr. Johnson, talked him out of it.

In a speech to the Rotary Club, the new football coach stated that the 1946 team would have only two players who had played football before. Since there was no activity bus, several club members volunteered to furnish transportation to the first game at Farmville.

Naming the brothers who played for the Tornadoes would take several pages. If I added cousins to the list, another book may be required. Now and again they played together on the same team and at other times a younger brother had to wait his turn. The Bullock brothers and their family arrived on the scene in 1944 after their dad, who worked for the Department of Agriculture, was transferred to Ayden from Faison, North Carolina.

**1949 Annual king and queen Janice Turnage and Tommy Bullock.** *(The Wheel)*

**1949 Co-Captains Jimmy McCormick & Teedy Bullock.** *(The Wheel)*

Like Bear Baldree, Tommy Bullock ('49) played on Coach Tripp's first team. "None of us knew anything about football. We had to be taught how to get down in a stance. [We] needed to be taught the fundamentals of fundamentals. There wasn't anything in football, basketball, or baseball that Coach didn't know how to demonstrate," Tommy said. Tripp was not exaggerating at the Rotary Club meeting when he reported on the inexperience of the upcoming players. "We had players that played in the first football game they ever saw," Tommy emphasized.

The Tornadoes' season started with a bang; halfway through the ten-game schedule, the record was 4-1, but AHS lost the final five games to finish, 4-6. The final scores in all the games were close with the exception of the famous "ringer game" lost to Columbia, 34-0. Farmville was defeated twice, 20-6 and 26-6.

A similar fate awaited the Tornadoes the following year, 1947. After six games their record was 4-2. As in the previous year, AHS faltered toward the end and finished with a losing record. After 16 boys and 13 girls participated in graduation exercises, the Athletic Banquet was held at the Airport Inn in Greenville. The records from the years' teams were reported: football, 4-5; boys' basketball, 11-8 during the regular season and 2-2 in the Pitt County Tournament; girls' basketball, 18-1 and 1-2 in the Pitt County Tournament. The baseball team had just completed its season with a record of 7-2. The evening concluded with a film of the North Carolina State – St. John's basketball game. State won. (The football record coincides with the archives available to me. The boys' and girls' basketball do not. The 7-2 record in baseball is the only info I've been able to locate on Ayden High School baseball in the three years immediately following the war.)

In the eighth game of the 1947 season on a wet muddy field in Clinton, the Tornadoes were defeated, 12-0. Because of an injury to an offensive lineman, Doug Stocks ('48) had to be moved to another position. R.H. Mason ('50) took his place. The Clinton defensive lineman opposite R.H. was 20-30 pounds heavier than he was. On first down, the quarterback called a play over R.H. No gain. When R.H. returned to the huddle, mud was splattered across his face and helmet. The quarterback again called a play to be run off R.H.'s side of the line. No gain. For the third consecutive time, the signal-caller called for an off-tackle play over R.H. Tommy Bullock was in the same huddle. "At that time if you didn't understand the play, you'd say 'check.' Everybody would come back to the huddle quickly and the quarterback would make the call again. R.H. called check and, when the play was called again, R.H. didn't move." The fact that R.H.'s dad was a minister didn't deter him from being emphatic, "I'll be &%# !*$@ if we're going that way again."

More than once, I heard Coach Stewart Tripp asked the question, "What was your best team ever?" He mentioned two "eras:" The "Teedy" Bullock era and the Paul Miller era. Those two periods of time were not only special to him, but they were also special to the fans. I never heard Coach Tripp go on and on about Teedy or Paul. Instead, he bragged about "his boys." His boys – that was the special part to Coach Tripp. We are about to launch into the first of those two times.

## Chapter 20
Cowboy Spurs

Dennis "Dink" Mills ('61) finished his remarks at the Community Foundation's fourth annual golf tournament by saying, "Please join me in honoring Leonard S. "Teedy" "Len" Bullock as the Community Foundation, Inc.'s 2011 Legend Award recipient. I invite his family to come up and be with him at this time." Danny Sapp's article in *The Times-Leader* detailed the award's standards: "The legend award recognizes an alumnus, principal, athletic director, coach, player, manager, statistician/scorekeeper, announcer, or sports bus driver in the Ayden or Grifton communities, who achieved – through a sports experience – a work ethic, spirit and attitude that continues in their day to day life. The recipients celebrate the virtues of a career and a service to others."

The quarterback on the muddy field in the Clinton game in 1947 was Teedy Bullock, Tommy's younger brother. I have heard Coach Tripp asked a question several times: Which teams were your favorite or which were your best? Coach always answered, "There was the Teedy Bullock era and there was the Paul Miller era." I never heard him use the terms "best" or "favorite" or "special" or any expressions that he thought might show partiality. So, any superlatives which are applied to individuals and to this time period are mine, alone.

We've all heard of "growth spurts." When Teedy was in the $7^{th}$ grade, he was 5'7" tall. During the next three to four months and by the $8^{th}$ grade, he grew to 6'1" and 165 pounds. He remembered his mom placing hot wet compresses on his aching legs at night. At about the same time that his body decided to surge ahead, Teedy began practicing with Ayden's varsity football team. He never missed a practice in 1947 although he was too young to play in the games.

Not to be outdone by his brother, Tommy experienced a growth spurt of his own; his playing weight jumped from 120 to 132 pounds between his junior and senior years. It was Tommy's speed that kept him on the field. From his tailback position in the single wing attack, he once ran for 65 yards and a touchdown. The speedster could not have made it, however, without the benefit of his father who "reached paydirt" two steps before his son did. Mr. Bullock had been running down the sidelines yelling encouragement all the way. The tailback was not only speedy on the gridiron, he was fast on his feet. Along with Helen Joyce Whitehurst, Tommy was voted the best dancer in the class of 1949.

More and more, the community was pulling together to support the Tornadoes. Bonnie Ruth McCormick, Coach Tripp's sister and the mother of one of the football players, made a plea to promote the team by urging the fans to attend the games. As in innumerable times before, the Rotarians led the way. Each club member "guaranteed the sale of three tickets" by pledging to purchase them if they were not sold.

The senior, Tommy, and the freshman, Teedy, played in the same backfield during the 1948 season. After the Mt. Olive Panthers shellacked the Tornadoes 49-0 in the first game of the year, the team won four straight. In the fourth game, a 56-6 victory over Warsaw at Guy Smith Stadium in Greenville, Teedy threw 5 touchdown passes. The exhilaration of the 4-1 start was dashed when AHS lost its last two games to complete the season, 4-3.

For a number of years Coach Tripp did it all. There was no official assistant coach, but volunteers not only provided transportation to the away games, they helped on the field. Hal Edwards, a starter on Ayden's first football team in 1926, taught Teedy how to punt.

Ayden entered a new conference in 1949. The nine-team East Central Conference of the year before was replaced with a five-team league that included Farmville, Robersonville, South Edgecombe, and Vanceboro. The new conference was called the Coastal Conference. The emphasis on fundamental skills development on the field and community support off the field must have paid off. Ayden's record of 7-1 was the best since the team finished 8-1-1 in 1932. The only blemish was a 14-13 loss to Greenville in the second game.

With only one player lost from last year's team, the 1950 Tornadoes expected to be good. They were better than good. For the first time in school history, the team completed the season undefeated at 9-0. Teedy Bullock and Walter Meeks ('51) were the co-captains.

### 1950-1951: Ayden High School Football Season
### (9-0)

| Ayden | 13 | Williamston | 7 |
|-------|-----|-------------|---|
| Ayden | 40 | Robersonville | 0 |
| Ayden | 42 | Vanceboro | 0 |
| Ayden | 46 | Farmville | 6 |
| Ayden | 36 | South Edgecombe | 6 |
| Ayden | 25 | Tarboro | 0 |
| Ayden | 14 | Ahoskie | 2 |
| Ayden | 7 | Fuquay Springs | 6 |
| Ayden | 19 | Central of Elizabeth City | 0 |

**1950-51 Ayden High School's First Undefeated football team** *(The Wheel)*

No team scored over one touchdown and four teams were shut out. AHS won its second consecutive Coastal Conference championship. Against conference opponents, Ayden averaged 41 points per game to their foes 3 per game. The second team played over one-half of several of the games because the first team was so far ahead. We'd have to turn our history clocks back to the first four years of football in the late 1920s and the two year period of 1931 and 1932 to find teams that were as dominant as the 1949 and 1950 teams. None of the previous teams had completed the season undefeated. Utilization of the descriptive term, dominant, would certainly fit the 1931 edition of the AHS Tornadoes; the team finished 10-1-1 with 10 shut outs.

An example of the 1950 team's domination occurred in its 40-0 win over Robersonville. Ayden finished with 11 first downs to Robersonville's 2. Robersonville gained 31 yards on the ground and -2 yards passing on 2 of 17 attempts. Two of those passes were intercepted. The Tornadoes amassed 400 yards in total offense.

With some exceptions, I have been unable to list the players on specific teams throughout the years, usually because that information was not accessible. Even if available, providing a directory of players for every squad would make the book read more like a report; the narrative would become more and more difficult if page after page contained an endless number of names. Additionally, recording the starters on a particular team would invariably leave someone out. No problem existed when pictures of the entire group could be located. I feel obligated to indicate the players on Ayden's first undefeated team. The following "probable starters" were listed in the local newspaper for the historic game under the lights:

| | |
|---|---|
| Willis Manning ('52) | Left end |
| Jerry Britt ('51) | Left tackle |
| James Hemby ('51) | Left guard |
| Greg Davis ("51) | Center |
| Walter Meeks ('51) | Right guard |
| Troy Jackson ('51) | Right tackle |
| Mac Whitehurst ('53) | Right end |

| | |
|---|---|
| Teedy Bullock ('52)* | Quarterback |
| B.L. Byrd ('51) | Right halfback |
| Darrell Worthington ('53) | Left halfback |
| Mac Hardee ('51) | Fullback |

*Attended Fork Union Military Academy for his senior year.

Playing on the school's first lighted field set another record for attendance. The win marked the 13th straight victory over the last two years. Coach Tripp and the Tornadoes began receiving accolades outside the area. Teedy Bullock was selected to play in the Optimist Bowl in High Point on Thanksgiving Day. This game pitted the East All-Stars against the West All-Stars. So far, he was 40-83 passing for 781 yards as the "T" formation quarterback. Teedy also played safety on defense. At 158 pounds, Greg Davis ('51) was considered the leader on defense.

The homecoming game saw Ayden face a non-conference opponent that was 5-1-1. The Fuquay Springs Falcons took a 6-0 lead into the 4th quarter. The crowd of 1,100 looked on as the Tornadoes drove toward the goal line. A succession of passes from Teedy Bullock to Darrell Worthington and Willis Manning moved the "T" formation down field. Mac Hardee scored on a running play and Teedy Bullock made the all-important extra point on an end run. The 7-6 victory kept the undefeated, untied season alive.

Central High of Elizabeth City, another strong team with a 6-1 record, was the final opponent. Their only defeat had come at the hands of Plymouth, 21-13. The teams from northeastern North Carolina – the schools north of the Albemarle Sound – had been tough opponents. Although not traditional rivals, when the Tornadoes played Ahoskie, Edenton, and Elizabeth City, AHS had come up on the short end of the final score. Not this time. Ayden dominated the game, holding Central to 57 yards rushing and 40 yards passing. A goal line stand that ended at the two yard line preserved the shutout, 19-0.

Ten seniors had played the last football game for their alma mater. And, a junior Tornado had taken his final snap from center. The following year Teedy Bullock would enroll at Fork Union Military Academy in Fork Union, Virginia. The University of North Carolina Tar

Heels had shown interest in Teedy and had suggested that he attend a year of prep school to better prepare him athletically and academically.

Teedy received his Ayden High School diploma in a unique way. He entered Fork Union and when it became time to apply to the University of North Carolina, Teedy's parents contacted Mr. Johnson, principal at AHS, and made arrangements to have their son's grades transferred to Ayden High School.

**Leonard "Teedy" Bullock during his UNC days.** *(Photo Courtesy of Teedy and Anne Bullock)* **Leonard "Teedy" Bullock after receiving the Legend Award from Community Foundation, Inc.** *(Photo Courtesy of Community Foundation, Inc.)*

Playing on the first team as a freshman, the Ayden quarterback participated for three years on the varsity at the University of North Carolina. "Without that year at Fork Union, I never would have been a starter," Teedy said. He played safety on the defensive unit during his first year in 1952. "[UNC] had a freshman team but, if you could make the varsity, you could play." Carl Snavely, a teammate of Charlie "Choo Choo" Justice, was Teedy's coach. When Snavely left UNC, he took the single wing with him, and George Barclay was brought in to teach the

"T" formation. For his sophomore and junior years – 1953 and 1954 – Teedy played quarterback in the "T" and safety on defense. After skipping his senior year at UNC, Teedy began a career in the theater in New York. After Jim Tatum replaced Barclay as UNC's coach, he contacted Teedy in New York and asked him if he'd return for his final year of eligibility. He declined, telling Coach Tatum that he was married and had started his career.

One more time, let's return with the Legend Award winner to Ayden.

*Hop in the red car with Teedy and me. I want to show you a famous place. You'll never guess where we're headed, so I'll tell you. We're going to skip the athletic venues where he played and go somewhere that holds fond memories for the quarterback and his teammates. There will be no engraved plaque or trophy to mark the spot, but the little room is well-known; at least, to the ones who remember. It is located at the Ayden High School building in the auditorium, the same place that was opened in 1929. And yes, the same place where our journey started. Teedy ... it's your story; you take it from here.*

"After World War II, all the football uniforms were stored in the projection room. I was the youngest guy on the team. The cleats [to the football shoes] screwed on and they had rusted. When I ran it sounded like I had spurs on ... cowboy spurs. They would jingle. I was more proud of that pair of shoes than any I ever wore." Thinking back to the time when he was a 7th grader, Teedy says, "I've really made it now. I got these shoes. It was great."

Although I didn't know it when I walked into Panera Bread in Raleigh to meet with him, James "Jim" Hemby also played on the 1949 and 1950 teams that only lost one game by one point. He played offensive guard and linebacker on defense. I knew him as James; but like me, his name got changed when he "left home." I'm William in Ayden and Bill everywhere else. Even so, I'm going to call Jim by his Ayden name, James. With Teedy at quarterback, the Tornadoes ran from the "T" formation. On occasion they'd switch to the double wing. At that point Greg Davis, the offensive center, moved to the backfield and James moved over to snap the ball.

Like Teedy, James described the team members as "tight off the field," as good friends. When Troy Jackson moved to Ayden, he used to ride to school on the back of James' bicycle. Ayden friendships often started early and lasted forever. I presume that means Troy, offensive tackle, must have been forgiven on the following occasion: "Troy couldn't see very well. [After a play] Teedy came limping back to the huddle. Troy said 'what happened, I got my man.' Teedy [responded], 'you damn right you did, *me*.' Troy hit the first thing around."

"James," I asked, "what did playing sports mean to you?"

"The one thing it meant to me was discipline … organizational patterns that accentuated discipline. [The] organization of a team. I thought that Stuart Tripp was exceptionally good at that. In a subtle way, [he] taught us reliance on each other. Recognizing everybody's dependence on somebody. It's deeper than what I'm saying. I'm not sure it's something you learn; it's something you absorb … something you experience and it sorta gels. Helped me a lot in my academic administration."

After receiving his Ph.D. in English from Texas Christian University, James held several administration and teaching positions before becoming president of Barton College in 1983. He also officiated collegiate and high school football, basketball, and baseball games. Playing three sports at Ayden Highs School; refereeing and umpiring those same games; sitting in an uncountable number of classrooms; plus his career in higher education have all become concentrated in the person James has become. He went on to answer my question concerning the meaning of sports to him. "[Sports taught me] the notion of timing or court presence or field presence. Instilling the importance of where you are; what your role is; and the importance of timing. What your role is in relation to everybody else – to your opponents and teammates. Carries over into life."

Before we leave James sipping on his coffee at Panera, I want to re-visit a blacksmith shop in Ayden. As he said to me, "I hold a unique distinction in football." By that he meant an exclusive place in *Ayden* football. Across Park Avenue from the Hembys lived the Dunns. The oldest sibling, Jimmy Dunn ('51), and James were playing sandlot football in a famous side yard in the neighborhood when Jimmy accidentally kicked his friend in the nose. When getting his physical to play football, the doctor stated that James would have to have some type of protection for his broken nose. As far as I know, the bar that was welded onto his helmet won James a place in Ayden's history books – the first player to wear a face mask. It was so unusual that the referees had to examine it before every game. In at least one game, the strange looking contraption came in handy.

James said, "Linemen would try some tricky things. The defensive player across from me came straight up and was going to hit me in the head with his fist." Needless to say, the steel bar did not feel good when the offensive lineman's opponent struck it with the back of his hand. "He didn't know what had happened; it was hurting so bad." James' friend and fellow lineman, Greg Davis, got a kick out of the whole thing. "I thought he was gonna die; he was laughing so hard."

To start the 1951-1952 school year, Ayden had won 15 consecutive games and was 16-1 over the previous two seasons. How long would the streak last?

That question was answered in the first game: Williamston 18, Ayden 13. The 1951 edition of the Tornadoes won the next five to take a 5-1 record into the final four games. Ties against Plymouth and Hertford plus losses to Beaufort and Weldon lead to a 5-3-2 season.

The following year, the 1952 Tornadoes were 4 and 5. For the second successive year, the co-captains were Mac Whitehurst ('53) and Darrell Worthington ('53). Mac accomplished a milestone that few have achieved; he was voted to the All-conference team for the 4th time. My first cousin, Randall Harrington ('53) made the All-conference team for the 2nd year. Another senior, Wesley Cannon ('53) was also chosen All-Conference.

The Tornadoes again won the Coastal Conference championship with a 4-0 record, but admiration of the trophy was short-lived. Soon after the season, AHS discovered that it had played all of its games with an ineligible player. As a result, the second place finisher, Farmville, was awarded the crown. In a bizarre turn of events, the Red Devils also discovered that they had used an ineligible player. Finally, the third place team in the five-member conference was declared the winner. Instead of 4-5, the official record became 0-9.

## May 1947: Picture Shows at the Myers Theater

**Saturday**    *Lone Hand Texan* starring Charles Starrett
        *Blondie's Big Moment* starring Penny Singleton

**Sunday**    *Song of the South* in color
        a Disney Feature Cartoon
        a Short: *Wacky Talky Gawky*
        and the News

**Wednesday** *Hit the Saddle* starring The Three Mesquiteers
        *The 13th Hour* starring Richard Dix and Karen Morley
        Serial: *Chick Carter, Detective*

**Thursday**    *Margie* in color starring Alan Young and Jeanne Crain
        Short: *Amusement Park*
        and the News

## Other News in Late 1940s

Garland Little: A pitcher on the baseball team at ECTC strikes out 19 batters in a game against the Little Creek Amphibians, a team from Virginia. Little also plays right field and is currently hitting .350.

The first Southern Conference tournament games to be broadcast on WPTF radio.

Mr. C.E. Myers has moved the seats and equipment from the Princess Theater to Hookerton where a new movie house will be opened.

Ayden High School graduating class of 1947: 15 boys and 14 girls.

School enrollment: High school = 136; Grade school = 427

New cooling system installed at the Myers Theater.

Pitt County, the leading tobacco grower in the United States in 1945.

Faust Johnson to be principal for the 6th straight year beginning with the 1948 school term.

October 1948: Inauguration of postal delivery service in Ayden.

Thirty girls go out for Faust Johnson's basketball team.

**"Slim" Short and "Cactus" Jim**

## Chapter 21
### The Black and White Box in the Living Room

On December 22, 1953, a piece of "furniture" was added to Ayden's living rooms – at least for the households that could afford the leap into the world of television. Like the telephone it would take a few years before nearly every family would own the gizmo that was predicted to end a night out at the movies. That date is not exactly correct. There were television sets in Ayden prior to that time. The problem; the wind had to be blowing at precisely the right speed, from precisely the right direction with no interference from sunspots to enable the folks in their homes to get a picture from a station miles away. And that's not all. Someone had to adjust the "rabbit ears" at just the right angle to take advantage of the ideal atmospheric conditions outside of the house. In the event that you've never experienced rabbit ears, envision a ball of plastic about the size of a tennis ball. Sticking out of the opposing sides of the "ball" were two long silver extensions about the circumference of a pencil. "Adjusting" meant turning the ball around and around while extending or shortening the ears to find just the right spot. Wrapping the ends of the rabbit ears with tinfoil and hanging coat hangers on them tended to help, slightly.

*The only "remote" was the family member in the back of the house who was usually summoned by hollering, "Hey Mabel, come look at this thing. We finally got a picture." She would come running to see what all the fuss was about.*

*"Well, what is it?"*

*"I ain't quite sure, but it's something."*

The "thing" on the little black and white screen would be engrossed in what came to be called "snow" because that's what it looked like. Just as the snow would let up and the viewers could make out a face or a scene of some kind, the picture would start jumping around uncontrollably like an angry giant had reached through the window to violently shake the confounded machine. Just when the image in the little box began to resemble the advertisement in the store window, the station would sign off for the day. At that moment, the meteorological circumstances would become ideal just in time to see the beautiful American flag waving in the make-believe breeze and to hear a rousing rendition of the National Anthem. Right after that, the test pattern would come on. The family usually stayed after the official closing ceremonies to watch this final attraction. I never knew what the test pattern was for and I could never understand why it was so clear. Most baffling was the sound; the image was always accompanied by a humming noise. Picture perfect. And then, the last thing the television person at the station had to do before he closed up shop for the night was turn off the test pattern. The last act; the screen would be completely filled with snow – which is precisely where the night had begun.

The date, December 22, was actually the day that WNCT, Channel 9 signed onto the air. The Greenville station was the first to serve eastern North Carolina. The emphasis was on the provision of "crop news" for the farmers of the area; that is, the reporting of weather conditions affecting their lives. A former Navy officer, Sherman Housted, became the first weatherman.

In the 1950s, local programming was more important than it is today. One of the first television "personalities" I remember was Slim Short on *Carolina Today*, a program that ran from 1959 to 1998, featuring local news and weather. Cactus Jim emceed an afternoon program. When the show started, he would be sitting on a bale of hay. I vaguely remember paying a visit to the studio to see Cactus in person. I'm not sure if that trip to Greenville was imagined or real. Once the Greenville station went on the air, we could get local and national programming without all the snow. My classmates and I would gather in the hallways to talk about the most recent episode of *Gunsmoke*, *I Love Lucy*, *The Hit Parade*, *Red*

*Skelton*, *The Ed Sullivan Show*, and a few others. Before cable-TV, however, there remained problems for a number of years if one desired to get a far off station. The conditions had to be "picture perfect."

By the spring of 1954, Channel 9 estimated that there were 45,000 television sets within a 60-mile radius of the new station. The four networks available were CBS, NBC, ABC, and the DuMont Network. Aydenites who were fortunate to have the new piece of technology in their homes were enjoying an expanded schedule of programs. They could tune in anytime between 7:00 am and the national anthem at 11:30 pm. After that, the snow and its familiar hissing sound would mysteriously engulf the screen.

My most vivid memory of 1950s television was the North Carolina Tar Heel's run through the NCAA Tournament on their way to an undefeated season in 1957. I do not think any of the regular season games were televised that year – only the national tournament. I can still see in my mind's eye Tommy Kerns, at 5'7," jumping center against the University of Kansas' Wilt Chamberlain, a 7 footer, to start the '57 national championship game. That same year Johnny Taylor ('62) and his dad, P.R. Taylor, my dad, and I drove to Chapel Hill to see Carolina play N.C. State in Woolen Gym. Carolina jumped out to a commanding lead in the first half. Everett Case decided to try something that was relatively commonplace at that time. He put two defenders on Lennie Rosenbluth, UNC's best offensive player. What happened next was not so commonplace; Rosenbluth went over and stood on the sidelines, folded his arms and watched the game; the two State players went with him. The three watched the game together for a while. I don't remember for how long. We got to talk to a tall lanky fellow who sat near us. We asked Bones McKinney, the Wake Forest Demon Deacons' coach, how he was going to beat Frank McGuire's team that year. Whatever he said didn't work. The Tar Heels won four games against his team: two home and home games, a game in the Dixie Classic, and the championship game of the Atlantic Coast Conference Tournament. The Heels defeated State that night, 86-57. What a trip for a 13 year-old boy!

Just the name *Dixie Classic* brings back fond memories of the greatest holiday tournament of them all. I was fortunate to attend some of the Classic games in the 1950s. During the heyday of the tournament, the big four (Duke, North Carolina, State, and Wake Forest) hosted four out-of-state teams – many of them nationally ranked. No "outside" team ever won the trophy. From her home base in Greenville, Bethany Bradsher authored the book to read: *The Classic: How Everett Case and His Tournament Brought Big-Time Basketball to the South*. It is one of those books that I couldn't put down. Bradsher covers each separate tournament in all of its glory and, at the same time, chronicles two evils of the era. One was the racism that the invitees faced when they attempted to locate accommodations for their African American players in Raleigh. And, the other was the scandals that finally brought an end to the holiday classic.

## Class of '52 Reunion
(Graduating class = 27)

The class of '52 celebrated the 45th anniversary of its high school graduation in 1997. The booklet handed out to each attendee reminded them of the "then and now."

The classmates were born before penicillin and the polio vaccine; their favorite radio stations were confined to the AM band; and pizzas, hamburgers at McDonald's, and instant coffee were foods of the future.

In their hometown at Worthington's 5 and 10 cents store, items could actually be purchased for 5 and 10 cents. Edward's Pharmacy and the Sky Light Inn sold hot dogs and sandwiches for 10 and 15 cents.

Five cents would buy you a phone call in a real phone booth or a Pepsi-Cola or stamps for a letter with enough pennies left over for two post cards.

The price of a gallon of gasoline was 16 cents.

## From *The Wheel*, 1952

**Faculty: Faust Johnson**, Principal & Coach; **Virginia Belle Cooper**, Piano; **Sullivan Nelson**, Science; **Charles Brown**, English; **Mrs. Nora Lee Craft**, Home Economics; **Stuart Tripp**, History, Physical Education & Coach; **Heber Adams**, Mathematics; **Mrs. C.C. Little**, English; **Mrs. Rosa Little**, Public School Music; **Mrs. Carolyn Howard**, French & Librarian; **Mrs. Hannah Allen**, Commerce.

**Sr. Class Officers: Harold Spencer**, President; **Delano Cox**, Vice President; **Jo Ann Padley**, Honorary President; **Charlene Smith**, Secretary; **Juanita Garris**, Treasurer; **Sybil Lee Meeks**, Reporter; **Linwood Little**, Representative.

**Who's Who: Sybil Lee Meeks & James Jenkins**, Best Dressed; **Jo Ann Padley & John David Stocks**, Most Likely To Succeed; **Hannah Jackson & Delano Cox**, Most Popular; **Dorothy Thomas & Willis Manning**, Wittiest; **Juanita Garris & Harold Spencer**, Most Sincere; **Charlene Smith & Delano Cox**, Best Looking; **Charlene Smith & Curtis Dennis**, Most Athletic; **Hannah Jackson & Delano Cox**, Best All-Round; **Hannah Jackson & Curtis Dennis**, Cutest; **Juanita Garris & Linwood Little**, Most Dependable; **Dorothy Thomas & Norman Skinner**, Friendliest; **Louise Beddard & Curtis Dennis**, Best Sport.

**Mascots: Martha Gooding & Sidney Jolly**

## Chapter 22
### Sandlots and Little League Baseball

Just about the time Teedy was galloping along the football trail in his "new" old shoes with the jingly spurs, my first memory comes alive. I can now add those recollections to the stories of playing and living in tobacco country. I cannot guarantee that I will be able to distinguish between what actually happened to me and the stories that my family and friends have told about me; in some cases, on me. I've decided to leave out the questionable descriptions of my behavior – chiefly the ones that depict me in a somewhat dubious light – and emphasize the ones that paint the true picture of me as I really was.

I remember nothing before the age of five. My first recollection of an event was a painful one. As I walked out of my hospital room in Greenville, I felt an aching sensation in my right eye when I turned to look down the hallway. A surgeon at Pitt Memorial Hospital had performed a miracle. I could still see out of that eye. Michael Dale ('63) and I were performing an experiment with a milk bottle on the front porch of Miss Lena Dawson's brick house on Snow Hill Street across from the tennis courts. This goes back to the time when milk in glass containers was delivered to a family's home. The milkman would replace the empties with fresh milk-filled containers. *Somebody* threw one of Miss Lena's bottles against the brick wall of her house, and a tiny sliver of glass popped into my right eye. I instinctively rubbed my eye, making a tiny cut across the pupil. Obviously, our investigation went awry. Literally for decades I was absolutely sure that the empty round vessel had been thrown by Michael. One day recently I asked my two brothers,

"Who threw that bottle?" In unison, they both replied, "You did." Since my friend from so many years ago was not present at the time so that I could ask him, I guess I had to be the culprit. To be honest about all this, I'm still not convinced; I think it is a possibility that Michael was the professor directing the research and I was his assistant.

Until a memorable early morning in 1969, I hadn't seen my co-conspirator since my days at Ayden High School. During the summer of that year, my son, Paul, and I set out in a rubber raft a few miles north of Durham to navigate a short distance on the Neuse River. Night overtook us and we had to sleep near the water. Needless to say, my family was very worried. I will always be grateful to all the rescuers who rowed down the river and drudged along the riverbank during the wee hours of the morning. One of the boats picked us up, and we completed our trip. As Paul and I were walking up to the road from the rescue boat, I heard someone yell out. I'll never forget the encouraging words that were uttered. "@!! $%#*, if I'd known it was you, I never would've been out *here* all night!" Michael Wingate Dale had been one of my rescuers – reluctantly – when he realized who he had been trying to save.

For 1955, the first season of little league baseball in Ayden was deemed the town's third most important story of the year – immediately behind the inadequate sewage system (#1) and the hurricanes (#2).

The president of the Ayden Little League, Corey Stokes, called the Board of Directors' meeting to order. Stokes had taken over for Till Chauncey, the league's second president. The first president was Clay Stroud ('34). The topic of discussion was season number two – the summer of 1956.

The first year, four civic clubs had sponsored the teams: the American Legion, the Jaycees, the Lions Club, and the Rotary Club. Each of the 80 players was issued a jersey and a cap. Under the tutelage of Red Nobles and with the power hitting of William Harrington, the Jaycees had won the crown in '55. Harrington went on to have a mediocre baseball career for AHS. (The only written records available on the first season of Little League Baseball in Ayden are the 1956 accounts in *The Ayden Dispatch*. The miniscule snippets of information from the first season in 1955 were included as background information in the 1956 editions of the Ayden newspaper.)

Mayor Corey Stokes threw out the first pitch on May 29, 1956 and the "boys of summer," decked out in their spiffy new uniforms, were ready to play the first games of their 22-game schedule. The same four civic clubs from the inaugural year sponsored one team each:

**American Legion**: Sam McLawhorn, Coach
**Jaycees:** Red Nobles, Coach
**Lions Club**: Robert Benford and Charles Deal, Coaches
**Rotary Club**: Preston "Lefty" Dunn, Coach
(See player rosters for each team at end of this chapter.)

**1956 American Legion Little League Baseball Team**
Member of the team include: First row (l-r): Godfrey Little, Joe Tripp, Wayne Hart, Elmer Dail, Johnny Barfield, and Dickie Perkins. Second row: Jimmy Persinger, Garland Rouse, Emmitt Gibson, Coach Sam McLawhorn, Bob Harrington, Bobby Griffin, and William Harrington. (*Photo Contributed by William Harrington*)

The local newspaper was teeming with box scores, up-to-date standings, and other pertinent baseball statistics. Not since the 1930s Coastal Plain League had there been so much tabloid space dedicated to America's pastime. The high school diamond must have been alive with flying baseballs every night. In addition to the Little League, the Pony League and Junior League teams were also sharing the same field.

**Members of the American Legion Little League Team**
Members of the team include: First row (l-r): Lewis Tripp, Billy Stokes, Monte Little, Bud Faulkner, Cherry Stokes, Danny Cleaton, George Kite and Jim Booth. Second row: Unknown, Bill Booth, Joe Tripp, Godfrey Little, Leroy Denton, Unknown, Johnny Barfield, Jimmy McLawhorn, and Duane Gwyn. Back row: Coaches Sam McLawhorn and Kenneth Jesneck. (*Photo Courtesy of Sandra McLawhorn Reed, Date Unknown*)

**Ayden Junior League Team Sponsored by the Ayden Fire Department**
Members of the team include: Front row (l-r): Donald "Bud" Carman, Robert Cannon, Jimmy Wingate, Bob Harrington, Bob Smith, Dink Mills, Tommy Dunn, and J.D. Willoughby. Second row: David "Clem" McLawhorn, Bobby Lang, Bobby Bateman, Bobby Sanders, William Harrington, and Alvin Wingate. Third row: Coaches Gene Smith and Joel "Wimp" Wingate, Tony Blackwell, Don Braxton, Frank Merritt, and Coach Ham Lang. (*Photo Contributed by William Harrington*)

The summer of '56 was a memorable one. At a cost of $3,440, the cyclone fence was erected around the football and baseball fields. R.L. Collins reminded me that Frank Peterson and his agriculture classes were given the responsibility of erecting the new fence: "So we went out and dug holes for the posts to go in. Mr. Peterson was very particular about his tools. His tools started disappearing. People were dropping hammers and crowbars in the holes. There are tools in all of those holes."

The old tin fence, built at a cost of $2,000, had lasted for only six years. The hurricanes of the first half of the decade had taken their toll. Bill Norris ('58) remembered school officials standing over the not-so-secret entry points that had been dug out to provide an unofficial entrance into the game. Now, a person without the necessary cash could peer through the new fence. Another innovation was installed behind the bleachers by the Town of Ayden. The bill for the new water fountain and the costs to light the field nearly every night were footed by the Town.

Back to the diamond; history was being made on the pitcher's mound. Clem McLawhorn ('62) pitched the first one-hit shutout in Little League history when his team, the Lions, defeated the Rotary, 7-0. Two weeks later, Tommy Dunn ('62) almost equaled Clem's feat. He hurled a 2-hit shutout – Lions 13, Rotary 0. Another entry had to be made in the record book when Rudolph Cannon ('63) took to the mound in early August; his no-hitter topped them both. Only one Rotarian reached first base on an error; Jaycees 8, Rotary 0. The "year of the pitcher" continued in the post-season tournament. A pitching duel between Clem McLawhorn and William Edwards ('62) produced only one run. Clem's team, the Lions, eked out a 1-0 win over William's team, the Rotary. William struck out 13 batters in the losing cause.

The America Legion, the team on which I was playing, led most of the summer, but the Lions came on strong during the second half and won the regular season. The best 3 out of 5 tournament was played between the first and second place teams, the Lions and the American Legion. In the first game, Godfrey Little ('64) and I doubled in some runs, only to have my brother Joe Harrington ('64) single with the bases loaded to beat us, 7-6 in extra innings. In the "rubber" game of the series, the Lions won, 5-0, to take the tournament.

Besides the high school ballpark, where else was baseball played? The answer, just about everywhere: cow pastures, side yards, back yards – anyplace there was room for four bases. When I was talking to Tommy Edwards in Maryland by phone, he mentioned a field on which he used to play baseball. He described the field as being near Dr. Gooding's house. We normally thought of sandlot *baseball*, but those kinds of "unofficial" games also included softball, football, and "shooting hoops." Only basketball required a piece of equipment that was not portable. The gloves, bats, and balls could obviously be moved from place to place.

"So, let's find us a field and play some ball."

Tommy's brother, Kemp ('54), and several of his schoolmates played baseball on a lot at the corner of 4th Street and Montague Avenue. "We used all personally owned equipment. Often, someone would have a broken bat from a high school game. We'd tape the crack with black tire tape and it was as 'good as new' to us. If the ball seams had worn so badly that the threads were broken, we'd tape the ball, also with black tire tape." Tommy and his friends used the baseball field that he would later play on in high school. "We also used the far center field portion near the football goal posts where we sort of set up a field that faced the regular baseball field."

"Did any girls ever play?" I asked.

"It's very possible that Carole Faye Harper ('56) played some [baseball] with us, but I don't have a specific memory of it. She did play "sandlot" football with us often. Carole Faye was fast and ran without fear! You had to really put a good tackle on her to bring her down. You wanted to have her on your side," Tommy answered.

Tommy recalled playing football in "someone's large back yard area near where Joe ('58) and Kay Dunn ('58) and Wayland McGlohon ('58) used to live." Playing football at that time always meant tackle football. I doubt tag football had been invented by then. At least, Tommy, his buddies and Carole Faye didn't know about it at the time. I wonder if that back yard was actually the McGlohon's side yard. I played many football games there. So did James Hemby – at a different time and when a different family lived there. I always liked Wayland to be on my side. When I got to carry the ball, I would grab onto his belt and we'd run in unison toward the goal line. In the end zone near Park Avenue stood a tiny spruce tree, an evergreen that Mrs. McGlohon loved with a great passion. It was easy to recognize her concern when she came rushing out of her backdoor to remind us of that fact. I have no explanation for how the sapling managed to survive. It is currently taller than anything else in the neighborhood.

One final anecdote about Carole Faye. Tommy's sophomore year at the Citadel, his team upset West Virginia University in Morgantown, West Virginia. Suddenly, his former sandlot teammate, Carole Faye, "showed up out on the field to greet me before we got off the field."

I grew up around the corner from the McGlohon family. Tommy Sumrell ('61) and I used to shoot basketball on a goal behind the Dunn's house. Once we had asked and as long as we supplied the basketball, Tommy and I were granted permission to play there anytime. I'm not sure if Mr. and Mrs. Dunn realized just how many hours we'd spend in their back yard. Playing throughout the warm months of the summer was great. During the winter and especially if it had rained recently, our cold fingers would become caked with a thin layer of mud. It didn't matter; quitting time was when the sun went down and we were unable to see the basket.

I am sure that an endless number of accounts of sandlot ball could fill these pages. We are all familiar with the broken window that could occur in neighborhoods as the result of a "pick up" baseball game that got out of hand. I doubt many of those episodes made the newspaper, but at least one did. In 1936 a plot of ground between $2^{nd}$ and $3^{rd}$ streets near the railroad tracks was beautified by the Ayden Woman's Club. Apparently, the boys playing on that parcel of land were not overwhelmed by the esthetics of the property and thought that it made a nice football field. Mayor Eure instructed the police officers to end that practice. Evidently, the mayor and the Woman's Club had not discussed the matter with Tris Speaker (Major League baseball player in the 1910s and 1920s) and Eliot Ness (the organized crime fighter most famous for Al Capone's arrest.) Speaker thought that "as sandlot baseball increases in a community, its juvenile crime disappears." Ness reported that Cleveland's juvenile crime would triple if not for sandlot ball.

Ayden has had a long history of baseball. In addition to "every crossroads had a baseball team" to the sandlot ball that was played anywhere two teams could get together. I was fortunate to play on the town's first little league team. I imagine Coach Tripp had a good idea about which players would be starting at what positions when we reached high school. My teammates and I had played several summers on Ayden High School's diamond by the time we entered the ninth grade. And many friendships were begun on that field – the home of little league, junior league, and high school baseball. I wonder how many baseball and church softball games have been played on AHS's field.

### Rosters of the Four Little League Teams in 1956

The following team rosters were taken from two consecutive issues of *The Ayden Dispatch*. The names were listed under the pictures of each team; hence, they are in the order that the players appeared in the snapshots. It was not possible to reproduce all of the pictures because of their poor quality. It is conceivable that some of the players who were on the teams were left out of the actual photographs. Also, I cannot vouch for all of the spellings.

**Jaycees:** "Red" Nobles, Coach; Rudolph Cannon, Elbert Buck, Carroll McLawhorn, Bobby Sanders, Charles Dunn, Brunson Tripp, Terry Allen, Johnny Taylor, Jimmy Cavanaugh, Ronnie Craft, Leonard Gibson, Henry Wood, and Jimmy Cannon.

**Rotary:** Preston "Lefty" Dunn, Coach; Donnie Wilson, Robert Cannon, William Edwards, Rob Roy Turnage, Jackie Collins, Billy Bateman, Meryl Thompson, Wayne Smith, Terry Smith, Jimmie Carman, Mac Carmichael, Bill Booth, Don Craft, and Terry Denton.

**American Legion:** Sam McLawhorn, Coach; Jimmy Persinger, Garland Rouse, Emmitt Gibson, Bobby Griffin, William Harrington, Wayne Dail, Godfrey Little, Joe Tripp, Wayne Hart, Elmer Dail, Johnny Barfield, and Dickie Perkins.

**Lions:** Robert Benford & Charles Deal, Coaches; David "Clem" McLawhorn, Artie, McGlohon, Charles Skinner, Tommy Dunn, Michael Taylor, Dwayne Gwyn, Douglas Tyson, Monty Little, Joe Harrington, Frankie Hart, Lloyd Allen, and Randle Mozingo.

**Ayden Lions Little League Baseball Team**
Members of the team are: First row (l-r) Terry Allen, John Bulow, Lloyd Allen, Johnny Gravely, Unknown, Johnny Taylor, Dickie Schott, and Henry Wood. Second row: Coach William F. "Fred" Bulow, Billy Everette, Bobby Griffin, Mearl Thompson, Wayland Loftin, William Edwards, Elbert Buck and Coach Harry Cleaton. *(Photo Courtesy of Tony Dail, Date Unknown)*

**Ayden Jaycees Little League Team**
Members of the team are: First row (l-r): David McGlohon (batboy), Terry Smith, Tony Dail, Hall 'Buster" Miller, Ronnie Craft, Sammy Reynolds, Terry Craft and Paul Miller (batboy). Second row: Wayne Smith, Artie McGlohon, Frankie Hart, Wayne Dail, Sonny McLawhorn, Mac Carmichael, and Jimmy Cannon. Back row: Coaches Elwood 'Red' Nobles and Hall C. Miller. *(Photo Courtesy of Tony Dail, Date Unknown)*

## Other News of 1956

Ayden Clinic sustains $25,000 worth of damage in fire; to be housed temporarily in the American Legion Hut.

Ayden High School graduation class = 35.

Mr. L.G. Baldree's City Barber Shop is now air conditioned for your comfort.

Ayden's sewer system condemned by the state.

Stevenson carries North Carolina by narrow margin in 1956 presidential election; vote in Ayden: Stevenson = 1,238 votes and Eisenhower = 246 votes.

Ball point pens replace staff pens at the Ayden Post Office.

See Elvis Presley in *Love Me Tender* at the Myers Theater.

## Chapter 23
### Baseball: Post World War II

I couldn't wait. I parked the old car in the deck and started up the hill. Walking too fast was a no-no; the "trick" knee that I injured in football practice before the first football game of my sophomore year might "go out" on me. Then, somebody would have to pick me up off the sidewalk. I slowed down. For the first time, Momma and Daddy's names would be on the wall outside the entrance to The Bosh, the renovated baseball stadium on the campus of the University of North Carolina in Chapel Hill.

Retirement in early 2008 meant several things to me. Mainly, I wanted to do "what I wanted to do." Right in the middle of all those desires was having season tickets to Carolina baseball. While Boshamer Stadium was being redone, fans had had to travel to Cary for the season. Yes, I wanted to see the new place, but more than that I wanted to find the inscription

I was surprised when I answered the phone and the voice asked me to verify the lettering. Yes, that's right: *Bill and Retha Harrington*. I wanted my parents' names close to the place where I'd be spending lots of time. Momma was not the biggest sports fan. She sometimes sat in the living room with her husband and her boys because she wanted to "participate" in something that her family enjoyed so much. That is, when we were glued to some sports event on television.

More than anything, I wanted Daddy's name to be close to Carolina's "new" baseball field. Maybe he could take some time out from watching spring practice near the Pearly Gates. Collegiate baseball started in

February, and I'm sure the season up there doesn't start until the first pitch of the major league baseball season. What I'm trying to say is, "Heaven wouldn't be Heaven for Daddy if there was no baseball." I wanted him close to me as I enjoyed my retirement. Sometimes I think he's there sitting next to me, cheering the Tar Heels on and whispering in Coach Fox's ear: "It's the right time. Lay down a bunt. That's the right way to play baseball." There was only one way to play the game, he always said and, that was "the right way."

Daddy really did sit with me in that stadium once. You should have heard my father-in-law and Daddy comparing the "good old days" with modern-day college baseball. "Why, if I'd had a glove like that, I'd never made an error." I knew I'd hear something about the aluminum bats, and it wasn't long before one of them exclaimed, "Listen to them bats. Don't sound right." Metal bats were not the right way to play baseball.

Finding the engraving was not as easy as I thought. Took me a while, but I finally spotted "Bill and Retha Harrington" right where I was told it would be. I just stood there for a few moments with tears in my eyes. Finally, I said to myself, "Daddy, let's go see the Tar Heels play some baseball."

Telling the narrative of Ayden High School baseball has been one of the thorniest of my pursuits. The archives are so fragmented that I've had to leave out some seasons altogether. The primary sources that have been used to write this book contain little about America's pastime, at least the local variety. Coverage in *The Ayden Dispatch* and *The Daily Reflector* varied greatly from season to season. An outstanding pitching achievement, such as a no-hitter or a series of high strikeout games, was more likely than impressive hitting to receive the printer's ink. It would be easy to be critical of the newspaper staff for their poor coverage. There simply weren't enough reporters to go around, so the staff would have relied on summaries of the various games to either be phoned in or sent in by a representative of at least one of the participating schools. If the school failed to follow through, then the individual games vanished from the radar. In basketball when games went unreported, I was able to rely on conference standings to provide me with a team's conference and approximate overall record. Not true with baseball. Entire seasons went by without a report of won-loss records.

As the years went by, the availability of sports news improved. By and large, this was true of football and basketball for Ayden High School and South Ayden High School. The accessibility of Tornado baseball facts and figures was more erratic. For instance, the coverage of AHS baseball games was more complete in the early 1950s than in the latter part of the decade.

*The Wheel* always went to press before the baseball season started. The baseball schedule was hardly ever included in the annuals. A sentence or two would sometimes be written about the prior season's team. The sparse information about AHS baseball varied from annual to annual. In the 1950s and into the early 1960s, eight to ten games were played each spring. I'm going to utilize what crumbs I've been able to find to take us from the revitalization of baseball in the mid-1940s through the early 1960s. Making it coherent will be a real challenge, so hang with me. This is going to be much like a Boeing 747 flying over Ayden dropping thousands of leaflets – with each one of them containing a piece of the AHS baseball story. Envision me running around with my bad knee and overused and sometimes malfunctioning back trying to find all of them. Get the picture?

The first sport to be resurrected after being discontinued around the start of World War II was basketball; baseball was next, and then football.

In the spring of 1946, the merchants of Ayden donated funds to two baseball teams simultaneously. Suits for the town team called the Ayden Aces were financed by 16 firms whose names were publicized in the local newspaper. Likewise, 20 firms were listed as supporting the purchase of suits for the high school team. Since both teams were identified only as "Ayden" in the available archives, separating scores and players for the two teams required some "reading between the lines." Obviously, the readers of that time would have been able to sort out such statements as "Coach F. Johnson to start on April 2 against Washington Pam-Pack." Now, it ain't so easy. Was Coach Johnson the coach of the Ayden Aces or Ayden High School? Was he the AHS coach who was going to start for the town team? Or, was he the Aces' coach who also pitched for the town team? Could he have been the coach *and* the pitcher for the high school team? Don't be too hasty with what must seem like an obvious answer to this last question. It was a different day. I do know at the time that Mr. Johnson was also the principal of Ayden High School. Whichever the case, the pitcher had a rough day on the mound; Washington won the game, 11-7.

Provided that the principal, Faust Johnson, was not doubling as the coach of the AHS team, there is no mention of a "paid" high school baseball or basketball coach during or after the war until Stuart Tripp was hired for the 1946-1947 school term. I assume that whoever was coaching those teams was volunteering his services. We know that Leslie Stocks and Till Chauncey volunteered as basketball coaches, but there's no record of a volunteer baseball coach. Additionally, no records exist of conference alignments until after World War II.

During the same week that the Rotary Club was organizing a search committee to locate Ayden High School's first post-war coach, the Tornadoes defeated Grifton 7-3 and tied New Bern 5-5. At about the same time, the Aces won a game against Selma, 8-2.

The high school baseball coverage disappeared from the local newspaper, but write-ups on the Ayden Aces' games continued: the reason; probably because the high school Tornadoes didn't have a very good year and the Aces did. Here's a summary of the recorded scores and the scarce morsels of info provided:

### 1946: Sample of Games Played by the Ayden Aces, with Scores and Game Info:

Aces 7, Washington 11

Aces 8, New Bern 2

Aces 8, Selma 2

Aces 9, Robersonville 8

Aces 8, Williamston 3

(Winning pitcher: Crack Rogerson)

Aces 6, Deep Run 5
(Players: Brice McKay, Harry Mumford, Gene McLawhon, & Dick
Paul. Team's 5th win of season)

Aces 3, La Grange 4
(First home loss)

Aces 7, La Grange 5
(Players: Dick Paul, Stuart Tripp, James Ray McLawhorn, & Crack
Rogerson)

Aces 7, Bues Creek 2
(Players: "Punk" Jones, Lefty Dunn, Crack Rogerson, Joe Sumrell,
"Wyck" White, & James Ray McLawhorn. Grand slam by "Punk" Jones)

Aces 8, Faison 2

Aces 1, Mt. Olive 0
(Team's 9th win)

Aces 9, Faison 6
(To players above add Joe Hatem. Team's 5th straight win)

Aces 4, Mt. Olive 1
("Punk" Jones' 4th straight win. Team's 11th win & 6th straight)

The surviving records do not offer us an editorial synopsis of the
Ayden Aces' season. So, we don't know how many total games they
played or what their final record was. Interestingly, Faust Johnson was
never mentioned in the game summaries as a coach or as a player. Is it
possible that the principal pitched for his high school team, after all? I
doubt it. Mr. Johnson would go on to wear many hats in his 19 years as
principal but principal, coach, and player at the same time at the same
school – more than likely not.

The 1950 baseball Tornadoes finished second in the Coastal Conference. Coach Bob Lee's Robersonville Rams won the title.

### 1949-1950: Ayden High School Baseball Season
### (6-4)

| Ayden | 5 | South Edgecombe | 3 |
|-------|-----|-----------------|-----|
| Ayden | 3 | Robersonville | 4 |
| Ayden | 13 | Grifton | 2* |
| Ayden | 2 | Vanceboro | 1 |
| Ayden | 8 | Vanceboro | 4 |
| Ayden | 2 | Farmville | 1 |
| Ayden | 0 | Robersonville | 9 |
| Ayden | 6 | South Edgecombe | 5 |
| Ayden | 6 | Grifton | 4* |
| Ayden | 0 | Farmville | 6 |

*Grifton was a non-conference opponent.

The following year's team (1951) improved its record to 8-2 and won the Coastal Conference championship over South Edgecombe (Pinetops). The fight for first place was not resolved until Ayden's final game against Farmville on the Red Devil's home field. Coach Tripp handed the ball to Darrell Worthington ('53), and the Tornadoes' ace struck out 14 batters while throwing a 2-hitter. This was Darrell's fifth victory against one defeat.

Ayden's 7 hits and the losers' 4 errors were all the Tornadoes needed for the 4-0 win. AHS's hitting leader was Randall Harrington ('53) with a 2 for 3 day. David Manning ('51) went 2-4 and was credited with a triple, the game's longest hit. The score was 2-0 going into the top of the $7^{th}$ inning. Willis Manning ('52) landed on $1^{st}$ base via an error; then, David Manning and Darrell Worthington singled to load the bases. Teedy Bullock's walk forced in a run, and Lee Webb, Farmville's hurler, flung a wild pitch to score the $2^{nd}$ run of the final inning.

The first and second place teams during the regular season were scheduled to play a best 2 out of 3 game tournament to crown the conference winner. Game #1 was played on the Pinetoppers' field. The only team to defeat the Tornadoes during the regular season did it again: South Edgecombe 5, Ayden 3. The winner's pitcher, Earl Deal, had beaten Ayden in the first game of the year by the score of 5-2. With the score tied 1-1, South Edgecombe sent 4 runners across the plate in the bottom of the 5$^{th}$ inning. The big blow was a bases-loaded triple. Another triple had scored the Pinetoppers' first run. Teedy Bullock took the loss.

Down by a game, the Tornadoes faced a must-win situation in the second game of the series played in Ayden. South Edgecombe scored one in the top of the first inning, but Ayden came back to get 4 in the bottom of the 2$^{nd}$. With the score 4-2 going into AHS's half of the 3$^{rd}$, the bottom fell out for the visitors. Ayden sent 15 men to the plate and scored 10 runs on 6 walks and 4 hits. For the game, Todd Kittrell ('53), Willis Manning, and Darrell Worthington got 2 hits apiece. Both of Darrell's hits were two-baggers. Worthington also picked up the victory with help from Teedy Bullock.

The morning following Ayden's 19-5 victory, South Edgecombe's coach made an announcement; the school forfeited the rubber game of the series. AHS was awarded the conference trophy.

The '51 team was known primarily for its pitching. Darrell Worthington finished the season with a 6-1 record. Prior to the tournament, he had fanned 72 hitters in 42 innings. Worthington allowed only 8 earned runs and pitched 3 shutouts in regular season play. Teedy Bullock was the reliever. He pitched 11 innings, gave up 6 hits, and struck out 14 men. Teedy allowed only 4 earned runs.

The hitters provided ample support for the pitching of Worthington and Bullock. Ayden's center fielder, David Manning, led the regular season attack with a .448 batting average. Randall Harrington was second with a .353 average. The two teammates each had 9 runs batted in. David also led his team in runs scored with 12. (All of these stats are for the regular season with the exception of Darrell Worthington's pitching record, which includes his victory in the tournament. No overall season records are available.)

## 1950-1951: Ayden High School Baseball Season
## (8-2)

| Ayden | 2 | South Edgecombe | 5 |
|-------|-----|-----------------|---|
| Ayden | 14 | Vanceboro | 6 |
| Ayden | 5 | Robersonville | 2 |
| Ayden | 5 | Farmville | 0 |
| Ayden | 8 | Grifton | 2 |
| Ayden | 7 | South Edgecombe | 3 |
| Ayden | 3 | Robersonville | 0 |
| Ayden | 4 | Farmville | 0 |
| (Tournament) | | | |
| Ayden | 3 | South Edgecombe | 5 |
| Ayden | 19 | South Edgecombe | 5 |

**1950-51 Ayden High School Baseball Team**
Members of the team include: First row (l-r): Norman Skinner, Hal Edwards Jr., Billy P. McLawhorn, A.T. Venters, Todd Kittrell, and Willis Earl Manning. Second row: Ham Lang, Carroll Vandiford, Jimmy Wall, Billy McGlohon, Randall Harrington, Mack Allen and Coach Stuart Tripp. *(The Wheel)*

The high caliber pitching continued during the next year. For the 1952 team, Willis Manning pitched 3 consecutive one-hitters. The defending Coastal Conference champs' schedule included a total of eight games – all conference games. The coaching staff hoped to fill the two open dates with non-conference opponents. If the Tornadoes were going to again win the trophy, they would have to do it during the regular season. There would be no post-season tournament.

Ayden had only six lettermen returning, but the returnees would form the nucleus of what potentially could be another successful year. In the first game played on AHS's field, the Tornadoes were outhit 6 to 8 by South Edgecombe. However, 9 errors by the Pinetops' team awarded the victory to the home team, 10-5.

Ayden traveled to fellow Coastal Conference foe, Vanceboro, the following week. Things didn't look good for the visitors in the first two innings; Claude Davis struck out the first five Tornadoes to face him. In the 7 inning contest, he gave up single runs in the first, fourth, and fifth inning, but AHS's pitcher, Willis Manning, was better. He pitched a one-hit shutout, and the Tornadoes came away with a 3-0 victory. Like the week before, the losers made too many errors (6) to win the contest.

The following week, Willis Manning got the call again against the Robersonville Rams, another conference team. Only a double that landed squarely on the left field chalk line in the 6$^{th}$ inning deprived Willis of a no-hitter. He again threw another one-hit complete game shutout. Randall Harrington led the hitting attack with two singles and a double; Ham Lang was 2-4, and Willis Manning and Darrell Worthington collected a double each. In all, the home team picked up 9 hits in the 6-0 victory.

As Willis Manning strode to the mound in his next start against Farmville, his teammates must have wondered what he would do for an encore. Again, Willis gave up only one hit; however, his teammates' sloppy fielding denied him his 3$^{rd}$ straight shutout. Five errors led to 3 unearned runs. The Tornado hurler did not help his cause as he walked 5 batters. The right-hander seemed to turn up the heat when it counted the most, though. In the second inning, Willis walked the first two men he faced and then struck out the side. Two bases-loaded hits spelled the difference for Ayden. Catcher Hal Edwards ('53) hit one over the right fielder's head to score three in the 3$^{rd}$ inning. In the 6$^{th}$, Randall Harrington cleared the bases again with a double to left-center field. The score: Ayden 9, Farmville 3.

Darrell Worthington, Ayden's chief pitcher during the previous season, started his 2$^{nd}$ game of the campaign, a non-conference encounter against the Bethel Indians. With a runner on first base via a single and one out, Worthington strained a muscle in his pitching arm when he struck out the 3$^{rd}$ batter in the 1$^{st}$ inning. Willis Manning came in at that point and pitched the remainder of the contest. He struck out 10 and did not give up a walk.

As it turned out, AHS won the game in the bottom of the 4$^{th}$ inning. The bases were full of Tornadoes when Willis came to bat. His inside-the-park home run traveled 400 feet into center field. The drive scored A.T. Venters ('53), W.O. Jolly ('55), and Mack Allen ('54) ahead of him. The first run of the inning was scored when Allen walked with the bases loaded, scoring Todd Kittrell. In all, 5 runs scored, and Ayden led 5-2. Manning won his 4$^{th}$ game of the year, 7-3.

In the home and home series with South Edgecombe, Ayden was defeated by the Pinetops team on their home field. The results of that game are unavailable. Halfway through the '52 campaign, Ayden and Robersonville were tied for the lead:

### 1951-1952: Coastal Conference Baseball Standings at the Halfway Mark

| | |
|---|---|
| Ayden | 4-1 |
| Robersonville | 4-1 |
| South Edgecombe | 3-2 |
| Farmville | 1-3 |
| Vanceboro | 0-5 |

Ayden traveled to Rams' country to play for the Coastal Conference lead against Robersonville. Willis Manning was on the mound again and Hal Edwards was behind the plate. These battery mates had enjoyed a good season so far. AHS's only loss had come at the hands of South Edgecombe. Could they keep it up? Willis hurled yet another great game, giving up only one run in the Tornadoes 2-1 victory. Randall Harrington was the leading hitter with a 3-4 day and scored both runs. A.T. Venters had two hits.

I remember visiting my cousin, Randall, when his family resided on Lee Street. He tied some kind of homemade ball on the end of a string and attached the other end of the string to the limb of a tree in his back yard. Randall showed me how he swung his bat and hit the ball. The blow would rap the string around and around the branch. Then, he'd unwind his pretend pitching machine and swing again. It must've worked. Randall was the first in our family to earn a college degree. He went on to receive his M.D. from Duke University and was a staff physician at the University of Alabama at Birmingham School of Medicine when he died. Every time I write his name, I wish he could be here to read these words.

Ayden arrived in Farmville riding high after taking the conference lead. Manning's 3$^{rd}$ one-hitter had been against the Red Devils. This time, the home team turned the tables; Roy Vick, the Farmville pitcher, threw a one-hitter at the league leaders for a 3-0 win.

In his next outing, Farmville's Roy Vick pitched a no-hitter against Robersonville. He struck out 12 batters in the seven innings and did not issue a walk; final score: Robersonville 2, Farmville 1. His teammates committed 7 errors behind him; thus denying him a victory.

Like the year before, the Coastal Conference regular season winner was not settled until the last day of the season. Unlike 1951, however, there would be no tournament, so the happenings on the last day would determine the league champion. South Edgecombe did Ayden a favor by defeating Robersonville, 10-3. The Tornadoes won the trophy with a 6-2 record, and the Rams finished 5-3. Farmville and South Edgecombe completed their seasons with 4-4 records. Vanceboro was 1-7. Overall, Ayden probably finished 8-2.

Very little is known about the next two years of Ayden High School baseball. One of the noted accomplishments of the '52-'53 season belongs to William Watson, ace pitcher for Belvoir-Falkland. He had not allowed an earned run for 35 innings when Watson and his team traveled to Chicod to play a conference game. Chicod broke his string in the first inning and went on to win, 7-4. In contrast, hitting made the headlines in the Robersonville-South Edgecombe game in the latter part of the season. Robersonville won the game, 22-9, and Maurice Everette led his team with a 5-5 day. He hit 3 home runs, a triple and added a single. I drew a big "0" on Ayden games during this year and could gather very little information on the following year, 1953-1954. It is difficult to explain why Ayden's print media coverage suffered such a decline during this time. Again, I believe it is because the teams were unsuccessful on the field. As the saying goes; "to the victor goes the spoils." Normally, the better teams get the most coverage. The old adage was true of local media – at least from the perspective of the sources available for my research. Even the editorial staffs of *The Wheel* adhered to this rationale when they made decisions pertaining to sports teams. It makes sense; when my favorite team is in the Super Bowl or in the playoffs or the World Series, more of my time is directed their way. "Everybody loves a winner," including sports fans.

In 1954, most of the good news was generated outside of Tornado country. Ayden did bring back a win from Robersonville, however. With two outs in the top of the $8^{th}$ inning, the Tornadoes scored twice. Ham Lang ('54) had the big hit in the deciding frame and finished 2-4 on the day. Billy Davidson ('54) went 2-3 and Bobby Harris ('55) was 2-2. Ayden was outhit by the Rams but garnered 10 walks to help their cause. The losing pitcher, Darrell Hurley, was the leading hitter for both teams. He was 4-5 and clouted a home run. The final score in the Coastal Conference contest was Ayden 11, Robersonville 9.

One of the sports stories that catches every baseball fan's eye is great pitching. Going into a contest against Ayden, Johnny Hinson had struck out 20 of 21 batters in his previous 7-inning outing against Snow Hill. This brought the Farmville lefthander's strike out total to 38 over his last two games. The visiting Tornadoes scored one run off the lefty in the first inning. The 1-0 pitching duel lasted until the top of the $5^{th}$ when Farmville scored 10 runs to ice the game away. The final score was 17-1, giving Hinson a 7-1 record. For 3 games, the Red Devil ace had an astonishing record; out of the 63 outs for the 21 innings he pitched during the 3-game stretch, he'd struck out 55. In those 3 games, only three balls were hit out of the infield.

The Ayden High Tornadoes rebounded from the previous two years' performance and won the Coastal Conference championship with an 8-1 record in 1954-1955. AHS defeated Robersonville by the score of 7-1 to win the title.

**1954-55 Ayden High School Baseball Team**
Members of the team include: First row (l-r): R.L. Collins, Horton Jolly, Bum Dennis, Lorenzo "Rink" Allen, Jim Simon and Glenn Bowen. Second row: Roy Salmon, Tommy Edwards, Leslie Stocks, Lindy Dunn, Ikey Baldree, and Dan Batemen. Third row: Cloyce "Shot" Braswell, Joe Dunn, Bobby Johnson and Coach Stuart Tripp.
*(The Wheel)*

Ayden's right fielder was Melvin Worthington ('55). The center fielder was Milton Worthington ('55). I flipped a coin and phoned Milton to set up an interview. I suggested that he and his brother could be interviewed at the same time. The moment I hung up, I realized what I'd done; it is not a good idea to interview identical twins at the same time. Luckily, there had been a mix-up in communication when I arrived at Melvin's house and I got to talk to each brother separately.

Melvin and Milton graduated from Ayden High School in 1955; they roomed together in college; both were married in 1959, and the brothers were called to the ministry. The brothers went their separate ways and pastored churches from Florida to Michigan. In 2002, they both retired and returned to the "old home place" on Golf Club Road near the Ayden Golf and Country Club.

When I asked Melvin to tell me where Milton lived, he said that would be easy. We walked toward my car together and he pointed across the road. Even with my non-existent sense of direction, it was impossible for me to get lost. I shook Melvin's hand, and he went to join his wife who was feeding a calf that had been rejected by its mother.

I unknowingly left my recorder running as I got into my car to drive to the brick house across the way. Talking out loud, I reminded myself, "this is gonna be Milton." I was continuing in my attempts to make sure I kept the twins apart. I asked Milton if he remembered a particular play or game or anything from his playing days. He immediately responded with the fond memory of the 1955 conference baseball championship.

After the '55 championship campaign, Coach Tripp had some worries about the 1955-1956 team: "We lost five of our best boys and only four lettermen will be back." Only two of the four letter winners were seniors: first baseman, Glenn Bowen, Jr. and right fielder, Lathan "Bum" Dennis. In fact, these two players were the only seniors on the team. There was good news as well; 25 boys turned out for the first practice, and the team's pitching would return. Lindy Dunn and Tommy Edwards were scheduled to divide the mound duties. Tripp's final statement to the reporter was, "We should have a fairly good defensive team, but we don't know much yet about our hitting. We lost most of our top batters last year."

The first game of the year was a Coastal Conference endeavor against Contentnea. The bats Coach Tripp was concerned about came alive as the Tornadoes won, 8-4. Lindy Dunn was the winning pitcher. Two of Ayden's nine hits were triples. Ikey Baldree topped the hitting with one of the triples and two singles. Sophomore Leslie Stocks had the other triple and added a single.

The starting lineup was as follows: Dan Bateman ('58), third base; Ikey Baldree ('57), catcher; Lindy Dunn ('57), pitcher; Tommy Edwards ('58), shortstop; Glenn Bowen, Jr. ('56), first base; Wayland McGlohon ('58), left field; Lathan "Bum" Dennis ('56), right field; Leslie Stocks ('58), center field; and Horton Jolly ('57), second base.

Ayden and Farmville were predicted to chase each other for the Coastal Conference crown. The two potential pace setters met, and the Red Devils came away with the win. Farmville routed its first three opponents: Farmville 20, Contentnea 4; Farmville 13, Ayden 2; Farmville 12, Vanceboro 3. In their fourth game, Snow Hill figured out a way to quiet Farmville's bats and won 3-2. The league leading Red Devils recovered their hitting shoes and took two more games from conference opponents: Farmville 12, Robersonville 5 and Farmville 12, Contentnea 5. These victories gave Farmville a 6-0 conference mark; 7-1 overall.

Ayden traveled to Farmville for their second meeting of the year. The Tornadoes could manage only one hit in the hour and forty-five minute contest. Coach Elbert Moye's team collected 12 hits, and their coach lauded their defensive play. The 9-0 win gave the Red Devils a 7-0 record in the Coastal Conference.

With the season winding down, the Robersonville Rams came to town to meet the Tornadoes. Lindy Dunn won his third game against three loses. In the 3-2 victory, Tommy Edwards was the difference-maker offensively with a single and a double; his two-base hit in the fourth knocked in two runs. The star at the plate for the game, however, was the Rams' pitcher, Murphy. He banged out a single, double, and a home run, accounting for his team's two runs.

In all likelihood, the Farmville Red Devils were conference champs. After Ayden's record reached 4-4, the remaining four games were cancelled. I was unable to ascertain why these games were not played. In addition, simple math gives us a 12-game schedule. I doubt those figures are correct. Ayden baseballers never played more than eight to ten games during this time period.

The archives of *The Daily Reflector* do not contain even one article on Coastal Conference baseball during the 1956-1957 school year. As I plowed through edition after edition of the newspaper, suddenly an article emerged from nowhere: "Gaylord Perry, young right hander for the Williamston Green Waves, has pitched five no-hitters this season." One of those 5 performances was a perfect game against the Ahoskie Indians. He struck out 14 of the 21 batters and didn't allow a ball to be hit out of the infield. Perry was 11-0 thus far with an ERA of 0.00. The future Hall of Famer was his team's cleanup hitter with what was termed a "well over .400 mark."

Ayden experienced two subpar years in 1958 and 1959. In the first of those two campaigns, the county teams were divided into two divisions. Ayden was in the division with Belvoir-Falkland, Farmville, and Winterville. Belvoir-Falkland won the division with a 7-0 mark. Belvoir-Falkland played the other division winner for the county championship. The results are unknown. At one point in the season, the Tornadoes were 1-4.

The '59 version of the diamond Tornadoes played an early game with Belvoir-Falkland hoping to end their opponent's eight game winning streak in conference play. In a game plagued by a total of 13 errors, Belvoir won 9-6. Donald "Bud" Carmen ('61) took the loss. Bobby Bateman ('59), George Jolly ('61), and Mack Tripp ('61) managed Ayden's three hits. Chicod finally ended Belvoir-Falkland's win streak by defeating them, 10-1. After losing its first game, Ayden's Bud Carman made sure of his team's 3rd victory by shutting out Farmville 6-0 on a two-hitter. Mack Tripp ('61) managed two hits and J.D. Willoughby ('61) scored three runs to pace the Tornadoes' attack.

The Chicod Hornets defeated Bethel in their final game of the season, 17-1. Chicod finished the season at 8-1, 7-1 in the conference. Winterville and Chicod tied for the regular season trophy with 7-1 records. On East Carolina College's field, Winterville won the tie-breaker game 9-5. Tommy Braxton was the winning pitcher. A Winterville player familiar to those of us who played on Ayden's first little league team, Wilton "Shake" McLawhorn, was the Wolves' hitting star. Shake connected on a bases-loaded triple in Winterville's 7-run fourth inning. Winterville represented Pitt County against Gatesville. The outcome of that game is unknown. The winner was to move on to the District 1 championship.

The 1959-1960 season was my junior year at Ayden High. The Belvoir-Falkland Eagles got the headlines, but the Tornadoes won the Pitt County Conference championship. The Eagles star pitcher, Ernest Lewis, threw a no-hitter at Grimesland, and his team was 2-0 in the league. After Lewis' one hitter beat Bethel 6-0, Belvoir-Falkland was 4-1 in the conference standings.

Ayden was undefeated when Belvoir-Falkland visited the Tornado's diamond. Donald "Bud" Carman ('61) got the nod against Cobby Deans. The home team was ahead by the score of 4-2 when the Eagles came to bat in their half of the 3$^{rd}$ inning. The Eagles' pitching star, Ernest Lewis, belted a 3-run homer to put his team ahead 5-4. Lewis also relieved Deans in the same inning and pitched the rest of the way. Nolan Norman ('61) came on in relief of Carman in the 3$^{rd}$ inning, and Tommy Dunn ('62) took over in the 6$^{th}$. Belvoir won the game 7-5 and left town with a 5-1 mark in the conference.

Coach Stuart Tripp flipped the ball to Tommy Dunn against Stokes-Pactolus as the season wound down. Tommy responded with a 3-hitter to lead the Tornadoes to a 9-1 win. Ayden was ahead 1-0 when Nolan Norman came to bat with the bases loaded in the home half of the 3$^{rd}$ inning. His double scored 3 runs. Gardner Faulkner ('61) and Norman had two hits apiece.

The following Friday, Ayden traveled to Winterville to face James Braxton, the Wolves tall and lanky right-hander. He was coming off of a one-hit shutout against Farmville. He struck out 12 Red Devils and issued only 2 walks in the 4-0 victory. The two teams were not having their greatest years; Winterville was 3-3 and Farmville was 3-4.

Tommy Dunn drew the pitching assignment against Winterville's ace. Tommy pitched a no-hitter, a gem that never made the Greenville newspaper. Ayden's pitcher saved his own accomplishment: "Bobby Hobgood ... he hit a line drive right back at me. I trapped the ball against the upper part of my left thigh. I caught it, although it never went in the glove. I pulled the ball out and doubled the guy at first base." Tommy's throw to me at first base resulted in a bang-bang play. We went on to win the conference crown and defeated an unknown team for what was called a district championship. Those two trophies are verified. This means that Belvoir-Falkland lost at least one game and probably finished second to us. My guess is that we were 7-1 in the conference and 9-1 overall. This team was one of Ayden's best. It's too bad that not more is known.

The archives are skinny on my senior year, 1960-1961. This is really too bad because I broke out of a five year hitting slump beginning after my Little League days. It lasted through Junior League and the first three years of high school. I am very happy that no one knows about this calamity and would appreciate it if you would keep my secret. I've seen at least a zillion baseball games in my 73 years, and I continue to wonder about players' ups and downs. I remember distinctly deciding to stop worrying about my stance, the position of my hands on the bat handle, and, most of all, to be aggressive at the plate. I'm sure Coach Tripp was astounded at my turn-around. I was too.

Donald Carman and Tommy Dunn were the pitchers in '61. Donald struck out 12 in our season's opener against Belvoir-Falkland, and Ayden won, 10-6. Tommy pitched the following week against Bethel. He gave up only 6 hits and struck out 6 batters in a complete game. He didn't have to be so particular. The Tornadoes won 24-2. I don't remember ever playing in a game that was so one-sided. The home team collected 21 hits against 3 Bethel pitchers. Donald Carman collected 4 hits: 2 singles, a double, and a homerun. William Edwards ('62) also got 4 hits: 2 singles, a double, and a triple.

In Ayden's third victory of the season, Tommy Dunn and I each collected 3 singles in route to defeating the Grimesland Panthers 12-0 on their field. Bud Carman pitched a two-hitter and struck out 12. Donald also carried a big stick that day; he delivered a bases-loaded triple. In an unusual twist, the Grimesland pitcher, Lindsay Hardee, went the distance giving up 15 hits.

The Tornadoes were riding high without a loss when the Farmville Red Devils rolled into Ayden. Donald Carman got the nod from his coach. Bobby Avery pitched for Farmville. The home team was ahead 1-0 until Donald gave up 2 runs in the top of the 6th. The Red Devils added 2 more in their half of the 7th and won the game, 4-1. In Farmville's final game of the season, the Red Devils handed James Braxton his first loss of the year when Ben Monk pitched a one-hit shutout; the score, 6-0. This was the winning team's 10th victory of the year.

Henceforth, the water gets very murky and I'll have to venture a guess, since my memory offers me no assistance. I do know that there were no playoffs that year. More than likely, Farmville won the conference with a final mark of 9-0; 10-0 overall. Since no district playoff games were held, the victory against Winterville ended the season. Ayden probably finished in second place with an 8-2 or maybe a 7-3 record.

*I have one more baseball season to cover, but my red Thunderbird has traveled a long way – over several decades and back again. I need to get it serviced. In 1961 there are numerous garages and service stations in Ayden that I can count on to do the job. I snuck my cell phone into the middle of the 20th century, so I'm gonna call PL 6-8081 to see if Hal's Gulf Service has time on short notice. This was an easy choice because my grandparents live right across Lee Street, and I'll have time to visit them while I wait. I have set my timer on the dashboard to just the right time. Granddaddy will be in his back yard picking up pecans, and Grandmamma will be frying shrimp for dinner. Oh, that's right ... I'm back home in 1961; it's supper. Either way, it'll be gooood.*

**Never Give Up: It Ain't Over 'Til the Fat Lady Sings**

## Chapter 24
## "The Dinky Mills Story" (or) *Never Give Up*, You May Still Get to Wear Gasoline-soaked Bloomers

*Here we go again – in style. It's my freshman year, 1957. Instead of walking to school as usual, we're taking my '55 Thunderbird. A bunch of students are gathered around the 6th Street entrance to the high school building. I downshift when I get to the entrance of the gym and turn sharply into a parking spot in the vacant lot across the street from my schoolmates. I wave nonchalantly as I pass by the crowd. I always wanted to do that.*

I'm not sure when Daddy took me to my first ballgame. Likewise, I do not recall if it was football or basketball. I walked along the sidelines of the football field with him and sat in the bleachers near the front door of the gym. In the 1950s, I watched many of the players who've appeared on these pages. To me, playing sports at Ayden High School was part of student life, part of growing up. I longed for the time that I could suit up. And then, all of a sudden it was 1961; my 55 classmates and I were graduating.

East Carolina College was next. During my four years of undergraduate studies, I attended many of Ayden's football games in the early to mid-1960s. I wanted to see my brothers and friends win, win, and win some more – to do what earlier teams had not been able to. I didn't have to wait long; the 1961-1962 football, basketball, and baseball teams would pull off something that no AHS team had done before. But first, let's return to a freezing night in Sea Dog territory at Beaufort High School near where many of us first swam in the ocean.

After we shift forward and revisit a few of my memories, we'll put the Thunderbird time machine in reverse and roar back to the post-war era again before I change gears for the final time and recreate the exceptional '61-'62 season.

Imagine you're walking next to me – one arm wrapped around a cheerleader on my left and the other around a cheerleader on my right – after winning the conference championship in the final regular season game of 1960. The wind had been blowing off the ocean throughout the football game; Ayden 0, Beaufort 0. Maintain that picture while you attempt to solve a riddle: How could the Tornadoes have won the trophy when Beaufort High School had been undefeated and unscored on in Coastal Conference play? I've asked that question over the years, and no one has ever answered it correctly, even after providing the following hint: By the early 60s, scoreless ties were rare but still occurred. The answer: Beaufort had tied two games, 0-0, and Ayden, while also going unbeaten, had tied only one game, 0-0.

On the field that night for Beaufort was a 150 pound sophomore, Mike Smith. Accelerate to January 28, 1986; I was working in a residential treatment facility, a program operated by the Durham County Mental Health Center. Suddenly, my world of work came to a screeching halt. The news was tragic. Just 73 seconds after launch, the Challenger Space Shuttle had broken apart. The pilot that day was Captain Michael J. Smith, United States Navy, a 1963 graduate of Beaufort High School. Captain Smith was posthumously awarded the Congressional Space Medal of Honor.

Vivid images of that game are still plastered to the inside of my skull. For one thing, I'd never had my arms around two girls at the same time before. Come to think of it, that hasn't happened since, either. I know you're wondering who the cheerleaders were. I confess; I do not know. I remember Jackie Collins ('64) blocking a punt within the shadow of Beaufort's goalposts. We still didn't score. I remember leaping up and trying to block a pass. I missed the ball, but fortunately time ran out before intermission. In any event, none of that really mattered. What mattered was walking off the field with the knowledge that we'd be going to the playoffs.

I forgot one thing in the Beaufort game; the wind was cold as hell. When you think about it, our language can be strange. Something can be cold as hell, hot as hell; a person can be mean as hell but not nice as hell. A person unfamiliar with the "vernacular of sports" would require an interpreter to read this and other sports publications. In football there's a nickel defense and a dime package. In basketball there's a fast break and a triple double. In comparison, it seems to me that the language of baseball would be the most difficult for a creature from another planet to understand. In case you run across a friendly extraterrestrial, one who is planning to attend a baseball game, suggest that he or she or it listen to a rendition of *Who's on First* by Bud Abbott and Lou Costello. The entity will probably take the next space ship home.

It's not only Martians who would have problems with understanding a TV commentator on ESPN. The language of athletics can be confounding to the unfamiliar here on earth. Maija is one of those – that is, a non-sports aficionado. I thought our marriage might be in trouble soon after our wedding day in 1992 when she asked me, "Where does the shortstop play in basketball?" Even though she remains uninformed, there are times when no one else is around that she has to listen to my ravings about a particular sports personality or a noteworthy event in a game I've just witnessed. I love her for many reasons; being a great listener is one of them. I must say, however, that talking to her about a subject that she knows so little about is trying at times. She simply does not understand the use of tricky words like offense and defense. More than once, I've had problems attempting to clarify such concepts as a zone defense versus man-to-man coverage. Explaining a triple double in basketball would take an entire semester of work. Recently, I had reason to be optimistic. While we were eating lunch, I was going on and on about a collegiate coach that I have deplored for years. I have a distinct category into which I have placed such people. Suddenly, she asked me, "Is he a son of a bitch?" She understood! And, I didn't even have to articulate the keyword. After 22 years of marriage, Maija has learned one of the most important words in my sports vocabulary. Once again, I am reminded that communication is an essential ingredient in a good marriage.

Back to my senior year. My biggest claim to fame during that season was throwing a block for Dennis Erastus Mills ('61) – springing him for a long touchdown run. Now you know why he was called "Dinky." From my right half position the quarterback faked to me on a dive play over tackle and pitched out to Dinky around right end. For some reason, I kept running downfield. Maybe I had faith that the fullback was going to break free. He did, running untouched past the hometown bleachers to paydirt. Right in front of the hometown bleachers, I threw a "hip block" that knocked the would-be tackler off his feet.

The "Dinky Mills Story" is one I've told since high school. Lately, I have been unable to tell it without having to stop periodically to hold back the tears. I'm far from the only one who's told my classmate's story when teaching and making speeches. Ikey Baldree had a long career in public school education; he spent 26 years in Grifton and 14 years at D.H. Conley High School. On occasion, a student would end up in Principal Baldree's office with a long face as a prelude to making excuses for what they could not accomplish. Mr. Baldree started off by asking them to listen as he told a story. The "bottom line" was, "Don't come in here and tell me you can't do something."

Tommy Dunn, Billy Everett ('62), and Carroll McLawhorn were the "witchweed boys" during a summer while they were in high school. (Witchweed was a parasitic plant that could destroy corn. Their job was to locate the weed so that it could be destroyed before it killed the entire field.) One morning the three "professional hunters" began their day by traveling on Highway 102. When they reached Cannon's Crossroads, they observed Dinky working out. One end of his rope was tied to a tree and the other end to an inner tube. Dinky "ran in place" for as long as possible until the contraption snatched him backwards. Then, he dried himself off and did it again. Tommy knows this story well. "I own my own company. I could call any of my employees in here [into his office] right now and they would know who Dinky Mills is."

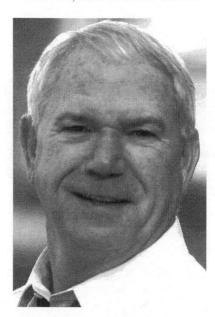

**Dink Mills**

**Dink Mills at East Carolina College and at Ayden High School**
*(Photos Courtesy of Dink Mills)*

I arrived at Dinky's home near Williamston with a big smile and a hand shake. We sat down in the den near the brick fireplace. Very soon thereafter, my host let me know that his name was Dink, now that he was an adult. I interpreted that to mean, "Now that I'm famous, it is appropriate and proper that I be addressed as Dink rather than Dinky." I tried to remember.

I was still trying to find the best place for my digital recorder when Donna walked in and let me know that her husband had provided me with the most uncomfortable chair in the room. When I explained that it was ideal for my bad back, she exited so that the two "old farts" could reminisce about the good old days.

Before I arrived at Dink and Donna's house, I thought about Coach Tripp's funeral and the remarks that Dink had made about Ayden's legendary coach – one legend telling the congregation what another legend had meant to him: "I was playing basketball near where the Myers Theater used to be when Coach Tripp and his wife drove up. They knew my situation. They gave me a pair of shoes for Christmas. Excuse me Reverend, but after that I would have run through hell with gasoline bloomers on for that man." A few months later in 2010, Dink was awarded the first Legend Award by the Community Foundation, Inc. at CFI's annual fundraiser, the Alumni Golf Tournament. Presenting the award to Dink, Mitchell Oakley repeated some of Coach Tripp's remarks. "… the hardest working young man he ever coached" and "… succeeded because of his awesome work ethic and his sheer will and determination." Mitchell went on to say that Dink Mills is "a product of what it means for a school and a community to cooperatively come together for excellence in sports and academics."

I'm not sure that Mitchell's last word – academics – pertains to Dink; at least, when he was in grades 10-12. If you set aside Dink's athletic prowess, the two of us have similar education-related backgrounds; neither high school pupil set the world ablaze academically, and we both attended East Carolina College in the fall of 1961. It was not until we actually matriculated at ECC that we "saw the light." Spring quarter of our sophomore year, Dink and I took Biology 106 together. Our teacher for Human Anatomy was Dr. Knight, one of my favorite teachers during my undergraduate work. We both made an "A" in that course. By the way, in case you desire to verify those grades, I wouldn't bother. I vaguely remember hearing that the grades for the spring quarter of 1963 for all the pupils with last names beginning with an "H" and an "M" were destroyed when the Tar River spilled over its banks in the flood of 1999. You'll just have to take our word for it.

"Dink, what did playing sports at Ayden High School mean to you?" I asked.

Dink went back even further than Coach Tripp. "Ham Lang ('54) was the first male who really showed an interest. Because of that, I started liking the attention I was getting because I was a pretty decent baseball player." Ham was Dink's coach during the first Little League season in 1955. "Even on the Little League level, you'd go uptown and people would say, 'I saw you play the other night … and they did that for everybody."

Our 8th grade teacher added another dimension to Dink's life. "LaRue Evans made me realize that I had to have some education. Once they lit the fire, I started working out. All because of the attention I was getting. It motivated me."

I was curious. I wondered if Mrs. Evans gave Dink any special attention.

"It was the way she went about teaching. It was the way she could compliment you. She had the knack of knowing whether you were understanding what she was teaching. She had a way of complimenting you even when you weren't exactly right. She would've made a helluva coach. She knew how to deal with kids and how to bring them along. I don't believe I ever heard her say anything negative to a student."

As I'm endeavoring to deposit words on this page, I am struck by the power of person to person compassion, even when the consequences of that kindness can only be hoped for. One sentence uttered at the right time, in the right place, in the right way, by the right person can have monumental aftereffects. Obviously, Mrs. Evans articulated more than one "right sentence" during a very short period of time in Dink's life. Soon, I will be viewing one of my all-time favorite movies at Christmas. In *It's a Wonderful Life*, Jimmy Stewart, as George Bailey, is visited by his guardian angel, Clarence. Having a difficult time proving to George that he is really an angel sent to help, he comes up with a brilliant idea.

All Clarence needs to do is to think about it; and, magically, George disappears from the lives of all his friends. Of course, his good deeds disappear as well. Lives are drastically changed – and not for the better. And then, magically, Clarence gives George his life back. To me, George Bailey's story is what teaching and coaching are all about. Both impart the knowledge of their respective disciplines but, most importantly, they show their players the X's and O's of life.

Even with the encouragement of many, Dink did not become a good student in high school, although, as he put it, "I was better."

Dink was not offered a scholarship. The people of Ayden, however, would not take "no" for an answer. He was encouraged to attend ECC and to go out for football as a walk-on. "I got money from some of the different clubs in Ayden and from Mr. Rowe, the banker. If it hadn't been for the clubs and him, I'd probably been in the tobacco patch."

"Who knows where Dink Mills would have been," I said. That was my way of asking Dink what would have happened without the support he received.

"Look, I know where I'd been. There's no telling. I could have gone the other way, so easy. I mean, so easy. My mom was taking care of four kids. There's no question if I hadn't had the support of the community of Ayden, I'd never made it. It's definitely an example of when the community actually made me."

N.C. State's coach, Jim Valvano, was famous for saying, "Never give up." I thought about that remark when Dink and I were talking and he said twice for emphasis, "Never give up on anybody. Never give up on anybody." I hope that there will always be room for the "late bloomer." When I returned to visit my family after departing Ayden for the beginning of my career, I would usually take my daily walk for exercise in the afternoon. On one visit, I happened to see J.D. Willoughby ('61) in his mother's yard, standing next to his Cadillac. I hadn't seen my fellow footballer and classmate in years, so we talked for quite some time. At one point, the same guy who had hung me from the tree in his Park Avenue front yard many years earlier, made reference to his membership on the Board of Education in Charlotte. At that, I burst out laughing. He wanted to know, "What in the world was so funny?" The answer was obvious to me; there stood two guys who barely made it out of high school and one of them is now advising the people of our state's largest city on how to run their education programs. Never give up on anybody.

Before I said good-bye to Dink, I had one more topic of discussion, the game at Chicod. But, I was reluctant. I told Dink that I didn't want to put anything in the book that he did not want me to. His answer gave me the green light. "My life's an open book," he said.

On a Thanksgiving morning, I was thinking about this conversation with Dink when I sat down to read the newspaper, a morning ritual for me since retirement. I tried to set aside my mental maneuverings so that I could concentrate on the news. I had ended the day before by writing the line, "Never give up on anybody," and I was thinking about how I might wrap up that part of the book. Since the beginning of time I have read the sports section first. The November 28, 2013 issue of *The News and Observer* included an insert entitled "Dean Smith: Beyond Basketball." I assumed that reading it from cover to cover would prevent me from thinking about Coach Tripp and Dink. It did the opposite, in fact; they jumped out at me over and over again. I had read all of the superlatives about Coach Smith before; surprisingly, one was new: In Coach Mike Krzyzewski's office, there's a picture of him and Dean Smith sitting next to each other at the Naismith Good Sportsmanship Awards in 2011. Both men received the award at the same time. Two bitter rivals during the game; eventual friends off the court. Since writing became a part of me on a daily basis, I've never read another author's work in the same way. I could *feel* the *N&O* journalist struggling to find the right words to express the very relationship that existed between Dink and his mentor, Coach Tripp. It's just as challenging – if not more so – for a coach's ex-players to find the words. Coach K's picture says it better than any words ever could.

Michael Jordon said, "Smith was father figure to everybody in the Carolina basketball family." Charles Scott said, "I base my life on the things Coach Smith taught me." Mike Krzyzewski said, "I love Dean. He's remarkable. Truly remarkable." When Coach K retires, the Duke basketball family will say the same things about him. They already are.

The Chicod story. Another reason I was reluctant to bring up a basketball game during our junior year was … it ain't pretty. I thought;

the best way to approach this is to tell Dink what I remembered and see if it coincided with his memory. It did.

The quietest bus ride I ever endured – in fact, the only quiet bus ride I ever experienced – lasted the short distance from Chicod High School to Ayden. I don't remember if we won or lost. The silence arose from what had happened after the game. It's better for Dink to take over at this point: "I had a temper. I fouled out pretty quick. I sat on the bench and got madder and madder and madder. After the game, I went out and confronted the guy [one of the referees]. All I had in my mind is that he had mistreated me. And, I wanted to tell him. We actually exchanged blows. After I'd done [that] … I thought … they're not gonna let me play anything else. I had a temper. I'd fight at the drop of a hat … if I felt like somebody mistreated me."

In my version of the story, I'd told Dink that I thought that night had changed him forever.

"You're right. It changed me. I thought, you dumb hick. You have worked up and worked out and now you've screwed it all up."

Afterwards, the unthinkable happened: no official reprimand, no suspension, no nothing … like the incident had never taken place. I asked Dink, "How did you not get suspended?"

"I don't know. Evidently, the guy didn't do anything about it."

All that can be said is that, apparently, the referee did not report the fray after the game. Coach Tripp obviously knew about it. All I know is that Dink was a different person, afterwards. One tiny blip in Dink's life – at the right time, at the right place, and "handled" by the right person or persons. What if that night had never happened? Who knows.

"It changed me," Dink said.

Right here is a good place to leave Dink Mills, the coach, the teacher, and the principal; the guy who made himself a chain harness and pulled a log along a dirt road to stay in shape; the guy who moved from # 5 to #1 on the ECC Pirate depth chart; the guy who became an inspiration to those players who came after him.

Clarence Stasavich was Dink's football coach at ECC. He apparently needed some guidance in "discovering" his player's potential. While scouting at an AHS football game, an Ayden fan, who did not know him, told the coach that "ECC has one of the best football players in the state, but the stupid head coach doesn't have sense enough to play him." Yet another example of a Dink Mills' supporter from Tornado country.

## Chapter 25
### Wayland's Foul Shots

The Ayden High School Tornadoes had so much to be proud of during the football season of my senior year, 1960-1961. For only the second time in school history, the team finished undefeated during the regular season. The 1950 team was undefeated and untied during the year. The 1960 Tornadoes were undefeated and once tied during the regular season.

**1960-1961: Ayden High School Football Season**
**(9-1-1)**

| Ayden | 27 | Havelock | 6 |
|---|---|---|---|
| Ayden | 39 | Snow Hill | 0 |
| Ayden | 47 | Vanceboro | 0 |
| Ayden | 25 | Robersonville | 6 |
| Ayden | 21 | Farmville | 6 |
| Ayden | 14 | Williamston | 0 |
| Ayden | 19 | LaGrange | 0 |
| Ayden | 20 | Contentnea | 0 |
| Ayden | 0 | Beaufort | 0 |
| | (State playoffs) | | |
| Ayden | 18 | Lillington | 0 |
| Ayden | 13 | James Kenan * | 19 |

*Eventual Class A State champions

**1960-61 Ayden High School football seniors.** *(The Wheel)*

**1960-61 Ayden High School football seniors.** *(The Wheel)*

The '50 and '60 teams won with overpowering defense. Through nine games, the footballers of 1950 allowed only 27 points, while the 1960 team allowed only 18 points through their nine-game regular season. The '50 team scored 27 points per game and the '60 team 24 points per game. In those two years during the regular season, no opponents scored more than one touchdown. There was no playoff series in '50, so Ayden's season ended with a 19-0 win over Elizabeth City. In '60, Ayden won the first playoff game against Lillington and then lost the second game 19-13 to James Kenan. James Kenan, the eventual state champions, managed to score more points than the ten previous teams combined.

The 1960 team proved to be a drastic turn-around from the previous two years when the records were 3-6 in 1959 and 1-7-1 in 1958. The 1957 Tornadoes fared better at 6-3. In '57, the last game of the season was canceled by Tarboro because of an outbreak of the flu. Robersonville agreed to play another game against Ayden, but the game was postponed due to inclement weather. When the two teams were finally able to play, the Tornadoes defeated the Rams for the second time that year.

As I watched from the sidelines, my freshman year turned into a basketball season to remember. The '57-'58 roundballers won their first game of the season on Robersonville's court, 57-44. The Tornadoes started four seniors and a junior: Joe Dunn ('58), Tommy Edwards ('58), Bill Norris ('58), Leslie Stocks ('58), and Bobby Gene Weathington ('59). With a 4-0 record and sporting victories over arch rivals Bethel and Farmville, Ayden traveled to Chicod and ran into Jimmy Fornes, a perennial high scorer. Fornes, a 5-9 guard, scored 40 points on 11 of 27 from the field and 18 of 19 from the foul line. The Tornadoes suffered their first loss, 65-61.

Halfway through Pitt County Conference play, Ayden, Belvoir-Falkland, and Chicod had spent time in first place. In mid-January, Ayden was in first place with a 7-2 record. The nine-team league was highly competitive.

The biggest individual story of the year continued to be the scoring of Jimmy Fornes. In a game against Grifton, Fornes set an individual conference single game scoring record with 56 points. The final score, 93-35 in favor of Chicod, also represented one of the highest team point totals in league history. At this point, Ayden continued in first place, however.

Heading into the Pitt County Conference Tournament, the final standings showed just how competitive the season had been:

## 1957-1958: Pitt County Conference Regular Season Basketball Standings

| | |
|---|---|
| Ayden | 12-2 |
| Chicod | 11-3 |
| Belvoir-Falkland | 10-6 |
| Bethel | 10-6 |
| Winterville | 9-7 |
| Stokes-Pactolus | 7-7 |
| Farmville | 5-7 |
| Grimesland | 2-12 |
| Grifton | 0-15 |

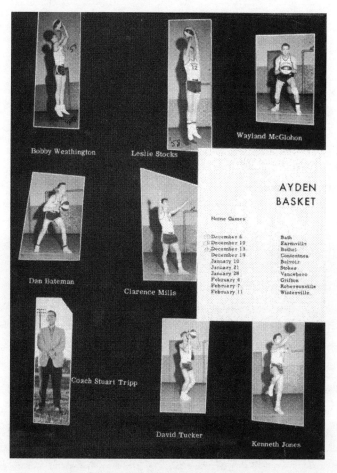

**1957-58 AHS Basketball Team** *(The Wheel)*

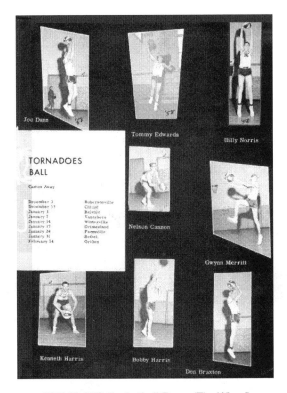

**1957-58 AHS Basketball Team** *(The Wheel)*

Ayden won the right to play in the finals with wins over Grimesland 55-31 and Winterville 56-35. The Tornadoes won the championship over Chicod, 53-46. After averaging over 30 points per game during the regular season, the Ayden five held Fornes to 16 points. But the Chicod team was not made up of just one superstar. I remember the play of Phillip Smith, who also scored 16 points in the tournament finals.

The tournament trophy provided Ayden with the right to enter the State Class A playoffs. Conference officials had corrected the internal league rules that had disqualified Ayden at the close of the previous season. (This disqualification will be discussed further in Chapter 29: '57.) Two teams from each league in the district were permitted: the regular season and the tournament winners. Since Ayden won both, Chicod, as the tournament runner-up, was invited as well.

Both Ayden and Chicod won their District 1 playoff openers. Ayden defeated Perquimans High School (Hertford) 48-34. Chicod beat Edenton 57-39. In the semifinals, the Williamston Green Wave defeated

Chicod 81-63. Gaylord Perry, who would later be voted into the Baseball Hall of Fame, scored 40 points – 26 in the first half. Jimmy Fornes finished with 25 points and Phillip Smith with 19.

The next night in the other semifinal game against Gatesville, Ayden's Wayland McGlohon ('58) stood at the foul line with no time left on the clock and the score tied. Wayland was the only sub to enter the game that night. As the time ticked off the clock in the final quarter, the Tornadoes were down by seven. Leslie Stocks hit two field goals and a foul shot, and then Tommy Edwards bucketed two field goals. With the score tied at 60, Ayden held the ball for the final shot. Edwards attempt missed the mark and McGlohon captured the rebound. He was fouled. The upperclassman I'd played football with in his side yard connected on both: Ayden 62, Gatesville 60. Ayden's scoring: Stocks 24, Edwards 21, Weathington 7, Dunn 6, Norris 2, and McGlohon 2.

The District 1 finals pitted Ayden against Williamston, the same team that had moved ahead the year before after the Tornadoes' disqualification. The underdog AHS team trailed the taller Williamston quintet for most of the game. With one minute left in the game, Bobby Weathington hit a ten-foot jumper to put his team ahead 35-33. Weathington and Dunn played catch in the backcourt as time ran out. Finally, Weathington was fouled. He hit one free throw to make the score 36-33. Perry dribbled the length of the court and hit the last shot. The Ayden Tornadoes had won their first Class A District 1 championship 36-35. All-State player, Gaylord Perry, tallied 23 points and pulled down 14 rebounds. Ayden scoring: Edwards 12, Weathington 9, Stocks 8, Dunn 6, McGlohon 1, Norris, 0. Bill Norris may not have reached the scoring column, but he pulled down a team-high eight rebounds.

In the first game of the state tournament in Southern Pines, Ayden led most of the game only to be eliminated by Allen Jay, 55-45. The victory was the Guilford County team's 27th in a row. Allen Jay lost in the semifinals to Zeb Vance 66-65. Lawrence "Cotton" Clayton, an eventual star athlete at East Carolina College, led the winners with 23 points. With a 29-1 record, Zeb Vance would play Valley Springs of Buncombe County for the Class A championship. The title was won by Valley Springs over Zeb Vance, 62-59. Swansboro defeated Allen Jay 73-61 for third place.

The '57-'58 basketball Tornadoes completed one of the best season's ever. Corralling the season's final record is a challenge. Newspaper accounts often leave out this important statistic. I will have to make a guess. The only documented record was the conference standings: 12-2. More than likely the team finished the regular season 17-2. They won three games to take the Pitt County Conference tournament and three games in the District 1 tournament. Their loss in the first round of the state tournament would have left them with a 23-3 overall record.

The basketball teams of my remaining years in high school could not match the '57-'58 accomplishments. Bobby Jean Weathington was the only starter to return from that team. The records are sketchy to be sure. The team probably finished slightly below .500. They were defeated by the Winterville Wolves by the score of 45-33 for the first time in four years and lost the first game in the Pitt County Conference Tournament to Farmville, 62-51. Bobby Gene Weathington made the 1959 All-County team.

The teams of my junior and senior years both finished 13-7. Like other years, this final record for both years may be off by one or two games. The big story of my senior year, '60-'61, belongs to Ayden's perennial arch rival, Bethel. The Indians swept through the regular season and the county tournament with a 19-0 conference mark, 27-2 overall. Bethel and Chicod represented the league in the Class A District 1 tournament. Chicod was ousted in their first game by West Bertie, 45-26. Bethel defeated Chowan 58-32 and Knapp 61-60. Bethel was defeated in the district finals by Pantego High School 65-59. The Pitt County champs finished 29-3.

*Putting the red time machine in reverse, we're gonna zoom back to the early 1950s and pick up football again. We will have to be careful with my little car; from time to time hurricanes will be lurking off the coast. Oftentimes, the monster storms skirt the coast and track north and then, if we're lucky, they make a turn to the northeast and disappear into the vastness of the Atlantic Ocean. I remember vividly one that clearly did not take the detour that Aydenites had hoped and prayed for.*

**Tornadoes Meet the Hurricanes**

# Chapter 26
Hazel

When we last lined up with the Tornado football team in 1952, Ayden had finished 4-0 in the Coastal Conference, but had lost all of its non-conference games to finish 4-5. At the end of the season, AHS discovered that an ineligible player had participated in all nine games. Robersonville was eventually crowned conference champs. For the first and only time, Ayden completed the season with a winless record.

Ayden footballers in '53-'54 and '54-'55 failed to reach .500, finishing 3-4-1 and 2-3-3, respectively. There were a few unusual twists to the '54 season. The first game against Benvenue was postponed from Friday to Monday night because of Hurricane Edna. Edna was followed by Hurricane Carol, but neither could match the ferocity of the third storm. The *big one*, Hurricane Hazel, struck the coast on October 15, 1954.

R.L. Collins played in at least two games that were adversely affected by the deluge of rain storms during that time. In the second game of the season at Vanceboro, the Tornadoes arrived to find the football field covered with grass at least one foot high and swarming with mosquitoes. Vanceboro won 13-0. I remember playing on Vanceboro's baseball field during the summer. There was only one way to tell the difference between the mosquitoes and the birds; the mosquitoes buzzed around our heads and the sparrows choose not to get so close. Illumination of the field was not a strong point of the field either. A high pop fly disappeared on the way up, so it was anyone's guess as to where it would come down.

In a 20-13 loss to Williamston on Ayden's field, R.L. recalled that it "rained so hard that the referee had to stand with his foot on the ball while we were huddling to keep the ball from floating away."

Over the years, old timers like me have referred to the October 15th storm simply as "Hazel." When someone asks, "Do you remember Hazel?" It hasn't taken much prodding for me to conjure up the angry winds that swirled around my family's house on that day. At the time, the family room, small porch, and carport had not been added. The two-bedroom cinder block house had two small dark green awnings, one over each of the front and back doors. Daddy noticed that they were flopping wildly up and down. The two of us went out and attempted to tie the fragile canopies down with a rope. Soon after our rescue efforts, the wind ripped them off. The Category 4 storm continued north through Virginia, leaving behind in North Carolina an estimated 136 million dollars in damage, 19 deaths, and 200 people injured. Fifteen thousand houses and other structures were destroyed and 39,000 structures were damaged. Football had to take a "back seat" to keeping one's family safe.

In '54, every game was decided by one touchdown or less with the exception of the loss to Vanceboro by a score of 13-0. Two games were tied 0-0, and the last game against Beaufort ended up in a 13-13 tie. In four out of the last five games, the Tornadoes scored 13 points. Two of the opponents during the season scored 13 points. Hurricane Edna to kick off the season plus all those unlucky 13s might lead one to become superstitious. The highlights of the season must have been the victories over two of Ayden's fiercest rivals: Ayden 6, Robersonville 0 and Ayden 13, Farmville 6.

The curse of hurricanes and unlucky 13s was lifted in 1955 – with the exception of a solitary play in Farmville. After the first five games, the Tornadoes were 2-2-1, but the team finished with four straight wins and completed the season at 6-2-1. Ayden lost a hard fought game on Farmville's home field by a 6-0 score. I was there to witness a play that has become part of AHS's folklore. With less than three minutes left to play and the score tied 0-0, the Red Devil's Carroll Wooten "intercepted" a pass and rambled 50 yards for the only touchdown. I remember Ayden's pass hit the ground and everybody relaxed. Wooten scooped the ball up on first bounce, but, when he heard no whistle, the defensive lineman ran for the score – a difficult way to lose a game, especially a conference game to the Tornadoes' arch rival.

After the loss at Farmville, the Tornadoes lost to Williamston 12-0 the following week before defeating Pamlico County and Contentnea. In the next to last regular season game, Ayden played a favored Tarboro team and upset them 20-19. Behind 19-14, Coach Tripps' defense recovered a fumble on their own 45 yard line. Quarterback Lindy "Leo" Dunn directed the winning drive as the clock wound down. He took turns handing off to R.L. Collins ('57) and Tommy Edwards. Dunn plunged over the goal line for the final touchdown.

Ayden defeated Beaufort 26-13 on homecoming night for its final victory. Always tough to play, Beaufort was down 26-0 when Coach Tripp cleared the bench. As so often is the case, the offensive linemen seem to get lost in the shuffle of players who get all of the newspaper ink. The backfield stars – Collins, Dunn, and Edwards – must have received superb blocking in this game; yet, the names of the "hogs" seldom appeared in *The Daily Reflector*. Possibly on the insistence of Coach Tripp, the defensive linemen standouts were often listed near the end of the article. For homecoming, Bum Dennis ('56), Sonny Smith ('56), and Burt Tripp ('57) were singled out for their stellar play on defense.

I have used three major sources of *written* documentation. In the 1950s, only the 1950, 1954, and 1956 issues of *The Ayden Dispatch* were available for review. Greenville's *Daily Reflector* has been one of the other two major written sources on Ayden High School sports. Frequently, however, the '50s journalists from Greenville and I have not agreed on what constituted informative sports reporting. If I'd had my way, every player who got into a game for the Tornadoes would have been listed. Of course, I realize that was never done in football. It is interesting to note that box scores have traditionally been completed in basketball and baseball. I guess there were simply too many football players to keep up with. Over and over again, I've used AHS's yearbooks to verify graduation dates, player names, and season statistics. Of course, *The Wheel* hasn't offered breakdowns of individual games or conference schedules.

At the end of the '55 season, the touchdown at Farmville that shouldn't have been but was must have been on the minds of the Ayden coaches at their end-of-the-year meeting in Greenville. Farmville and Robersonville tied for the Coastal Conference championship.

The 1956-1957 season proved to be one of Ayden's best. Many of the underclassmen who'd received accolades the year before were back. For the first time, the Tornadoes swept through the Coastal Conference without a blemish; the team was undefeated, untied, and unscored on in league play. The two regular season losses were to Williamston 13-7 and to Tarboro 12-6. The conference champs moved on to the playoffs and defeated Wendell in the first round, 20-0, before succumbing to Edenton 21-14. That year, the defensive efforts and line play could not be ignored. Ayden had shut out six of its ten opponents. The All-Conference team reflected the defensive prowess of the '56 team. In addition to Lindy Dunn at quarterback, the following made the all-conference team: Ikey Baldree ('57), Melvin Byrd ('57), Horton Jolly ('57), and Burt Tripp (two years). The co-captains were R.L. Collins and Lindy Dunn.

**1956-57 Ayden High School Football Team**
Members of the team include: First Row (l-r): Harold Worthington, Tommy Edwards, Horton Jolly, Burt Tripp, Ikey Baldree, and Joe Dunn. Second row: Coach Tommy Craft, Bobby Gene Weathington, Clarence Mills, and Ensley Carmichael. Third row: Herb Little, Wayland McGlohon, Kenneth Harris, Jimmy Griffin, Barry Moore, and Kay Dunn. *(The Wheel)*

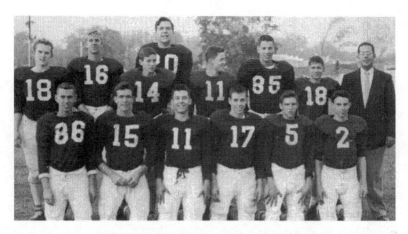

**1956-57 Ayden High School Football Team**
Members of the team include First Row (l-r): John Hart, Dan Bateman, James Willis, Les Stocks, Lindy Dunn and R.L. Collins. Second row: Roy Salmon, Sheridan Rutledge, and Coach Stuart Tripp. Third row: Ronnie Tripp, David Priddy, Bobby Bateman, Billy Vandiford, and Bill Cuthrell. *(The Wheel)*

Daddy and I attended the Edenton game. As far as I know, Coach Tripp's teams always ran for extra points. For some unidentifiable reason, I have clearly retained one of the two extra points Ayden scored. As usual, Lindy received the ball from center and stepped back; Leslie Stocks from his end position delayed a couple of counts and flared into the end zone, and the quarterback hit him with a perfectly thrown pass. The game was fun for a 13-year old to watch but sad for the players I looked up to. I remember Daddy's disappointment in the days that followed.

An important piece of this playoff game that did not make the newspapers occurred on a country road outside of Williamston. The principal, Faust Johnson, agreed to play the game on Edenton's home field when they guaranteed AHS a specific amount of money from the gate receipts and offered to provide the Tornadoes a fried chicken dinner after the game. Burt Tripp remembered the details: "We ate lunch in the cafeteria and left about 12:00. Got to the country club near Williamston and the bus gave out. We pushed the bus up and down three hills trying to get it started." The bus finally started, and it was repaired at a garage in Williamston. Finally, the team and its questionable transportation arrived at their destination a little past 7:00, less than one hour before game time. "If we hadn't had to push that bus, we'd won that game." I doubt the money and chicken dinner seemed like a very good deal after the game.

It's time for the "Brick through the Bus Window Story," a story that has survived long after the disappointing ending to the '56 year. The Tornadoes traveled to Pamlico County for the 6th game of the season. I'd already heard this story before some of the players on the team told it to me. As always, there are differences in the 60 year old tale. What I'll do is smash them all together and hope that reality will somehow come to the surface … maybe. Several common "threads" run through the various accounts. Everybody remembers the brick that was thrown through the back window of the activity bus. Nobody seems to recall what or who started the fight, but there is agreement that R.L. Collins ended it or, at least, he tried.

R.L. had a graphic memory of that night. "Pamlico County was just starting off in football and they had equipment problems. They had several players [whose] shoes must have been two or three sizes too big. The toes of their shoes were flapping as they ran. Their jerseys came down to their knees. Looked like a joke. We beat the tar out of them. They finally did score, and when he went to kick the football, the kicker missed the football and we were all in stitches … fans and players laughing. When we came out of the locker room, there was a whole bunch of people – not just players but fans – madder than hell [and] ready to whop our ass."

R.L. went on to say that he was the last one to get on the bus when someone grabbed him and tore his favorite jacket. When he did, R.L. turned around and "knocked the shit out of him and jumped on him. Coach pulled me off." R.L.'s uncle "grabbed the guy and drug him off to the side." He ended his story with "that was some night."

Ikey Baldree said that the fighting was so fierce that the door to the bus was kept shut until all the players were allowed in – one by one. "We won the game but nearly lost the fight." When R.L. and his corduroy jacket finally made it back onto the bus, "he didn't have to unzip his jacket to take it off. Someone had grabbed him and tore a strip all the way down the back of the jacket. He took the jacket off from back to front."

The Tornadoes won the game that night by the score of 27-7. The year before the score had been 33-7 in favor of AHS. The first game between Ayden and Pamlico County was during the '54 season: Pamlico County 14, Ayden 13. For the record, the two schools did not play again until the 1964 season when Ayden was victorious, 41-7. Between 1954 and 1970, a total of ten games were played between the contestants. Ayden owned the series, 8-2. In terms of fights between the two teams, I'm not sure whether to report a 1-0 or an 0-1 record – mainly because we don't know what actually happened to the poor fan that R.L.'s uncle drug off to the side.

*Time to change gears again and motor over to AHS's gym. For this stop, we'd better put the Thunderbird's top up. It's the first basketball season after World War II, and it might be cold outside. We should be able to keep warm, though. The Ayden High PTA is trying to get radiators for the school. Another thing ... the PTA is raising money to get a loud speaker for the gym. I hope they can do it.*

## Chapter 27
### Boys' Basketball: Post World War II

*The magical red car enables us to perform a small miracle; we can choose a year, travel to that time, and then we can stay awhile to gab about the goings-on. It's sort of like traveling to a drive-in movie. The two-seater Thunderbird is perfect for viewing the big screen. I remember traveling with my family through Wilson and getting excited because the outdoor movie faced the street and I was going to be able to catch a glimpse as we drove by. Pretend that we've clipped the speaker onto the window, and the picture show's about to begin. Once I've adjusted a few knobs on the dashboard, we'll be able to start the 1946 movie – to fast-forward or reverse the black and white performance whenever we want.*

Back then, we didn't use the word movies; we talked about picture shows or we said to our friends, "Let's go see the picture or let's go to the show" – much like the word television. The new box in the living room was called a television until a couple of decades later when "TV" became popular.

Before the main picture show starts, there is a short documentary about how *organized* basketball in Ayden was restarted after the war. By organized I mean a team participating in a conference or, at the least, starting the season with a pre-determined schedule. To this I would add playing in real uniforms (i.e. uniforms representing AHS) and being led by a paid coach; in essence, a team representing and sponsored by Ayden High School. Rather than a set of rigid criteria, it's safer to use these as a "jumping off place." There is some evidence that boys' and girls' basketball was played throughout the war years coached by community volunteers against some of AHS's traditional rivals. The school year of 1942-1943 may have been the only exception. The 1945 edition of *The Wheel* has this statement: "It was in this year that all extracurricular activities were left out of the school program. We put our shoulders to the wheel, to help win the war by devoting all our efforts toward doing what we could; such as, collecting paper, iron, tin cans, and buying war bonds and stamps."

That same edition of *The Wheel* from 1945 lists the seniors as having lettered for two years in boys' basketball. That means that a team played competitively in 1944 and 1945 but not the year before. Interestingly, several girls lettered in years previous to '44 and '45. So, it is conceivable that the girls played all through the war years but the boys did not.

In the winter of '44, Stuart Tripp, Ayden High's future coach, refereed AHS's first game of the season: Ayden 13, Winterville 11. This team's new uniforms had arrived complete with jackets that were purchased by Ayden merchants. The coaches were Faust Johnson and Till Chauncey. The Tornadoes went on to finish 7-10.

The following year (1945-1946) a basketball game sponsored by the AHS student body was played against Maury in January 1946. The game's outcome is unknown. We do know that it was played for a good cause; the proceeds of the contest went to the Student Activities Committee to purchase draperies for the auditorium. In addition to Maury, the opponents that year were Arthur, Belvoir, Bethel, and Stokes. Only two scores are available: Ayden 38, Arthur 22 and Stokes 29, Ayden 26. When the game against Bethel appeared in the local newspaper for an upcoming Friday night, the announcement stipulated that it was a regularly scheduled game. Here, the implication is that there was a schedule; plus, additional games that could have been arranged during the season. The overall record is unknown.

Soon after the game against Arthur, Lester Alvin Burnette appeared in person at the Princess Theater. Smiley Burnette was Gene Autry's sidekick in many, many westerns. He was Hal Edwards' guest at a Rotary Club meeting that had significance for us. The point was made that "the [high school] students now have basketball and Leslie Stocks was commemorated for coaching the boys' basketball team." I doubt that

Mr. Stocks received any enumeration for his efforts. Another statement pertained to the near future: "[the students] expect to have baseball this spring." Finally, Rand Smith said to his fellow Rotarians that he would provide a 100 dollar bill toward hiring a coach for next year. A committee was formed to begin the search.

Volume III of Ayden High School's maroon and white annual was dedicated to Miss Virginia Belle Cooper: "*The Wheel* of 1947 is lovingly dedicated to her for her outstanding kindness, interest and loyalty." Music was her thing, and teaching music was her passion.

Facing "Miss Virginia Belle" on the next page was an American flag and a memorial to those who never returned from World War II:

Leon Maurice Cannon, Navy Air Corps

Graham Coward, Army Air Corps

Jack Bright, Infantry

Edward Hatch, Infantry

Charles Hooks, U.S. Army

Prior to the war, basketball was not as successful as football. Ayden High School won 67% of its football games and had several outstanding teams on the gridiron between the inaugural season of 1926 and the last season prior to the war in 1939. It is impossible to reconstruct the annual pre-war basketball records. My best guess comes from reading everything I could find on those years on the hardwood. One outstanding year happened in 1932-1933 when the team finished 15-4-1. I'm not sure when the Tornadoes' tenacious rivalry started with Bethel. That year AHS defeated the Indians twice. The score of the first game is unknown; the second game score was 37-17. The team also defeated another rival that year: Ayden 40, Winterville 13. Because of the virtually random games covered in the local newspaper, the final records are challenging to discern. One of the best seasons on record was the 1934-1935 team that completed its season 25-8. The following year, '35-'36, the team was 10-2 at one point, but the records for the remainder of the season have been lost. It is possible that Ayden's best pre-war basketball team was the last to play before the sport was de-emphasized until after or near the end of WW II. The 1939-1940 team lost its only game to Farmville and finished 19-1.

Flipping the page to the dark-side, the Tornado team of '30-'31 finished the season, 0-19. It took five games into the next season before the team managed a win to end the 23-game drought. Outside of the exceptional years, AHS's pre-war basketball record was probably in the neighborhood of .500. Keep in mind that I do not know when basketball actually got started at AHS, so I've come to these conclusions beginning with the first recorded round ball team in the mid-twenties.

Rand Smith's $100 got the ball rolling, and Stuart Tripp was hired to coach all three sports in the fall of 1946. Coach Tripp's first basketball team completed the season with an 11-12 record. The 1947-1948 team finished 11-7. When Ayden played its 11th game of the season and lost to Bethel 50-20, I wonder if anyone thought that they had just been defeated by the eventual state champions.

On April 23, 1988, the stars of the 1948 Class B championship team gathered for their 40th reunion in the Bethel Rotary Club building. For decades, the Bethel Indians could boast of being the only Pitt County team to win a state championship in basketball. In addition to the state tournament, Bethel won two other tournaments: the Pitt County Conference Tournament and the Bethel Invitational. On the way to a 38-1 record, the Indians defeated such teams as Kinston, Needham Broughton (Raleigh), Elizabeth City and Chapel Hill. The only loss was to Morehead City. Eight teams competed in the state tournament. Bethel won their semifinal game easily against Cullowhee, 45-27. The finals were not so easy. For those unable to make the trip to Woolen Gym on the University of North Carolina's campus, an open telephone line was rigged up between Chapel Hill and Bethel. The Indians led most of the game, but Stanley tied the score with three minutes remaining. Bethel eventually won by the score of 43-39.

Ayden's 1948-1949 team completed the season 21-5, one of the best seasons on record. Strangely, *The Daily Reflector* covered none of AHS's regular season games; whereas, Ayden's newspaper covered several but not nearly all of the games. The starting five were Jimmy McCormick ('50), and Tommy Bullock ('49), at guards, Billy Jenkins ('50) at center, and Jack Harrington ('49), and Teedy Bullock at forwards. Daddy always told me when I asked that I was not related to

Jack, but I don't see how I couldn't have been. It seems to me that a Harrington is a Harrington.

**1946-47 Ayden High School Boys Basketball Team**
Members of the team (in no particular order) include: Hilliard Kinlaw and Edward Earl Cox, Gene Lang, J.W. Stocks, Frank Harrington, John C. Andrews, Tommy Bullock, L.L. Kittrell, Jimmy McCormick, Billy Jenkins, Leonard Bullock, Marvin Baldree, Bob Holland, R.H. Mason, and Jack Harrington. *(The Wheel)*

Going down the stretch, Ayden and Bethel were both 11-0 in Pitt County. In mid-February, the two teams played a best two out of three games to determine the county's representative in the State Class B playoffs. The defending state champs held Ayden to a total of four field goals and won the first game, 54-28. (AHS scored the remaining 20 points on foul shots.) The Indians won the second matchup by an almost identical score, 55-28.

Eastern District One was composed of Pitt, Bertie, Martin, and Craven counties. The Bertie County winner, Colerain, played Bethel; the Indians won 34-28. Jamesville of Martin County defeated Craven County's Vanceboro team, 35-20. Both games were played in the Farmville High School gym. Eight hundred fans showed up on Saturday in the Red Devil's gym for the district title game. Jamesville beat Bethel 32-25 to move on to the state finals.

Two local tournaments followed the state playoffs. In what I am assuming was the forerunner of the Coastal Conference, Ayden won the "Farmville Invitational Coastal Plain Basketball Tournament." In the finals of the Pitt County Tournament, Bethel won its third encounter with the Tornadoes, 56-36. Ayden's five defeats were to two teams. Besides the three loses to Bethel, Vanceboro defeated Ayden twice – 23-22 in the first game and 42-14 in the second game.

**1948-49 Ayden High School Boys Basketball Team**
**The starting lineup of this team was Co-Captain Jimmy McCormick and Tommy Bullock at guards, Billy Jenkins at center, and Jack Harrington and Co-Captain Leonard Bullock at forwards. No other players were identified.** *(The Wheel)*

To make plans for the upcoming 1949-1950 season, representatives from schools in the Coastal Athletic Conference met at the Olde Town Inn in Greenville in mid-November. Principal Faust Johnson offered Ayden High School's gym as the venue for the conference tournament to be held from February 27 through March 3. The invitation was accepted. The officials voted to utilize the North Carolina High School Athletic Association eligibility rules. This decision was important because the league had allowed eighth graders to play football and still have four years of eligibility in that sport. The reason: allowing the extra year allowed the smaller schools to field more competitive teams. The NCHSAA regulations did not allow eighth graders to play in basketball.

One of the agenda items pertained to fans sneaking into games by pretending to be players or managers. To resolve the problem, the delegates voted to provide 35 free tickets to each visiting school and to allow no admittance without a ticket. The exact price of admission was not dictated; however, the amount charged could not exceed 25 cents for students and 50 cents for adults.

For the three previous post-war years, I was able to rely on *The Wheel* to provide me with pictures and scores. The class of '50 did not publish a yearbook. The reason is somewhat of a mystery, but those I have interviewed contributed the decision to the small class size. The junior class in the '49 annual needed less than one page for its class pictures; 17 would go on to graduate in May 1950.

Ayden was joined by Farmville, Robersonville, South Edgecombe, and Vanceboro in the Coastal Conference. The Tornadoes also played in the Pitt County Conference, a ten-member confederation. With only a few games to play in the regular season in the latter league, the standings demonstrated just how tough the schedule had been, especially among the first three teams.

An end-of-the-season conference tournament followed at the termination of the regular season for each league. A third tournament, the State Class B District Tournament, was thrown into the mix. The following cart-before-the-horse chronologically will be useful in helping both of us keep up with the '49-'50 campaign; 1st event: the State Class B Tournament; the second event: the Coastal Conference Tournament; the 3rd event: the Pitt County Conference Tournament.

### 1949-1950: Pitt County Conference Regular Season Basketball Standings (partial)

| | |
|---|---|
| Farmville | 10-1 |
| Bethel | 14-2 |
| Ayden | 13-3 |
| Winterville | 11-6 |
| Grifton | 9-6 |
| Grimesland | 8-10 |
| Stokes | 5-10 |
| Chicod | 3-11 |
| Belvoir | 2-13 |
| Bell Arthur | 2-13 |

Viewing this early 1950s timeline seems odd to us today. One of the reasons for playing a conference tournament is to decide which team will represent the league in the playoffs. That reasoning obviously cannot be applied here. Based on the Pitt County standings, Farmville was invited to represent the county in the Class B District tourney, the first step in choosing the team that would go on to the state finals in Durham. Farmville was not only invited before their conference tournament started, but they were also offered the invitation before the end of the Red Devils' regular season. As the second place team, the conference rules allowed Coach Walter Latham's Bethel team to play the first place finishers a game to decide which team would represent Pitt County in the state playoffs. He decided not to make that challenge.

Some referred to this tournament as the Class B elimination tournament, the same tournament that Bethel had won in 1948. Hap Perry, the executive secretary of the state high school athletic association, announced the Class B tournament pairings. Farmville was scheduled to meet Manteo in the opening round. The Red Devil's principal, Sam Bundy, explained that the champion of this tournament would play the winner of another regional tournament to generate one of the teams for the state tournament.

In the first round of the eight-team district tournament, Ahoskie (Hertford County) defeated Hobucken, 44-29, and Vanceboro (Craven

County) beat Jamesville, 33-25. The next night in the second round, Farmville whipped Manteo, 51-32. In the evening's second contest, Colerain (Bertie County) won over Elm City, 47-32.

In the semifinals, Farmville was upset by Ahoskie by the score of 32-31, and Vanceboro defeated Colerain 48-34. The high school teams of today would seem like giants to the players of the early 50s. Vanceboro reportedly had a team that "averaged six feet," an unusually tall team for the times.

Ahoskie, described as the dark horse of the tournament, won over Vanceboro for the district tournament title. The Ahoskie five was led by their 6-3 center, Tom Umphlett, with 18 points. Ahoskie moved on to represent the district in the next round of the state playoffs.

A few days after representing Pitt County in the state elimination tournament, Farmville entered the Coastal Conference tournament. The regular season ended with the following standings.

### 1949-1950: Coastal Conference Final Basketball Standings

| | |
|---|---|
| Vanceboro | 6-1 |
| Ayden | 5-2 |
| Farmville | 5-3 |
| South Edgecombe | 1-6 |
| Robersonville | 1-6 |

Had Farmville or Vanceboro won the district championship, that team's games in the state playoffs would probably have conflicted with the upcoming Coastal Conference tournament and, for Farmville, in the Pitt County Conference tournament. In the Coastal Conference, Farmville had finished third at 5-3 behind Ayden at 5-2 and Vanceboro, the regular season winner with a 6-1 mark. Ayden was upset by last place Robersonville, 41-33. The championship game was a hard fought affair with Farmville winning the trophy, 44-41 over Robersonville.

Next stop for Ayden and Farmville was the Pitt County Conference Tournament. After Bethel ended Ayden's season 37-28 in the semifinals, Farmville and Bethel squared off in the finals. Bethel won the trophy, 31-27.

The Tornadoes' record of 20-6 would appear to anyone as a successful season. Yet, Ayden's round ball nemesis, Bethel, and another of the team's arch rivals, Farmville, had been a little better. For the '49-'50 season, AHS outscored its opponents by an average of 44.1 to 29.6. Jimmy McCormick and Teedy Bullock were voted All-Conference by Pitt County Conference officials. McCormick averaged 12.4 points per game and Bullock averaged 12 per game.

The winning ways for the Tornadoes continued in 1950-1951. Ayden returned seven lettermen: Teedy Bullock, Delano Cox ('52), Jimmy Dunn ('51), L.J. Griffin ('51), James Hemby, Troy Jackson ('51), and Mac Whitehurst. The Tornadoes were undefeated until overcome by Bethel 57-36 in their 10th game.

In the winter of 1949, a notion spawned by the Farmville Junior Chamber of Commerce turned into reality. The idea was to initiate an early basketball tournament with the proceeds going to the benefit of the Farmville athletic program. The plan was to invite teams from Pitt and the surrounding counties. The Gold Medal Tournament was an immediate success with capacity crowds numbering near 800 for each game. The Ayden Tornadoes won the first year's tournament, Farmville won the second, and Ayden again earned the title in 1951 with a win over Snow Hill in the finals. AHS's 28-21 victory in the championship game had an unusual statistic: no player from either side scored in double figures. In the regular season game that immediately followed the Gold Medal Tournament, Snow Hill avenged its loss to Ayden by winning 42-32.

Before the Coastal Conference and Pitt County tournaments were played, Ayden was invited to play Red Oak of Nash County in the State Class A playoffs. The winner was scheduled to go to the regional playoffs in Louisburg the following week. At the time, the Tornadoes were 19-2. Red Oak was victorious, 57-47.

The AHS Tornadoes then played in their second and third tournaments of the year. Ayden won the Coastal Conference Tournament by defeating Robersonville 48-45 and, in the championship game, by beating South Edgecombe 49-35. Bethel was the favorite going into the Pitt County Tournament at the East Carolina College gym. The Indians did not disappoint their fans. Walter Latham's team defeated Ayden in the finals 50-19, their fourth Pitt County tournament title in a row. Ayden finished with a record of 24-6.

Seventeen boys showed up for Ayden's first practice on a Monday night in November 1951. With one week to go before the first game of the year against Grimesland, Coach Tripp had to work fast to put together his team. Only two starters returned from the previous year; nonetheless, senior, Delano Cox, and junior, Mac Whitehurst, could form the nucleus of another formidable team. Curtis Dennis ('52), Hal Edwards, Jr. ('53), and Randall Harrington ('53), three lettermen from the previous season, would be fighting the following newcomers for playing time: Billy Holland ('53), Todd Kittrell ('53), Jamie "Ham" Lang ('54), Billy Powell McLawhorn ('53), and Darrell Worthington ('53).

The maestro of Ayden's three successive 20-win seasons did it again. Coach Tripp's Ayden team defeated Grimesland in its first game of the 1951-1952 season, 33-18. After winning the first three games, Bethel traveled to Ayden to play a Pitt County Conference game. After two of the Indians' first team players fouled out early in the fourth quarter, it appeared that the Tornadoes might win a game from its arch rival for the first time since before World War II. Bethel's subs saved the day and gave the visitors an early Christmas present, 36-34. The return match on Bethel's home court after the holiday break saw another hard fought match. Once again, it appeared that Ayden would come away with a victory after leading at halftime, 24-16. However, something happened to the Bethel five when they saw the maroon and white coming. The home team outscored the visitors 19-8 in the third quarter and won the game by the final score of 45-42.

Ayden quickly got back on the winning road and finished in first place in the Coastal Conference standings:

## 1951-1952: Coastal Conference Final Regular Season Basketball Standings

| | |
|---|---|
| Ayden | 7-1 |
| Vanceboro | 5-3 |
| Robersonville | 4-3 |
| Farmville | 2-5 |
| South Edgecombe | 1-7 |

After defeating Farmville 76-55 to earn the right to play Vanceboro for the tournament championship, Ayden was invited to play in the District Class A playoffs in Louisburg. The Ayden-Vanceboro game had to be postponed because of the conflict.

Before traveling to Louisburg to play against Rock Ridge, I need to make another statement about my kinfolk. In the 1950s, the Harringtons were related to half the people in Ayden, and we were probably related to the other half – they just didn't know it and probably would not have claimed it.

With the score tied at 37, Randall Harrington was fouled on a shot with two seconds remaining on the clock. Cousin Randall hit one out of two, and AHS advanced to the semifinals with a 38-37 victory over Rock Ridge, the number one team in Wilson County. Bethel had also been invited to the same Class A playoff venue. The Indians defeated the number two team in the Wilson County Conference: Bethel 49, Elm City 40. In the semifinals, Bethel was overpowered by Louisburg, 52-32. Ayden won its semifinals game by beating Franklinton by the score of 59-39. Randall won the scoring honors with 19 points and Whitehurst collected 16. Ayden's Curtis Dennis and Delano Cox were singled out for their defense.

Back in Pitt County, officials were trying to figure out how the Ayden-Vanceboro Coastal Conference championship game could be played. The contest had to be postponed a second time because Ayden had won two games in Louisburg. Meanwhile … Vanceboro entered the Craven County Tournament and would be busy for a week – *unless* they were eliminated early.

In the District finals, Ayden was behind at half 27 to 19. The Tornadoes fell further behind in the third quarter before rallying in the fourth. But, they couldn't catch up: Louisburg 44, Ayden 38. Whitehurst tallied 16 points, Dennis and Harrington scored 7, and Cox had 6. Delano Cox was again lauded for his defense. Hal Edwards also received accolades for his stellar defensive efforts.

With only three days to lick its wounds, Ayden returned home to participate in the Pitt County Conference Tournament at Wright Gymnasium on East Carolina College's campus. The Tornadoes easily won their first game against Stokes by the score of 64-41. Favored to win in the semifinals, Ayden almost faltered against Winterville, a team it had beaten twice during the regular season. Maybe the team was tired from its busy schedule in Louisburg or maybe it was looking ahead to the championship game with Bethel. For whatever the reasons, the Tornadoes could muster only 28 points on 21% shooting from the floor. Fortunately for the Ayden team, Winterville experienced an even more disastrous display of shooting. The Wolverines shot 13% and ended the evening with 22 points. After scoring 20 points in the previous game, Whitehurst registered four points. The night before, Harrington had failed to get into double figures, but he rediscovered his shooting touch and scored 18 points.

The tourney's largest crowd swarmed into East Carolina's gym to witness the two old rivals go at it for the third time. Bethel had won two close games from Ayden during the regular season and had completed its conference schedule undefeated. Only Delano Cox scored in double figures as the Indians won their fifth consecutive tournament title by a score of 51-42.

After Ayden was idle for over a week, the Tornadoes and Vanceboro were finally able to play in the finals of the Coastal Conference Tournament. The Ayden five were sluggish out of the locker room and managed only 9 points in the first quarter. With "Harrington and Cox paving the way," Ayden took the lead in the 2nd quarter and was never threatened thereafter: Ayden 50, Vanceboro 33. This title represented the "second consecutive championship in three years of competition in the Coastal Conference." Ayden's girls' team also defeated Vanceboro for the trophy, 60-45.

I had to go over the newspaper articles several times and draw myself a mental picture to keep the latter part of the season straight for this narrative. I'm not sure that the following quote from *The Daily Reflector* will help, but here goes: "The game [Ayden vs. Vanceboro] was originally scheduled to have been played on Friday, February 29, [1952] but was postponed in order that Ayden might participate in the district playoffs for the state championship. The mix-up was further confused when Vanceboro was host to an all-girls invitational tourney last week, while both teams played in their respective county tournaments week before last." Got it?

Ayden's final record of 22-6 marked the fourth straight year of 20 or more victories. Could Coach Tripp and "his boys" make it five?

## Chapter 28
### A First for Coach Tripp

The 1952-1953 Tornadoes finished 23-2, one of the best records in the history of the school. Five of those victories were experienced in the school's annual tournaments:

### Coastal Conference Tournament

| | |
|---|---|
| Ayden 73 | Vanceboro 48 |
| Ayden 65 | Robersonville 58 |

### Pitt County Conference Tournament

| | |
|---|---|
| Ayden 47 | Farmville 46 |
| Ayden 36 | Winterville 34 |
| Ayden 62 | Stokes 55 |

The victory over Stokes in the finals of the Pitt County Conference Tournament should have been an automatic entrée into the best two out of three with the Bethel Indians for the right to represent the county in the Class A playoffs in Ahoskie. On the contrary, Stokes played Bethel for that right. *Another mystery*. This is the same school year that Ayden finished atop the Coastal Conference standings in football only to find that the team had been inadvertently playing an ineligible player. All four league victories had to be forfeited and the team's official record was downgraded to 0-9. Could something like this have happened again in basketball? Before we comb the historical airwaves for the answer, let's recap a great season.

**1952-53 Ayden High School Boys Basketball Team**
First row (l-r) The starter five: Hal Edwards, Todd Kittrell, Co-Captain Mac Whitehurst, Co-Captain Randall Harrington, and Ham Lang. Second row: Thomas Heath, Melvin Worthington, Marshall Tripp, Robert Harris, Wilbur Jackson, Donnie Tripp, Billy Jolly, "Jaybird" Stokes, Gordon Hart and Coach Stuart Tripp. *(The Wheel)*

Four seniors anchored the staring five: Hal Edwards, Jr., Randall Harrington, Todd Kittrell, and Mac Whitehurst. Ham Lang, a junior, was the 5th starter. A sophomore, W.O. Jolly, started on occasion. The point spread was so wide in several games that many on the fourteen-player roster got to play.

Before Christmas, Ayden defeated Bethel 52-29. When I asked my former little league coach about the season, the first thing Ham told me was that the team had defeated the arch rivals and it was "Coach Tripp's first victory over Bethel." I hope the coach did something special in the next few days to commemorate the victory. The journalist for *The Daily Reflector* reported that this was Ayden's first victory over the Indians in 11 years. Once again, my numbers do not coincide with the Greenville paper's totals. The last time Ayden bested Bethel was during the 1939-1940 school year when Stuart Tripp was a player. Prior to the Christmas holidays of '39, Ayden won 18-16. This was Ayden's first game of the season and the Indians' sixth of the year. About one month later, the Tornadoes beat Bethel again, 19-15. There is no evidence that *organized* basketball was played after that season until the '44-'45 season. There were games played on AHS's gym floor, but those were more like "pick-up games" coached by volunteer coaches. I have no way of knowing if the writer was counting from the pre-war season or had some other configuration in mind. In any event, I'm sure Coach Tripp knew since I believe he played on the last team that defeated the arch rival.

After Mac Whitehurst hit the deciding basket to help Ayden defeat Winterville 45-43, Ayden was 6-0. In January 1953, the Tornadoes won the majority of their games while losing two. Narratives for the two losses are missing. The final Pitt County Conference standings had Bethel on top with a 14-2 record and Ayden in second place at 11-2. Although not verified, Bethel was probably the top seed in the Pitt County Conference Tournament. Stokes caught fire, beat Bethel, and ended up in the finals against Ayden. The 2$^{nd}$ seeded Tornadoes almost succumbed to Bethel's fate when they played 6$^{th}$ seeded Farmville. It took two foul shots in the closing seconds of the contest by Hal Edwards to win over the Red Devils by one. After beating Winterville, Ayden won the trophy by defeating Stokes in the finals. This victory should have pitted the tourney winner, Ayden, against Bethel, the regular season champs, in a best two out of three series to choose Pitt County's entrance into the state tournament; yet, Stokes was chosen to play against the Indians.

I'm afraid that I was unable to pin down the precise reason for AHS's disqualification. I spoke to members of the team and to others who usually have been able to fill in the cracks for me. Needless to say, all remembered not being able to move forward. Once I pushed the Ayden alumni for their best guesses, I was supplied with an array of possibilities – from playing in two conferences to Mr. Johnson wouldn't let us play to playing too many games in one week. I could not come up with a comprehensive set of events that led to the decision or, for that matter, who or what authority made that decision.

One story for which I take full responsibility is more rumor than fact. I remember being told over the years that a team in the '50s was disqualified because the responsible person at Ayden High School didn't send in the names of the players on time. The list of players (and a check to cover a required fee) was required for the state association to check the players' eligibility. As the story goes, there was a mix up and the names, etc. were never sent or arrived after the designated date. For whatever reason, one of Ayden's best basketball teams was unable to continue an excellent season for something that happened off-the-court, an occurrence over which the players had no control. It is safe to say that the "adults failed the kids" in some way.

After such a downer, it's time for a little humor. Truly, the following event is comical now; however, it wasn't so funny at the time.

*At the age of ten, I'm too young to drive the Thunderbird, so let's climb on our bicycles. Follow me. I want to show you around. It's 1953, probably about the time the Tornadoes were finishing up basketball and getting ready to start baseball.*

Joe, Bob and I were allowed to ride our bicycles all over town when Momma and Daddy thought we were old enough. Their instructions were always the same. "You be careful. Watch for cars."

*I could tell you the name of every family who lives on Snow Hill Street, but we're gonna be flying by too fast for me to do that.*

Passing by houses where the Sumrells, the McGlohons, the Hembys, and the Dunns lived, we turned left onto Park Avenue.

*I sure would like to have an apple. Wonder if Mrs. Phillips is at home?*

Then, I remembered the NO TRESSPASSING sign that Daddy had erected. The "Bill Harrington unwritten rule of misbehavior" learned through experience: "I don't need to tell you but once."

*Stop here. I gotta tell you what J.D. Willoughby ('61) did to me one time. See that tree.*

We were playing cowboys and Indians when he put a rope around my neck and pushed me off that limb right there. Mrs. Willoughby ran out of the house and cut me down. Saved my life, I guess. I tried to catch him, but he outran me. Later on, I couldn't catch him on the football field, either. Grandmamma Lou, Daddy's momma, lives right over there, but I guess she didn't see what happened.

*Let's stop at Mrs. Buck's store out in front of her house. I don't know about you ... I'm gonna get me an Orange Crush. We ride by Daddy's ice plant and wave to him and Earl Gay working on the platform, then head up the hill across Lee Street and by the Town Office where Granddaddy's working. Let's go see Jimmy Wingate ('63) and play in our fort in back of Grandmamma and Granddaddy's house across the railroad tracks down on 2ⁿᵈ Street. They won't mind.*

I've never known whether or not J.D.'s rope trick was on purpose. I'm really afraid to ask.

Back to the hardwood; twenty-win seasons were hard to come by – especially when teams only played a few more than 20 games in a season. The Ayden High School Tornadoes were hoping to make it six straight, but stumbled during the 1953-1954 season to finish 8-11. As in years past, the available written sources failed to embrace a team with a losing record – meaning less coverage through the local news media. Going into the sixth game of the young season in December 1953, Ayden was 0-5. The team scored its first victory of the season over Snow Hill in the next game, 47-25. Coach Tripp usually stuck with the same starting five throughout the season. This season was an anomaly. Thomas Heath, Jamie "Ham" Lang, and Elwood Stokes ('55) started every (recorded) game. Bobby Harris ('55), W.O. Jolly ('55), Burt Tripp, and Melvin Worthington ('55) also started games at times. The co-captains were Thomas Heath and Ham Lang. Teams that the Tornadoes had been beating with regularity in recent years were gaining their revenge – at least temporarily. Belvior, Chicod, Grimesland, and Robersonville recorded victories over the Tornadoes before the Pitt County Conference Tournament started in early March. Winterville eliminated Ayden in the second round.

I wish I knew what was on the minds of the Ayden Tornadoes as they took the court for the first game of the brand new season of 1954-1955. I would bet that improving on the previous season's 8-11 mark – the first losing record since '46-'47 – was given at least a thought as they went through their warm-ups. The Robersonville Rams came to town in an early December game and left disappointed. Elwood Stokes ('55) hit a shot with the clock ticking down in the 4th quarter to send his team ahead by one point. Two foul shots added to the final score of 52-49. A little later in the young season, Elwood led the scoring with 17 points against Stokes-Pactolus and Ayden won, 63-55. After this win, the Tornadoes were 2-1.

Winterville was the team to beat. Ayden's team was young; it included 3 youthful starters: a freshman, Tommy Edwards and two sophomores, Lindy Dunn and Burt Tripp – all stars on future teams. The youngsters were joined by two experienced upperclassmen: Elwood Stokes and Melvin Worthington. Bobby Harris came off the bench to lead Ayden in scoring with 17 points in a 63-37 win over Grifton.

In what must have been a much anticipated game, Winterville visited Ayden for a Pitt County Conference game in mid-January. The Tornadoes and the Wolves were deadlocked with 23 points apiece at half. Ayden went ahead by two after three quarters. The maroon and white clad boys held their neighborhood rivals to only 3 points in the final quarter to win 46-39. Bobby Harris led the team with 14 points.

Ayden was on top of the Pitt County standings by one game when the young Tornadoes traveled the three miles to take on the second place Winterville team on the Wolves home court. Winterville held the lead at half 28-19 and at the end of the 3$^{rd}$ quarter, 38-32. Ayden pulled even at the end of the 4$^{th}$ quarter to force a three-minute overtime period. Neither team could muster a rally. The Tornadoes did just enough to win, 54-52. Burt Tripp led the scoring with 17 points and Harris again came off the bench to get 11. This win in AHS's last game of the season gave them the regular season trophy. Ayden finished 10-3 in the Pitt County Conference, and Winterville completed its league schedule at 11-4.

Uncharacteristically, the Bethel Indians finished in fourth place, one game behind Stokes-Pactolus. Their record of 10-5 was respectable but did not represent their usual success in conference play. What was familiar was Bethel's continued success against the Tornadoes; two of Ayden's three conference losses were to Bethel. Even so, Ayden had every reason to be optimistic about their chances in the upcoming Pitt County Conference Tournament.

Chicod defeated Grifton for the right to play Ayden in the Farmville gym before the winner moved on to East Carolina College's court. The Tornadoes outscored Chicod in every quarter to win easily, 76-39. Next up, Bethel. The game was nip and tuck all the way; Bethel led at half but

Ayden pulled ahead by three at the end of three quarters. For the third time, Bethel defeated Ayden. This time, the final score was 55-52. Bobby Harris put on one of the best offensive performances in Ayden basketball history when he poured in 17 points in the second half. Ayden's sixth man led his team's scoring with 20 points for the game. Bethel edged Stokes-Pactolus 57-56 to add another tournament title to its trophy case.

Bobby Harris made the All-Coastal Conference team, and Melvin Worthington was named to the All-Pitt County Conference team.

The '54-'55 Tornadoes had opened the round ball season with a young team. I wonder what Coach Tripp realistically thought of his chances for a successful season. I have not been able to verify Ayden's final record, but I am reasonably sure it was 18-4. By the end of the year, the players weren't young any longer. In this case, the cliché of "wait 'til next year" that all sports fans use to dampen end-of-season disappointments was not just wishful thinking.

Mrs. Christine Tripp, Stuart Tripp's wife, loaned me her husband's 1956 annual. As I thumbed through the yearbook, I realized how many of the students I knew. I wondered where they all were and how they were doing. The Ayden businesses had been generous with their ads. Business after business brought back memories of clothing purchases, trips to the grocery store (with my mother), fountain cokes with vanilla, buying gas at unheard of prices, and wandering around the showroom gawking at the new Chevrolets at S. & E. Motor Service.

The only full-page ad was taken out by the DuPont Plant, the business that meant so much in terms of opportunities. The people of the community were not only able to procure jobs at the plant, but Ayden experienced an influx of citizens who added in incalculable ways to the town's quality of life. When the corporation brought its business to Kinston, it's probably safe to say that no one's "crystal ball" could have foretold the impact. In addition to mayor and other town officials, the "DuPonters," as I often heard them called, contributed an uncountable number of volunteer hours to sports at Ayden High School. Their sons and daughters played on teams, became cheerleaders, and eventually graduated from AHS. My two best friends in high school were

"DuPonters." I felt like a member of Ross and Happy Persinger's family. Their youngest son, Jimmy, and I were inseparable until we matriculated at different colleges. We remained the best of friends. I felt like if I didn't visit Tony Blackwell's ('61) mom and dad periodically that my life was somehow incomplete. Tony and I roomed together for a couple of years in Chapel Hill while we were both finishing up degrees and during our first jobs after college. Jimmy and his family rode in on the "DuPont train" from West Virginia, and Tony and his family moved in from Tennessee.

Time for the basketball season of 1955-1956. I amassed every copy of *The Wheel* that I could find. I naively assumed that the scores of all the basketball games would be included in every yearbook. This was the case with some years, but other annuals only included the schedules of the season. And, much to my dismay, a few of the books went to press during the basketball season and consequently no overall season records could be incorporated. The 1956 issue of *The Wheel* had one page of basketball news: "The Tornadoes, when this annual went to press, have won 10 without a defeat including a win over Bethel, 61-51. The team is young and there is but one senior, Jim Simons ('56), on the roster." Fourteen players were pictured. The co-captains were Lindy Dunn and Burt Tripp.

I caught up with R.L. Collins by phone at his home in Marietta, Georgia. One of the numerous questions I had for one of my favorite players was about a game that he'd played on Chicod High School's court. I verified the validity of the story and asked him if he was the one; R.L. said he was. Soon after the end of the football season, Coach Tripp put R.L. into the game. In five times up and down the floor, R.L. fouled out before Coach had a chance to take him out. "I fouled out. I was just so used to playing football. If somebody got in my way, I just ran over them."

After the Christmas break, Ayden was undefeated in the Coastal Conference and the Pitt County Conference. For the first time in the post-war years, the phrase "had an easy time of it" was uttered in connection with the ten point win over the Bethel Indians. With only a couple of close games on its resume, Ayden traveled to Bethel for its annual game against the Indians on their home floor. Bethel handed Ayden its first defeat of the season in convincing fashion, 80-63. This game gave Bethel the lead in the Pitt County Conference. Ayden remained undefeated in the Coastal Conference.

The Ayden five got back on the winning road with a 59-29 win over Grifton. The starting Tornado lineup had solidified by that time: Lindy Dunn, Tommy Edwards, Leslie Stocks, Burt Tripp, and Billy Vandiford. Another annual rival, Winterville, succumbed to the Tornado attack by the score of 50-37. Going into the Pitt County Conference Tournament, Ayden had only one blemish on its record, the loss at Bethel. The final conference standings had Bethel in the lead at 14-1 and Ayden in second place at 12-1. In its bracket, the Tornadoes easily dispensed with Belvoir-Falkland, 62-35, and Farmville, 53-37.

On their way to the title game, Bethel played Stokes in one of the most peculiar games I've ever witnessed. The Stokes-Pactolus boys had finished with a record of 5-9. No one in the stands expected a close game. In the 1$^{st}$ quarter, Stokes scored three points and Bethel scored four. In the 2$^{nd}$ quarter, Bethel scored three points and Stokes scored eight to lead 11-7 at half. The team that had overpowered Ayden and scored 83 points in the process had managed only seven points halfway through the game. The 3$^{rd}$ quarter wasn't quite as low scoring as the previous two, but Stokes continued to lead at the beginning of the 4$^{th}$ quarter, 24-21. It was like "a bad day at the office" for the Indians. I remember watching a particular play in which a Bethel player positioned himself perfectly for the rebound only to have it bounce over his head right into the hands of an opposing Stokes player. A team that could do no wrong against the Tornadoes could do little right versus a 5 and 9 team. You might be able to guess who the Tornado fans were pulling for – including the one writing these lines. The tide turned in the final stanza and Bethel prevailed, 32-29.

Ayden and Bethel found themselves in familiar territory – playing each other for the tournament championship. At the half with the score knotted at 22, the all-conference team was announced. Lindy Dunn, Tommy Edwards, and Burt Tripp received the honor. The game could not be settled during regulation; the score after the final buzzer was tied at 41. Ayden failed to score in the three-minute overtime and Bethel won, 44-41.

The Coastal Conference Tournament started the following week on Ayden's home court. AHS had finished regular season league play at 7-0, Farmville, Robersonville, and Vanceboro completed their seasons at 4-3, and Contentnea failed to win a game and finished at 0-4. *The Daily Reflector* reported that Farmville and Robersonville were in 2$^{rd}$ place and Vanceboro in 3$^{rd}$ place – with identical records. This could be a misprint or Vanceboro could have finished in 3$^{rd}$ place based on which teams defeated them. There is no way of sorting this out. I cannot explain the reason that Vanceboro only played four games in the conference.

Ayden's first regular season conference contest against Contentnea was one of the few close games it played all year. The Tornadoes won 53-50. In the semifinals, AHS defeated Contentnea for the third time, 58-45. In the championship game, the Tornadoes beat the Farmville Red Devils 47-25. This victory was Ayden's fourth over Farmville. The rivals were the only schools fielding teams in both the Pitt County and Coastal Conferences. So, the home and home series played each season counted in both leagues. Ayden won the two regular season games and the semifinal contests in the two conference tournaments.

There was no conference representing football in Pitt County because Ayden and Farmville were the only county schools fielding teams in that sport. The configuration of the Coastal Conference in football sometimes changed from one year to the next. The Ayden team participated in one conference in baseball, the Coastal Conference.

Ayden ended its season at 19-2. By virtue of its win in the Pitt County Conference finals, Bethel represented the league in the district playoffs in Smithfield.

*The next season, 1956-1957, the Ayden High School basketballers were so good that our Ford Motor Company time machine will spend a whole chapter there.*

# What If …

.

.

# Chapter 29
## '57

In the early summer of 1962, Stuart Tripp was cutting his lawn when Grady Elmore from *The News and Observer* arrived to interview him. Coach Tripp had just completed one of the most successful years in his 17-year coaching career – 16 at Ayden High School. Elmore must have inquired about his past teams. Coach Tripp rattled off the conference champions in football, basketball, and baseball. Next, he said, "Our best basketball team was the one that got disqualified about six years ago."

During the 1956-1957 school year, I was in the eighth grade. I remember the players more than I do particular games. Prior to my high school days, this is my most memorable team. The starters were Lindy Dunn, Tommy Edwards, Leslie Stocks, Burt Tripp, and Billy Vandiford. The co-captains were Burt and Lindy. Before one game during the season, the team made their entrance from the door next to the stage in the auditorium. Whoever was leading the Tornadoes, started dribbling the warm-up ball and I noticed something different. The normally orange-colored sphere was maroon and white. At my age, I thought that was great because I'd seen the Carolina Tar Heels warm up with their light blue and white basketball. What could be cooler than that?

Literally, while penning this chapter, I received word that Burt Tripp had passed away. One of Coach Tripp's favorite game-time sermons included rebounding. Like real estate and its emphasis on location, location, location, the three most important things in the game were rebounding, rebounding, and rebounding. Tommy Edwards remembered that "Coach Tripp would often get out on the court and demonstrate."

Tommy's description included Coach's habit of chewing on his stogie on one occasion when he was showing Burt how to block out – almost knocking his center down in the process. I believe every time Coach emphasized rebounding, he had Burt in mind. I certainly did. I have several images of the '57 team – gathered from my vantage point in the bleachers. One includes Burt using his wide body to block out his opponents just like Coach Tripp taught him to do. I can see him now stationing himself under the goal and pulling down yet another missed shot. Certain people are supposed to be with us for all time. And, in a way they are. Our heroes are part of who we are, forever.

Mitchell and I met with Burt at Bum's Restaurant loaded with questions for a star athlete who played on some of Ayden High School's best football and basketball teams. How about baseball?

"I played basketball and football and everybody wanted me to go out for baseball," Burt said. When he told us that he batted left handed, I asked him about that since I'd never seen him on the diamond.

"My grandmother and I used to chop cotton. She chopped right handed and she made me chop left handed so she could watch me."

I guess it felt more natural to hold the wooden bat like he had the hoe handle. In any event, nothing seemed to help when Coach Tripp asked each prospect to hit three pitches. On the 20th pitch from the coach, Burt finally hit one. Coach Tripp asked Burt to take a seat on the bench. That ended what may have been the shortest baseball career of all time.

When the team took the floor at home in their first game against Robersonville, only two weeks had elapsed since they'd lost to Edenton in the Class A Playoffs in football. All of the starting five had played in that game. I hope Coach Tripp gave them a week off. If so, the Tornadoes had had only about a week to prepare. Nevertheless, the Rams were defeated 56-44. In the next two games, Stokes-Pactolus and Farmville were held to single-digit scoring in each of their first two quarters of play. Moreover, Stokes-Pactolus never got into double figures in any quarter. Ayden held substantial leads going into the second half of each game, and the 2nd and 3rd stringers got into both games. In the Farmville game, 15 AHS players saw action.

**1956-57 Ayden High School Boys Basketball Team**
Starting at top row (l-r): R.L. Collins, Bill Norris, Billy Vandiford, Kenneth Jones, Tommy Edwards, Leslie Stocks, Joe Dunn, Ikey Baldree, Nelson Cannon, James Willis, Wayland McGlohon, Cloyce "Shot" Braswell, Lindy Dunn, Ronnie Tripp, Dan Bateman and Burt Tripp. *(The Wheel)*

The annual trip to play Bethel sidetracked the Tornadoes. Despite Burt Tripp's 23 points, the Indians won 61-54. The only consolation that night occurred in the preliminary game; the Ayden girls' team shellacked the Bethel girls by the score of 75-43 with Sue Sutton ('57) scoring 38 points.

Following a victory over Benvenue, the Ayden boys' team again held a team to single digits in all four quarters of play: Ayden 43, Winterville 28. This feat was impressive in view of the fact that the subs were seeing ample playing time.

Ayden picked off opponent after opponent and had only one loss when it was time to play Bethel again on the Tornadoes court. Before that, the Farmville Red Devils gave Ayden some assistance in the Pitt County Conference standings. Traveling to play Farmville on its home floor, Bethel was riding high. The defending league champions had won 26 straight in Pitt County Conference play, a streak that started during the regular season the year before. Bethel teams seemed to gain momentum as games progressed. Farmville led the entire game until near the end of the $4^{th}$ quarter. With the score 46-44 in Bethel's favor, Farmville's Norwood Wooten hit the final shot and was fouled as time ran out. He hit the foul shot and Bethel suffered its first loss, 47-46.

Coach Tripp's constant antagonist swooped into town on a Tuesday evening near the end of January 1957. Each team had one loss in conference play. Bethel led at halftime, 19-18 and at the end of the $3^{rd}$ quarter, 35-34. Ayden's starting five scored all of the points with Tripp getting 16 and Stocks scoring 14, but it wasn't quite enough. Bethel rolled out of town with a 48-46 victory.

Ayden cruised through the rest of its schedule without another loss. When the time arrived for the Pitt County Conference Tournament, Bethel was first in the standings with a 15-1 record, and Ayden was 11-2. As anticipated, Ayden had an easy time with its first and semifinal round opponents: Ayden 69, Grimesland 44 and Ayden 63, Winterville 48. It was Ayden versus the projected tournament winner, Bethel, in the finals.

The reporter for *The Daily Reflector* called Bethel the "heavy favorite." The Indians won the first quarter, 18-11. Burt Tripp went scoreless while Tommy Edwards and Billy Vandiford kept Ayden in the game. In the second quarter, Burt began rebounding and scoring points. Ronnie Tripp ('57) came off the bench to add offense. Vandiford continued to play well. At half, the score was tied at 24. The Indians pulled ahead again in the third quarter and led 34-32 going into the final stanza. Neither team could muster much offense thereafter. Bethel could manage only four points, but Ayden scored seven to win, 39-38.

In another upset that night, the Ayden girls' team came out of nowhere in the tournament to win the trophy. The Lady Tornadoes defeated Winterville 52-43. Sue Sutton scored 26 points, Carolyn Sumrell ('58) added17, and Ann Long ('57) chipped in 9. The guards (defense) were Sandra Basden ('57), Bonny Rutledge ('57), and Barbara Worthington.

The Pitt County Conference had a rule that required the regular season frontrunner to play the tournament champs – provided the two winners were different – to determine the school that would represent the league in the state playoffs. In the future, two teams from Pitt County would move on to the playoffs, but in 1957 only one team was eligible to go. The Greenville sports reporter must not have been convinced of Ayden's prowess: "... Bethel would avenge the championship loss and hand the Ayden club a harsh defeat." The game on Monday night was much like the previous Saturday's tilt; neither team could pull away from the other. Unlike the conference championship game, however, Ayden led at the half, 21-16. Almost as if Bethel had a second half script to follow, the Indians outscored the Tornadoes 13-10 and closed the gap by the end of the 3$^{rd}$ quarter: Ayden 31, Bethel 29. In defiance of the soothsayers, Ayden added to its lead in the 4$^{th}$ quarter and won 45-41. All the starters and Ronnie Tripp scored in single digits, and Tommy Edwards added ten points.

Then the trouble started.

The Tornadoes had won the battle but lost the war. Daddy remained upset about the next few days for the rest of his life. Just the mention of the controversy would bring on the same story over and over. *The Williamston Enterprise* reported the problem in its March 5$^{th}$ issue, the day after Ayden's 45-41 victory over Bethel: "The entry [into the District 1 Class A Playoffs] of Ayden raised another possibility. The state regulations do not permit more than three games in a week for any one team so that if Ayden should win its bracket down to the finals it would be compelled to forfeit the District Championship to the winner of the opposite bracket. This has happened in the State playoffs before but not in this District."

It appears from the quote in Williamston's local newspaper that the possibility of a disqualification was well known prior to the start of the tournament. Nonetheless, Ayden entered the first round game against Perquimans and won easily. Coach Tripp played a total of 15 players en route to his team's 71-45 victory.

In the semifinals, Ayden defeated Williamston and Gaylord Perry, 63-51. This 12-point spread might be the most famous 12 points in the history of AHS basketball. I've heard several close followers of Tornado country basketball reminisce about this game. All remembered two things: Gaylord Perry, the future baseball Hall of Famer, played for Williamston and "we beat them by 12 points." One of the benefits of Ayden's team in 1957 was the ability of all the starters and the 6th man, Ronnie Tripp, to score points. When one had an off-night or was guarded by a tough defender, others had the ability to take over. Ayden's victory over the Green Wave demonstrated the point. Lindy Dunn was high scorer with 21 points, Tommy Edwards scored 17, Burt Tripp 14, Billy Vandiford 5, and Leslie Stocks 4. For me, the MVP of the game would have been Billy; Ayden's 6'1" forward played Perry man-to-man and held him to nine points.

Prior to the final District 1 game against Scotland Neck, Ayden received word that it had been disqualified. Williamston was then chosen to play the winner of the other bracket and defeated Scotland Neck, 55-48. The two high scorers for Williamston were Gaylord Perry with 23 and Jimmy Rogers with 20.

Coach Tripp was interviewed and said, "The District 1 committee asked us to play off our tie at the end of the Pitt County Tournament to decide which team would represent our conference in the District 1 playoff at Williamston. Now, they disqualify us for playing that game." The committee that insisted Ayden and Bethel play on Monday for the fourth time was the same group that voted to disqualify the Tornadoes. Stuart Tripp's final statement to the reporter was, "It seems a shame to me that a team that has already been beaten would represent the District 1 in the state playoffs."

The local District 1 decision was appealed by Ayden officials to the State Committee on Class A basketball in Chapel Hill. The committee ruled that there was no basis for an appeal and the petition was denied. Coach Tripp was told that the decision was uncomplicated and straightforward: "… a simple case of not obeying the rules set up for conference play and district action." The committee members further stated that the Pitt County rules were in conflict with State rules by allowing their tournament to be played after February 23. All county tournaments leading to the district playoffs must be completed by that date. At the same time, the East Carolina College gym was not available to conference officials in time to meet the required deadline.

The resolution by the committee may have been simple for them, but it forever complicated the picture for the fans, coaches, and players who thought that "we had the best team in the state." There was reason to believe that conviction was true. Williamston eventually won the consolation game, while Mebane defeated Jonesville for the state title.

The most daunting question pertains to the viability of the conference "playoff" game. Why play a game that would eventually lead to the breaking of a high school rule? Truthfully, no one knows for sure. Innuendoes and the culpability for the decision to play the game have been hurled around since those infamous few days of the dispute. In one version, Walter Latham, Bethel's coach, got the blame. More specifically, it was rumored that he thought – prior to the final Ayden-Bethel game – he could get the pertinent rules waived so that the winner of the game could represent the district in the state tournament, provided the team won the District 1 title. The most egregious accusation was that he "juggled the books" behind the scenes and never really thought he could accomplish this; however, this account leads to an inconsistency: if Bethel had won, the Indians would have also been disqualified.

Burt Tripp's version of the story is the one that many Aydenites of that time still believe is true: "Walter Latham was on the committee with the state. Stuart [Tripp] knew if we played on Monday we'd be disqualified. Walter Latham told him, 'Don't worry, I'll cover for you.'" As a result of the controversy, Coach Tripp and Bethel's coach had a meeting with Hap Perry, a representative of the North Carolina Athletic Association. "Stuart said that Walter Latham never spoke up for us and we didn't get to go." Burt believes that if he had spoken up for us, as promised, that he and his teammates would have been able to continue in the playoffs.

Other versions of Burt's descriptions of events have been tossed around forever. One thing's for sure; it was a situation in which the "adults failed the kids." Which adults should be held responsible will always be up for grabs. The Tornado players who'd been so good would forever wonder if they could have won it all. The '57 basketball team's disqualification was the most difficult of the "near misses" to accept because the opportunity to be the best was taken away by circumstances off the court.

The '53 team had suffered a similar fate. The circumstances surrounding that year were different, but the outcome was the same: disqualification. These two groups of Tornadoes combined won 48 out of their 52 games. That's like winning nine out of every ten games. I cannot say with any certainty that these were the two best basketball teams up to this point. I wouldn't be going out on a limb too far to claim that they were the two best in the 1950s.

*The red convertible and I have one more stop. What a year! The athletes of the 1961-1962 school year are going to accomplish something that no other group of Tornados has ever achieved.*

## Chapter 30
### One

*The Wheel*, 1962: "Someday, perhaps, this will help you to remember these things. This book is an attempt to make permanent for us the many incidents of a year at Ayden High. Within the covers of this book are recorded the various aspects of high school life – life, not as it might have been, but as it actually was; sometimes happy, sometimes sad, sometimes leisurely, sometimes difficult; but always worth remembering."

My first year at East Carolina College coincided with an unforgettable year in sports at Ayden High School. I was a day student for all four years of my undergraduate work. That made it a little easier to attend games during the 1961-1962 school year. I didn't have to pack to "go home" like most of my ECC classmates. I was already there. Most of all, I wanted to see my brother Joe play. I knew every guy who played on every team. I'd played little league baseball with most of them. I called several of them friends – visiting in their homes, playing sandlot ball in their yards, and riding around in cars looking for girls on Saturday nights. The girls only came out on that one night of the weekend, so we had to be ready. Finally, it happened; four of us discovered several members of the opposite sex. Alas, we had neglected to discuss what to do next, and they insisted on being taken home.

Writing triggers insights that I do not believe could be achieved in any other way – at least for me. Looking back, I wanted my team, my school, my friends, my brother to accomplish more than we'd been able to. I longed for the Tornadoes to win every game. And they almost did.

Coach Stuart Tripp seemed to play it cool when he was asked by a reporter to say a few words about the upcoming football season. "It is hard to say just what will happen. We are thin and not in the best of shape." I think he was just "playing possum." It's true that 12 veterans had graduated, but there were 11 returnees from one of Ayden's deepest teams. He must have known that Coach Hoyt Hayes of Havelock would be reading the newspaper. Coach Tripp may have been trying to "slip up" on his first opponent. Coach Hayes wasn't buying it, however. He said, "They are strong" and then he added, "They lack the depth they had last season.

**1961-62 Ayden High School Football Team**
**Starting Offensive Unit (l-r): David "Clem" McLawhorn, Carroll McLawhorn, Robert Cannon, Joe Tripp, Wayland McGlohon, Jackie Collins, and Emmitt Gibson. Backfield: Rudolph Cannon, Tommy Dunn, William Edwards, and Joe Harrington.** *(The Wheel)*

Before there was a two-point conversion, Ayden defeated Havelock 8-0. William Edwards scored the only touchdown, and Havelock's center snapped the ball over his punter's head and out of the end zone for a safety in the fourth quarter. The lone score in the first quarter held up for the win. Among other accolades, Coach Tripp had made a name for himself as a defensive coach. His 16th AHS football team would go on to be one of his best. Havelock managed only 90 yards rushing and 15 passing. It was obvious that much work still needed to be done; the Tornadoes had over 200 yards in penalties.

Against Greene Central High School (Snow Hill), William Edwards ran the opening kickoff back for a touchdown and the 40-0 route got off to a flying start. The starting offensive unit never played in the second half, and every member of the Tornado team participated. Even so, Greene Central was held to only two first downs.

Ayden's defending Coastal Conference champions made an even more compelling statement in its third game, a 55-0 shellacking of Vanceboro. The Tornadoes scored on every possession. Ayden's "teamwork" on its first touchdown set the stage for the remainder of the contest. On the second play of the game from midfield, William Edwards raced around right end and headed for the end zone. He was caught from behind at the five yard line, but managed to lateral the ball to tackle Jackie Collins who rambled over for the score. After Collins' touchdown, numerous players got into the scoring column. Rudolph Cannon ('63), Mac Carmichael ('64), Tommy Dunn, Joe Harrington, George Kite ('65), and Clem McLawhorn crossed the goal line. The AHS coach cleared his bench again. The man who wasn't sure how his team would fare once the season began, made an uncharacteristic statement at the conclusion of the game: "You can't call this football. This game tonight and last week's against Greene Central have been nothing but scrimmages for us. Things will be tougher from here on in. When we meet Robersonville next week, it will be just like starting the season all over again."

The Ayden coach's prediction came true. The Robersonville Rams were tougher. The end result was the same: Ayden 18, Robersonville 0. Rudolph Cannon scampered for 53 yards for Ayden's first touchdown; William Edwards intercepted a pass to set up the second score; and quarterback Tommy Dunn's pass to Edwards covered 73 yards to the Rams' five yard line. Edwards scored the final touchdown.

In basketball, Bethel was *the* arch rival. In football, it was the Farmville Red Devils. Game number five was played on Farmville's turf. Threatening to score first, the home team was on Ayden's seven yard line when Clem McLawhorn broke through and sacked Dean Oglesby, the Farmville quarterback. It appeared the defense that had put up four zeroes in as many games would hold. On fourth and 14, Oglesby pitched out to Danny Dilda. Instead of running, Dilda passed to a teammate who was open in the end zone. For the first time, the '61 Tornadoes were behind.

In the 2nd quarter, Rudolph Cannon ran 30 yards for AHS's first touchdown. Edwards added the extra point. The score at half: Ayden 7, Farmville 6. In the third quarter, Edwards and Cannon took turns plunging through Farmville's line with Edwards going the final yard. Tommy Dunn passed to Emmitt Gibson ('62) for the extra point. On the first play of the fourth quarter, a 21-yard pass for a touchdown put Farmville within two points of the visitors. Ayden fumbled away an opportunity to salt away the game, and Farmville began to march downfield with less than four minutes remaining. With time ticking away, Edwards intercepted a pass on the Red Devil's 25 yard line. Ayden earned the right to be in first place in the Coastal Conference standings: Ayden 14, Farmville 12.

In the next game, a non-conference contest versus Williamston, Ayden again fell behind after Linwood Rogerson picked off a Tommy Dunn pass and raced 70 yards for a touchdown. Rogerson enjoyed an unusual stat; he had scored all of his team's points up to that time in the season. Emmitt Gibson blocked the extra point attempt. In the second quarter, Gibson stepped up again and caught a Dunn pass to put Ayden ahead at half 7-6.

Ayden marched down the field on the first drive of the second half to put themselves ahead 13-6. Unbelievably, Rogers again intercepted a deflected pass and ran all the way to make the score 13-12. Just as unlikely, Gibson crashed through the Green Wave's defense to block his second extra point. On the ensuing kickoff, Ayden put together a sustained drive of 68 yards to make the score 20-12. A long pass by the Williamston quarterback was intercepted by Edwards as the game ended.

Ayden pitched another shutout the following week against La Grange to gain their seventh win, 13-0. The next game Ayden spoiled the Contentnea Wildcats' homecoming on a frigid night in mid-October by whipping them, 36-0. Once again, the Tornadoes defense was the story of the game. Two sophomores, Joe Harrington and Duane Gwynn, teamed up for a play that led to their team's first touchdown. Gwynn partially blocked the home team's first punt on the 25 yard line and Joe scooped it up and returned it to the 20.

Ayden picked up its second safety of the season when a Contentnea player tried to run an Edwards' punt out of his own end zone. AHS intercepted three passes: Edwards picked off two and Clem McLawhorn ran 70 yards for a touchdown with another. Harrington was the leading ground gainer for the Tornadoes.

The Beaufort Seadogs arrived in town hoping to spoil Ayden High School's homecoming. By that time, Beaufort had moved to double A. Scoreless until the second quarter, Joe Harrington received a handoff from Tommy Dunn and ran 65 yards to the visitor's 25 yard line. On second down, Dunn hit Emmitt Gibson with a pass for Ayden's only touchdown of the night. On Beaufort's first drive of the second half, tailback Ray Hassell took a double reverse and scampered for 38 yards to Ayden's 31. On the next play, Clem McLawhorn recovered a fumble to thwart the drive. The two defenses stymied the offenses in the second half until Ray Hassell picked up three straight first downs. From the three yard line, the Seadogs were unable to get off another play before time ran out.

Homecoming was a success and the Tornadoes were 9-0. Cannon, Edwards, and Harrington were singled out on offense and Carroll McLawhorn and Clem McLawhorn on defense. As usual, the journalist chose only a handful of players to honor for the game. I'd like to add everybody else. The Ayden team had kept a perennial powerhouse out of the end zone.

Ayden defeated Bath 19-6 in the final game. For the second consecutive year, the Tornadoes were undefeated during the regular season, the only blemish the 0-0 tie with Beaufort in 1960. This was a first at Ayden High School. Early in September, Coach Tripp was concerned about the struggle his players might encounter, "Cars and girls will give a great deal of competition." I'm not sure what happened with the girls and cars off the field, but on the field the Tornadoes were 10-0 and headed to the playoffs.

The single A playoffs started against the Camp Lejeune Devil Dogs, winners of the Waterway Conference with a 9-0 mark. Playing in Kinston at Grainger Memorial Stadium, Ayden found itself up against one of its strongest opponents. The Tornadoes scored first and took a 6-0 lead. Camp Lejeune then scored on a sustained 63 yard drive. The extra point put the Devil Dogs ahead, 7-6. The two teams traded touchdowns. At the half, Ayden's opponents held the lead, 14-12. Peering back after all of these years, the two clubs appeared evenly matched. Camp Lejeune's four turnovers spelled doom for the losers. Their second fumble led to the winning touchdown. Running behind the blocking of Edwards, Harrington scored the winning touchdown: Ayden 19, Camp Lejeune 14.

Next, Ayden faced Rohanen High School of Rockingham for the Eastern Single A title. Like Ayden, Rohanen had squeaked past its first playoff opponent; Mount Olive was defeated 20-13. Rohanen scored in the final minute of the first half and held on to win, 7-0. An overused football phrase fits the game summary from the Tornadoes' perspective: "We ran all up and down the field but couldn't score." Four times Ayden threatened, but the strong Rohanen defense shut the door each time. On one occasion, Ayden recovered a fumble on their opponent's 21 yard line. William Edwards carried to the one-foot line and, on the next play, Tommy Dunn's quarterback plunge was unsuccessful. On third down, William was thrown for a three yard loss. On fourth down, William's pass to Rudolph Cannon was knocked down in the end zone. This "near miss" was just that – a few inches away.

For several years to come, the year before ("60-'61) was the final year of the state playoff system in football. So, this regional championship was the last game of the season for both teams.

The individual honors for the football players on this team read like a Who's Who of eastern North Carolina football. I have not indicated the All-Conference *Honorable Mention* awards before, but for the '61-'62 team I will make an exception.

**William Edwards**, Fullback     All-Conference and All-Eastern
**Carroll McLawhorn**, Tackle     All-Conference and All-Eastern
**Rudolph Cannon**, Halfback      All-Conference and All-Eastern
                                  Honorable Mention

**Artie McGlohon**, Guard         All-Conference
**Clem McLawhorn**, End           All-Conference

**Robert Cannon**, Guard      All-Conference Honorable Mention
**Tommy Dunn**, Quarterback      All-Conference Honorable Mention
**Emmitt Gibson**, End      All-Conference Honorable Mention

*Senior Players . . .*

TOMMY DUNN
Quarterback
All-Conference Honorable Mention

*Co - Captains*

CARROLL McLAWHORN
Tackle
All-Eastern

WILLIAM EDWARDS
Fullback
All-Eastern

EMMITT GIBSON
End
All-Conference
Honorable Mention

CLEM McLAWHORN
End
All-Conference

ARTIE McGLOHON
Guard
All-Conference

ROBERT CANNON
Guard
All-Conference
Honorable Mention

**1961-62 Ayden High School senior football players.** *(The Wheel)*

My guess is that Stuart Tripp would have chosen all of the starters to receive end-of-season honors. When interviewed for the upcoming Rohanen game, Coach Tripp paid tribute to his senior linemen: "… these five have been the backbone of the team all year."

I don't know if the first basketball game of the season brought happiness or relief to Ayden's athletes. With a little over 200 students in grades 9-12, most of the boys played two sports and many participated in all three: football, basketball, and baseball. There was little time to recuperate after the maroon and white had played 12 football games. Of the 12 players on the roundball roster, 11 played on the football team. Based on my playing days with most of the players, I'm sure they were eager to take the court in their first game against Belvoir-Falkland. Tommy Dunn remembered the non-existent transition. "[We] lost to Rohanen on Friday night. On Monday we had basketball practice. We handed out uniforms. Tuesday night we played Belvoir-Falkland and beat them without practicing one minute." Final score: Ayden 74, Belvoir-Falkland 41.

Behind James Braxton's 29 points, the Winterville Wolves won Ayden's second game of the young season by the score of 64-49; Ayden had lost its first regular season game. The starting five in this game would also be the starters in the final game: Wayne Dail ('63), Tommy Dunn, William Edwards, Duane Gwynn, and Clem McLawhorn: a junior, senior, senior, sophomore, and a senior respectively. Changing into their street clothes after the game, I doubt if even one Tornado considered what would happen over the next several weeks.

Bethel came to town a couple of weeks before Christmas. Too many times before, the Indians had invaded Tornado country and left Ayden with a victory. The long-time rivals led at halftime 33-23, and the history that had repeated itself over and over looked as if it would occur again. Coach Tripp must have known what to do: Ayden slowed the game down and outscored the visitors 41-27 in the second half. The Tornadoes gave their fans an early Christmas gift, a 64-60 victory.

Starting Five

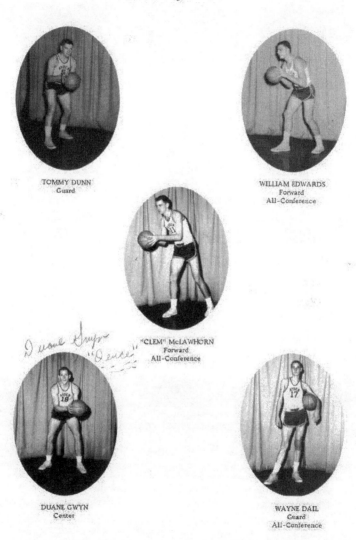

TOMMY DUNN
Guard

WILLIAM EDWARDS
Forward
All-Conference

"CLEM" McLAWHORN
Forward
All-Conference

DUANE GWYN
Center

WAYNE DAIL
Guard
All-Conference

**1961-62 Ayden High School basketball team starters.** *(The Wheel)*

*Conference Champions. . .*

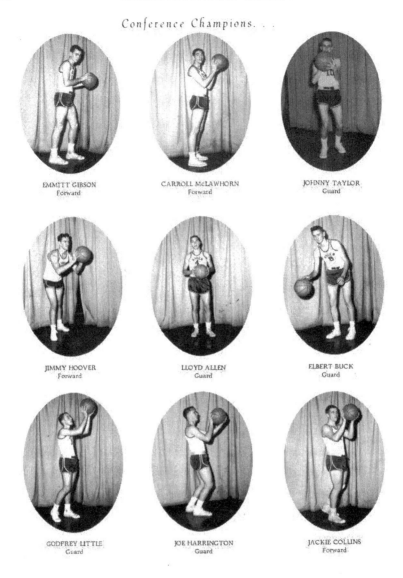

**1961-62 Ayden High School basketball team members.** *(The Wheel)*

The home and home series meant a return match with the Indians at the end of January 1962. I remember the year before when Bethel pasted us by 39 points on their home court. They were tough to beat anywhere, but winning on their home floor for any opponent was always a huge challenge. Ayden won 59-53. Tommy Dunn told me that this win was the first for a Coach Tripp team on Bethel's home court. Although there remains an insufficient number of frames to assemble the entire old movie, I believe the last time this happened was when Stuart Tripp, the *player*, was among the starting five during the '39-'40 school year.

The rising star for the Ayden Tornadoes, junior Wayne Dail, was high scorer for both sides with 19 points. Bethel, the defending conference champ, was 10-2 in the Pitt County Conference and Ayden was 10-1.

Ayden continued to roll over most of its competition by double figures. Besides the two games with Bethel, Grifton was defeated 47-44 on its home court, and Winterville was beaten by the score of 57-51 in Ayden. The Farmville Red Devils rolled into town for the last game of the regular season. Compared to the game in Red Devil country earlier, Ayden had a relatively difficult game before winning by eight: 45-37. These were the only hotly contested contests until the Pitt County Conference Tournament in early March.

The tournament was being played in Wright Gym on East Carolina College's campus. I felt like the Tornadoes were visiting me in my living room. It had been just a year since I'd played on a team that had been unable to win its final game on that same court. Looking back, I had unpleasant memories about that game. My senior year, our first game in the tournament had been against Winterville, a team we'd defeated twice during the regular season. The games were close, and we knew we'd have to play at our best to win. Basketball players know that tournament play is different. Every team plays its best because a loss usually means the season is over. As a senior, it means the end of a high school career. I'd managed to work my way up to being Coach Tripp's sixth man – not much on offense but not bad on defense. The Wolves never trailed by more than four points. In the fourth quarter, we managed to pull away for a 46-42 win. Two of my senior classmates, Ted Norris and Dink Mills, were high scorers for Ayden while James Braxton took high scoring honors for Winterville. I'd managed just two points on 2-3 at the foul line. Bethel was next up for us. The game turned out to be one of the hardest fought games of the year. Two of Bethel's starters fouled out, and Mills fouled out for us. Dink had played one of his best defensive games. All the 50-50 balls rolling on the floor were his. Ted Norris hit nine out of AHS's 15 field goals and scored 19 points. I went 0-3 at the foul line, Bethel's final margin of victory. Although his name is not listed in the final totals, I remember that it was J.D. Willoughby who yelled at me on my last attempt at the charity stripe. I was unable to hear him because of the constant roar from the crowd. I hit that last one, but the ref blew his whistle and took it away. My foot was over the foul line. It looks like he could have overlooked such a tiny transgression. The 0-3 at the foul line and the Indian's 46-43 victory will be stamped on my brain until someone sings *Amazing Grace* at my funeral.

I was in the winter quarter of my freshman year, a time of important decisions in my young life. I started out as a chemistry major only because one of my friends, Jerry Henderson, was a senior about to graduate from that department. Before I was able – miraculously – to make a "C" in my General Chemistry course, I switched to a Health and Physical Education major. That made the venue of the Pitt County Tournament my home department. I would go on to take a number of courses in the classrooms in the building surrounding the gym floor.

William Edwards was the only Tornado in double figures with 23 points in Ayden's 71-35 opening round win over Stokes-Pactolus. Ayden's subs continued to add to the margin of victory in the 4th quarter. The Tornadoes beat Farmville for the third time that season in the semifinals, 54-41. The championship game was next.

The two teams that were expected to be in the finals were there. Ayden led Bethel throughout the game. In the last quarter on cue, Bethel started closing the gap, but the Tornadoes held them off to win the conference trophy, 52-50. Clem McLawhorn turned his game up a notch with 19 points on five field goals and 9 of 12 at the line. Both of the two finalists would represent the conference in the district tourney.

Ayden placed three players on the Coach's All-County team: Wayne Dail, William Edwards, and Clem McLawhorn. Wayne was the only junior on the 10-member team.

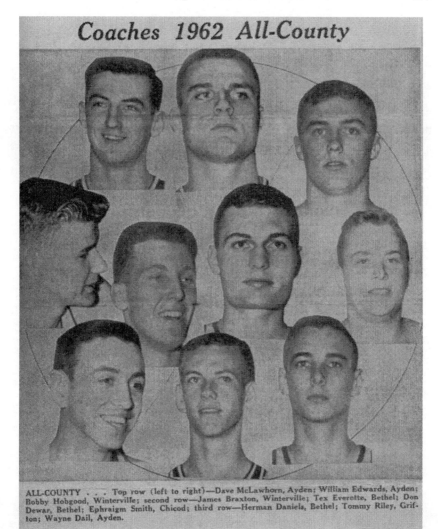

ALL-COUNTY . . . Top row (left to right)—Dave McLawhorn, Ayden; William Edwards, Ayden; Bobby Hobgood, Winterville; second row—James Braxton, Winterville; Tex Everette, Bethel; Don Dewar, Bethel; Ephraigm Smith, Chicod; third row—Herman Daniels, Bethel; Tommy Riley, Grifton; Wayne Dail, Ayden.

**1962 All-County Boys Basketball Team** *(The Daily Reflector Newspaper Clipping, Scrapbook Courtesy of William Edwards)*

In the first round of the District 1 Class A Tournament, Ayden defeated Pasquotank Central High School 49-32. Clem McLawhorn was again high scorer with 18 points. When Ayden needed it the most, Tommy Dunn scored seven of his 11 points in the fourth quarter to help his team pull away.

In their first round game, Bethel beat Beaufort County's Pantego Warriors to gain the semifinals against the Windsor Lions. Windsor's

6'8" center, Al Pierce, led his team with 21 points and a 59-49 victory over the Bethel Indians.

Ayden's semifinal game against the Knapp Knights turned into a methodical contest. After Knapp scored in the early seconds to take a 2-1 lead, Ayden made it 3-2 and held the lead throughout the remainder of the contest. The Knights speeded the game up in the last quarter and narrowed the gap, but the Tornadoes won 44-39. Edwards and McLawhorn were the high scorers. Ayden was where it wanted to be – in the district championship game. But, how was it to cope with Windsor's 6-8 center?

I knew about Al Pierce. I walked down on the court during warm-ups to see if he was really 6-8. It's difficult to believe that now *every* college team has 6-8 forwards. At that time, a 6-8 player was a rarity – especially in Class A high school basketball. He was every bit as big as advertised. I was worried right away. Ayden's tallest starter was 6-2. Maybe Coach Tripp, the mentor who put so much emphasis on defense, would be able to figure out a way.

Windsor's largest lead in the first half was seven points – the same as the 13-6 margin at the end of the 1st quarter. Four minutes into the 2nd quarter, Coach Tripp switched from his customary zone defense to a man-to-man defense. This move was rare but not unheard of. I remember Coach Tripp coming to me my senior year and telling me that he wanted me to play man-to-man against Grifton's Allan Jackson. The wheels of defensive strategy were always turning in his head. The change started to work. At the half, the Lions were still ahead, 18-14. I'll never forget watching Clem as he "climbed into Pierce's back pocket." I remember thinking that the big center looked so much taller than Clem. Maybe he was closer to 6-10. Going into the final stanza, the score was knotted at 23. In the slow-moving game, Edwards hit a field goal with three minutes left in the game to put his team ahead, 27-25. Eventually, Windsor scored to give them a one point lead. After Clem hit a shot to put the Tornadoes ahead 29-28, William hit a field goal and Wayne Dail tossed in two foul shots. Ayden won the District 1 Class A championship by defeating Al Pierce and his Windsor Lions by the score of 33-31.

The Class A State Tournament at Durham High School's gym pitted Ayden against Tryon in the first round. Coach Tripp returned to his traditional zone defense and held the Tigers' leading scorer to 13 points, the only player to hit in double figures for the opponents. The Sports Editor for *The Daily Reflector* pointed out a statistic that he thought may have been a record in tournament play. Ayden made good on 26 of 28 free throws. Tryon began a full court man-to-man press in the last quarter. This led to numerous free shot attempts. The Tornadoes went 19-20 in that period. Wayne Dail was high scorer with 22 points on 16 of 17 from the line. The final score: Ayden 54, Tryon 44.

Coach Stuart Tripp was interviewed after the game. The reporter, George Bryant, recounted remarks that the coach made earlier in the day. Tripp told him that the current year had been the happiest of his life. He indicated his pleasure with the football team and his joy with the success of the basketball team. Coach Tripp was quoted as saying, "We also had a son this year."

The 1962 semifinal game against the Warrenton Yellow Jackets has become part of the lore of Ayden High School basketball. When a bunch of guys with grey hair and wider bodies than their playing days get together for a reunion or meet somewhere for whatever purpose, *the shot* to tie the score at 49 at the end of regulation brings back a ton of memories. It may be the most famous shot in Ayden's round ball history. To the dismay of all Aydenites, it was made by the opposition. Chocky White hit the 25-footer as the final second ticked off the clock. Like the biggest fish I ever caught, the shot has gotten longer over time. One thing's for sure, it was a "Hail Mary" that went in. The "bad break," as the newspaper called it, was particularly disconcerting because the Tornadoes had led for most of the game.

The two teams played four three-minute overtimes. In the fourth extra period, Warrenton grabbed the lead for good and won 54-51. The dream season had ended with the knowledge that "we should have won it." As compared to the '53 and '57 basketball off-the-court fiascos, it was a different kind of loss but still another "near miss." The consolation game remained to be played. Ayden defeated the Valley Springs Panthers 58-57 for third place.

The Colfax Bulldogs won the championship game by whipping Warrenton 53-47. The Bulldogs' Larry Morgan scorched the nets for 30 points. He made 10 field goals and went 10-10 at the foul stripe.

The Ayden Police Department hosted a barbecue dinner at the Community Building to honor the Tornadoes. First, Reverend Bennie Pledger gave the invocation and then Mayor Frank Peterson took over as MC. Fifty-one players, family members, cheerleaders, policemen, Jaycees, and school officials attended the event.

Baseball was next for many of the players who had been on the diamond for Ayden's first Little League team. It is sad that there is no archive of Ayden High School baseball stashed away somewhere. There is more known about the '56 Little League season than about the '62 team. Could the Tornadoes duplicate the '60 squad and go undefeated? Senior, Tommy Dunn, and two sophomores, Godfrey Little ('64) and Gene Bowen, carried the pitching load. I've been able to round up information on five of the eight games. Ayden's eventual Pitt County Conference champs defeated Farmville 10-7. Either the next game or two games later, Winterville's James Braxton pitched a no-hitter against the Red Devils. He walked four and struck out 15.

Ayden didn't give Stokes-Pactolus much of a chance in their encounter. Gene Bowen started the game and retired the side in the first inning. In the second, two Stokes batters reached base, but Bowen struck out the side to end the threat. Godfrey Little pitched the final five innings, striking out the first 5 batters he faced. In total, 12 of Stokes batters went down via strike outs. Rudolph Cannon ('63) had a home run and a single; William Edwards stroked a triple, and Godfrey Little and Clem McLawhorn had doubles.

In the next game, Grifton had an afternoon to forget; their pitchers' gave up 14 hits and 7 walks, and the defense committed 8 errors. Grifton took a 3-2 lead in the second, but two 5-run innings put it away for the Tornadoes. The leading hitters were William Edwards with 3 singles, Robert Cannon ('62) with 2 doubles, Rudolph Cannon with a single and a double, and Tommy Dunn with two singles. In addition to winning his third game, Little collected two singles. After defeating Grifton 16-8, Ayden was 5-0.

In '62, the two best teams in the conference were Ayden and Winterville. The two schools were tied for first place when they met at the mid-point of the season. Godfrey Little got the call on the mound for the Tornadoes, and James Braxton pitched for the Wolves. After three innings, Winterville surged ahead when three errors and a single led to 3 unearned runs. Braxton did not allow a hit until his mound opponent, Godfrey Little, singled in the 4$^{th}$ inning. Another single and a walk eventually brought across 2 runs. In the 5$^{th}$, Ayden went ahead 4-3. In the next inning, William Edwards' triple chased across 2 runs. The final score was 8-3. The two hurlers went all the way. Godfrey hurled a 6-hitter, walked 6 and struck out 7. Braxton was tagged with his first loss of the year. He walked 5 and struck out 12. The Tornadoes were 6-0.

Belvoir-Falkland rolled into town for the 7$^{th}$ game of the season, Gene Bowen took over for Godfrey Little after 2 innings and won his first game of the year. In his 5 innings, Bowen allowed only two hits, struck out 4 and walked 5. There were several hitting stars in Ayden's 13-2 victory. A total of 10 runs were scored in the 2$^{nd}$ and 5$^{th}$ innings. Wayne Dail, William Edwards, and Godfrey Little had two singles each. Robert Cannon and Rudolph Cannon chipped in with triples. Ayden was 7-0.

Ayden traveled to Bethel for its final game, but the particulars of the game are unknown. The Tornadoes won the game and finished 8-0 for the season.

When Coach Tripp had a decision to make on who to play, he usually went with experience. There were exceptions; R.L. Collins ('57) started at linebacker his freshman year. "I fit Stuart's mold for playing linebacker," Collins told me. "Tripp thought I was the meanest guy imaginable. I was hard as a rock and mean as a snake." I remember that Carroll McLawhorn was so good on defense as an underclassman that Coach couldn't "keep him off the field." Mac Whitehurst made All-Conference for four years in football. Tommy Edwards played early in all three sports. A senior in 1962, Tommy Dunn's pitching ability was so obvious as a freshman that he won a starting position.

Tommy's freshman pitching debut was a memorable one. In a game at Belvoir-Falkland, Jimmy Little, one of Belvoir's best athletes, came to bat with the bases loaded. For the first time in the season, Coach Tripp summoned for Tommy to enter the game. "Coach Tripp said 'do not walk this guy.'" Tommy threw two or three pitches. "The last one went over the pine trees in left center field. When I came off the field, Coach said 'you did exactly what I asked you to do.'"

The next game in Grifton, Donald Carman started the game and got two outs before he lost his control. "I went in and pitched the last 6 1/3 innings. From then on, I pitched most games that we played." Tommy lost only one game to Currituck County in his AHS career.

In the nearby Martin County Conference, Robersonville's Jimmy Rogers also finished up his astounding four years in high school in 1962. In the county tournament, he defeated Jamesville, the only team to beat him – ever. Rogers finished 26-1 in his career.

With the Bethel Indians final strike out or fly ball or grounder in the bottom of the 7th inning of the eighth game, the best overall year a bunch of Ayden athletes had ever experienced came to an end.

Another super performance came to an end within days of Ayden's final baseball game. Principal E.F. "Faust" Johnson resigned to accept a position as Field Consultant at the North Carolina Education Association in Raleigh. Mr. Johnson had been principal for 19 years. Somewhere around 1970, my family and I were having dinner in Raleigh when I spotted Mr. Johnson sitting nearby. He said to me, "You know, William, I was the only principal you ever had." That was true. He was the principal of two buildings – the grammar school building and the high school building.

As I write these words about Faust Johnson on a snowy day in Durham, it's impossible to complete this paragraph without thinking about Tommy Craft. I was prevented from attending his funeral this week because of the bad weather. He was my 8th grade teacher and the assistant coach during my days on the football team. Today, there are few educators like Mr. Johnson and Mr. Craft – men who wore multiple hats during their careers. Tommy Craft was a teacher, a coach, a principal, and assistant superintendent for the county.

There are those of us who will never forget these two giants of the Ayden community – two men who meant so much to so many.

Now you know why this chapter is entitled "One." The 1961-1962 teams lost only one regular season game, the second game of the young basketball season in Winterville. *The News and Observer* journalist, Grady Elmore, called it the "Best Season for Successful Coach Tripp." Counting the playoff games, Ayden finished 45-3 in all three sports. "We've had better individual teams, but never a year like this one," Coach Tripp said. After that, he bragged about some of "his boys."

On occasion writing can be downright weird. For months I tried to think of a way to compose a tiny chunk of this book – how to turn things over to Mitchell for Act 2 (Volume 2) of our play. And then, I woke up at 3:30 one morning with an idea. So, here goes. The time has come for me to pass the keys to a friend of mine. Attempting to tell you how much fun and, at the same time, what an honor it has been for me to take us this far is like trying to sleep with someone who has the hiccups. Impossible!

I am required to give credit where credit is due – to cite my references. The inspiration for this passage must go to someone who has no idea what a great help she was. She happened to be asleep. My wife, Maija, was the one with the hiccups.

Mitchell Oakley's beginning:
BIRTH ANNOUNCEMENT: Mr. and Mrs. W.H. Oakley, Jr. of Ayden announce the birth of a son, Vicki *Mitchell*, August 1, 1947. Mrs. Oakley is the former Miss Christine Vandiford of Grifton.

### *The Wheel*, 1962
(Graduating Class = 46)

Nicknames must have been important to the Class of '62 …

| | |
|---|---|
| **William Charles Everett** | Reverend |
| **Artie Campbell McGlohon** | Snow White |
| **Thomas Parker Dunn** | Big Dunn |
| **Patricia Lee Braxton** | Loretta Young |
| **Carolyn Stocks** | Pig |
| **Peggy Ann Mills** | Lucy |
| **David McLawhorn** | Clem |
| **Barbara Ann Greene** | Bag |
| **Linwood Earl Branch** | Sweetwater |

Some very important people who were not always recognized …

| | |
|---|---|
| **Mrs. George Bullock** | Secretary |
| **Ralph and Omira** | Custodians |
| **Mrs. W.O. Jolly, Manager** | Lunchroom staff |
| **Mary King** | |
| **Maude Willis** | |
| **Bernice Shackleford** | |
| **Joyce Wainwright** | |

Junior-Senior Prom: **Nina Jane & Randall, Laura & Carroll, Nancy & Rudolph, Martha & Wayne, Trillis & Frankie, Mary Catherine & Walter, Mara Ruggles & Lloyd, Laura & Randall**

# Acknowledgements

*Ayden, the Sports Town* represents the accumulated wisdom and experiences of so many people. Maybe that's why Mitchell and I have waited until the last possible moment, just before we go to press – to complete this section. We've put it off because we don't want to leave anyone out. Writing a book that covers so much ground is sort of like putting together a 500-piece puzzle; for it to be complete, all of the pieces must be in place for the whole picture to emerge. Some of the pieces were difficult to locate and others we realized are gone forever. For everyone who assisted Mitchell and me – thank you.

Old newspapers and other important papers live in libraries and hidden archives. Special thanks go to Pat Nichols and Alice Cannon-Parker at the Ayden Library. I lost track of the number of times I visited the back room, unlocked the door, and carefully turned the old yellow pages of *The Ayden Dispatch*. Pat – and Alice when Pat was not there – answered dozens of questions. They did their work with a smile – always. Thanks to the Reference Librarian Sharon Vaughn, Sheppard Memorial Library in Greenville, to the staff of the library at Lenoir Community College in Kinston. Mitchell and I also did work at the Joyner Library on campus at East Carolina University. Sherri Scharf at the Town of Ayden office assisted me in locating documents from as far back as 1907. She knew right where they were.

Graduates of Ayden High School and South Ayden High School trusted us with their annuals. We kept them much too long but, without them, there would have been no book and fewer pictures.

Individuals loaned us their scrapbooks containing mostly old newspaper clippings not available anywhere else. Thanks to those who shared boxes of pictures and souvenirs from their high school days. Some of the pictures and other items had been handed down from their parents and relatives. Like the annuals, these prized possessions contained invaluable information that added enormously to the narrative of *Ayden, the Sports Town*.

On countless occasions Mitchell and I met at Bum's Restaurant where we ate a delicious home-cooked meal, discussed topics relative to this book and traded various stories. We also were able to interview countless individuals in Bum's side room. Bum Dennis not only welcomed us to his place of business, but his knowledge and memories also helped us with our research.

Mitchell and I worked in *The Times-Leader* office in Grifton on countless occasions. Kyle Stephens was always gracious in allowing us to use the space and the equipment. Every picture in the book owes its presence to the software Mitchell (mostly Mitchell) and I used to place the photos in their proper places.

Volume 1 is written mostly by me, but Mitchell not only edited the writing but he surprised me one day when we were having lunch near the Shepard Library by sliding a one-inch thick bundle of papers across the table. Without my even asking, he had completed all of the research I needed from the 1960s and early 1970s to complete the chapters of the book on girls' basketball.

Stuart Albright, creative writing teacher at Jordan High School in Durham, edited every word of the manuscript. I have worked with Stuart before. He's more than an editor; Stuart is my friend and one of the reasons writing has been so much fun for me.

There are two people who I want to thank – two individuals that did not contribute directly to this book but who helped me get started in my writing career after I retired. I learned so much from Jane Hoover, a writing teacher who helped me realize that maybe I could do this thing. A very good friend of mine, Phyllis May, edited my very early work, met with me on so many occasions, and gave me advice that I will always treasure. Although Phyllis is no longer with us, sometimes I think she's looking over my shoulder and pushing me – as she did in life – to do better and better.

I want to add one more person; oh, how I wish Jimmy Persinger could be here today. I lost the best friend any person could have when Jimmy passed away suddenly when he was 58 years old. I wish I could send him a copy of *Ayden, the Sports Town*.

My wife Maija edited parts of the manuscript and – being a non-sports fan – forced me to realize that some of the wording needed to be altered so that it could be more easily understood by all. She helps me more than she knows – by her encouragement when I'm tired and cranky and need to talk to my best friend about my work.

Thank you to all of the interviewees who made this book possible. The stories that made the book special came from the men and women who lived them. They are far too numerous to list all of them here. Almost all are mentioned in the text. For those who are not, the Chapter Notes appendix indicates each by name.

**Appendices**

## Appendix 1
Chapter Notes

11 *Ayden High School song: The Wheel,* p.2, 1949.

INTRODUCTION

*Page*

18 *Princess Theater:* personal communication, Bum Dennis, 9-23-2011.

20 *scored in a game:* personal communication, Nolan Norman, 10-8-2014.

23 *a week longer than expected: The Ayden Dispatch,* p.1, 7-25-1929.

CHAPTER 1: A BALOON RIDE

*Page*

27 *South Ayden High: The News-Leader,* p.1, 1-31-1991

28 *new-fangled contraption: The Ayden Dispatch,* p.1, 3-21-1929.

29 *frontier was over: The Wisdom of History* by Rufus Fears; DVD, The Teaching Company, 2007.

29 *two years in the future: From Dawn to Decadence* by Jacques Barzun, HarperCollins Publisher, 2000.

29 *loved to fight:* "Facts About the Town of Ayden," undated brochure.

29 *Farmer's Funeral Home:* undated and unnamed newspaper article.

29 *in the name: The Ayden Dispatch,* p.4, 1-31-1929.

29 *Scotland Neck to Kinston: The Ayden Dispatch,* 2nd Section, p.1, 2-25-1937.

30 *community's main street:* www.aydencollardfestival.com.

30 *dignify the name:* www.aydencollardfetival.com.

31 *at least that early: Chronicles of Pitt County North Carolina,* 1982.

31 *the postmaster: The News-Leader,* p.13, 1-31-1991.

31 *Kinston and Weldon:* undated and unnamed newspaper article.

31 *druggists in abundance: Chronicles of Pitt County North Carolina* (contributed by Russell Wooten from issues of *The Ayden News-Leader* and personal knowledge), 1982.

33 "Early Ayden:" *The Ayden Dispatch,* 1926 – 1939, 1956; *The Times-Leader,* 1991.

37 *to said gate or gates: The Ayden Dispatch,* 1st Section, p.8, 2-25-1937.

37 *chickens to run free:* Ibid., p.7.

37 *chickens at home: The Ayden Dispatch,* p.1, 2-22-1940.

37 *at least for now: The Times-Leader,* p.1, 2-19-2014.

38 *at another location: The Ayden Dispatch,* 1st Section, p.7, 2-25-1937.

38 *offense was $5.00:* Ibid.

38 *horse cost $250.00:* Ibid.

38 *middle of the streets:* Ibid.

38 *$225,000 bond issue:* Ibid., p.1.

38 *published a booklet: Ayden North Carolina: One of the Most Progressive Small Cities in the State,* Chamber of Commerce, 1916 (?).

42 *a big heart: The Ayden Magazine,* p.23, summer/fall 2014.

42 *and living appeal: The Ayden Dispatch,* p.1, 3-2-1950.

42 *17 years old at the time: The Ayden Magazine,* p.24, summer/fall 2014.

42 *in Pitt County: The Ayden Dispatch,* 1st Section, p.10, 2-25-1937.

43 "Start-ups in Early Ayden:" *The Ayden Dispatch,* 2-25-1937; *Chronicles of Pitt County North Carolina,* 1982; *The Ayden News-Leader,* 1-31-1991; Census reports.

## CHAPTER 2: AYDEN, THE EDUCATION TOWN

*Page*

47 *it was Annie:* personal communication, Helen Joyce (Whitehurst) Stroud, 8-3-2014.

47 *in September 1990:* personal communication, James Hemby, 3-7-2013.

47 *Atlantic Christian College:* Ibid.

47 *Wilson, N.C.:* www.livingplaces.com.

47 *Atlantic Christian College:* "Educational Highlights in Ayden to 1944," unpublished and undated paper, unknown author.

48 *in the 1920s:* www.livingplaces.com.

48 *adding an auditorium: A History of Ayden Seminary and Eureka College* by Michael Pelt, Division of Humanities, Mt. Olive College, pp.1&2, date unknown.

48 *Bible courses: The Free Will Baptist,* p.4, 2-27-1926.

49 *Eureka College:* Ibid., p.5.

49 *75 cents was charged:* Pelt, *A History of Ayden Seminary and Eureka College,* p.15.

49 *closed in 1931:* Ibid.

49 *and Wilmington:* www.umo.edu, 9-15-14.

49 *Ayden-Grifton High School:* "Educatinal Highlights in Ayden to 1944," p.344.

50 *American Legion Post 289:* personal communication, Sammy Anson Pierce, 3-6&7-2014.

50 *day ended at 4:00:* unpublished paper written for accreditation review, author unknown, 1985/1986.

50 *behind the building:* Ibid.

51 *3$^{rd}$ Street:* "Educational Highlights in Ayden to 1944," p.344.

51 *to cost $100,000: The Ayden Dispatch,* p.1, 3-14-1929.

51 *900-seat auditorium: The Ayden Dispatch,* p.1, 8-22-1929.

52 *class of 1931: The Ayden Dispatch*, p.4, 4-2-1931.

52 *old lunchroom tables:* "Ayden Elementary School" by Tommy Craft, p.2, unpublished and undated.

53 *for lunch break:* Ibid.

53 *a new year began!:* Ibid., p. 3.

54 "Early Education in Ayden" - *The Ayden Dispatch,* 1926-1939.

CHAPTER 3: THE FIRST FOOTBALL SEASON

*Page*

59 *to be like 'em:* personal communication, Ikey Baldree, 9-6-12.

60 *for its patrons:* "Chip Off the Old Block" by William Harrington, *Ayden Magazine*, vol. 6, no. 1, p 31, 2009.

60 *Princess Theater Ad: The Ayden Dispatch,* 10-7-1926.

61 *in 21 seconds: The Ayden Dispatch,* 7-1-1926.

62 *designed to be deceptive:* www.wikipedia.org, 11-17-2014 and *The Steve Logan Show*. WRAL, 11-23-2014.

63 *moved underneath the center:* Ibid.

63 "Ayden Plays Williamston to Scoreless Tie," *The Ayden Dispatch,* 10-14-1926.

63 "The Foot Ball Game, Were You There?" *The Ayden Dispatch,* 10-21-1926.

64 "Ayden Wins," *The Ayden Dispatch,* 10-28-1926.

65 "Ayden Defeats LaGrange," *The Ayden Dispatch,* 11-4-1926.

65 "Ayden Defeats Robersonville," *The Ayden Dispatch,* 11-18-1926.

66 "Ayden Defeats Williamston," *The Ayden Dispatch,* 11-25-1926.

66 "Ayden Wins Again," *The Ayden Dispatch,* 12-2-1926.

68 "Mr. H.G. Mumford Entertains Foot Ball Squad At An Oyster Roast," *The Ayden Dispatch,* 12-9-1926.

69 *for Ayden High: The Wheel,* p.41, 1928.

69 1927-1928: Ayden High School's Second Football Season: Ibid.

70 *of Ayden football:* Ibid.

70 *maroon and white: The Ayden Dispatch,* p.3, 10-13-1927.

71 *were held scoreless:* compilation from *The Wheel,* 1928 and *The Ayden Dispatch,* 1926-1929.

72 "Advertisements in *The Ayden Dispatch*: Late 1920s, Early 1930s" and "Sports and Other Notations from *The Ayden Dispatch*: Late 1920s, Early 1930s," *The Ayden Dispatch,* 1926-1932.

CHAPTER 4: BOYS' BASKETBALL

*Page*

81 *in every player: The Wheel,* p.43, 1928.

81 *not been stellar:* Ibid.

81 1927-1928: Ayden High School Basketball Season, Ibid.

82 *faced 2nd street:* "Ayden Sports History" by Stuart Tripp, p.3, unpublished and undated paper.

82 *in the warehouse:* Ibid.

82 *on a dirt floor: The Ayden Dispatch,* p.4, 1-17-1929.

83 *on the wet spots:* Ibid.

83 *ball handling mistakes: The Ayden Dispatch,* p.4, 2-28-1929.

83 *necessitated dressing elsewhere: The Ayden Dispatch,* p.4, 1-17-1929.

83 *of the cold weather: The Ayden Dispatch,* p.8, 1-30-1936.

83 *in the late 1940s:* personal communication, Bear Baldree, 8-23-2013.

83 *in the mid-50s:* personal communication, Sue Sutton, 8-12-2014.

83 *season was over: The Ayden Dispatch,* p.2, 3-8-1928.

84 *high school basketball coach: The Ayden Dispatch,* p.8, 1-28-1926.

84 *until 1930: The Ayden Dispatch,* p.4, 10-2-1930.

84 *New Bern 27, Ayden 9: The Ayden Dispatch,* p.3, 1-22-1931.

84 *in 23 games: The Ayden Dispatch,* p.1, 1-28-1932.

85 *to Hertford, 23-21: The Ayden Dispatch,* p.1, 2-16-1933.

85 *against Beulaville, 52-25: The Ayden Dispatch,* p.1, 2-13-1933.

85 *Grimesland, 24-14: The Ayden Dispatch,* p.1, 3-3-1933.

85 *for the state championship:* Ibid.

85 *finished 15-4-1: The Ayden Dispatch,* p.1, 3-16-1933.

85 *completing their season, 25-8: The Ayden Dispatch,* January-May, 1935.

85 *of the season: The Ayden Dispatch,* p.8, 1-17-1935.

85 *in the championship game: The Ayden Dispatch,* p.1, 2-14-1935.

85 *Dover, 32-13: The Ayden Dispatch,* p.8, 3-14-1935.

85 *Pitt County Tournament: The Ayden Dispatch,* p.4, 3-19-1936.

86 *in December: The Ayden Dispatch,* January-March, 1939.

86 *against Farmville, 29-16:* Ibid.

86 *defeated Farmville, 31-13:* Ibid.

8 *team's leading scorer:* Ibid.

CHAPTER 5: BASEBALL

*Page*

87 *Ayden 15, Winterville 14: The Ayden Dispatch,* p.8, 3-24-1927.

87 *AHS team: The Ayden Dispatch,* March-May, 1927.

87 *who is interested: The Ayden Dispatch,* p.4, 3-15-1928.

87 *Durham Luckies, 6-5: The Ayden Dispatch,* p.1, 4-21-1938.

87 *Tobacco County League: The Ayden Dispatch,* p.1, 6-15-1950.

87 *Bright Belt League: The Ayden Dispatch,* p.1, 6-26-1947.

87 *Pitt-Greene League: The Ayden Dispatch,* p.4, 6-3-1948.

87 *Coastal Amateur League: The Ayden Dispatch,* p.1, 6-4-1942.

87 *Goober Belt Baseball League: The Ayden Dispatch,* p.4, 3-27-1957.

88 *lived to regret it:* personal communication, Thomas Heath, 6-6-11.

88 *to their patrons:* "Imagining the Action: Audiovisual Baseball Game Reproductions in Richmond, Virginia, 1895-1935" by Eric Dewberry; chapter in *The Cooperstown Symposium on Baseball and American Culture,* McFarland and Company, Inc., Jefferson, N.C., William M. Simmons, Editor, p.141, 2003-2004.

88 *of newspaper offices:* Ibid.

88 *from behind the board:* Ibid.

89 *no cost to fans: The Ayden Dispatch,* p.1, 9-30-1926.

89 *defeating Winterville, 16-2: The Ayden Dispatch,* p.4, 3-28-1929.

89 *twice been runners-up:* Ibid.

89 *their two games: The Ayden Dispatch,* p.4, 4-4-1929.

89 *academically ineligible: The Ayden Dispatch,* p.4, 4-18-1929.

89 *courses to play:* Ibid.

89 *was not reported: The Ayden Dispatch,* p.4, 4-25-1929.

89 *do its best: The Ayden Dispatch,* p.3, 3-19-1931.

90 *was Hawaii: The Ayden Dispatch,* p.4, 4-21-1932.

90 *by 20%: The Ayden Dispatch,* p.1, 3-23-1933.

90 *and Williamston: The Ayden Dispatch,* June-September, 1932.

90 1932: The Cotton Belt Final Regular Season Standings, *The Ayden Dispatch,* p.1,7-28-1932.

91 *remain unknown: The Ayden Dispatch,* p.1, 8-25-1932.

91 *one nigh each week: The Ayden Dispatch,* p.4, 3-1-1933.

91 *with a .500 record: The Ayden Dispatch,* p.4, 4-13-1933.

92 *in July 1930: The Ayden Dispatch,* p.1, 7-3-1930.

92 *was defeated, 10-9: The Ayden Dispatch,* p.4, 5-5-1932.

92 *and lost, 12-5: The Ayden Dispatch,* p.1, 5-12-1932.

92 *came to Ayden:* Ibid.

93 *Greenville Water and Light Department 3: The Ayden Dispatch,* p.1, 5-25-1933.

93 *Durham Luckies 5: The Ayden Dispatch,* p.1, 4-21-1938.

93 *for their support: The Ayden Dispatch,* p.1, 6-15-1939.

93 *summer of 1942: The Ayden Dispatch,* p.1, 6-4-1942.

93 *the final score: The Ayden Dispatch,* p.1, 9-10-1942.

93 *London International Baseball League:* p.1, 8-12-1943.

93 *the Baseball Medallion: The Ayden Dispatch,* p.1, 1-20-1944 and personal communication, Loys Sumrell, 10-9-2013.

94 *I am unfamiliar: The Ayden Dispatch,* p.1, 8-10-1939.

94 *giant flood lights: The Ayden Dispatch,* p.1, 9-14-1939.

94 *good shape: The Ayden Dispatch,* p.1, 8-17-1939.

94 *called the game: The Ayden Dispatch,* p.1, 8-24-1939.

94 "Advertisements in *The Ayden Dispatch*: 1930s," *The Ayden Dispatch,* decade of the 1930s

CHAPTER 6: THE COASTAL PLAIN LEAGUE

*Page*

98 *early 1960s:* www.negroleaguebaseball.com, 8-12-2014.

98 *in a tree: The Ayden Dispatch,* p.1, 8-10-1939.

98 *people watching: We Could Have Played Forever: The Story of the Coastal Plain Baseball League* by Robert Gaunt, p.8, 1997.

99 *for the league: The Ayden Dispatch,* p.1, 5-18-1933.

99 *J. Bruce Eure:* Gaunt, *We Could Have Played Forever,* p.16.

99 *Municipal Recorder's Court: The Ayden Dispatch,* 2$^{nd}$ *Section,* p.1, 2-25-1937.

99 *the charter members: The Ayden Dispatch,* p.1, 5-18-1933.

99 *Claxton "Crack" Rogerson: The Ayden Dispatch,* p.1, 6-8-1933.

99 *in their town: The Ayden Dispatch,* p.1, 6-15-1933.

99 1933: Inaugural Year of the Coastal Plain League Final Regular Season Standings, p.1, 8-31-1933.

100 *a .390 average:* Ibid.

100 *the Coastal Plain League:* personal communication, Robert Gaunt, 10-11-13.

100 *on the highway:* Ibid.

100 *real barbecue:* Ibid.

100 *four charter members: The Ayden Dispatch,* p.1, 4-19-1934.

100 *started 11-1:* Gaunt, *We Could Have Played Forever,* p.16.

100 *the Ayden team:* Ibid., p.17.

101 *Tar Heels:* Ibid.

101 *the offer down:* Ibid.

101 *the next four:* Ibid., p.18.

102 *"Never Wrong" Greene:* The nicknames in this paragraph were taken from various pages of Dr. Gaunt's book including the Acknowledgments.

102 *in 1934:* Gaunt, *We Could Have Played Forever,* p.19.

102 *into the league:* Ibid., p.20.

102 *each contest:* Ibid., p.22.

102 *on successive days:* Ibid., p.21.

102 *of the game:* Ibid., p.22.

102 *Goldsboro 8:* Ibid., p.23.

103 *exiting the field:* Ibid., p.25.

103  *4 games to 1:* Ibid., p.26.

103  *on the market:* Ibid., pp.27 and 28.

103  *of the formula:* Ibid., pp. 28 and 29.

104  *an envelope:* personal communication, Robert Gaunt, 10-11-13.

104  *the Ayden Aces: The Ayden Dispatch,* p.1, 4-30-1936.

104  *lifetime batting average:* Gaunt, *We Could Have Played Forever,* p.30.

104  *times at bat:* Ibid., p.32.

104  *today's collegiate world:* Ibid.

104  *University of Georgia:* Ibid.

105  *a late inning run:* Ibid., p.33.

105  *the series, 3-1:* Ibid.

105  *his team needed:* Ibid.

## CHAPTER 7: CLASS D BASEBALL COMES TO TOWN

*Page*

107  *the lowest: We Could Have Played Forever: The Story of the Coastal Plain Baseball League* by Robert Gaunt, p.39, 1997.

107  *under control:* Ibid., p.37.

108  *receiving team:* Ibid.

108  *in the summer of 1937:* Ibid., p.38.

108  *an eight-team league:* Ibid.

108 *cleared that fence:* Ibid., p.43.

110  *worthwhile civic projects:* Ibid., p.48.

110  *over the franchise:* Ibid.

110  *winning percentage:* Ibid., p. 52.

110  *showed inconsistency:* Ibid., p.48.

110  *to the plate:* Ibid., p.52.

110  *the victory, 11-10:* Ibid., p.51.

112  *other semifinal series:* Ibid., p.52.

111  *and the Athletics:* Ibid., pp. 438 and 439.

111  *of Edgecombe:* Ibid., p.44.

111  *"Snake" Henry:* Ibid., p.46.

111  *from Ayden:* Ibid., p.55.

111  *of the league:* Ibid., p.57.

111  *Snow Hill:* Ibid.

111  *in the standings:* Ibid., p.73.

112  *hit .332:* Ibid., p.69.

112  *unofficial standings:* Ibid., p.73.

112  *not to mention:* Ibid., p.61.

112  *somewhat vague:* Ibid.

112  *to leave the league:* Ibid., p.63.

113  *penalties were imposed:* Ibid.

113  *to make the playoffs:* ibid.

113  *won the playoff championship:* Ibid., pp.76 and 77.

113  *six years in the league:* Ibid., p.81.

114  *for the upcoming summer: The Ayden Dispatch,* p.1, 1-26-1939.

114  *to Wilson:* Gaunt, *We Could Have Played Forever,* p.81.

114  *Wilson "Tobs":* Ibid., pp. 81 and 82.

114  *1943, 1944, and 1945:* Ibid., p.175.

114  *shutting down for good:* Ibid., p.399.

114  "Morsels of Information from *We Could Have Played Forever* by Robert Gaunt" This end-of-chapter summary was taken from Dr. Gaunt's book – with two exceptions:

1)    The sentence ending with *a .390 batting average* was taken from the following source: *The Ayden Dispatch,* p.1, 8-31-1933.

2)    The phrase *Charter member, 1933* was taken from the following source: *The Ayden Dispatch,* p.1, 5-18-1933.

CHAPTER 8: THE GOLDEN AGE OF GIRLS' BASKETBALL

*Page*

121  *Ayden 12: The Ayden Dispatch,* p.8, 2-4-1926.

121  *Fountain, 12-6: The Ayden Dispatch,* p.2, 2-23-1928.

121  *Ayden's girls, 48-2: The Ayden Dispatch,* p.3, 1-11-1934.

121  *South River, 20-8: The Ayden Dispatch,* p.1, 1-25-1934.

121  *Vanceboro, 33-7: The Ayden Dispatch,* p.3, 2-8-1934.

122  *in the coming years: The Wheel,* p.44, 1928.

122  *in the other game: The Daily Reflector,* p.8, 1-4-1958.

123 *in later editions: The Daily Reflector,* p.5, 1-11-1958; *The Daily Reflector,* p.8, 1-15-1958.

124 1946-1952: The Golden Age of Girls' Basketball at Ayden High School: OverallSeason Records, *The Wheel:* 1947, 1948, 1949, 1951 and *The Daily Reflector,* p.6, 3-26-1952. In '47-'48, the season record could have been 19-3. After much consternation, doubling back on my original research, and consulting with my Ouija Board, I made the decision to go with 20-3.

124 *never be duplicated:* Ibid.

125 *Forwards: Martha Fleming ('47):* Players and coach from *The Wheel,* p.34, 1947.

126 *Chicod 6: The Wheel,* p.32, 1948; *The Ayden Dispatch,* p.4, 1-8-1948.

126 *Farmville 3$^{rd}$: The Daily Reflector,* p.7, 2-23-1948.

127 *of 23 to 16: The Daily Reflector,* p.7, 3-2-1948.

127 *Grimesland, 17-12: The Daily Reflector,* p.7, 3-3-1948.

127 *up to that time: The Daily Reflector,* pp.1 and 4, 2-26-1948; *The Daily Reflector,* pp.1 and 4, 3-4-1948.

127 *Forwards: Patricia Fleming ('48):* Players and coach from *The Wheel,* p.32, 1948.

128 *clothes off line: Aydenites,* back page, 1943-1944.

129 *Pitt County Conference Tournament: The Wheel,* p.30, 1949.

129 *Forwards: Unreported:* Players and coach from *The Wheel,* p.30, 1949.

CHAPTER 9: "BUGGY" AND MAE

*Page*

132 *one that stuck:* personal communication, Alice Jean (Cox) Smith, 6-4-2014.

132 *Jean at DuPont:* Ibid.

133 *matrimonial occasion:* Ibid.

134 *a game she loved:* personal communication, Suzanne (Wilson) Gray, 10-9-2014.

135 *every minute of it:* personal communication, Anne Mae (Cox) Eichorn, 6-11-2014.

135 *of the time:* Ibid.

135 *Buggy told me:* personal communication, Alice Jean (Cox) Smith, 6-4-2014.

135 *last four seconds:* Ibid. and *The Daily Reflector,* p.6, 3-13-1950.

136 *started at 10:30: The Daily Reflector,* p.6, 2-4-1950.

136 *before Christmas: The Daily Reflector,* p.10, 12-14-1949.

136 1949-1950: Coastal Conference Regular Season Girls' Basketball Standings, *The Ayden Dispatch,* p.1, 2-23-1950.

137 *Farmville, 36-32: The Wheel,* p. unknown, 1951.

138 *championship game:* Ibid.

138 *to Chicod: The Ayden Dispatch,* p.1, 3-9-1950.

138 *Southern Pines: The Wheel,* p. unknown, 1951.

138 *Lady Tornadoes, 48-36: The Ayden Dispatch,* p.1, 3-16-1950.

138 *All Coastal Conference teams: The Wheel,* p. unknown, 1951.

138 *a 22-6 overall record: The Wheel,* p.28, 1951.

138 Coastal Conference, Gold Metal, and Pitt County Conference scores, Ibid.

138 *close behind at 18: The Daily Reflector,* p.12, 12-5-1951.

138 *scoring 27 points: The Daily Reflector,* p.6, 12-8-1951.

138 *Liverman added 22: The Daily Reflector,* p.6, 1-9-1952.

138 *Bethel 45-37: The Daily Reflector,* p.6, 1-12-1952.

138 *record was 8-3: The Daily Reflector,* p.6, 1-19-1952.

138 *South Edgecombe 38-36: The Daily Reflector,* p.6, 2-4-1952.

138 *score of 40-37: The Daily Reflector,* p.6, 2-9-1952.

138 *South Edgecombe 36: The Daily Reflector,* p.6, 2-16-1952.

138 1951-1952: Coastal Conference Regular Season Girls' Basketball Standings, *The Daily Reflector,* p.6, 2-25-1952.

139 *to win again:* Ibid.

139 *the state playoffs: The Daily Reflector,* p.6, 2-28-1952.

139 *Wilma Stocks ('54): The Daily Reflector,* p.6, 3-18-1952.

139 *Chicod 61-42: The Daily Reflector,* p.5, 3-4-1952.

139 *second time, 66-49: The Daily Reflector,* p.6, 3-8-1952.

139 *Katherine Wooten (20): The Daily Reflector,* p.6, 3-10-1952.

139 *to replace her:* memorabilia collection from *The Daily Reflector*, Alice Jean (Cox) Smith.

140 *a single season:* Ibid.

## CHAPTER 10: FRUSTRATING TIMES

*Page*

141 *Pitt County Conference: The Daily Reflector,* December 1952-April 1956.

141 *over Walstonburg: The Daily Reflector,* p.6, 3-3-1953.

142 *the defensive chores: The Wheel,* 1957 and 1958.

142 *highest scoring average: The Daily Reflector,* December 1956-April 1957.

142 *in the league: The Daily Reflector,* p.8, 3-2-1957.

142 *fourth at 9-4:* Ibid.

142 *Stokes-Pactolus 63-46: The Daily Reflector,* p.8, 12-8-1956.

142 *team that year: The Daily Reflector,* p.7, 12-12-1956.

142 *against Farmville: The Daily Reflector,* p.7, 1-23-1957.

142 *defeated Bethel twice: The Daily Reflector,* p.8, 12-15-1956; p.7, 1-30-1957.

142 *by one point: The Daily Reflector,* p.8, 2-2-1957.

142 *the boys played one: The Daily Reflector,* p.6, 2-25-1957.

142 *a close one, 40-38: The Daily Reflector,* p.7, 2-26-1957.

142 *Stokes-Pactolus 37: The Daily Reflector,* p.6, 3-1-1957.

142 *championship game, 52-43: The Daily Reflector,* p.6, 3-4-1957.

142 *honor at guard: The Daily Reflector,* p.6, 3-4-1957.

143 *averaged more points:* personal communication, Sue (Sutton) Turnage, 8-12-2014.

143 *Farmville, 48-38: The Daily Reflector,* December 1957-April 1958 and p.7, 2-19-1958.

143 *All-Conference team: The Daily Reflector,* p.5, 2-22-1958.

143 *in the conference: The Daily Reflector,* December 1958-February 1959.

144 *the game 41-33: The Daily Reflector,* 2-16-1959.

144 *netted 8: The Daily Reflector,* p.6, 2-16-1959.

144  *scored 29 points: The Daily Reflector*, p.5, 2-21-1959.

144  *as a guard: The Daily Reflector*, p.6, 2-23-1959.

144  *Tornadoes 73-39: The Daily Reflector*, p.13, 12-3-1959.

144  *handily, 90-60: The Daily Reflector*, p.5, 12-5-1959.

144  *against Grimesland:* Ibid.

144  *double overtime, 65-61: The Daily Reflector*, p.10, 12-16-1959.

144  *Chicod 71-44: The Daily Reflector*, p.5, 12-19-1959.

144  *over the same team: The Daily Reflector*, p.7, 1-16-1960.

144  *Robersonville, 49-30: The Daily Reflector*, p.5, 1-9-1960.

144  *Belvoir-Falkland, 71-63: The Daily Reflector*, p.7, 1-20-1960.

144  *against Stokes-Pactolus: The Daily Reflector*, p.5, 1-23-1960.

144  *to get 4 points: The Daily Reflector*, p.11, 2-18-1960.

144  *of the tournament: The Daily Reflector*, p.5, 2-20-1960.

145  *in conference play: The Daily Reflector*, p.7, 2-23-1960.

145  *team at guard: The Daily Reflector*, Ibid.

145  *Andrea (Harris) Norris: The Daily Reflector*, December 1960-February 1961.

145  *of her career: The Daily Reflector*, p.5, 2-18-1961.

145  *the Bethel Indians:* personal communication and scrapbook, Andrea (Harris) Norris, 8-10-2014.

145  *in first place: The Daily Reflector*, p.5, 2-23-1963. Ayden's record for '62-'63 was more difficult than usual to pin down. *The Daily Reflector* reported Ayden's early season record to be 4-4 in the conference and shortly thereafter to be 13-3 overall. Then, at the end of the season it was 11-3. Suddenly the record became 11-5. I hope the final overall record of 12-6 is close to reality.

145  *6-10 conference record: The Daily Reflector*, p.5, 2-23-1963.

146  *Tornadoes 40-38:* Ibid.

146  *to win the title: The Daily Reflector*, p.8, 3-4-1963.

146  *All-Conference honors:* Ibid.

146  *rather than two:* personal communication, Suzanne (Wilson) Gray, 10-9-2014.

146  *10 of their first 11 games: The Wheel*, p.58, 1964.

146  *12-4 conference record: The Daily Reflector*, December 1963-March 1964.

146 *Stokes-Pactolus handily 41-24: The Daily Reflector,* p.1, Sports Section, 2-25-1964.

146 *in the finals: The Daily Reflector,* p.1, Sports Section, 2-28-1964.

146 *the score, 56-28: The Daily Reflector,* p.1, Sports Section, 3-2-1964.

146 *All-Conference at guard: The Daily Reflector,* p.8, 3-2-1964.

146 *Ayden 15: The Daily Reflector,* p.1, Sports Section, 2-22 through 2-27, 1965.

146 *All-Conference at forward: The Daily Reflector,* p.1, Sports Section, 3-2-1965.

146 *record was 11-6: The Daily Reflector,* December 1964-February 1965.

146 *Pitt County Conference tournament: The Daily Reflector,* p.1, Sports Section, 2-22-1966 and p.1, Sports Section, 2-23-1967.

146 *as a guard: The Daily Reflector,* p.1, Sports Section, 2-28-1966.

146 *All-Conference team: The Daily Reflector,* p.12, 2-26-1967.

147 *Pitt County Conference standings: The Daily Reflector,* p.15, 2-28-1968.

147 *in overtime, 37-35: The Daily Reflector,* p.11, 1-3-1968.

147 *by 21 points: The Daily Reflector,* p.15, 1-7-1968.

147 *with a loss, 36-30: The Daily Reflector,* p.13, 1-10-1968.

148 *before tourney time: The Daily Reflector,* January and February 1968.

148 *Indians had 3: The Daily Reflector,* p.14, 2-14-1968.

148 *finished 9-3: The Daily Reflector,* p.13, 2-18-1968.

148 *Grifton, 26-19: The Daily Reflector,* p.8, 2-23-1968.

148 *in the finals, 41-18: The Daily Reflector,* p.6, 2-27-1968.

148 *with 5 points: The Daily Reflector,* p.15, 2-11-1968.

148 *All-Conference team: The Daily Reflector,* p.14, 2-25-1968.

148 *All-County team: The Daily Reflector,* p.14, 3-24-1968.

148 *record was 12-4: The Daily Reflector,* December 1967-February 1968.

148 *the year 12-8: The Daily Reflector,* December 1968-March 1969.

148 *an earlier loss: The Daily Reflector,* p.15, 1-22-1969.

148 *the scoring column: The Daily Reflector,* p.15, 2-2-1969.

148 *Wolf Gals!: The Daily Reflector,* p.15, 2-9-1969.

148 *behind the leaders: The Daily Reflector,* p.7, 2-6-1969.

148 *10 to 12 points: The Daily Reflector,* p.7, 2-6-1969.

148 *Indians won, 46-39: The Daily Reflector,* p.1, Sports Section, 1-8-1969.

148 *score was 42-34: The Daily Reflector:* p.14, 2-12-1969.

148 *in the conference: The Daily Reflector,* p.15, 2-16-1969.

149 *wining 37-20: The Daily Reflector,* p.13, 2-26-1969.

150 *scored 7: The Daily Reflector,* p.15, 3-2-1969.

150 *a 26-0 record: The Daily Reflector,* Ibid., p.13.

150 *All-Conference team: The Daily Reflector,* Ibid., p.14.

150 *no one in double figures: The Daily Reflector,* p.1, Sports Section, 12-17-1969.

150 *scored in double figures: The Daily Reflector,* p.8, 1-5-1970.

150 *next tourney game: The Daily Reflector,* p.1, Sports Section, 2-26-1970.

150 *Judy Dail graduated: The Daily Reflector,* p1, Sports Section, 3-1-1970.

150 *my best guess: The Daily Reflector,* December 1969-March 1970.

150 *2 points each: The Daily Reflector,* p.16, 1-2-1971.

150 *Grifton, 34-19: The Daily Reflector,* p.1, Sports Section, 2-18-1971.

150 *Lynn Langston and Patsy Loftin: The Daily Reflector,* p.16, 2-21-1971.

150 Unbelievable Numbers during Six on Six Girls' Basketball Era, www.luckyshow.org/basketball/NC6histories.htm

CHAPTER 11: GROWING UP WHITE DURING JIM CROW

(no citations)

CHAPTER 12: SOUTH AYDEN SCHOOL

*Page*

163 *on the other: South Ayden School: History and Memories* by Charles L. Becton, p.24, 2007.

165 *columns are new:* Ibid., p.14.

166 *pictures of those teams: The Eagle,* pp unnumbered, 1955.

166 *when I was a boy: The Eagle,* pp unnumbered, 1966.

167 *school's last yearbook publication: The Eagle,* 1970.

168 *South Ayden School:* Becton, *South Ayden School: History and Memories*, p. iv.

168 *of its existence:* Ibid., p. v.

168 *in ignorance:* Ibid., p.1.

168 *the Civil War:* Ibid., p.3.

168 *offered none:* Ibid.

168 *a Band room:* Ibid.

170 *all the costs thereof:* Ibid., pp. 9 and 10.

170 *and Shiloh:* Ibid.

170 *same time period:* Ibid., p.8.

170 *World War II:* Ibid., p.18.

170 *the school's history:* Ibid., p.13.

170 *better library facilities:* Ibid., p.18.

170 *Ayden Colored School:* Ibid., p.19.

170 *the white enrollment:* Ibid., p.18.

171 *of $11,417.48:* Ibid., p.19.

171 *South Ayden School:* Ibid., p.13.

171 *attending South Ayden School:* personal communication, Charles Becton, 5-26-2014.

174 *I will see him again:* The fictional dialogue between Charles Becton and me is taken from *South Ayden School: History and Memories* and an interview I did with him on 5-26-2014.

174 "Additional Information from *South Ayden School: History and Memories"* taken from Charles Becton's book.

CHAPTER 13: SOUTH AYDEN EAGLE FOOTBALL

*Page*

179 *were exceptional athletes:* personal communication, Charles Becton, 5-26-2014.

179 *educational opportunities:* Ibid.

179 *by his classmates:* personal communication, Huey Lawrence, 8-13-2014.

180 *fall of 1965:* The Daily Reflector, p.10, 8-27-1965; p.11, 9-2-1965; p.7, 9-3-1965; p.6, 9-6-1965.

180 *Becton remembered:* personal communication, Charles Becton, 5-26-2014

180 *experienced football program:* The Kinston Daily Free Press, p.2, 9-8-1965.

180 *from whence he started:* personal communication, Charles Becton, 5-26-2014.

181 *at safety:* The Daily Reflector, p.6, 9-6-1965.

181 *on the ground:* The Kinston Daily Free Press, p.2, 9-8-1965.

181 *Grainger Stadium:* The Kinston Daily Free Press, p.2, 9-9-1965.

181 *never threatened:* The Kinston Daily Free Press, p.3, 9-13-1965.

182 *now 2-2:* The Kinston Daily Free Press, p.3, 9-29-1965.

182 *football in North Carolina:* Sidelines: A North Carolina Story of Community, Race, and High School Football by Stuart Albright, pp.65 and 66, 2009.

182 *won going away:* The Kinston Daily Free Press, p. 3, 10-4-1965.

182 *for a touchdown:* The Daily Reflector, p.6, 10-9-1965.

182 *of the ball:* The Kinston Daily Free Press, p.2, 10-13-1965.

183 *South Ayden 6:* The Daily Reflector, p.8, 10-25-1965.

183 *the following week:* The Kinston Daily Free Press, p.3, 10-27-1965.

183 *in New Bern:* The Kinston Daily Free Press, p.2, 11-10-1965.

183 *of 2-7:* The Kinston Daily Free Press, p.2, 11-17-1965

183 *experienced football program:* The Daily Reflector, p.20, 9-1-1966.

183 *Carver, 58-0:* The Daily Reflector, p.9, 9-3-1966.

183 *the end zone:* The Daily Reflector, p.4, 9-11-1966.

184 *team's only score: The Daily Reflector,* p.15, 9-18-1966.

184 *the only touchdown: The Daily Reflector,* p.17, 9-25-1966.

184 *Dunn 6: The Kinston Daily Free Press,* p.2, 10-1-1966.

184 *by Eppes High: The Daily Reflector,* p.3, 10-9-1966.

184 *for the contest: The Kinston Daily Free Press,* p.3, 10-8-1966.

184 *Glenn Whitehurst: The Kinston Daily Free Press,* p.3, 10-15-1966.

184 *for 20 yards: The Kinston Daily Free Press,* p. 2, 10-22-1966.

185 *through the air: The Kinston Daily Free Press,* p.3, 10-31-1966.

185 *Wake Forest, 8-6: The Daily Reflector,* p.17, 11-6-1966.

185 *All-Conference honors: The Daily Reflector,* p.1, Sports Section, 11-16-1966.

185 *boys are working: The Daily Reflector,* p.7, 9-4-1967.

185 *7-6 score stood up: The Kinston Daily Free Press,* p.3, 9-5-1967.

185 *Clinton Sampson 25, South Ayden 0: The Daily Reflector,* p.16, 9-10-1967.

185 *Sugg 20, South Ayden 0: The Daily Reflector,* p.14, 9-17-1967.

185 *Eppes 25, South Ayden 0: The Daily Reflector,* p.14, 10-8-1967.

185 *the final tally: The Daily Reflector,* p.14, 9-17-1967.

186 *without an interception: The Daily Reflector,* p.14, 10-8-1967.

186 *300 yards rushing: The Kinston Daily Free Press,* p.2, 10-28-1967.

186 *to win 9-6: The Daily Reflector,* p.14, 9-8-1968.

187 *Patillo 32, South Ayden 0: The Daily Reflector,* p.17, 9-15-1968.

187 *rest of the game: The Daily Reflector,* p.15, 9-22-1968.

187 *Sampson High 25, South Ayden 0: The Kinston Daily Free Press,* p.3, 9-28-1968.

187 *65 yard pass play: The Daily Reflector,* p.15, 10-6-1968.

187 *2-4 on the season: The Daily Reflector,* p.15, 10-13-1968.

188 *Glenn Williams: The Kinston Daily Free Press,* p.3, 10-19-1968.

188 *3-5 after their win: The Daily Reflector,* p.15, 10-27-1968.

188 *The record: 3-6: The Daily Reflector,* p.15, 11-3-1968.

188 *two old rivals: The Daily Reflector,* p.14, 11-7-1968.

188 *season's record: 3-6-1: The Daily Reflector,* p.14, 11-10-1968.

189 *Bethel Union High School:* personal communication, Johnny Davis, 8-6-2014.

189 *World War II: The Forgotten First: B-1 and the Integration of the Modern Navy,* by Alex Albright, 2013.

189 *to his future wife:* personal communication, Johnny Davis, 8-6-2014.

189 *the following Friday: The Daily Reflector,* p.15, 9-7-1969.

189 *1-1 for the year: The Daily Reflector,* p.14, 9-14-1969.

189 *for 16 yards: The Daily Reflector,* p.15, 9-28-1969.

189 *last year's 3-6-1 team: The Daily Reflector,* p.18, 10-5-1969.

190 *for 3 TDs:* Ibid.

190 *Kevin King, end:* Ibid.

190 *High School Athletic Conference:* Ibid.

191 *20-0, the final score: The Kinston Daily Free Press,* p.3, 10-6-1969.

192 *in a tie: The Daily Reflector,* p.15, 10-12-1969.

192 *South Ayden won 24-20: The Daily Reflector,* p.15, 10-19-1969.

192 *20 first downs: The Kinston Daily Free Press:* p.3, 10-27-1969.

192 *the game at 14: The Daily Reflector,* p.15, 11-2-1969.

192 *move against them: The Kinston Daily Free Press,* p.2, 11-10-1969.

193 *South Ayden High:* personal communication, Johnny Davis, 8-6-2014.

## CHAPTER 14: SOUTH AYDEN EAGLE BASKETBALL

*Page*

195 *a record of 8-0: The Daily Reflector,* p.7, 2-13-1962 and personal communication, Charles Becton, 5-16-2014.

195 1961-1962: South Ayden Final Regular Season Basketball Standings, *The Daily Reflector,* p.7, 2-13-1962.

196 *Charles Becton, 10:* Scrapbook (newspaper article): Charles Becton.

196 *overall record was 13-4:* Ibid.

196 *Charles Becton scored 21: The Daily Reflector,* p.6, 2-16-1962.

196 *Coach of the Year: The Daily Reflector,* p.9, 2-20-1962.

196 *a 7-1 mark: The Daily Reflector,* p.9, 2-20-1962.

196 *Faye Woods:* Ibid.

196 *with 11 points: The Daily Reflector,* p.6, 3-9-1962.

197 *17 points apiece:* Scrapbook (*The Kinston Daily Free Press,* p. unknown, 11-23-1961), Charles Becton.

197 *Charles Becton scored 20:* Scrapbook (*The Kinston Daily Free Press,* page and date unknown), Charles Becton.

197 *for two decades:* personal communication, Charles Becton, 5-26-2014.

197 *to arrange a game:* Ibid.

198 *lost only two: The Ayden Dispatch,* p.8, 1st Section, 2-25-1937.

198 *on the team: South Ayden School: History and Memories* by Charles Becton, pp. 20 and 21, 2007.

199 *around .500: The Daily Reflector,* December 1964-March 1965; December 1965-March 1966.

199 *home and home series: The Daily Reflector,* p.1, Sports Section, 1-8-1966; p.8, 2-4-1966.

199 *Linwood Best got 15: The Daily Reflector,* p.1, Sports Section, 2-19-1966.

199 *of 68-53: The Daily Reflector:* p.1, Sports Section, 2-21-1966.

199 *over Bethel Union, 36-32: The Daily Reflector,* Ibid.

200 *with a .500 record: The Daily Reflector,* December 1966-March 1967.

200 *Bethel Union, 48-41: The Daily Reflector,* p.11, 2-19-1967.

200 *for the Eagles: The Daily Reflector,* Ibid.

200 *District Tournament: The Daily Reflector,* p.14, 3-12-1967.

201 *were seniors: The Daily Reflector,* p.15, 12-13-1967.

201 *the Greenville paper: The Daily Reflector,* Ibid.

201 *Eppes High School of Greenville: The Daily Reflector,* p.1, Sports Section, 12-8-1967.

201 *their rivals, 56-54: The Daily Reflector,* p.15, 12-13-1967.

201 *mid-season game: The Daily Reflector,* p.8, 2-9-1968.

201 *over Hargrave, 61-34: The Daily Reflector,* p.1, Sports Section, 2-21-1968.

201  *defeated Central, 66-51: The Daily Reflector,* p.1, Sports Sectin, 2-22-1968.

201  *Woodington High School Longhorns: The Kinston Daily Free Press,* p.2, 2-21-1968.

201  *James Lowry with 15: The Daily Reflector,* p.15, 2-25-1968.

202  *defeated Deans, 80-48: The Daily Reflector,* p.9, 2-29-1968.

202  *John Roundtree added 15: The Daily Reflector,* p.13, 3-1-1968.

202  *Hornets' home floor:* personal communication, Johnny Davis, 8-6-2014.

202  *wasn't nearly enough: The Daily Reflector,* p.13, 3-6-1968.

202  *the Eagles' shots:* Ibid.

202  *over 1,000 rebounds:* www.seminoles.com, 8-10-2014.

202  *season's record of 21-6: The Daily Reflector,* p.13, 3-6-1968.

202  *All-Conference team: The Daily Reflector,* p.14, 3-24-1968.

202  *head basketball coach:* person communication, Johnny Davis, 8-6-2014.

202  *69-68 in overtime: The Daily Reflector,* p.16, 12-4-1968.

202  *the team was 4-1: The Daily Reflector,* p.19, 12-18-1968.

202  *SAH was 4-3: The Daily Reflector,* p.15, 1-5-1969.

203  *Leon Mayo got 12: The Daily Reflector,* p.9, 2-7-1969.

203  *tournament was next: The Daily Reflector,* p.15, 2-9-1969.

203  *upset in its first game: The Daily Reflector,* p.9, 2-13-1969.

203  *tourney championship: The Daily Reflector,* p.15, 2-16-1969.

204  *in Goldsboro:* Ibid., p.13.

204  *with 22 points: The Daily Reflector,* p.13, 2-19-1969.

204  *first matchup, 85-82: The Daily Reflector,* p.15, 1-13-1969.

204  *78-76 in overtime: The Daily Reflector,* p.14, 1-29-1969.

204  *Jesse Woods hit 11: The Daily Reflector,* p.13, 2-20-1969.

204  *a 15-4 record: The Daily Reflector,* December 1968-February 1969.

204  *the neighborhood of .500:* December 1969-March 1970.

204  *Robinson 99: The Daily Reflector,* p.1, Sports Section, 12-10-1969.

204  *Robinson won 54-46: The Daily Reflector,* p.14, 2-22-1970.

204  *Robinson 52: The Daily Reflector,* p.1, Sports Section, 3-5-1970.

204 *19.9 scoring average: The Kinston Daily Free Press,* p.2, 3-17-1970. This statement was taken from the Kinston newspaper. It is conceivable that this statistic would have been different if the Greenville newspaper had compared Mayo's scoring average in its "area."

204 *All-Conference team: The Daily Reflector,* p.15, 3-22-1970.

203 *only two wins: The Daily Reflector,* December 1970-March 1971.

205 *several "firsts": The Historic Architecture of Pitt County, North Carolina* by P. Power (Ed.), 1970.

205 *first encounter 61-49: The Daily Reflector,* p.19, 12-12-1970.

205 *the second, 48-32: The Daily Reflector,* p.1, Sports Section, 2-16-1971.

205 *beat that year: The Daily Reflector,* December 1970-March 1971.

205 *in early February: The Daily Reflector,* p.18, 12-9-1970; p.14, 1-2-1971; p.15, 1-10-1971.

205 *21 points in Farmville: The Daily Reflector,* p.18, 12-9-1970.

205 *its first loss, 68-67: The Daily Reflector,* p.2, 2-3-1971.

205 *into the state playoffs: The Daily Reflector,* February-March 1971.

205 *John Ormond: The Daily Reflector,* p.16, 2-21-1971; p.3, 3-21-1971.

206 *been torn down:* Becton, *South Ayden History,* p. v, 2007.

206 *Ayden-Grifton standout:* personal communication, Charles Becton, 12-24-2014.

CHAPTER 15: TWO OF THE BEST FOOTBALL TEAMS EVER (AND THEN, THE MYSTERY OF MYSTERIES)

*Page*

209 *His book called: The Great Depression* by Lionel Robbins, 1934.

209 *"buy local": The Ayden Dispatch,* p.1, 1-5-1931.

209 *$60.00 per month: The Ayden Dispatch,* p.1, 1-29-1931.

208 *everybody can afford: The Ayden Dispatch,* p.3, 1-8-1931.

209 *sold at auction: The Ayden Dispatch,* p.5, 10-15-1931.

209 *the former institution: The Ayden Dispatch,* p.1, 11-5-1931.

209 *team went 4-5: The Ayden Dispatch,* September-December 1930.

209 1931-1932: Ayden High School Football Season, *The Ayden Dispatch,* September-December 1931.

211 *Elizabeth City, 32-0:* Ibid.

211 *field a team: The Ayden Dispatch,* p.3, 10-1-1931.

211 *both to Elizabeth City: The Ayden Dispatch,* September-December 1931; September-December 1932.

211 *shows each morning: The Ayden Dispatch,* p.1, 10-29-1931.

211 *on WPTF: The Ayden Dispatch,* p.1, 9-18-1930.

211 *Saturday night: The Ayden Dispatch,* p.3, 2-20-1930.

212 *North Carolina plow horse: The Ayden Dispatch,* p.1, 10-2-1930.

212 *all talking movie:* Ibid.

212 *Sunday School Class: The Ayden Dispatch,* p.1, 11-19-1931.

212 *by late afternoon: The Ayden Dispatch,* p.1, 9-1-1932.

212 *squealing white pit: The Ayden Dispatch,* p.6, 10-1-1936.

213 *team finished 1-6: The Ayden Dispatch,* October-December 1933.

213 *in 1934, 6-3-1: The Ayden Dispatch,* October-December 1934.

213 *no first downs: The Ayden Dispatch,* p.1, 10-11-1934.

213 *and Greenville, The Ayden Dispatch,* Special Supplement, 9-26-1935.

213 *Vanceboro game was next: The Ayden Dispatch,* September-November 1935.

214 *play other schools: The Ayden Dispatch,* p.6, 10-8-1936.

214 *in December: The Ayden Dispatch,* November and December 1936.

214 *in interest and spirit: The Ayden Dispatch,* 3$^{rd}$ Section, p.2, 2-25-1937.

215 *in two years: The Ayden Dispatch,* September-November 1938 and September-November 1939.

CHAPTER 16: *THE WHEEL*

*Page*

217 *stock market crash: The Wheel,* pp.9-13, 1928.

218 *the 1928 annual:* personal communication, Tommy Edwards and William Edwards, 10-16-2013.

219 *Dedication: The Wheel,* p.6, 1928.

220 *Staff:* Ibid., p.5.

220 *We've won the first mile* (poem): Ibid., p.14.

221 *riding in Pontiacs:* Ibid., p.21.

226 *the Glee Club:* Ibid., p.38.

234 *J.J. McClees and Company:* Ibid., pp. unnumbered.

235 *And bring you all prosperity* (poem): Ibid., p. unnumbered.

236 *our Last Will and Testament:* Ibid., pp. 19 and 20.

236 *become a tradition: The Ayden Dispatch,* p.6, 10-20-1938.

236 *a softback version:* personal communication, Helen Joyce (Whitehurst) Stroud, 10-26-2014.

236 *the annual queen: The Wheel,* p. unnumbered, 1945.

236 *as the mascots:* Ibid.

236 *war bonds and stamps:* Ibid.

236 *no annual:* personal communication, Helen Joyce (Whitehurst) Stroud.

237 *to be sold:* personal communication, Loys Sumrell, 10-9-2013.

237 *of the Aydenites:* These *Aydenites* entries were taken from two issues of the newspaper. Both were undated but content dictates that they were published between 1943 and 1945.

238 *so small:* personal communication, Elmer Tripp, 11-1-2013.

240 *Wipe Out: Wipe Out,* 1966.

241 "1928: Selected Advertisements: *The Wheel, Volume I"*

CHAPTER 17: DECEMBER 7, 1941

*Page*

245 *to the mainland: The Ayden Dispatch,* p.1, 2-5-1942; reprinted from *The Chapel Hill Weekly.*

246 *'06 magazine article:* The Ayden Magazine, p.2, volume 3, number 1, 2006.

246 *Medal of Honor:* personal communication, Sammy Anson Pierce, 9-9-2013.

248 *during the mid-1930s:* personal communication, Sammy Anson Pierce, 1-29-14.

248 *the designation of ace:* personal communication, Sammy Anson Pierce, 1-31-2014.

249 *at the white parachute:* Ibid.

250 *the Pierce family:* Ibid.

250 *Eagles' football team:* personal communication, Huey Lawrence, 8-13-2014.

250 *segregated college:* Ibid.

250 *and Atlanta:* The Forgotten First: B-1 and the Integration of the Modern Navy by Alex Albright, p.138, 2013.

250 *Ted Williams trained there:* Ibid., pp. 78 and 120.

250 *to the bandsmen:* Ibid., p.73.

250 *the oppressive past:* Ibid.,, p.75.

251 *of the flag:* Ibid., p.87.

251 *formal drill practice:* Ibid., p.85.

251 *some more:* Ibid., p.86.

251 *married local women:* Ibid., pp.88 and 89.

251 *Woolen Gymnasium:* Ibid., p.89.

251 *band's barracks:* Ibid., p.93.

251 *some white girls:* Ibid.

251 *Marines had arrived:* Ibid.

251 *were dismissed:* Ibid.

252 *best part of Hawaii:* Ibid., p.113.

252 *on the island:* Ibid., p.122.

252 *band on campus:* Ibid., p.94.

252 *Marching Tar Heels:* Ibid., p.94 and 95.

252 *first colored band:* Ibid., p.153.

252 *Victory Medal:* Ibid., p.130.

253 *National Day of Prayer:* The Ayden Dispatch, p.1, 1-1-1942.

253 *to signal the time:* The Ayden Dispatch, p.1, 4-9-1942.

253 *Episcopal Church in Ayden: The Ayden Dispatch,* p.1, 3-11-1943.

253 *local aircraft observers: The Ayden Dispatch,* p.1, 1-8-1942.

253 *two-person teams: The Ayden Dispatch,* p.1, 10-7-1943.

253 *turn out the lights: The Ayden Dispatch,* p.1, 1-15-1942.

253 *of the war: The Ayden Dispatch,* p.1, 3-26-1942.

253 *April 25, 1942: The Ayden Dispatch,* p.1, 4-16-1942.

253 *scrap metal drives: The Ayden Dispatch,* p.1, 10-15-1942.

253 *under army control: The Ayden Dispatch,* p.1, 12-30-1943.

254 *her hometown:* personal communication, Helen Joyce (Whitehurst) Stroud, 8-3-2014.

254 *to purchase retreads: The Ayden Dispatch,* p.1, 1-1-1942.

254 *to June 1942: The Ayden Dispatch,* p.2, 7-30-1942.

254 *at periodic intervals: The Ayden Dispatch,* p.1, 11-12-1942.

254 *their tires inspected: The Ayden Dispatch,* p.1, 1-7-1943.

254 *in February 1943: The Ayden Dispatch,* p.1, 12-31-1942.

254 *U.S. Defense Bonds: The Ayden Dispatch,* p.1, 1-1-1942.

254 *week of sales: The Ayden Dispatch,* p.1, 9-17-1942.

254 *in its first month: The Ayden Dispatch,* p.1, 10-1-1942.

254 *$1,900 had been collected: The Ayden Dispatch,* p.1, 9-24-1942.

254 *conducted the auction: The Ayden Dispatch,* p.1, 11-19-1942.

255 *bid of $2,000: The Ayden Dispatch,* p.1, 11-26-1942.

255 *in the United States: The Ayden Dispatch,* p.1, 7-16-1942.

255 *collection hosts: The Ayden Dispatch,* p.1, 6-25-1942.

255 *for a half day: The Ayden Dispatch,* p.1, 10-29-1942.

255 *Saturday matinee: The Ayden Dispatch,* p.1, 11-5-1942.

255 *before the carnival:* Ibid., p.4.

255 *$1.00 worth of defense stamps:* Ibid.

255 *"Tin Can Week" was held: The Ayden Dispatch,* p.1, 11-4-1943.

255 *home-packed produce: The Ayden Dispatch,* p.1, 1-14-1943.

255 *the previous year: The Ayden Dispatch,* p.1, 9-3-1942.

255 *on the farms: The Ayden Dispatch,* p.1, 10-8-1942.

255 *sweet potato fields: The Ayden Dispatch,* p.4, 10-14-1943.

255 *September 1942: The Ayden Dispatch,* p.4, 10-1-1942.

255 *paper in 1942: The Ayden Dispatch,* p.1, 3-12-1942.

255 *to save gasoline: The Ayden Dispatch,* p.1, 3-18-1943.

256 *May 10 in 1944: The Ayden Dispatch,* p.1, 9-2-1943.

256 *school year 1943-44: The Ayden Dispatch,* p.3, 5-20-1943.

256 *soldiers at sea: The Ayden Dispatch,* p.1, 3-25-1943.

256 *campaign was started: The Ayden Dispatch,* p.1, 4-15-1943.

256 *65,000 new student nurses: The Ayden Dispatch,* p.4, 8-26-1943.

256 *to save cloth: The Ayden Dispatch,* p.1, 4-2-1942.

## CHAPTER 18: THE VIEW FROM AYDEN AROUND 1946

*Page*

258 *on the inside: The Ayden Dispatch,* p.2, 1-27-1938.

258 *"healing" electricity: From Dawn to Decadence* by Jacques Barzun, p.601, 2000.

258 *and many, many others:* Ibid., pp.601 and 602.

258 *The first electric chair:* Ibid., p.603.

259 *not have been encouraging: The Ayden Dispatch,* p.4, 12-12-1940.

259 *Ayden 8: The Ayden Dispatch,* p.4, 12-12-1940.

259 *Fountain, 19-12: The Ayden Dispatch,* p.4, 1-22-1942.

259 *to coach teams:* unpublished paper by Stuart Tripp, p.2.

259 *refereed by Stuart Tripp: The Ayden Dispatch,* 12-2-1944.

259 *Till Chauncey: The Ayden Dispatch,* p.1, 2-28-1946 and unpublished paper by Stuart Tripp, p.2.

259 *spring of 1942: The Ayden Dispatch,* p.1, 4-2-1942.

259 *Coastal Amateur League: The Ayden Dispatch,* p.1, 6-4-1942.

259 *in September: The Ayden Dispatch:* p.1, 9-10-1942.

259 *a volunteer coach: The Ayden Dispatch,* p.1, 5-2-1946.

259 *Faust Johnson: The Ayden Dispatch,* p.4, 4-4-1946.

260 *would be needed: The Ayden Dispatch,* p1, 5-9-1946.

## CHAPTER 19: FRIDAY NIGHT LIGHTS

*Page*

263 *good sportsmanship: The Ayden Dispatch,* p.6, 1-20-1949.

263 *part of that: The Ayden Dispatch,* p.1, 10-13-1949.

263 *1953-1954 school year: The Daily Reflector,* p.3, 2-27-1954.

264 *Durham in 1962:* Scrapbook (*The Daily Reflector),* William Edwards.

264 *have a team: The Ayden Dispatch,* p.3, 3-8-1934.

264 *conference championship: The Ayden Dispatch,* p.1, 10-26-1950.

264 *new fire truck: The Ayden Dispatch,* p.1, 12-28-1950.

264 *football team on the field: The Ayden Dispatch,* p.1, 5-9-1946.

264 *the upcoming season: The Ayden Dispatch,* p.1, 8-1-1946.

265 *shoes didn't have cleats:* remarks at Ayden Golf Tournament, Bear Baldree, 9-13-2012 and personal communication, Bear Baldree, 11-2-2012.

265 *his broken nose:* personal communication, Bear Baldree, 11-2-2012.

266 *high school auditorium:* personal communication, Elmer Tripp, 11-1-2013.

266 *in the war:* personal communication, Bear Baldree, 11-2-2012.

266 *talked him out of it:* Ibid.

266 *first game at Farmville: The Ayden Dispatch,* p.1, 9-19-1946.

266 *Faison, North Carolina:* personal communication, Tommy Bullock, 5-22-2011.

268 *Tommy said:* Ibid.

268 *20-6 and 26-6: The Ayden Dispatch,* September-December 1946 and *The Wheel,* p.33, 1947.

268 *a losing record: The Ayden Dispatch,* September-December 1947 and *The Wheel,* p.35, 1948.

268 *in graduation exercises: The Ayden Dispatch,* p.1, 6-3-1948.

268 *State won: The Ayden Dispatch,* p.1, 6-17-1948.

269 *that way again:* personal communication, Tommy Bullock, 5-22-2011.

CHAPTER 20: COWBOY SPURS

*Page*

273 *him at this time:* personal communication, Mitchell Oakley, 6-27-2011.

273 *a service to others: The Times-Leader,* p.9, 7-1-2011.

273 *aching legs at night:* personal communication, Teedy Bullock, 5-28-2011.

274 *in the games:* personal communication, Mitchell Oakley, 6-27-2011.

274 *junior and senior years: The Ayden Dispatch,* p.1, 10-7-1948.

274 *before his son did:* personal communication, Teedy Bullock, 5-28-2011.

274 *in the class of 1949: The Wheel,* p. , 1949.

274 *attend the games: The Ayden Dispatch,* p.1, 10-28-1948.

274 *were not sold: The Ayden Dispatch,* p.7, 10-14-1948.

274 *5 touchdown passes: The Ayden Dispatch,* p.1, 11-4-1948.

274 *the season, 4-3: The Wheel,* p.33, 1949.

274 *Teedy how to punt:* personal communication, Teedy Bullock, 5-28-2011.

274 *and Vanceboro: The Ayden Dispatch,* p.1, 9-1-1949.

274 *the Coastal Conference: The Wheel,* pp. unnumbered, 1951.

275 *Greenville in the second game: The Ayden Dispatch,* Septe5ber-December 1949.

275 1950-1951: Ayden High School Football Season, *The Wheel,* pp. unnumbered, 1951.

276 *3 per game:* Ibid.

276 *so far ahead:* personal communication, Teedy Bullock, 5-28-2011.

276 *400 yards in total offense: The Ayden Dispatch,* p.1, 9-28-1950.

276 *following "probable starters": The Ayden Dispatch,* p.1, 10-19-1950.

277 *leader on defense: The Ayden Dispatch,* p.1, 11-9-1950.

277 *untied season alive: The Ayden Dispatch,* p.1, 11-16-1950.

277 *the shutout, 19-0: The Ayden Dispatch,* p.1, 11-23-1950.

278 *athletically and academically:* personal communication, Teedy Bullock, 5-28-2011.

278 *son's grades transferred to Ayden High School:* personal communication, Teedy Bullock, 1-29-2015.

278 *started his career:* Ibid.

279 *It was great:* Ibid.

279 *to snap the ball:* personal communication, James Hemby, 12-12-2011.

279 *James said:* Ibid.

279 *academic administration:* Ibid.

280 *Carries over into life:* Ibid.

280 *came in handy:* Ibid.

280 *laughing so hard:* Ibid.

281 *a 5-3-2 season: The Wheel,* pp. unnumbered, 1952.

281 *All-Conference: The Wheel,* pp. unknown, 1953.

281 *became 0-9: The Daily Reflector,* p.6, 11-26-1952

281 "May 1947: Picture Shows at the Myers Theater," *The Ayden Dispatch,* p.3, 5-1-1947.

282 "Other News in Late 1940s," *The Ayden Dispatch,* March 1947-November 1948.

CHAPTER 21: THE BLACK AND WHITE BOX IN THE LIVING ROOM

*Page*

282 *the first weatherman:* www.wnct.com, 11-10-2013.

282 *news and weather:* Ibid.

282 *at 11:30 pm: The Ayden Dispatch,* p.1, 3-11-1954.

282 *to the holiday classic: The Classic: How Everett Case Brought Big-Time Basketball To the South* by Bethany Bradsher, 2011.

282 "Class of '52 Reunion," unpublished booklet by class of 1952.

282 "From *The Wheel,* 1952," excerpts from the 1952 annual.

CHAPTER 22: SANDLOTS AND LITTLE LEAGUE BASEBALL

*Page*

292 *the hurricanes (#2):* The Ayden Dispatch, p.1, 1-5-1956.

292 *meeting to order:* The Ayden Dispatch, p.1, 2-16-1956.

292 *Till Chauncey:* The Ayden Dispatch, p.1, 5-1-1956.

292 *Clay Stroud:* The Ayden Dispatch, p.1, 8-30-1956.

292 *summer of 1956:* The Ayden Dispatch, p.1, 2-16-1956.

292 *the Rotary Club:* The Ayden Dispatch, p.1, 4-26-1956 and p.1, 5-29-1956.

292 *jersey and a cap:* The Ayden Dispatch, p.1, 2-15-1956.

292 *the crown in '55:* The Ayden Dispatch, p.1, 5-24-1956.

293 *May 25, 1956:* The Ayden Dispatch, p.5, 5-31-1956.

293 *spiffy new uniforms:* The Ayden Dispatch, p.1, 3-1-1956.

293 *22-game schedule:* The Ayden Dispatch, p.1, 4-29-1956.

293 *four civic clubs:* The Ayden Dispatch, p.1, 8-2-1956.

295 *of those holes:* personal communication, R.L. Collins, 10-14-2014.

295 *into the game:* personal communication, Bill Norris, 8-20-2014.

295 *by the Town:* The Ayden Dispatch, p.1, 7-19-1956.

295 *the Rotary, 7-0:* The Ayden Dispatch, p.5, 7-12-1956.

295 *Lions 13, Rotary 0:* The Ayden Dispatch, p.2, 7-26-1956.

295 *Jaycees 8, Rotary 0:* The Ayden Dispatch, p.5, 8-9-1956.

295 *the losing cause:* The Ayden Dispatch, p.1, 8-16-1956.

295 *won the regular season:* The Ayden Dispatch, p.1, 8-30-1956.

295 *to take the tournament:* Ibid.

295 *Dr. Gooding's house:* personal communication, Tommy Edwards, 3-16-2013.

296 *black tire tape:* personal communication, Tommy Edwards, 3-18-2013.

296 *regular baseball field:* Ibid.

296 *Tommy answered:* Ibid.

296 *at the time:* Ibid.

297 *off the field:* Ibid.

297 *to end that practice:* The Ayden Dispatch, p.1, 11-26-1936.

298 *for sandlot ball:* The Ayden Dispatch, p.4, 4-13-1939.

298 "Rosters of the Four Little League Teams in 1956," *The Ayden Dispatch,* p.1, 8-26-1956.

299 "Other News of 1956," *The Ayden Dispatch,* 1956 editions.

CHAPTER 23: BASEBALL: POST WORLD WAR II

*Page*

303 *of World War II was basketball: The Ayden Dispatch,* p.1, 12-7-1944.

303 *baseball was next: The Ayden Dispatch,* p.1, 2-28-1946.

303 *and then baseball:* personal communication, Tommy Bullock, 5-22-2011.

303 *high school team: The Ayden Dispatch,* p.4, 4-4-1946 and p.1, 4-11-1946.

303 *Washington Pam-Pack: The Ayden Dispatch,* p.4, 4-4-1946.

304 *won the game:* Ibid.

304 *Selma, 8-2: The Ayden Dispatch,* p.1, 5-2-1946.

304 1946: Sample of Games Played By the Ayden Aces, *The Ayden Dispatch,* summer of 1946.

304 *Coastal Conference: The Wheel,* pp. unnumbered, 1951.

306 *won the title: The Daily Reflector,* p.6, 4-24-1952.

306 1949-1950: Ayden High School Baseball Season, *The Wheel,* pp. unnumbered, 1951.

306 *South Edgecombe (Pinetops): The Wheel,* pp. unnumbered, 1952.

306 *against one defeat: The Daily Reflector,* p.10, 5-3-1951.

306 *the final inning: The Daily Reflector,* Ibid.

306 *the conference winner: The Daily Reflector,* p.6, 3-9-1951.

306 *took the loss: The Daily Reflector,* p.6, 5-15-1951.

307 *Teedy Bullock, The Daily Reflector,* p.6, 5-16-1951.

307 *conference trophy:* Ibid.

307 *4 earned runs: The Daily Reflector,* p.6, 5-9-1951.

307 *with 12:* Ibid.

308 1950-1951: Ayden High School Baseball Season, *The Wheel,* p.30, 1952.

309 *no post-season tournament: The Daily Reflector,* p.6, 3-15-1952.

309 *the home team, 10-5: The Daily Reflector,* p.6, 4-3-1952.

309 *win the contest: The Daily Reflector,* p.6, 4-9-1952.

309 *6-0 victory: The Daily Reflector,* p.6, 4-12-1952.

309 *Farmville 3: The Daily Reflector,* p.6, 4-16-1952.

310 *not give up a walk: The Daily Reflector,* p.6, 4-19-1952.

310 *of the year, 7-3:* Ibid.

310 1951-1952: Coastal Conference Baseball Standings at the Halfway Mark, *The Daily Reflector,* p.6, 4-24-1952.

310 *A.T. Venters had two hits: The Daily Reflector,* p.6, 5-1-1952.

311 *for a 3-0 win: The Daily Reflector,* p.6, 5-3-1952.

311 *denying him a victory: The Daily Reflector,* p.6, 5-9-1952.

311 *probably finished 8-2: The Daily Reflector,* p.6, 5-15-1952.

311 *to win, 7-4: The Daily Reflector,* p.7, 4-15-1953.

312 *added a single: The Daily Reflector,* p.6, 4-27-1953.

312 *Robersonville 9: The Daily Reflector,* p.8, 4-8-1954.

312 *38 over the last two games: The Daily Reflector,* p.6, 5-14-1954.

312 *of the infield: The Daily Reflector,* p.8, 5-19-1954.

313 *7-1 to win the title: The Wheel,* pp. unnumbered, 1956.

313 *Country Club:* personal communication, Melvin Worthington, 11-1-2013.

314 *by its mother:* Ibid.

314 *1955 conference baseball championship:* personal communication, Milton Worthington, 11-1-2013.

314 *will be back: The Daily Reflector,* p.6, 3-15-1956.

314 *top batters last year:* Ibid.

314 *added a single: The Daily Reflector,* p.6, 3-29-1956.

314 *second base:* Ibid.

314 *Coastal Conference crown: The Daily Reflector,* p.6, 4-9-1956.

315 *won 3-2: The Daily Reflector,* p.8, 4-19-1956.

315 *7-1 overall: The Daily Reflector,* p.6, 4-24-1956.

315 *7-0 record in the Coastal Conference: The Daily Reflector,* p.6, 4-27-1956.

315 *team's two runs: The Daily Reflector,* p.6, 5-2-1956.

315 *games were canceled: The Wheel,* pp. unnumbered, 1957.

316 *.400 mark: The Daily Reflector,* p.9, 5-23-1957.

316 *county championship: The Daily Reflector,* p.7, 5-9-1958.

316 *Tornadoes were 1-4: The Daily Reflector*, p.5, 4-26-1958.

316 *Ayden's three hits: The Daily Reflector*, p.7, 4-7-1959.

316 *defeating them, 10-1: The Daily Reflector*, p.9, 4-8-1959.

316 *Tornadoes' attack: The Daily Reflector*, p.7, 4-20-1959.

316 *7-1 in the conference: The Daily Reflector*, p.11, 4-29-1959.

316 *District 1 championship: The Daily Reflector*, p.9, 5-6-1959.

316 *2-0 in the league: The Daily Reflector:* p.5, 4-9-1960.

317 *4-1 in the conference standings: The Daily Reflector*, p.9, 4-20-1960.

317 *5-1 mark in the conference: The Daily Reflector*, p.11, 4-21-1960.

317 *two hits apiece: The Daily Reflector*, p.7, 4-26-1960.

317 *Farmville was 3-4: The Daily Reflector*, p.9, 4-27-1960.

317 *at first base:* personal communication, Tommy Dunn, 10-14-2014.

317 *a district championship: The Daily Reflector*, p.5, 4-8-1961.

318 *Ayden won, 10-6:* Ibid.

318 *and a triple:* Ibid.

318 *giving up 15 hits: The Daily Reflector*, p.5, 4-15-1961.

318 *won the game, 4-1: The Daily Reflector*, p.11, 4-19-1961.

318 *10^th victory of the year: The Daily Reflector*, p.11, 5-17-1961.

318 *playoffs that year: The Daily Reflector*, p.11, 5-10-1961.


CHAPTER 24: "THE DINKY MILLS STORY" (OR) *NEVER GIVE UP,* YOU MAY STILL GET TO WEAR GASOLINE-SOAKED BLOOMERS

*Page*

324 *Space Medal of Honor:* www.nasa.gov, 10-15-2014; www.jsc.nasa.gov, 11-4-2014; personal communication, Clem McLawhorn, 10-5-2014.

326 *can't do something:* personal communication, Ikey Baldree, 9-6-2012.

326 *who Dinky Mills is:* personal communication, Tommy Dunn, 10-14-2014.

328 *I tried to remember:* personal communication, Dink Mills, 4-29-2010.

328 *sports and academics: The Times-Leader,* p.9, Mitchell Oakley, 6-2-2010.

329 *for everybody:* personal communication, Dink Mills, 4-29-2910.

329 *It motivated me:* Ibid.

329 *to a student:* Ibid.

330 *I was better:* Ibid.

330 *tobacco patch:* Ibid.

331 *community actually made me:* Ibid.

331 *any words ever could: The News and Observer,* p.1E, 11-28-2013.

331 *Truly remarkable:* Ibid.

332 *mistreated me:* personal communication, Dink Mills, 4-29-2010.

332 *you've screwed it all up:* Ibid.

332 *anything about it:* Ibid.

332 *Dink said:* Ibid.


CHAPTER 25: WAYLAND'S FOUL SHOTS

*Page*


335 1960-1961: Ayden High School Football Season, *The Wheel,* pp.52 and 53, 1961.

336 *to inclement weather: The Daily Reflector,* p.6, 11-1-1957.

336 *second time that year:* personal communication, Bill Norris, 1-29-2014.

337 *Bobby Gene Weathington, The Daily Reflector,* p.9, 12-4-1957 and *The Wheel,* pp. unnumbered, 1958.

337 *their first loss: The Daily Reflector,* p.9, 12-18-1957.

337 *highly competitive: The Daily Reflector,* p.5, 1-18-1958.

337 1957-1958: Pitt County Conference Regular Season Standings, *The Daily Reflector,* p.5, 2-15-1958.

339 *over Grimesland: The Daily Reflector,* p.7, 2-18-1958.

339 *and Winterville: The Daily Reflector,* p.9, 2-20-1958.

339 *in the tournament finals: The Daily Reflector,* p.5, 2-22-1958.

339  *Edenton 57-39: The Daily Reflector,* p.10, 3-6-1958.

339  *Phillip Smith with 19: The Daily Reflector,* p.7, 3-7-1958.

341  *and McGlohon 2: The Daily Reflector,* p.5, 3-8-1958.

341  *team-high eight rebounds: The Daily Reflector,* p.7, 3-10-1958.

341  *27th in a row: The Daily Reflector,* 3-13-1958.

341  *Class A championship: The Daily Reflector,* p.5, 3-15-1958.

341  *73-61 for third place: The Daily Reflector,* p.6, 3-17-1958.

341  *1959 All-County team: The Daily Reflector,* December 1958-February 1959.

343  *champs finished 29-3: The Daily Reflector,* December 1960-March 1961.


CHAPTER 26: HAZEL


*Page*


345  *and 2-3-3, respectively: The Daily Reflector,* September-December 1953 and September-December 1954.

345  *October 15, 1954: The Daily Reflector,* p.10, 9-11-1954; www.noaa.gov, 2-1-2014; *Southern New England Tropical Storms and Hurricanes, A Ninety-eight Year Summary 1909-1997* by David R. Valee and Michael R. Dion, National Weather Service, Tauton, Maine.

345  *swarming with mosquitoes:* personal communication, R.L. Collins, 10-14-2014.

345  *won 13-0: The Daily Reflector,* p.10, 9-18-1954.

346  *from floating away:* personal communication, R.L. Collins, 10-14-2014.

346  *39,000 structures were damaged:* www.4ncsu.edu, 2-2-2014, "Event Summary: National Weather Service, Raleigh, N.C., Case Study Team: Michael Strickler, Douglas Schneider, and Johnathan Blaes.

346  *to become superstitious: The Daily Reflector,* September-December 1954.

346  *Robersonville 0: The Daily Reflector,* p.10, 9-25-1954.

346  *Farmville 6: The Daily Reflector,* p.10, 10-2-1954.

346  *50 yards for the only touchdown: The Daily Reflector,* p.10, 10-1-1955.

347 *and Contentnea: The Wheel,* pp. unnumbered, 1956.

347 *the final touchdown: The Daily Reflector,* p.10, 11-5-1955.

347 *play on defense: The Daily Reflector,* p.10, 11-12-1955.

348 *Coastal Conference championship: The Daily Reflector,* p.6, 11-18-1955.

348 *and Lindy Dunn: The Wheel,* pp. unnumbered, 1957.

350 *we'd won the game:* personal communication, Burt Tripp, 2-11-2011.

350 *ready to whop our ass:* personal communication, R.L. Collins, 10-14-2014.

350 *that was some night:* Ibid.

350 *from back to front:* personal communication, Ikey Baldree, 9-6-2012.

351 *I hope they can do it: The Ayden Dispatch,* p.1, 2-14-1946.

CHAPTER 27: BOYS' BASKETBALL: POST WORLD WAR II

*Page*

354 *war bonds and stamps: The Wheel,* pp. unnumbered, 1945.

354 *by Ayden merchants: The Ayden Dispatch,* p.1, 12-7-1945 and *The Wheel,* pp. unnumbered, 1945.

354 *finish 7-10: The Wheel,* pp. unnumbered, 1945.

354 *for the auditorium: The Ayden Dispatch,* p.4, 1-24-1946.

354 *regularly scheduled game: The Ayden Dispatch,* p.1, 2-21-1946.

354 *many westerns:* Ibid.

355 *to begin the search: The Ayden Dispatch,* p.1, 2-28-1946.

355 *was her passion: The Wheel,* p.2, 1947.

355 *to those who never returned from World War II:* Ibid., p.3.

355 *Winterville 13: The Ayden Dispatch,* December 1932-March 1933.

355 *its season 25-8: The Ayden Dispatch,* December 1934-March 1935.

355 *have been lost: The Ayden Dispatch,* December 1935-March 1936.

355 *finished 19-1: The Ayden Dispatch,* December 1939-March 1940.

356 *season, 0-19: The Ayden Dispatch,* December 1930-March 1931.

356 *23-game drought: The Ayden Dispatch,* p.1, 1-28-1932.

356 *an 11-12 record: The Wheel,* p.35, 1947.

356 *finished 11-7: The Wheel,* p.33, 1948.

356 *Bethel 50-20: The Ayden Dispatch,* p.4, 1-29-1948.

356 *score of 43-39: The Bethel Herald,* p.1, 4-20-1988.

356 *21-5, one of the best seasons on record: The Wheel,* p.35, 1949.

356 *Teedy Bullock at forwards:* Ibid.

357 *State Class B playoffs: The Daily Reflector,* p.6, 2-13-1949.

357 *first game, 54-28: The Daily Reflector,* p.6, 2-14-1949.

357 *identical score, 55-28: The Daily Reflector,* p.8, 2-15-1949.

357 *Farmville High School gym: The Daily Reflector,* p.6, 2-26-1949.

358 *to the state finals: The Daily Reflector:* p.6, 2-28-1949.

358 *"Farmville Invitational Coastal Plain Basketball Tournament":* *The Wheel,* p.35, 1949.

358 *Tornadoes, 56-36:* Ibid.

358 *42-14 in the second game:* Ibid.

359 *to play in basketball: The Daily Reflector,* p.8, 11-16-1949.

359 *50 cents for adults:* Ibid.

359 *in May 1950: The Ayden Dispatch,* p.1, 5-25-1950.

359 1949-1950: Pitt County Conference Regular Season Basketball Standings (partial), *The Daily Reflector,* p.6, 2-21-1950.

360 *Pitt County Conference Tournament: The Daily Reflector,* February-March, 1950.

360 *not to make the challenge: The Ayden Dispatch,* p.8, 2-15-1950.

360 *for the state tournament: The Daily Reflector,* p.6, 2-21-1950.

360 *Jamesville, 33-25: The Daily Reflector,* p.10, 2-23-1950.

360 *Elm City, 47-32: The Daily Reflector,* p. 6, 2-24-1950.

361 *for the times: The Daily Reflector,* p.6, 2-25-1950.

361 *of the state playoffs: The Daily Reflector,* p.6, 2-27-1950.

361 1949-1950: Coastal Conference Final Basketball Standings, *The Ayden Dispatch,* p.1, 2-16-1950.

361 *with a 6-1 mark:* Ibid.

361 *Robersonville, 41-33: The Daily Reflector,* p.6, 3-1-1950.

361 *44-41 over Robersonville: The Daily Reflector,* p.6, 3-3-1950.

361 *37-28 in the semifinals: The Daily Reflector,* p.6, 3-11-1950.

361 *Bethel won the trophy: The Daily Reflector,* p.6, 3-13-1950.

362 *Bullock averaged 12 per game: The Ayden Dispatch,* p.1, 3-23-1950.

362 *Mac Whitehurst: The Ayden Dispatch,* p.1, 11-30-1950.

362 *in their 10$^{th}$ game: The Daily Reflector,* p.6, 1-17-1951.

362 *Farmville won the second: The Daily Reflector,* p.5, 1-27-1951.

362 *in double figures: The Daily Reflector,* p.10, 1-31-1951.

362 *by winning 42-32:* Ibid.

362 *Red Oak was victorious, 57-47: The Daily Reflector,* p.8, 2-22-1951.

362 *South Edgecombe, 49-35: The Daily Dispatch,* p.10, 2-28-1951 and p.8, 3-1-1951.

362 *title in a row: The Daily Reflector,* p.6, 3-10-1951.

362 *of 24-6: The Wheel,* pp. unnumbered, 1952.

363 *Darrell Worthington ('53): The Daily Reflector,* p.12, 11-28-1951; *The Wheel,* p.29, 1952 and personal communication, Ham Lang, 9-23-2011.

363 *1951-1952 season, 33-18: The Daily Reflector,* p.12, 12-5-1951.

363 *Christmas present, 36-34: The Daily Reflector,* p.8, 12-19-1951.

363 *final score of 45-42: The Daily Reflector,* p.6, 1-12-1952.

363 1951-1952: Coastal Conference Final Regular Season Basketball Standings, *The Daily Reflector,* p.6, 2-25-1952.

364 *tournament championship: The Daily Reflector,* p.6, 2-27-1952.

364 *of the conflict: The Daily Reflector,* p.6, 2-28-1952.

364 *in Wilson County: The Daily Reflector,* p.6, 2-29-1952.

364 *Elm City 40:* Ibid.

364 *score of 59-39: The Daily Reflector,* p.6, 3-1-1952.

364 *for their defense:* Ibid.

364 *eliminated early: The Daily Reflector* p.6, 3-3-1952.

364 *stellar defensive efforts:* Ibid.

365 *of 64-41: The Daily Reflector,* p.11, 3-6-1952.

365 *scored 18 points: The Daily Reflector,* p.6, 3-7-1952.

365  *of 51-42: The Daily Reflector,* p.6, 3-10-1952.

365  *the Coastal Conference: The Daily Reflector,* p.6, 3-18-1952.

365  *trophy, 60-45:* Ibid.

366  *Got it?:* Ibid.

## CHAPTER 28: A FIRST FOR COACH TRIPP

*Page*

367  *annual tournaments: The Wheel,* pp. unnumbered, 1954.

368  *roster got to play: The Daily Reflector,* December 1952-Februoary 1953.

368  *first victory over Bethel:* personal communication, Ham Lang, 6-27-2014.

368  *Indians in 11 years: The Daily Reflector,* p.8, 12-19-1952.

368  *Ayden won 18-16: The Ayden Dispatch,* p. unknown, 12-14-1939.

369  *Bethel again, 19-15: The Ayden Dispatch,* p. unknown, 1-18-1940.

369  *Ayden was 6-0: The Daily Reflector,* p.8, 12-19-1952.

369  *second place at 11-2: The Daily Reflector,* p.6, 2-16-1953.

369  *Red Devils by one: The Daily Reflector,* p.9, 2-18-1953.

369  *Stokes in the finals: The Daily Reflector,* p.9, 2-23-1953.

369  *to finish 8-11: The Ayden Dispatch,* p.1, 3-4-1954.

369  *next game, 47-25: The Daily Reflector,* p.8, 12-19-1953.

369  *games at times: The Daily Reflector,* November 1953-February 1954.

371 *and Ham Lang: The Wheel,* pp. unnumbered, 1954.

371  *over the Tornadoes: The Daily Reflector* and *The Ayden Dispatch,* November and December 1953.

371  *the second round: The Ayden Dispatch,* p.1, 3-4-1954.

372  *final score of 52-49: The Daily Reflector,* p.10, 12-4-1954.

372  *Tornadoes were 2-1: The Daily Reflector,* p.13, 12-9-1954.

372  *a 63-37 win over Grifton: The Daily Reflector,* p.10, 2-5-1955.

372  *with 14 points: The Daily Reflector,* p.10, 1-15-1955.

372  *to get 11: The Daily Reflector,* p.10, 2-15-1955.

372 *league schedule at 11-4: The Daily Reflector*, p.8, 2-29-1955.

372 *record of 10-5:* Ibid.

372 *were to Bethel: The Daily Reflector*, p.6, 2-22-1955.

372 *to win easily: The Daily Reflector*, p.6, 2-21-1955.

373 *for the game: The Daily Reflector*, p.6, 2-22-1955.

373 *to its trophy case: The Daily Reflector*, p.12, 2-24-1955.

373 *All-Coastal Conference team: The Daily Reflector*, p.8, 2-29-1955.

373 *All-Pitt County Conference team: The Daily Reflector*, p.12, 2-24-1955.

373 *it was 18-4: The Daily Reflector*, December 1954-February 1955.

374 *and Burt Tripp: The Wheel*, pp. unnumbered, 1956.

375 *ran over them:* personal communication, R.L. Collins, 10-14-2014.

375 *over the Bethel Indians: The Daily Reflector*, p.9, 12-15-1955.

375 *the Coastal Conference: The Daily Reflector*, p.6, 2-1-1956.

375 *Billy Vandiford: The Daily Reflector*, p.10, 2-4-1956.

375 *score of 50-37: The Daily Reflector*, p.10, 2-11-1956.

375 *Farmville, 53-37: The Daily Reflector*, p.6, 2-17-1956 and p.6, 2-22-1956.

375 *Bethel prevailed, 32-29: The Daily Reflector*, p.10, 2-18-1956.

376 *and won 44-41: The Daily Reflector*, p.6, 2-22-1956.

376 *finished at 0-4: The Daily Reflector*, p.6, 2-24-1956.

376 *in the conference:* Ibid.

376 *Tornadoes won: The Daily Reflector*, p.10, 1-7-1956.

376 *Red Devils 47-25: The Daily Reflector*, p.6, 3-1-1956.

376 *two conference tournaments: The Daily Reflector*, December 1955-March 1956.

376 *playoffs in Smithfield: The Daily Reflector*, p.6, 2-29-1956.

CHAPTER 29: '57

*Page*

379 *six years ago: The News and Observer,* Section II, p.5, 7-1-1962.

380 *in the process:* personal communication, Tommy Edwards, 3-16-2013.

381 *How about baseball?:* personal communication, Burt Tripp, 2-11-2011.

381 *Rams were defeated 56-44: The Daily Reflector,* p.9, 12-5-1956.

381 *15 AHS players saw action: The Daily Reflector,* p.8, 12-8-1956 and p.7, 12-12-1956.

381 *scored 38 points: The Daily Reflector,* p.8, 12-15-1956.

381 *ample playing time: The Daily Reflector,* p.8, 12-15-1956 and p.8, 1-12-1957.

382 *its first loss, 47-46: The Daily Reflector,* p.8, 1-26-1957.

382 *a 48-46 victory: The Daily Reflector,* p.7, 1-30-1957.

382 *Ayden was 11-2: The Daily Reflector,* p.8, 3-2-1957.

382 *Winterville 48: The Daily Reflector,* p.9, 2-28-1957 and p.6, 3-1-1957.

382 *to win, 39-38: The Daily Reflector,* p.6, 3-4-1957.

382 *Barbara Worthington ('58):* Ibid.

383 *the state playoffs: The News and Observer,* Section II, p.5, 7-1-1962.

383 *a harsh defeat: The Daily Reflector,* p.6, 3-5-1957.

383 *added ten points:* Ibid.

383 *not in this District: The Williamston Enterprise,* p.3, 3-5-1957.

383 *his team's 71-45 victory: The Daily Reflector,* p.6, 3-8-1957.

384 *Leslie Stocks 4: The Williamston Enterprise,* p.4, 3-12-1957.

384 *to nine points:* personal communication, Billy Vandiford, 2-11-2011.

384 *Jimmy Rogers with 20: The Daily Reflector,* p.6, 3-11-1957 and p.4, 3-12-1957.

384 *District 1 in the state playoffs: The Daily Reflector,* p.6, 3-11-1957.

384 *the required deadline: The Daily Reflector,* p.6, 3-12-1957.

385 *Jonesville for the state title: The Williamston Enterprise,* p.9, 3-19-1957.

385 *continue in the playoffs:* personal communication, Burt Tripp, 2-11-2011.

CHAPTER 30: ONE

*Page*

387 *always worth remembering: The Wheel,* pp. 4 and 5, 1962.

388 *depth they had last season: The Daily Reflector,* p.9, 9-1-1961.

388 *200 yards in penalties: The Daily Reflector,* p.5, 9-2-1961.

388 *only two first downs: The Daily Reflector,* p.5, 9-9-1961.

389 *all over again: The Daily Reflector,* p.5, 9-16-1961.

389 *the final touchdown: The Daily Reflector,* p.5, 9-23-1961.

389 *in the end zone: The Daily Reflector,* p.5, 9-30-1961.

390 *Farmville 6:* Ibid.

390 *Farmville 12:* Ibid.

390 *Ayden ahead at half 7-6: The Daily Reflector,* p.5, 10-7-1961.

390 *Edwards as the game ended:* Ibid.

390 *seventh win, 13-0: The Daily Reflector,* p.5, 10-14-1961.

391 *returned it to the 20: The Daily Reflector,* p.6, 10-21-1961.

391 *for the Tornadoes:* Ibid.

391 *before time ran out: The Daily Reflector,* p.5, 10-28-1961.

391 *Clem McLawhorn on defense:* Ibid.

391 *10-0 and headed to the playoffs: The Daily Reflector,* p.5, 11-4-1961.

392 *Camp Lejeune 14: The Daily Reflector,* p.7, 11-13-1961.

392 *Mount Olive was defeated 20-13: The Daily Reflector,* p.13, 11-16-1961.

392 *a few inches away: The Daily Reflector,* p.5, 11-18-1961.

392 *I will make an exception: The Daily Reflector,* p.13, 11-16-1961 and *The Wheel,* pp.50, 51, and 52, 1962.

393 *of the team all year: The Daily Reflector,* p.13, 11-16-1961.

393 *in grades 9-12: The Wheel,* pp.13-30, 1962.

393 *and baseball: The News and Observer,* Section II, p.5, 7-1-1962.

393 *11 played on the football team: The Daily Reflector*, p.7, 12-23-1961.

394 *without practicing one minute:* personal communication, Tommy Dunn, 10-14-2014.

394 *Belvoir-Falkland 41: The Daily Reflector,* p.5, 12-2-1961.

394 *Clem McLawhorn: The Daily Reflector,* p.12, 12-6-1961.

394 *a senior respectively: The Wheel,* pp.13-30, 1962.

396 *a 64-60 victory: The Daily Reflector,* p.11, 12-13-1961.

396 *Ayden won 59-53: The Daily Reflector,* p.9, 1-31-1962.

396 *Bethel's home court:* personal communication, 10-14-2014.

396 *Ayden was 10-1: The Daily Reflector,* p.9, 1-31-1962.

396 *47-44 on its home court: The Daily Reflector,* p.5, 1-6-1962.

396 *of the regular season: The Daily Reflector,* December 1961 and January 1962.

396 *by eight, 45-37: The Daily Reflector,* p.6, 3-3-1962.

397 *2-3 at the foul line: The Daily Reflector,* p.7, 2-24-1961.

397 *Amazing Grace at my funeral: The Daily Reflector,* p.5, 2-25-1961.

398 *Ayden's 71-35: The Daily Reflector,* p.9, 3-8-1962.

398 *the semifinals, 54-41: The Daily Reflector,* p.5, 3-10-1962.

398 *in the district tourney: The Daily Reflector,* p.7, 3-12-1962.

398 *on the 10-member team: The Daily Reflector,* p.5, 3-10-1962.

398 *team pull away: The Daily Reflector,* p.9, 3-15-1962.

398 *Bethel Indians: The Daily Reflector,* p.5, 3-17-1962.

398 *Windsor's 6-8 center?:* Ibid.

399 *score of 33-31: The Daily Reflector,* p.7, 3-19-1962.

400 *Tryon 44: The Daily Reflector,* p.9, 3-22-1962.

400 *a son this year:* Ibid.

400 *most of the game: The Daily Reflector,* p.5, 3-24-1962.

400 *58-57 for third place: The Daily Reflector,* p.7, 3-26-1962.

400 *at the foul stripe:* Ibid.

401 *attended the event:* Scrapbook (*The Daily Reflector* article), William Edwards.

401 *Farmville 10-7: The Daily Reflector,* p.7, 4-27-1962.

401 *streak out 15: The Daily Reflector,* p.12, 5-2-1962.

401 *had doubles:* Scrapbook (*The Ayden News-Leader,* 5-4-1962), Godfrey Little.

401 *Ayden was 5-0:* Ibid.

402 *The Tornadoes were 6-0:* Scrapbook (*The Ayden News-Leader,* 5-11-1962), Godfrey Little.

402 *Ayden was 7-0:* Ibid.

402 *mean as a snake:* personal communication, R.L. Collins, 10-14-2014.

402 *I asked you to do:* personal communication, Tommy Dunn, 10-14-2014.

403 *games that we played:* Ibid.

403 *in his AHS career:* Ibid.

403 *26-1 in his career:* The Daily Reflector, p.9, 5-25-1962.

403 *for 19 years:* The Daily Reflector, p.24, 5-23-1962.

405 *some of his boys:* The News and Observer: Section II, p.5, 7-1-1962.

405 *Miss Christine Vandiford of Grifton:* The Ayden Dispatch, p.3, 8-7-1947.

405 *"The Wheel, 1962"*

## Appendix 2

Ayden High School Football Game Scores and Season Records
from 1926-1971

**Blank = No score reported.**

### 1926 – 1927: 5-1-1

| | | | | |
|---|---|---|---|---|
| 10-8-26 | Ayden | 0 | Williamston | 0 |
| 10-15-26 | Ayden | 0 | Greenville | 35 |
| 10-22-26 | Ayden | 6* | La Grange | 0 |
| 10-29-26 | Ayden | 12 | La Grange | 0 |
| 11-16-26 | Ayden | 7 | Robersonville | 0 |
| 11-19-26 | Ayden | 6 | Williamston | 0 |
| 11-24-26 | Ayden | 3 | Tarboro | 0 |

*One touchdown for Ayden reported but not actual score; assume 6 points; La Grange held scoreless was reported.

## 1927 – 1928: 6-1-2

| Ayden | 6 | Kinston | 6 |
|-------|-----|--------------|----|
| Ayden | 20 | La Grange | 0 |
| Ayden | 12 | Robersonville | 0 |
| Ayden | 49 | Farmville | 0 |
| Ayden | 0 | Wilson | 0 |
| Ayden | 6 | Kinston | 2 |
| Ayden | 18 | Robersonville | 0 |
| Ayden | 12 | Morehead City | 0 |
| Ayden | 7 | Washington | 13 |

## 1928 – 1929: 7-3

| Ayden | 0 | Roanoke Rapids | 26 |
|-------|-----|--------------|----|
| Ayden | 26 | Nashville | 0 |
| Ayden | 25 | Robersonville | 0 |
| Ayden | 32 | La Grange | 0 |
| Ayden | 0 | Williamston | 20 |
| Ayden | 26 | Tarboro | 0 |
| Ayden | 20 | Vanceboro | 0 |
| Ayden | 0 | Wilmington | 19 |
| Ayden | 19 | Smithfield | 7 |
| Ayden | 14 | Greenville | 0 |

## 1929 – 1930: 8-2-1

| | | | |
|---|---|---|---|
| Ayden | 31 | Beaufort | 0 |
| Ayden | 31 | La Grange | 0 |
| Ayden | 38 | Rocky Mount | 0 |
| Ayden | 13 | Tarboro | 13 |
| Ayden | 6 | Vanceboro | 0 |
| Ayden (L) | | Weldon | |
| Ayden | 27 | Vanceboro | 0 |
| Ayden | 14 | New Bern | 0 |
| Ayden (W) | | Hertford | 0 |
| Ayden (W) | | Smithfield | |
| Ayden (L) | | Oxford | |

## 1930 – 1931: 4-5

| | | | |
|---|---|---|---|
| Ayden | 0 | Roanoke Rapids | 7 |
| Ayden | 0 | Elizabeth City | 13 |
| Ayden | 6 | Washington | 0 |
| Ayden (W) | | Tarboro | |
| Ayden | 30 | Farmville | 0 |
| Ayden | 0 | New Bern | 7 |
| Ayden | 12 | Chapel Hill | 0 |
| Ayden (L) | | Greenville | |
| Ayden (L) | | Kinston | |

## 1931 – 1932: 10-1-1

| | | | |
|---|---|---|---|
| Ayden | 12 | Aulander | 0 |
| Ayden | 0 | Elizabeth City | 32 |
| Ayden | 2 | Washington | 0 |
| Ayden | 21 | Beaufort | 0 |
| Ayden | 0 | Washington | 0 |
| Ayden (W) | * | New Bern | 0 |
| Ayden | 35 | Farmville | 0 |
| Ayden | 80 | Clayton | 0 |
| Ayden | 18 | Rich Square | 0 |
| Ayden | 6 | Plymouth | 0 |
| Ayden | 73 | Roper High | 0 |
| Ayden | 31 | Smithfield | 7 |

*Final score unreported; New Bern held scoreless was reported.

## 1932 – 1933: 8-1-1

| | | | |
|---|---|---|---|
| Ayden | 19 | Windsor | 7 |
| Ayden | 7 | Scotland Neck | 0 |
| Ayden | 19 | Beaufort | 0 |
| Ayden | 25 | Hertford | 0 |
| Ayden | 6 | Elizabeth City | 28 |
| Ayden | 0 | Edenton | 0 |
| Ayden | 33 | Enfield | 0 |
| Ayden | 33 | Rich Square | 0 |
| Ayden | 14 | Morehead City | 0 |
| Ayden | 7 | Henderson | 0 |

### 1933 – 1934: 1-6

| Ayden | 0 | Tarboro | 40 |
|-------|---|---------|-----|
| Ayden | 0 | Scotland Neck | 13 |
| Ayden | 6 | Williamston | 33 |
| Ayden (L) | | La Grange | |
| Ayden (L) | | Mt. Olive | |
| Ayden | 0 | Mt. Olive | 12 |
| Ayden | 12 | Snow Hill | 0 |

### 1934 – 1935: 6-3-1

| Ayden (?) | * | Washington | |
|-----------|---|------------|---|
| Ayden | 88 | Snow Hill | 0 |
| Ayden | 6 | Greenville | 7 |
| Ayden | 31 | Farmville | 0 |
| Ayden | 32 | Snow Hill | 0 |
| Ayden | 33 | Windsor | 6 |
| Ayden (?) | * | Scotland Neck | |
| Ayden | 7 | Morehead City | 0 |
| Ayden | 24 | Morehead City | 0 |
| Ayden (?) | * | Kinston | |

*Winners/losers and scores of three games unreported; two lost and one tied, 0-0

## 1935 – 1936: 3-1-1*

| Ayden | 6  | Beaufort      | 7 |
|-------|----|---------------|---|
| Ayden | 7  | Mt. Olive     | 0 |
| Ayden | 19 | Tarboro       | 0 |
| Ayden | 19 | Ahoskie       | 0 |
| Ayden | 0  | Morehead City | 0 |
| Ayden | ?  | Vanceboro     | ? |

*After starting season 3-1-1, *The Ayden Dispatch* reported that AHS's next game was an away game at Vanceboro. After that, nothing; football was never mentioned again. It appears that the remainder of the season was cancelled. I was unable to solve this mystery, but I do speculate in the narrative as to what may have happened. When calculating overall statistics, the record of 3-1-1 before the Vanceboro game will be used. Based on the newspaper's account of the upcoming season, the Tornadoes had remaining games with Farmville, Greenville, Kinston, Washington, Williamston, and Windsor. The actual week by week schedule was not provided.

## 1936 – 1937: 0-1*

| Ayden | 0 | New Bern | 19 |
|-------|---|----------|----|

*There was no football season in 1936. The players were divided into four teams that played each other. One "outside" game was lost to New Bern.

## 1937 – 1938*

*The records for the 1937 football season were unavailable.

### 1938 – 1939: 3-3-1

| Ayden (?) | | (team unk) | |
|-----------|---|------------|---|
| Ayden (?) | | La Grange | |
| Ayden (?) | | Plymouth | |
| Ayden | 0 | (team unk) | 19 |
| Ayden | 34 | Farmville | 0 |
| Ayden | 6* | Greenville | 6 |
| Ayden | 6 | Kinston | 26 |

*One touchdown per team reported but final score unreported; 6-6 tie assumed.

### 1939 – 1940: 1-3

| Ayden | 0 | Greenville | 12 |
|-------|---|------------|----|
| Ayden | 13 | Vanceboro | 0 |
| Ayden | 12 | Snow Hill | 21 |
| Ayden | 0 | Farmville | 13 |

### 1939 – 1946*

*Football was discontinued from 1939 (1939-1940) until 1946 (1946-1947).

### 1946 – 1947: 4-6

| | | | |
|---|---|---|---|
| Ayden | 20 | Farmville | 6 |
| Ayden | 20 | Mt. Olive | 13 |
| Ayden | 6 | Wallace | 7 |
| Ayden | 26 | Farmville | 6 |
| Ayden | 14 | Williamston | 0 |
| Ayden | 7 | Spring Hope | 13 |
| Ayden | 13 | Wake Forest | 20 |
| Ayden | 7 | Selma | 21 |
| Ayden | 0 | Columbia | 34 |
| Ayden | 0 | Wallace | 13 |

### 1947 – 1948: 4-5

| | | | |
|---|---|---|---|
| Ayden | 13 | Mt. Olive | 6 |
| Ayden | 49 | Warsaw | 0 |
| Ayden | 7 | La Grange | 27 |
| Ayden | 14 | Wake Forest | 13 |
| Ayden | 13 | Selma | 0 |
| Ayden | 31 | Farmville | 6 |
| Ayden | 0 | Wallace | 18 |
| Ayden | 0 | Clinton | 12 |
| Ayden | 7 | Williamston | 32 |

### 1948 – 1949: 4-3

| | | | |
|---|---|---|---|
| Ayden | 0 | Mt. Olive | 49 |
| Ayden | 6 | Smithfield | 0 |
| Ayden | 21 | Jacksonville | 0 |
| Ayden | 13 | Selma | 7 |
| Ayden | 56 | Warsaw | 6 |
| Ayden | 0 | Wallace | 13 |
| Ayden | 13 | Clinton | 18 |

## 1949 – 1950: 7-1

| Ayden | 34 | Wakelon | 0 |
|---|---|---|---|
| Ayden | 13 | Greenville | 14 |
| Ayden | 35 | South Edgecombe | 7 |
| Ayden | 28 | Vanceboro | 7 |
| Ayden | 13 | Farmville | 0 |
| Ayden | 26 | Tarboro | 7 |
| Ayden | 26 | Central of Elizabeth City | 0 |
| Ayden | 34 | Robersonville | 0 |

## 1950 – 1951: 9-0

| Ayden | 13 | Williamston | 7 |
|---|---|---|---|
| Ayden | 40 | Robersonville | 0 |
| Ayden | 42 | Vanceboro | 0 |
| Ayden | 46 | Farmville | 6 |
| Ayden | 36 | South Edgecombe | 6 |
| Ayden | 25 | Tarboro | 0 |
| Ayden | 14 | Ahoskie | 2 |
| Ayden | 7 | Fuquay Springs | 6 |
| Ayden | 19 | Central of Elizabeth City | 0 |

## 1951 – 1952: 5-3-2

| Ayden | 13 | Williamston | 18 |
|---|---|---|---|
| Ayden | 27 | Robersonville | 6 |
| Ayden | 14 | South Edgecombe | 6 |
| Ayden | 32 | Vanceboro | 12 |
| Ayden | 28 | Farmville | 6 |
| Ayden | 14 | Tarboro | 0 |
| Ayden | 6 | Plymouth | 6 |
| Ayden | 7 | Beaufort | 19 |
| Ayden | 14 | Hertford | 14 |
| Ayden | 7 | Weldon | 22 |

## 1952 – 1953: 4-5; 0-9*

| | | | |
|---|---|---|---|
| Ayden | 14 | Robersonville | 0 |
| Ayden | 55 | South Edgecombe | 0 |
| Ayden | 7 | Williamston | 13 |
| Ayden | 14 | Farmville | 6 |
| Ayden (W) | | Vanceboro | |
| Ayden (L) | | Tarboro | |
| Ayden | 7 | Plymouth | 20 |
| Ayden | 6 | Beaufort | 20 |
| Ayden (L) | | Hertford | |

*After completing the season with a 4-5 record (4-0 in Coastal Conference), Ayden discovered that it had played all games with an ineligible player. The four games were forfeited, thus, awarding the conference title to Farmville. Soon after that decision, Farmville also discovered that it had played the season with an ineligible player. Robersonville became the conference champions.

## 1953 – 1954: 3-4-1

| | | | |
|---|---|---|---|
| Ayden | 0 | Vanceboro | 0 |
| Ayden (L) | | Robersonville | |
| Ayden | 26 | South Edgecombe | 0 |
| Ayden | 0 | Williamston | 27 |
| Ayden | 7 | Farmville | 48 |
| Ayden | 7 | Jamesville | 0 |
| Ayden (cancelled) | | Dunn | |
| Ayden | 26 | Snow Hill | 0 |
| Ayden | 13 | Beaufort | 26 |

### 1954 – 1955: 2-3-3

| Ayden | 0 | Benvenue | 0 |
|-------|---|----------|---|
| Ayden | 0 | Vanceboro | 13 |
| Ayden | 6 | Robersonville | 0 |
| Ayden | 13 | Farmville | 6 |
| Ayden | 13 | Williamston | 20 |
| Ayden | 13 | Pamlico County | 14 |
| Ayden | 0 | Contentnea | 0 |
| Ayden | 13 | Beaufort | 13 |

### 1955 – 1956: 6-2-1

| Ayden | 13 | Benvenue | 0 |
|-------|----|----------|---|
| Ayden | 26 | Vanceboro | 0 |
| Ayden | 0 | Robersonville | 0 |
| Ayden | 0 | Farmville | 6 |
| Ayden | 0 | Williamston | 12 |
| Ayden | 33 | Pamlico County | 7 |
| Ayden | 26 | Contentnea | 0 |
| Ayden | 20 | Tarboro | 19 |
| Ayden | 26 | Beaufort | 13 |

### 1956 – 1957: 7-3

| Ayden | 20 | Benvenue | 0 |
|-------|----|----------|---|
| Ayden | 27 | Vanceboro | 0 |
| Ayden | 20 | Robersonville | 0 |
| Ayden | 19 | Farmville | 0 |
| Ayden | 7 | Williamston | 13 |
| Ayden | 27 | Pamlico County | 7 |
| Ayden | 40 | Contentnea | 0 |
| Ayden | 6 | Tarboro | 12 |

(STATE PLAYOFFS)

| Ayden | 20 | Wendell | 0 |
|-------|----|---------|---|
| Ayden | 14 | Edenton | 21 |

## 1957 – 1958: 6-3

| Ayden (W) | | (team unk) | |
|-----------|-----|----------------|-----|
| Ayden | 13 | Vanceboro | 14 |
| Ayden | 19 | Robersonville | 0 |
| Ayden | 0 | Farmville | 12 |
| Ayden | 0 | Williamston | 18 |
| Ayden | 33 | Selma | 13 |
| Ayden | 27 | Contentnea | 0 |
| Ayden | 26 | Elizabeth City | 13 |
| Ayden | * | Tarboro | |
| Ayden (W) | ** | Robersonville | |

*Game cancelled and not rescheduled because of flu.

**Robersonville agreed to play Ayden another game to make up for cancelation of Tarboro game. The second Ayden-Robersonville game was postponed because of inclement weather and then rescheduled again. Ayden won but score not available.

## 1958 – 1959: 1-7-1

| Ayden | 0 | Benvenue | 13 |
|-----------|-----|---------------|-----|
| Ayden (?) | | Vanceboro | |
| Ayden | 6 | Robersonville | 19 |
| Ayden | 0 | Farmville | 7 |
| Ayden (?) | | Williamston | |
| Ayden (L) | | La Grange | |
| Ayden (?) | | Contentnea | |
| Ayden (?) | | Beaufort | |
| Ayden (?) | | Tarboro | |
| Ayden (?) | | Havelock | |

### 1959 – 1960: 3-6

| | | | |
|---|---|---|---|
| Ayden | 14 | Havelock | 7 |
| Ayden | 7 | Benvenue | 19 |
| Ayden | 51 | Vanceboro | 6 |
| Ayden | 7 | Robersonville | 23 |
| Ayden | 0 | Farmville | 25 |
| Ayden | 6 | Williamston | 31 |
| Ayden | 0 | La Grange | 15 |
| Ayden | 27 | Contentnea | 14 |
| Ayden | 0 | Beaufort | 48 |

### 1960 – 1961: 9-1-1

| | | | |
|---|---|---|---|
| Ayden | 27 | Havelock | 6 |
| Ayden | 39 | Snow Hill | 0 |
| Ayden | 47 | Vanceboro | 0 |
| Ayden | 25 | Robersonville | 6 |
| Ayden | 21 | Farmville | 6 |
| Ayden | 14 | Williamston | 0 |
| Ayden | 19 | La Grange | 0 |
| Ayden | 20 | Contentnea | 0 |
| Ayden | 0 | Beaufort | 0 |

(STATE PLAYOFFS)

| | | | |
|---|---|---|---|
| Ayden | 18 | Lillington | 0 |
| Ayden | 13 | James Kenan* | 19 |

(*Eastern Champions and eventual State Champions)

## 1961 – 1962: 11-1

| | | | |
|---|---|---|---|
| Ayden | 8 | Havelock | 0 |
| Ayden | 40 | Snow Hill | 0 |
| Ayden | 55 | Vanceboro | 0 |
| Ayden | 18 | Robersonville | 0 |
| Ayden | 14 | Farmville | 12 |
| Ayden | 20 | Williamston | 12 |
| Ayden | 13 | La Grange | 0 |
| Ayden | 36 | Contentnea | 0 |
| Ayden | 7 | Beaufort | 0 |
| Ayden | 19 | Bath | 6 |
| (STATE PLAYOFFS) | | | |
| Ayden | 19 | Camp Lejeune | 14 |
| Ayden | 0 | Rohanen* | 7 |
| | | (*Regional Champions) | |

## 1962 – 1963: 8-3-1

| | | | |
|---|---|---|---|
| Ayden | 7 | Havelock | 13 |
| Ayden | 47 | Greene Central | 0 |
| Ayden | 56 | Vanceboro | 6 |
| Ayden | 13 | Robersonville | 13 |
| Ayden | 13 | Farmville | 0 |
| Ayden | 43 | Elm City | 7 |
| Ayden | 72 | La Grange | 0 |
| Ayden | 41 | Contentnea | 0 |
| Ayden | 0 | Beaufort | 13 |
| Ayden | 34 | Bath | 0 |
| (STATE PLAYOFFS) | | | |
| Ayden | 19 | Robersonville | 6 |
| Ayden | 27 | Windsor* | 28 |
| | | (*Regional Champions) | |

## 1963 – 1964: 8-1-1

| | | | |
|---|---|---|---|
| Ayden | 6 | Havelock | 6 |
| Ayden | 61 | Dixon | 0 |
| Ayden | 45 | Vanceboro | 0 |
| Ayden | 35 | Robersonville | 0 |
| Ayden | 0 | Farmville | 6 |
| Ayden | 21 | Elm City | 0 |
| Ayden | 27 | La Grange | 12 |
| Ayden | 52 | Contentnea | 0 |
| Ayden | 20 | Beaufort | 6 |
| Ayden | 28 | Bath | 6 |

## 1964 – 1965: 8-1-1

| | | | |
|---|---|---|---|
| Ayden | 18 | Havelock | 13 |
| Ayden | 48 | Dixon | 0 |
| Ayden | 16 | C.B. Aycock | 12 |
| Ayden | 33 | Robersonville | 0 |
| Ayden | 26 | Camp Lejeune | 0 |
| Ayden | 0 | Farmville | 13 |
| Ayden | 13 | Beaufort | 13 |
| Ayden | 62 | Bath* | 0 |
| Ayden | 8 | Zebulon | 7 |
| Ayden | 41 | Pamlico County | 7 |

(*Beginning of 45 game win streak)

### 1965 – 1966: 12-0

| | | | |
|---|---|---|---|
| Ayden | 31 | Havelock | 12 |
| Ayden | 46 | C.B. Aycock | 13 |
| Ayden | 61 | Robersonville | 0 |
| Ayden | 45 | North Lenoir | 0 |
| Ayden | 43 | Camp Lejeune | 0 |
| Ayden | 14 | Farmville | 0 |
| Ayden | 27 | Greene Central | 0 |
| Ayden | 60 | Bath | 0 |
| Ayden | 65 | Wakelon | 6 |
| Ayden | 28 | East Carteret | 6 |

(STATE PLAYOFFS)

| | | | |
|---|---|---|---|
| Ayden | 45 | Belhaven | 9 |
| Ayden** | 40 | Weldon | 21 |

(**Regional Champions)

### 1966 – 1967: 12-0

| | | | |
|---|---|---|---|
| Ayden | 21 | Grifton | 0 |
| Ayden | 46 | Charles B. Aycock | 0 |
| Ayden | 28 | Robersonville | 0 |
| Ayden | 32 | North Lenoir | 0 |
| Ayden | 33 | Camden | 0 |
| Ayden | 39 | Northern Nash | 0 |
| Ayden | 32 | Farmville | 6 |
| Ayden | 46 | Greene Central | 14 |
| Ayden | 46 | Bath | 13 |
| Ayden | 39 | East Carteret | 13 |

(STATE PLAYOFFS)

| | | | |
|---|---|---|---|
| Ayden | 39 | Vanceboro | 6 |
| Ayden | 21* | Weldon | 0 |

(*Regional Champions)

## 1967 – 1968: 13-0
### (Eastern Class A Champions)

| Ayden | 33 | Grifton | 0 |
|---|---|---|---|
| Ayden | 47 | Wakelon | 13 |
| Ayden | 38 | Robersonville | 0 |
| Ayden | 34 | North Lenoir | 0 |
| Ayden | 38 | Camden | 7 |
| Ayden | 12 | Northern Nash | 6 |
| Ayden | 35 | Farmville | 0 |
| Ayden | 19 | Greene Central | 6 |
| Ayden | 40 | Bath | 0 |
| Ayden | 34 | Pamlico County | 19 |

(STATE PLAYOFFS)

| Ayden | 42 | Grifton | 0 |
|---|---|---|---|
| Ayden | 33 | Weldon | 14 |
| Ayden | 20* | Liberty | 14 |

(*Eastern Class A Champions)

## 1968 – 1969: 11-2
## (State Class A Champions)

| Ayden | 73 | Gaston | 0 |
|---|---|---|---|
| Ayden | 40 | Knapp | 0 |
| Ayden | 41 | Swansboro | 6 |
| Ayden | 20 | North Lenoir | 0 |
| Ayden | 25 | Camden | 0 |
| Ayden | 7 | Farmville* | 24 |
| Ayden | 27 | Greene Central | 12 |
| Ayden | 40 | Bath | 0 |
| Ayden | 12 | Pamlico County | 13 |
| Ayden | 19 | Manteo | 6 |
| (STATE PLAYOFFS) | | | |
| Ayden | 47 | Robersonville | 9 |
| Ayden | 22 | Weldon | 21 |
| Ayden** | 14 | Red Springs | 13 |

(**State Class A Champions)

*Ayden High School's 45-game winning streak ended by Farmville High School

## 1969 – 1970: 5-5

| Ayden | 18 | Greene Central | 13 |
|---|---|---|---|
| Ayden | 19 | Swansboro | 23 |
| Ayden | 12 | Manteo | 14 |
| Ayden | 6 | Camden | 0 |
| Ayden | 12 | Grifton | 13 |
| Ayden | 6 | Farmville | 28 |
| Ayden | 20 | Weldon | 22 |
| Ayden | 13 | Louisburg | 12 |
| Ayden | 25 | Pamlico County | 18 |
| Ayden | 27 | Knapp | 20 |

## 1970 – 1971: 8-1-1

| Ayden | 6 | Greene Central | 0 |
|-------|-----|----------------|-----|
| Ayden | 26 | Columbia | 0 |
| Ayden | 14 | Manteo | 20 |
| Ayden | 41 | Camden | 6 |
| Ayden | 21 | Grifton | 12 |
| Ayden | 20 | Farmville | 16 |
| Ayden | 12 | Ahoskie | 12 |
| Ayden | 43 | Louisburg | 18 |
| Ayden | 34 | Pamlico County | 28 |
| Ayden | 27 | Knapp | 14 |

.

## Appendix 3
Ayden High School Basketball Season Records from
1946-47 thru 1970-71*

| | |
|---|---|
| 1946-1947 | 11-12 |
| 1947-1948 | 11-7 |
| 1948-1949 | 21-5 |
| 1949-1950 | 20-6 |
| 1950-1951 | 24-6 |
| 1951-1952 | 22-6 |
| 1952-1953 | 23-2 |
| 1953-1954 | 8-11 |
| 1954-1955 | 18-4 |
| 1955-1956 | 19-2 |
| 1956-1957 | 25-2 |
| 1957-1958 | 23-3 |

| | |
|---|---|
| 1958-1959 | 9-10 |
| 1959-1960 | 13-7 |
| 1960-1961 | 13-7 |
| 1961-1962 | 26-2 |
| 1962-1963 | 13-5 |
| 1963-1964 | 10-8 |
| 1964-1965 | 19-4 |
| 1965-1966 | 28-0 |
| 1966-1967 | 28-0 |
| 1967-1968 | 22-4 |
| 1968-1969 | 8-14 |
| 1969-1970 | 8-11** |
| 1970-1971 | 18-9 |

* These records include regular season and playoff games.

**The '69-'70 team had a 6-13 record until Vanceboro had to forfeit their games because of an ineligible player. This removed two losses from the loss column and added them to the win column.

## Appendix 4
## Notes on the Writing of *Ayden, the Sports Town*

*Writing a book like this one means the making of dozens – maybe hundreds of decisions. Mitchell and I discussed some and made some on our own. The controversies such as the disqualification of the basketball teams in the 1950s are the most difficult to write about. The fading of memories and the emotions surrounding these issues make a final non-contentious decision very unlikely. Telling the various stories that I documented during interviews and phone calls – a kind of analysis – and leaving the final decision to the reader seems like the most reasonable solution to the problem. In many cases, I have my own beliefs, but I do not want to impose them on you. Whenever I ran across one of these many-sided situations, I chose to call them mysteries. It's like putting a thousand-piece jigsaw puzzle together and realizing that the most prominent pieces are missing. The large majority of decisions do not relate to controversies. In comparison, they are easy. And on occasion, I was able to amass enough information to make a guess that I felt confident about. In any event, Mitchell and I take full responsibility for the numerous decisions that we made.*

**Sources**

*The Ayden Dispatch.* Prior to World War II, our primary source was *The Ayden Dispatch*, supplemented with interview accounts and memories of person's stories from those times. Copies of the Ayden newspapers from the beginning of publication in 1912 until 1925 have been lost. Available copies of *The Ayden Dispatch* start in 1926 and run through 1956. The following years are missing: 1937 (except for the 20th year anniversary issue described below), 1941, 1945, 1951, 1952, 1953, and 1955. From 1957 through 1971, the Ayden papers were unavailable except for some issues that were part of scrapbooks and individual memorabilia collections.

In 1937, a special 20th anniversary issue of *The Ayden Dispatch* was released in four sections. This publication was in celebration of the 20-year ownership of the newspaper by John C. Andrews. Mr. Andrews had tried twice before to put together a special issue, but the two men hired to collect the money from merchants absconded with the money. This edition is the most complete history of early Ayden ever assembled. The articles include info on how Ayden was named and how it got started, histories of Ayden businesses and pictures of the merchants, accounts of the town's public and private educational institutions, narrations and pictures of important people, and much more. The early African American community is left out completely with the exception of one article.

*The Daily Reflector. The Daily Reflector* (Greenville) did not begin its coverage of Ayden High School sports until the late 1940s. Luckily, the Greenville paper's coverage started at about the same time the Ayden newspaper accounts became unavailable. The reportage by the Greenville newspaper of South Ayden School sports was sketchy until the 1960s when the coverage improved dramatically.

*The Kinston Daily Free Press.* The Kinston newspaper started covering Ayden High School sports in the 1960s. Fortunately, the Kinston paper reported on the South Ayden High football games (1965-1970) that did not appear in the Greenville paper. By investigating both newspapers, I was able to put together four of the five seasons. I could locate info on only half of the games played during the third season.

The three primary newspapers that were researched found it easier to report on football than basketball. There were two reasons: 1) fewer games were played in football and 2) fewer teams in the area played football.

The archive availability for South Ayden boys' basketball appeared almost random for some years. Beginning in the early 60s, the Eagles' round ball seasons became more complete in both the Greenville and Kinston newspapers. The info for the girls' basketball program at South Ayden High School was very nearly non-existent. At about the same time that the coverage improved for SAH boys' basketball, girls' basketball was discontinued.

*The Wheel.* Another invaluable source of information was Ayden High School's yearbooks. At first, I assumed I could rely on *The Wheel* to report on individual game scores and end-of-season records. The facts and figures included in the annuals were inconsistent, however. Some yearbooks included scores of every game, others provided the schedule without the scores, and still others a brief narrative only. To complicate matters further, the provision of sports info varied from sport to sport. Even when sources were available, documenting basic information – such as a team's final record – proved a challenge. In the final analysis, the Sherlock Holmes method was employed; that meant assembling all the available clues from all the sources I could muster and making a decision on what to write.

Whenever the content of a document was suspect, I attempted to verify the information from other sources – either by asking people if they could remember the event in question or by researching other sources.

In total, my post-World War II sources were *The Ayden Dispatch* (late 40s, early 50s), *The Daily Reflector* (late 40s, 50s, and 60s), *The Kinston Daily Free Press*, personal communications (interviews, blogs, emails, Facebook, and phone calls), books, and websites. I collected as many unpublished papers as I could locate. For example, some of Ayden's historical information came from an accreditation report that was assembled in 1984/1985 in preparation for a review at the Ayden

Elementary School. I was also provided with unpublished papers that included the author's name and some that were anonymously written.

## Coverage

Many times newspapers were the *only* source of info – *The Ayden Dispatch* prior to World War II and *The Daily Reflector* and *Kinston Daily Free Press* after the war. This means, of course, that Mitchell and I had to rely almost solely on the coverage – on the games and other sports stories that appeared in the paper. The sports covered are as follows:

### Ayden High School

- Football
- Boys' Basketball
- Girls' Basketball
- Baseball

### South Ayden School

- Football
- Boys' Basketball

Periodically in the narrative, I have chosen to remind the reader of our trials and tribulations in relation to the availability and usage of resource materials. A good example is the end-of-the-year basketball tournaments in Pitt County. I was sometimes able to tell the reader what happened to a team after they won their conference tournament in basketball and why sometimes I could not. The variation from year to year was stark. One year the trophy winner's every game all the way through the district tournament and to the state finals would be written up, and the following year the Pitt County champion would disappear completely from the sports section.

It would be easy to "scapegoat" the local newspapers for their meager and sporadic coverage, but I suspect the "shoe should be placed on the other foot." I'm sure that the papers did not have nearly enough reporters for live coverage of every sporting event in the area. They relied on school-based reporters to call in the results of each game. Failure to phone meant no article. A school experiencing a good year in whatever sport would be more likely to have their games written up. Throughout the book, this may explain why teams sometimes disappeared from the radar. Under these circumstances if I were a betting man, I'd put my cash on the following supposition: an unreported game = a loss. Without some kind of proof, however, I could not translate my thesis into actual numbers.

One final word on information availability; based on the aforementioned reasoning, I have more confidence in the win column than the loss column. If my responsibility is to contact the newspaper with Friday night's game totals, I'm more likely to report a game that my team has won. So, games won are more likely to appear in print. Often, I had to count up the games that made the sports section. Since the games won appeared more frequently, the count could be skewed in an erroneous direction. At this point, I pulled out my Ouija Board, started talking to said inanimate object, and made a decision.

**Footnotes**

Mitchell and I chose the footnoting format that we thought would be least disruptive to the reader. No notation appears in the narrative. Instead, the last 3-4 words of a sentence along with its source are italicized in "Appendix 1: Chapter Notes." For the listings that occur primarily at the end of chapters, a "summary" footnote of the sources is documented in the "Chapter Notes." Fairly frequently, several sources are used in the same paragraph, so use of the usual number above a word or placing footnotes at the bottom of a page would have been distracting.

**Names**

Some high school athletes have "grown up" and assumed new names. R.L. Collins has become Ray; Tommy Edwards has become Tom;

William Edwards has become Bill; James Hemby has become Jim; Ikey Baldree has become Ike; Billy Norris has become Bill. I am familiar with this since I am Bill everywhere but in Ayden where I am still William. I actually like it that way. In most cases, I used the alumni's "Ayden name" because I thought it would be less confusing.

### Pictures

Mitchell deserves the credit for the pictures in *Ayden, the Sports Town*. We both worked tirelessly to locate the ones that appear in these pages. Once we had a photograph, it had to be scanned, cleaned up, and placed on a flash drive that was, in turn, handed over to our publisher. Mitchell did this tedious work for hours as I mostly watched. The technology was amazing to me, but some of the stains, signatures etc. could not be removed without distorting the photograph. There were times when we could not locate a particular photo. At other times, we chose to use a picture that is not of very high quality because it was the only one available. Some of the pictures and/or the accompanying narrative were too small when they were reproduced in the book. Some could be changed so that they were more readable and some could not. When faced with using or not using one of these pictures, we almost always chose to publish it. If you wonder why a certain team or individual portrait does not appear in these pages, it's probably because we simply could not locate it. Some team photos had all of the names of the players in order and some photos had no names at all. Several of the pictures had the names but not in any particular order. In some cases, Mitchell and I could identify the players and in some cases we could not. More than once, we were able to identify all of the team members but two or three.

The Acknowledgments spells out the numerous people who assisted us in this endeavor.

### Mistakes

I need to approach this topic from two perspectives. First of all, Mitchell and I knew that we'd run into inaccuracies, contradictions, and outright mistakes in our sources. That's just part of the writing game, so to speak. I for one, however, was surprised at both the number of miscues and the gravity of some of the misstatements. Newspaper accounts included incorrect first and last names of players, pictures with wrong players' names underneath, erroneous won-lost records, and numerous typos. One AHS annual listed the football season's individual game scores incorrectly; the final score of every game was misstated except one. And, the sports editor reported that the Tornadoes had defeated our arch rival, Farmville, when, in reality, the Red Devils won the game.

Secondly, Mitchell and I have been quite diligent in our verification of the events and statistics in this book. To accomplish this, we've made hundreds and hundreds of decisions along the way. Yet, I'm sure there are mistakes. My only hope is that we've managed to keep them to a minimum.

**Graduation Dates**

I had hoped to place the Ayden High School graduation dates behind each player and Ayden citizen. Unfortunately, I was unable to verify whether or not some individuals were AHS graduates or graduates of other schools. If a person does not have a date of graduation date next to his or her name, it means one of two things: The person did not graduate from Ayden High School or I was unable to learn from where he/she graduated.

## Appendix 5
### Bibliography and Further Reading

**Blackbirds: The Glory Days of Rocky Mount Athletics** by Lee Pace (2007)

**Cyclone Country: The Time, the Town, the Team** by Russell Rawlings (2000).

*Cyclone Country is written about Coach Henry Trevathan and the Fike High School Cyclones of Wilson, N.C. during a run of three straight state championships (1967-1969) in football.*

**The Coach J.G. (Choppy) Wagner: A Legend and a Loved Man** by Milton Parker

*The Coach ... is a booklet about a beloved coach, J.G. "Choppy" Wagner, coach, athletic director, and assistant principal, of Washington High School from 1946 to 1976. The publication is without a specified author or date of publication. The name, Milton Parker, is taken from the "Forward."(Judging by the contents, I am relatively sure that Mr. Parker was responsible for the book. My guess is that it was released in 2006 or soon thereafter.)*

******

*A History of Ayden Seminary and Eureka College* by Michael Pelt (undated)

**Ayden Magazine** (4th Edition, 2006)

**Ayden Magazine** (Summer/Fall 2014)

**Ayden North Carolina** Ayden Chamber of Commerce (1916)

**Chronicles of Pitt County** (1982)

**From Dawn to Decadence: 1500 to the Present** by Jacques Barzun (2000)

**Hurricane Hazel in the Carolinas** by Jay Barnes (2010)

**Sidelines: A North Carolina Story of Community, Race, and High School Football** by Stuart Albright (2009)

**South Ayden School: History and Memories** by Charles Becton (2007)

**The Ayden Dispatch** Special 4-Section Anniversary Edition (1937)

**The Classic: How Everett Case and His Tournament Brought Big-Time Basketball to the South** by Bethany Bradsher (2011)

**The Cooperstown Symposium on Baseball and American Culture** (2003-2004)

**The Forgotten First: B-1 and the Integration of the Modern Navy** by Alex Albright (2013)

**The Free Will Baptist** (February 1926)

**The Great Depression** by Lionel Robbins (1934).

**The Wisdom of History** by Rufus Fears, DVD, The Teaching Company (2007)

**The World at Arms** by Gerhard Weinberg (2005)

**We Could Have Played Forever: The Story of the Coastal Plain League** by Robert Gaunt (1997)

## About the Authors

WILLIAM HARRINGTON grew up in Ayden and graduated from Ayden High School in 1961. He earned his B.S. from East Carolina University in Health and Physical Education and Psychology, his M.Ed. in Guidance and Counseling from UNC-Chapel Hill, and his Dr.P.H. from the School of Public Health at UNC. Dr. Harrington retired in 2008 after a 40-year career in the mental health field. William and his wife, Maija, live in Durham, N.C.

MITCHELL OAKLEY grew up in southern rural Pitt County and graduated from Ayden High School in 1965. He earned an Associate of Applied Science degree in Accounting from Wayne Community College, then entered the business world in 1967 as a bookkeeper at Pitt-Greene Fertilizer & Fuel Company, Inc. where he advanced to office manager. In 1971 he became city editor of *The Ayden News-Leader* where he covered every aspect of community news, from town board discussions to sporting events. Upon his retirement in 2011, Oakley served as group publisher of *The Times-Leader*, *The Farmville Enterprise* and *The Standard Laconic*. Mitchell and wife, Dottie, live on a farm near Ayden.

43794667R00294

Made in the USA
Middletown, DE
19 May 2017